AWS Certified Develope
Associate Guide

Your one-stop solution to passing the AWS
developer's certification

Vipul Tankariya
Bhavin Parmar

BIRMINGHAM - MUMBAI

AWS Certified Developer – Associate Guide

First published: September 2017

Production reference: 1250917

Published by Packt Publishing Ltd.
Livery Place
35 Livery Street
Birmingham
B3 2PB, UK.

ISBN 978-1-78712-562-9

www.packtpub.com

Credits

Authors
Vipul Tankariya
Bhavin Parmar

Reviewer
Gajanan Chandgadkar

Commissioning Editor
Vijin Boricha

Acquisition Editor
Heramb Bhavsar

Content Development Editor
Abhishek Jadhav

Technical Editor
Swathy Mohan

Copy Editor
Juliana Nair

Project Coordinator
Judie Jose

Proofreader
Safis Editing

Indexer
Aishwarya Gangawane

Graphics
Kirk D'Penha

Production Coordinator
Aparna Bhagat

About the Author

Vipul Tankariya comes with a very broad experience in cloud consulting, development, and training. He has worked with a number of customers across the globe for solving real-life business problems in terms of technology and strategy. He is also a public speaker in various AWS events and meetups. He has not only extensively worked on AWS, but is also certified in five AWS certifications:

- AWS Certified DevOps Engineer – Professional
- AWS Certified Solution Architect – Professional
- AWS Certified Developer – Associate
- AWS Certified Solution Architect – Associate
- AWS Certified SysOps Administrator – Associate

This book combines his AWS experience in solving real-life business problems along with his hands-on development experience in various programming languages. Vipul is an accomplished senior cloud consultant and technologist focused on strategic thought leadership concentrated around next generation cloud-based solutions with more than 21 years of experience.

He has been involved in conceptualizing, designing, and implementing large-scale cloud solutions on a variety of public/private/hybrid clouds. He has also been instrumental in setting up cloud migration strategies for customers, building enterprise-class cloud solutions, Go-To market collateral, and AWS training as well as cloud pre-sales activities.

Vipul has a wide range of experience working on DevOps, CI/CD, and automation at each level of the delivery life cycle of products, solutions, and services on the cloud as well as on-premises.

Acknowledgments

There are many people in my personal and professional life who made me what I am today. Though many of the names that I am going to mention in this book may not even know what AWS is, but without their support, I would not have even developed many of the basic life skills, leave aside the capability of writing an AWS book.

First and foremost I would like to thank my father who taught me how important it is to be a good human being before being anything in life. I would always be indebted to my mother who taught me how to work hard and what a strong will power is. I would also like to specially mention the name of my wife, Priya, without her support this book would not have been possible. My son, Arav, also deserves a special mention here, as I have spent some of his share of my time on this book.

I would also like to thank my sisters, Asha and Bina, who taught me what is compassion. I must thank my brother, Vijay, who has always protected me in every course of life.

I would also like to thank Badrinarayan Ramanujan, my friend, who has always motivated me and helped me assess my real value. Jaymin Jhala, a very special thanks to him as I don't think my IT career would have started without him.

I must thank my friend, Jay Punjani, my brother from another mother, who has taught me to dream big and understand unspoken words. I would also like to thank Mr, BSGK Shastry, my Guru, who cultivated the professional approach in me.

I would also like to thank Mr. Ira Sheinwald, my friend and mentor, who showed confidence in me and gave me a chance to work on my first AWS project. Heartfelt thanks also goes to my friend, Shashikant Kuwar, along with Ira, as we have worked together to solve many technical and strategic challenges on AWS.

I must show my gratitude to Mr. Vivek Raju, my friend and mentor in my AWS journey. My AWS journey would not have been enriched without the support of Varun Dube and Vikas Goel who have been a part of my AWS journey.

My heartfelt thanks also go to my friends Satyajit Das, Jhalak Modi, Appasaheb Bagali, Ajaykumar Kakumanu, Pushpraj Singh, Chandrasekhar Singh, and Rakesh Sing who have been part of my AWS certification journey. Also, a very special thanks to Gajanan Chandgadkar who has been with me in multiple counts for not only technically reviewing this book, but also for being there in my AWS certification journey. We all worked together for almost a year to get our five AWS certifications.

I would also like to thank Heramb Bhavsar, Abhishek Jadhav, Swathy Mohan, and the entire team at Packt for making this book a reality.

Last but not least, I would like to thank my friend and co-author of this book, Bhavin Parmar, who saw the dream of writing this book with me. If it was not for him, I would not have taken this book as a project.

About the Author

Bhavin Parmar comes with a very broad experience in cloud consulting, development, training. He has an active participation in solving real-life business problems. Bhavin has not only extensively worked on AWS, but he is also certified in AWS and Red Hat:

- AWS Certified DevOps Engineer – Professional
- AWS Certified Solution Architect – Professional
- AWS Certified Developer – Associate
- AWS Certified Solution Architect – Associate
- AWS Certified SysOps Administrator – Associate
- Red Hat Certified Architect

This book combines his AWS experience in solving real-life business problems along with his hands-on deployment and development experience. Bhavin is an accomplished technologist and senior cloud consultant and focused on strategic thought leadership concentrated around next generation cloud-based & DevOps solutions with more than 11 years of experience.

He has been involved in conceptualizing, designing, and implementing large-scale cloud solutions on a variety of public/private/hybrid Clouds. Bhavin has also been instrumental in setting up cloud migration strategies for customers, building enterprise-class cloud solutions, Go-To market collateral, and AWS training as well as cloud pre-sales activities.

He has a wide range of experience working at each level of the delivery life cycle of products, solutions, and services on the cloud as well as on-premises.

About the Reviewer

Gajanan Chandgadkar has more than 12 years of IT experience. He has spent more than 6 years in the USA, helping large enterprise architect, migrate, and deploy applications in AWS. He's been running production workloads on AWS for over 6 years. He is an AWS certified solutions architect professional and a certified DevOps professional with more than seven certifications in trending technologies. Gajanan is also a technology enthusiast who has extended interest and experience in different topics, such as application development, container technology, and continuous delivery.

Currently, he is working with Happiest Minds Technologies as an Associate DevOps Architect. He has worked with Wipro Technologies Corporation in the past.

www.PacktPub.com

For support files and downloads related to your book, please visit www.PacktPub.com.

Did you know that Packt offers eBook versions of every book published, with PDF and ePub files available? You can upgrade to the eBook version at www.PacktPub.com and as a print book customer, you are entitled to a discount on the eBook copy. Get in touch with us at service@packtpub.com for more details.

At www.PacktPub.com, you can also read a collection of free technical articles, sign up for a range of free newsletters and receive exclusive discounts and offers on Packt books and eBooks.

https://www.packtpub.com/mapt

Get the most in-demand software skills with Mapt. Mapt gives you full access to all Packt books and video courses, as well as industry-leading tools to help you plan your personal development and advance your career.

Why subscribe?

- Fully searchable across every book published by Packt
- Copy and paste, print, and bookmark content
- On demand and accessible via a web browser

Customer Feedback

Thanks for purchasing this Packt book. At Packt, quality is at the heart of our editorial process. To help us improve, please leave us an honest review on this book's Amazon page at https://www.amazon.com/dp/1787125629.

If you'd like to join our team of regular reviewers, you can e-mail us at customerreviews@packtpub.com. We award our regular reviewers with free eBooks and videos in exchange for their valuable feedback. Help us be relentless in improving our products!

I would like to dedicate this book to my parents, friends, and knowledge.

-Bhavin Parmar

Table of Contents

Preface

This book starts with a quick introduction to AWS and the prerequisites to get you started. It gives you a fair understanding of core AWS services and the basic architecture. Next, you get familiar with Identity and Access Management (IAM) along with Virtual Private Cloud (VPC). Moving ahead, you will learn about Elastic Compute Cloud (EC2) and handling application traffic with Elastic Load Balancing (ELB). We will also talk about Monitoring with CloudWatch, Simple Storage Service (S3), and Glacier and CloudFront, along with other AWS storage options. Next, we will take you through AWS DynamoDB – A NoSQL Database Service, Amazon Simple Queue Service (SQS), and have an overview of CloudFormation. Finally, you will understand Elastic Beanstalk and go through an overview of AWS lambda.

At the end of this book, we will cover enough topics, tips, and tricks along with mock tests for you to be able to pass the AWS Certified Developer - Associate exam and deploy as well as manage your applications on the AWS platform.

With the rapid adaptation of the cloud platform, the need for cloud certifications has also increased. This is your one-stop solutions and will help you transform from zero to certified. This guide will help you gain technical expertise in the AWS platform and help you start working with various AWS services.

What this book covers

Chapter 1, *Overview of AWS Certified Developer - Associate Certification*, outlines the AWS Certified Developer – Associate exam and highlights the critical aspects, knowledge area, and services covered in the blueprint.

Chapter 2, *Introduction to Cloud Computing and AWS*, elaborates the fundamentals of AWS. The chapter starts by giving you a basic understanding of what cloud is and takes you through a brief journey of familiarizing yourself with the basic building blocks of AWS. It highlights some of the critical aspects of how AWS works and provides an overview of the AWS core infrastructure.

Chapter 3, *Getting Familiar with Identity and Access Management*, covers all critical aspects of Identity and Access Management (IAM) and provides sufficient details to allow you to work with IAM.

Chapter 4, *Virtual Private Cloud*, explains how one can create a Virtual Private Cloud and start building a secure network with a number of the components of AWS networking services.

Chapter 5, *Getting Started with Elastic Compute Cloud*, describes what EC2 is and how one can start provisioning servers with various Windows and Linux operating system flavors. It also describes how to connect and work with these servers.

Chapter 6, *Handling Application Traffic with Elastic Load Balancing*, describes how to create an ELB, how it works, and what the critical aspects of an ELB service are.

Chapter 7, *Monitoring with CloudWatch*, describes how you can use Amazon CloudWatch to collect and track metrics, collect and monitor log files, set alarms, and automatically react to changes in your AWS resources.

Chapter 8, *Simple Storage Service, Glacier, and CloudFront*, provides an understanding of Amazon Simple Storage Service (S3), Glacier, and CloudFront services, and takes you through CloudFront, a CDN (Content Distribution Network) service.

Chapter 9, *Other AWS Storage Options*, touches upon AWS Storage Gateway, which is a network appliance or a server residing on a customer premises. It provides an overview of AWS Snowball, which is a service that accelerates transferring large amounts of data into and out of AWS using physical storage appliances. It also provides a basic understanding of AWS Snowmobile, which is an Exabyte-scale data transfer service used to move extremely large amounts of data to and from AWS.

Chapter 10, *AWS Relation Database Services*, provides an understanding of AWS Relation Database Services (RDS). It explains different types of engine supported by AWS RDS and how to efficiently and effectively create and manage RDS instances on AWS cloud.

Chapter 11, *AWS DynamoDB – A NoSQL Database Service*, describes various components of DynamoDB with the best practices to manage it.

Chapter 12, *Amazon Simple Queue Service*, provides an understanding of what SQS is and how to create and manage it with relevant examples.

Chapter 13, *Simple Notification Service*, talks about fully managed messaging service that can be used to send messages, alarms, and notifications from various AWS services such as Amazon RDS, CloudWatch, and S3 to other AWS services such as SQS and Lambda.

Chapter 14, *Simple Workflow Service*, provides a basic understanding of SWF, its various components, and how to use them.

Chapter 15, *AWS CloudFormation*, provides an overview of the AWS CloudFormation service. CloudFormation templates provide a simpler and efficient way to manage your resources on AWS cloud.

Chapter 16, *Elastic Beanstalk*, gives an introduction to Elastic Beanstalk and describes how to create and manage applications using the service.

Chapter 17, *Overview of AWS Lambda*, provides an overview of Lambda and describes how it runs code in response to events and how it automatically manages the compute resources required by that code.

Chapter 18, *Mock Tests*, consists of two mock tests for you to test your knowledge. It tries to cover all the topics from the scope of the exam and challenges your understanding of the topics. Each mock test contains 50 questions. You should try to complete a mock test in 90 minutes.

What you need for this book

As the practical examples involve the use of AWS, an AWS account is required.

Who this book is for

This book is for IT professionals and developers looking to clear the AWS Certified Developer – Associate 2017 exam. Developers looking to deploy and manage their applications on the AWS platform will find this book useful too. No prior AWS experience is needed.

Conventions

In this book, you will find a number of text styles that distinguish between different kinds of information. Here are some examples of these styles and an explanation of their meaning. Code words in text, database table names, folder names, filenames, file extensions, pathnames, dummy URLs, user input, and Twitter handles are shown as follows: "For Amazon RDS MySQL DB instances, the default port is 3306".

A block of code is set as follows:

```
mysql -h <endpoit> -p 3306 -u <masteruser> -p
```

Any command-line input or output is written as follows:

```
$ pip install --upgrade --user awscli
```

New terms and **important words** are shown in bold. Words that you see on the screen, for example, in menus or dialog boxes, appear in the text like this: "Select **IAM** under **Security, Identity & Compliance** group from the AWS dashboard".

Warnings or important notes appear like this.

Tips and tricks appear like this.

Reader feedback

Feedback from our readers is always welcome. Let us know what you think about this book-what you liked or disliked. Reader feedback is important for us as it helps us develop titles that you will really get the most out of.

To send us general feedback, simply email feedback@packtpub.com, and mention the book's title in the subject of your message.

If there is a topic that you have expertise in and you are interested in either writing or contributing to a book, see our author guide at www.packtpub.com/authors.

Customer support

Now that you are the proud owner of a Packt book, we have a number of things to help you to get the most from your purchase.

Downloading the color images of this book

We also provide you with a PDF file that has color images of the screenshots/diagrams used in this book. The color images will help you better understand the changes in the output. You can download this file from https://www.packtpub.com/sites/default/files/downloads/AWSCertifiedDeveloperAssociateGuide_ColorImages.pdf.

Errata

Although we have taken every care to ensure the accuracy of our content, mistakes do happen. If you find a mistake in one of our books-maybe a mistake in the text or the code-we would be grateful if you could report this to us. By doing so, you can save other readers from frustration and help us improve subsequent versions of this book. If you find any errata, please report them by visiting http://www.packtpub.com/submit-errata, selecting your book, clicking on the **Errata Submission Form** link, and entering the details of your errata. Once your errata are verified, your submission will be accepted and the errata will be uploaded to our website or added to any list of existing errata under the Errata section of that title. To view the previously submitted errata, go to https://www.packtpub.com/books/content/support and enter the name of the book in the search field. The required information will appear under the **Errata** section.

Piracy

Piracy of copyrighted material on the internet is an ongoing problem across all media. At Packt, we take the protection of our copyright and licenses very seriously. If you come across any illegal copies of our works in any form on the internet, please provide us with the location address or website name immediately so that we can pursue a remedy. Please contact us at copyright@packtpub.com with a link to the suspected pirated material. We appreciate your help in protecting our authors and our ability to bring you valuable content.

Questions

If you have a problem with any aspect of this book, you can contact us at questions@packtpub.com, and we will do our best to address the problem.

1

Overview of AWS Certified Developer - Associate Certification

First of all, congratulations for choosing this book and beginning your journey to earn **AWS Certified Developer - Associate Certification**. As the saying goes, a *good beginning is half done*. You have set a target and taken the first step towards the target. If you follow the instructions in this book, it would certainly help you in completing the certification exam.

As you begin, you may have a number of questions running in your mind. This chapter covers a number of such questions that are frequently asked by beginners. To begin with, let us understand how you should start preparing for the exam.

Amazon publishes an official blueprint for each certification exam. The blueprint elaborates the scope of the exam, prerequisites to attend the exam, and the knowledge required to successfully complete the exam. This blueprint may change from time to time and you should look out for the latest copy of the blueprint for the exam from Amazon.

While publishing this book, the official blueprint for AWS Certified Developer - Associate exam is available at the following URL:

```
https://d0.awsstatic.com/training-and-certification/docs-dev-
associate/AWS_certified_developer_associate_blueprint.pdf.
```

This chapter outlines the AWS Certified Developer - Associate level exam and highlights the critical aspects, knowledge area, and services covered in the blueprint.

Let's begin with understanding the scope of the exam. The exam scope is divided into four domains as given in the following table with their respective weight in the exam:

Sr. No.	Domain	% Weightage in exam
1.0	AWS fundamentals	10%
2.0	Designing and developing	40%
3.0	Deployment and security	30%
4.0	Debugging	20%
Total		100%

The topics and the content covered in these domains as per the blueprint are given in the following section.

Domain 1.0 – AWS fundamentals

Identify and recognize cloud architecture considerations, such as fundamental components and effective designs. Content may include the following:

- How to design cloud services
- Database concepts
- Planning and design
- Familiarity with architectural trade-off decisions, high availability versus cost, Amazon **Relational Database Service (RDS)** versus installing your own database on Amazon **Elastic Compute Cloud (EC2)**
- Amazon **Simple Storage Service (S3)**, Amazon **Simple Workflow Service (SWF)**, and Messaging
- DynamoDB, AWS Elastic Beanstalk, AWS CloudFormation
- Elasticity and scalability

Domain 2.0 – Designing and developing

Identify the appropriate techniques to code a cloud solution. Content may include the following:

- Configure an **Amazon Machine Image (AMI)**
- Programming with AWS APIs

Domain 3.0 – Deployment and security

Recognize and implement secure procedures for optimum cloud deployment and maintenance. Content may include the following:

- Cloud security best practices

Demonstrate ability to implement the right architecture for development, testing, and staging environments. Content may include the following:

- Shared security responsibility model
- AWS platform compliance
- AWS security attributes (customer workloads down to physical layer)
- Security services
- AWS **Identity and Access Management (IAM)**
- Amazon **Virtual Private Cloud (VPC)**
- CIA and AAA models, ingress versus egress filtering, and which AWS services and features fit

Domain 4.0 – Debugging

Content may include the following:

- General troubleshooting information and questions
- Best practices in debugging

If you haven't earlier worked with **Amazon Web Services (AWS)** and cannot understand the topics given in the blueprint, do not worry. This book covers all these domains and each of the blueprint topics in detail. These topics are very carefully elaborated in the subsequent chapters. Some of the frequently asked questions are covered in following pages and will answer most of the queries you may have about the exam and how to get started with the preparation.

Frequently asked questions about the exam

- **Are there any prerequisites for AWS Certified Developer Associate exam?**

  There are no prerequisites for getting started with AWS Certified Developer Associate level exam preparation; however, it is recommended that the person preparing for this exam has knowledge or training in at least one high-level programming language.

- **What is the total duration of the exam?**

  A total of 80 minutes are given to you to complete the exam.

- **How many questions are asked in the exam?**

  The exam has around 55 questions that you need to complete in the given time. As per our experience, this number may vary at times.

- **What types of questions are asked in the exam?**

  The exam asks multiple choice questions. It gives a question with multiple answers and you have to choose one or more right answers from the given list of answers.

  You can refer to the following link for officially published sample questions:

  https://d0.awsstatic.com/training-and-certification/docs-dev-associate/AWS_certified_developer_associate_examsample.pdf.

  We have also given mock tests for you to practice and test your knowledge after you have finished reading the book.

- **Where can I register for the exam?**

  Amazon has tied up with **Kryterion** for the certification exams. Kryterion centers are spread across the globe. You can go to `https://www.webassessor.com` and create an account if you do not already have one or log on with your existing account. After logging in to the site you can follow the exam registration process given on the site to register for the exam in a Kryterion center near you.

- **How much does it cost to register for the exam?**

  There are two types of exam, practice exam and final exam. The associate level practice exam costs $20 and the final exam costs $150.

- **How should I prepare for the exam?**

  You can refer to all the chapters in this book and follow all the tips and tricks in the book to prepare for the exam. Also, go through the mock tests given at the end of the book. You can also refer to some of the reference materials pointed out in the reference section of the book to deep dive on some topics.

- **What is the passing score of the exam?**

  AWS does not publish the passing score of the exam as it is set by statistical analysis of the exam. This score is subject to change. Based on our experience, this score currently hovers around 65% to 70%. If more candidates start scoring higher marks, the statistical model may set the minimum marks to a higher limit. Similarly, if more candidates start failing in the exam or scoring lower marks, then minimum passing marks may change based on this statistical data.

- **How should I answer the questions in the exam?**

  The exam poses you with scenario-based questions. There may be more than one right answer, but you have to choose the most suitable answer out of the given answers. We suggest you choose elimination theory whenever you face difficulties in answering a question. Start discarding wrong answers first. When you start eliminating the wrong answers, you may automatically be able to find the right answer as eliminated answers will reduce your confusion. Also, do not spend more time on a question if you do not know the answer to it. Instead, mark the question for review. The exam interface keeps track of all the questions marked for review, which you can revisit before submitting the final exam.

2

Introduction to Cloud Computing and AWS

Clouds, as we know from our childhood, are tiny droplets of frozen crystals of water that are high in the sky hovering around our planet earth. What do these clouds do? They provide a service to the residents of planet earth. They bring us rain. *Something* (clouds) that is *somewhere* (up into the sky) provides us a service by bringing rain. This same concept of *something somewhere* can be applied to understand **cloud computing**.

Let's understand how we can imagine the concept of *something somewhere* with respect to cloud computing. In cloud computing, *something* is IT services such as compute, database, storage, network, security, and so on. These services are hosted somewhere at a secured place (that is, a data center) and are accessible without us needing to worry and even think about how they are configured and licensed. Thus, cloud computing is a host of services that are hosted at a remote location instead of a local server or personal computer and they are remotely accessible to us.

Let's look at some of the simple examples of accessing cloud services:

- Fill in a registration form and start using public email services (such as Gmail, Hotmail, Yahoo, and so on). In this case, we start using a service, we don't worry on how the mail services are configured, how the infrastructure is secured, how the software is licensed, whether highly qualified staff are available to maintain the infrastructure, and so on. We just start using email services by providing a secure password.
- Another example could be a mobile phone or electricity at home or the office. We just buy a SIM card from a telecom provider or electrical connection from a local power company, and we don't worry about how the telecom network works or how power is generated and reaches our place. We just use them and pay the bills per month, only for the services that we have actually consumed.

The AWS cloud can be imagined the same way as a public email, mobile network, or electricity providing company. AWS is a public cloud, wherein we can fill a form and start using the cloud services (that is, IT services). It can be used to host personal, commercial, or enterprise-grade IT infrastructures. Various IT services (such as compute, database, network, storage, NoSQL, and so on) can be used as a building blocks to create the desired IT infrastructure to match with the business requirement and compliance need of an enterprise.

At a higher level, clouds are of three types:

- **Private cloud**: A host of infrastructure, platform, and application services located in secured remote facilities providing compute, platform, or other IT services on-demand, accessible and controlled only by a single specific organization is called a private cloud. It is preferred by companies needing a secure and dedicated data center or hosting space. Constant upgrade of staff's skills and data center infrastructure is required. It is generally very costly and time-consuming to maintain a private cloud.

- **Public cloud**: A host of infrastructure, platform, and application services located in secure remote facilities providing compute, platform, or other IT services on-demand on a shared but isolated platform that is open and accessible to the public for subscription is called a public cloud. It is preferred by start-ups, MNCs, government organizations, military, scientific, and pharmaceutical companies intending to utilize on-demand cloud computing. Cloud computing enables the organizations to focus on their actual business rather than periodically getting engaged in upgrading existing IT infrastructure to design cutting-edge solutions to compete with their competitors in the market. In a public cloud, all services are provided on a *pay as you go* model. Hence, it is easy and economical to try various different architectures to test and finalize the optimum solution to accelerate organizational growth. Another important characteristic of the public cloud is having virtually an unlimited pool of resources as and when it is required to expand IT infrastructure for short or long-term needs.

- **Hybrid cloud**: Hybrid cloud is a cloud environment that uses a combination of on-premises, private cloud, and public cloud services to fulfill organizational needs. In this model, a private cloud can use a public cloud's resources to meet a sudden spike in resource requirement. Since private data centers have limited resources, these data centers are extended to a third-party service provider's public cloud. Such hybrid models can be used for any reason such as, budget, unusual requirement, infrastructure constraints, or any organizational need.

History of the cloud

The history of the evolution of the cloud is shown in the following *Figure 2.1*:

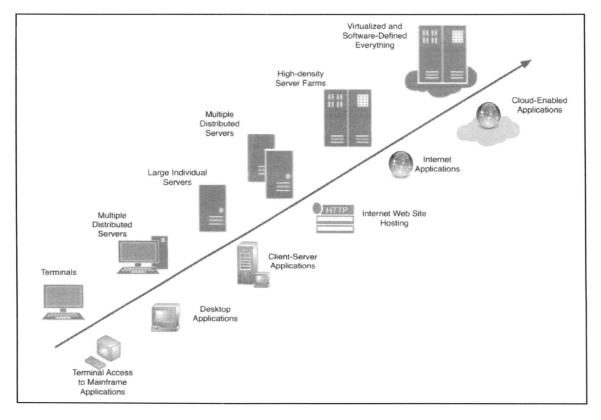

Figure 2.1: Cloud evolution

Image source: https://mycloudblog7.wordpress.com/2015/05/29/the-evolution-to-cloud-computing-how-did-we-get-here

Evolution of cloud computing

The following table describes how the cloud computing has evolved over the period of time:

Year	Event
1950	Mainframe, dumb terminals
1970	**Virtual machines (VMs)**
1990	**Virtual Private Network (VPN)**
1997	Cloud defined by Ramnath Chellappa
1999	`www.salesforce.com`
2000	Amazon's modernized data centers
2000	Google docs service
2006	Launch of AWS services
2008	Launch of Google app engine
2010	Launch of Microsoft Azure

The evolution of the cloud started in the 1950s and concepts such as service-oriented architecture, virtualization, and autonomic and utility computing are the stepping stones of today's cloud computing:

1. In the 1950s, mainframe computers were shared among various users through dumb terminals for saving cost and enabling efficient usage of the resources.

2. In the 1970s, VMs were developed to overcome the disadvantages of earlier technologies. VMs enabled us to run more than one different operating system simultaneously in isolated environments, providing all essential resources such as CPU, disk, RAM, and NIC individually to all VMs.

3. In the 1990s, telecom companies started dedicated *point-to-point* data circuits called VPN. It was offered at the fraction of the cost of the then available technologies. This invention made it possible to utilize bandwidth optimally. VPN made it possible to provide shared access to the same physical infrastructure to multiple users in shared but isolated environments.

4. In 1997, professor Ramnath Chellappa defined cloud computing as follows:

Computing paradigm where the boundaries of computing will be determined by economic rationale rather than technical limits alone.

5. In 1999, `https://www.salesforce.com` started delivering enterprise-level application services over the internet. This was one of the major moves in cloud history.
6. In the early 2000s, Amazon introduced web-based retail services on its modernized data centers. While Amazon was hardly using 10% of its data center capacity, they realized that new cloud computing infrastructure models can make them more efficient and cost-effective.
7. In the late 2000s, Google introduced their docs services directly to end users. This gave the taste of cloud computing and document sharing to end users.
8. In 2006, Amazon formally launched EC2 and S3. Subsequently, over the years, Amazon released various cloud services under the name AWS.
9. In 2008, Google announced the launch of its app engine services as beta service. This was the beginning of *Google Cloud services*.
10. In 2010, Microsoft Azure was formally released, followed by a number of cloud services in subsequent years.

Basic AWS concepts

AWS is a public cloud. It provides a range of IT services that can be used as building blocks for creating cutting-edge, robust, and scalable enterprise-grade solutions. It can be used to host everything from simple static websites to complex three-tier architectures, scientific applications to modern ERPs, online training to live broadcasting events (that is, sports events, political elections, and so on).

According to *Gartner's Magic Quadrant*, AWS is a leader in cloud IaaS. AWS is way ahead of its competitors after it pioneered the cloud IaaS market in 2006:

Figure 2.2: Gartner Magic Quadrant, rates various public cloud providers

Image source : https://www.gartner.com/doc/reprints?id=1-2G2O5FC&ct=150519

The **Magic Quadrant (MQ)** is a series of market research reports published by Gartner, the United States based research and advisory firm. It aims to provide a qualitative analysis into a market, its direction, maturity, and participants. Gartner's reports and MQs are respected in industries worldwide.

Benefits of using AWS over traditional data center

The benefits of AWS are significant and are listed as follows:

- **Switch Capital Expenditure (CapEx) to Operational Expenditure (OpEx)**: No need to bear the huge upfront cost of purchasing hardware or software and provision CapEx for the same in the budget. With AWS, pay only for what services you use on a monthly basis as OpEx.
- **Cost benefit from massive economies of scale**: Since AWS purchases everything in bulk, it gives them a cost advantage. AWS passes on the benefit from this cost advantage to their customers by offering the services at low cost. As the AWS cloud becomes larger and larger, these massive economies of scale benefit AWS as well as end customers.
- **No need to guess required infrastructure capacity**: Most of the time, before actual IT implementation, guessing IT infrastructure requirement leads to either scarcity of resources or wastage of resources when actual production begins. AWS makes it possible to scale the environment up or down as needed without guessing infrastructure need.
- **Increased speed and agility**: While building an on-premises data center, businesses have to wait to get the desired hardware or software from vendors for an extended period of time. With AWS, it becomes easier for the business to quickly get started and provision the required infrastructure on AWS immediately, without depending on third party vendors. They neither need to raise a purchase order nor wait for delivery, just log in to their AWS account and have everything at their disposal.
- **Global access**: AWS has data centers and edge locations across the globe. Take advantage and host your infrastructure near to your target market or at multiple locations across the globe at a very nominal cost.

Almost every IT need of an organization can be satisfied using AWS services, but there are still a few limitations, such as mainframe computing, which is not supported by AWS at the moment.

Accessing AWS services

Users can access AWS services in multiple ways. Individual services or the whole infrastructure can be accessed using any of the following means:

- **AWS Management Console**: This is a simple to use, browser-based graphical user interface that customers can use to manage their AWS resources.
- **AWS Command Line Interface (CLI)**: Mostly used by system administrators to perform day-to-day administration activities. There are individual sets of commands available for each AWS service.
- **AWS Software Development Kits (SDKs)**: AWS helps the user to take complexity out of the coding by providing SDKs for a number of programming languages including Android, iOS, Java, Python, PHP, .NET, Node.js, Go, Ruby, and so on. These SDKs can be used to create custom applications to meet specific organizational needs.
- **Query APIs**: AWS provides a number of HTTP endpoints. These endpoints can be used to send GET and PUT HTTP requests to AWS for obtaining present status and information for various AWS resources.

Most of the AWS services can be accessed with all of the preceding means. Yet some of the AWS services may not have one or two of the previously mentioned access methods.

AWS overview

AWS provides a highly reliable, scalable, low-cost infrastructure platform in the cloud that powers hundreds of thousands of businesses in 190 countries across the world. The following portion of the chapter provides a high-level overview of the basic AWS concepts that you should understand before you start working with AWS services.

AWS global infrastructure

AWS services are available at multiple locations across the globe. AWS provides these services with their infrastructure spread across the globe. The AWS infrastructure is connected and isolated in the form of **Regions**, **Availability Zones** (**AZs**), and **Edge Locations** based on geography. Let's understand some of the basic concepts of the AWS global infrastructure.

Regions and AZs

Each region, as shown in the following *Figure 2.3*, is a collection of at least two or more AZs. Each region is independent and they are isolated from each other to keep each of them safe in case of catastrophic events. Such regions actually correlate with geographical areas such as Asia, Europe, and North America:

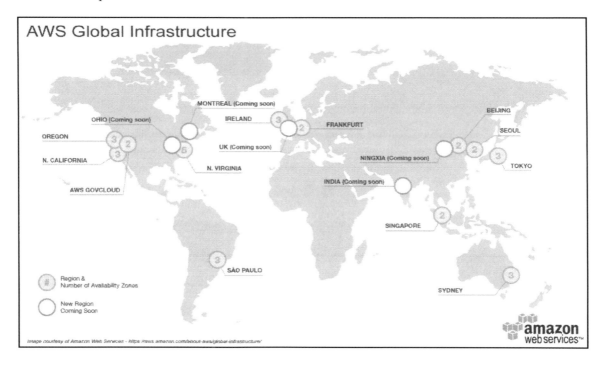

Figure 2.3: Reference image is taken from the official AWS site

Each AZ, as shown in the following *Figure 2.4* is separated based on a metropolitan area within a region, but they are internally connected with each other through dedicated low-latency networks within the same region to provide failover architecture:

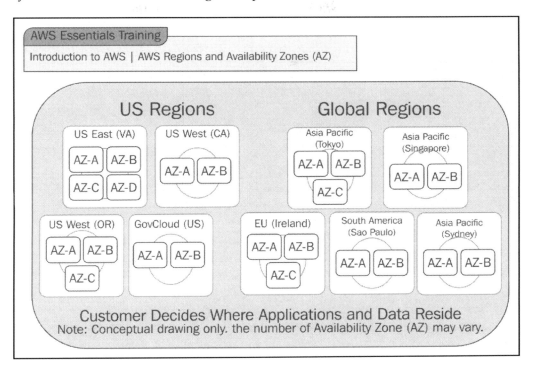

Figure 2.4: Example of AWS region and AZ configuration

Image source: http://www.slideshare.net/AmazonWebServicesLATAM/awsome-daybrbfreis201409

It is highly recommended to select an AWS region based on distance to the targeted market or based on legal compliance. For example, if a client's e-commerce website is selling goods and services only in the EU then it is suggested to host the website in Frankfurt or Ireland to minimize latency. One should also consider compliance requirements specific to a region while deciding on a region for hosting the application infrastructure. For example, if a client is running a website for betting, it may be illegal in one region, but it could be permitted in another region in line with the legal compliance requirements of a region.

AWS constantly evolves its service offerings. New services are launched in specific regions and then gradually supported in other regions. Due to the gradual approach of AWS in launching a service, there is a chance that not all the services may be available in all regions. It is a best practice to review available services in each region before planning, designing, or proposing any architecture.

 Physical access to AWS data centers is strictly controlled, monitored, and audited.

What are SaaS, PaaS, and IaaS?

Cloud computing is a broad term and covers many services. Common cloud computing models are **Infrastructure as a Service (IaaS)**, **Platform as a Service (PaaS)**, and **Software as a Service (SaaS)**.

Let's broadly understand these models:

- **IaaS**: When a service provider offers virtualized hardware or computing infrastructure as a service, such an offering is called IaaS.
- **PaaS**: PaaS is a type of cloud service in which a service provider offers application platforms and tools over the cloud, usually to enable application development. In this service model, underlined hardware and software are hosted on the service provider's infrastructure.
- **SaaS:** In the SaaS model, the service provider offers software or applications as services. Such services are hosted by the providers and the end customer simply consumes this SaaS without worrying about the underlying hosting platform, infrastructure, and maintenance.

The line of responsibilities in IaaS, PaaS, and SaaS is explained in the following *Figure 2.5*:

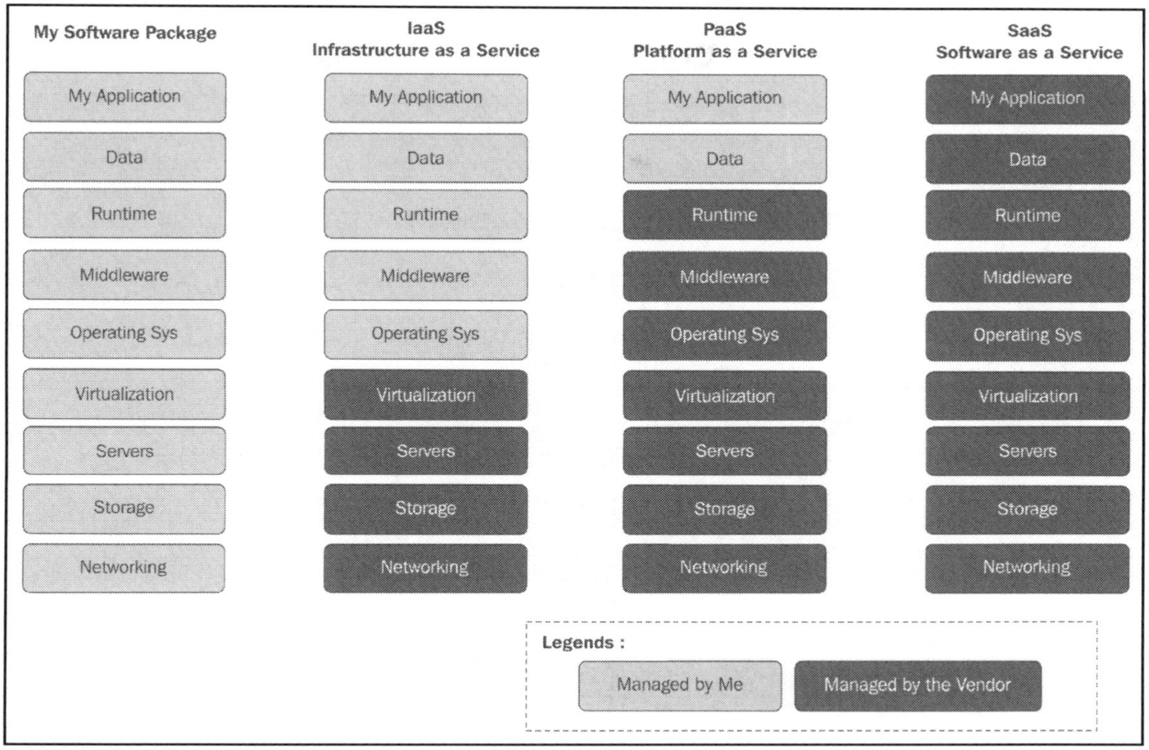

Figure 2.5: Stack and responsibility separation between cloud and customer among various cloud terms such as IaaS, PaaS and SaaS

Image source: https://thebpmfreak.wordpress.com/2012/09/28/iaas-paas-saas-a-pictorial-representation/

Understanding virtualization

Virtualization is a process of virtually segregating physical hardware resources into a set of virtual resources that can independently work as a computing resource and provide customized and dedicated CPU, RAM, storage, and so on. Each server and its resources is created in an isolated environment. Each isolated environment is abstracted from a physical operating system and underlying hardware configuration. Such resources are called VMs or instances.

Virtualization is achieved using virtualization software that maintains the abstract and virtual layers on top of physical hardware. Let us understand these virtualization software and virtualization types in the following sections.

Virtualization types based on virtualization software

As shown in the following *Figure 2.6*, virtualization software can be broadly categorized into two categories, class 1 and class 2:

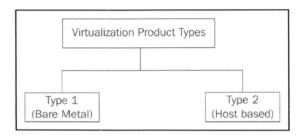

Figure 2.6: Virtualization types based on virtualization software

- **Class 1 type**: This is also known as bare metal virtualization type. Very thin (that is of a small size) virtualization software called a hypervisor is installed directly on the physical server. The AWS cloud uses a customized **Xen hypervisor**. Class 1 hypervisors are faster than class 2 hypervisors. Examples of class 1 hypervisors are Xen, OpenStack, Hyper-V, and vSphere.
- **Class 2 type**: This is also called a hosted hypervisor. These types of hypervisors are installed above the base operating system such as Windows or Linux. Examples of class 2 hypervisors are VMware Workstation, VirtualBox, and Virtual PC.

Virtualization types based on virtualization methods

As shown in the following *Figure 2.7*, virtualization can also be categorized as per the virtualization methods, as follows:

- **OS-level virtualization**: Host machine and VMs have the same OS with the same patch level
- **Software virtualization** (hypervisor):
    - **Binary translation**: Sensitive instructions of VMs are replaced by hypervisor calls.
    - **Para Virtualization Mode (PVM)**: Guest OS is modified to deliver performance.
    - **Hardware Assisted Virtual Machine (HVM)**: Creates an abstract layer between host and guest VMs. Uses CPU's special instruction sets (that is, Intel-VT and AMD-V) to boost guest VMs performance.
  - **Hardware emulation**: Makes it possible to run an unsupported OS, such as running Android on a PC:

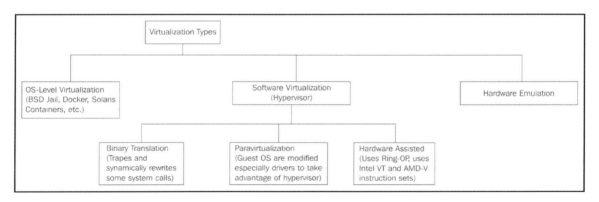

Figure 2.7: Virtualization types based on virtualization methods

Elasticity versus scalability

Elasticity and scalability are two important characteristics of cloud computing. They describe the way cloud infrastructure is able to expand and shrink to match the actual dynamic workload and are discussed as follows:

- **Scalability**: This means adding resources either to the existing instance (scale up) or in parallel to an existing instance (scale out). Scalability is essential to achieve elasticity:

  - **Scale up**: Changing instance type from small to large (that is, changing to more memory or compute) is called scaling up. It is also called **Vertical Scaling**. It may require stopping the existing and running instance. Usually, scaling up is done to get more compute and memory on the same instance. Scaling up is usually suggested for an application that does not support clustering mode easily such as, RDBMS. Usually, scaling up is achieved manually and requires downtime.

  - **Scale out**: By placing one or more new instances parallel to the existing instance is called scale out. It is also referred to as **Horizontal Scaling**. It gives good performance and availability as instances can be placed across multiple AZs. By having individual resources such as NIC and disk controller for each instance, much better performance can be achieved compared to scaling up. Usually, scaling out is suggested for clustering enabled applications such as stateless web servers, big data, and NoSQL. Scaling out generally does not require any downtime.

- **Elasticity**: In physics, elasticity can be defined as a *material's ability to expand and shrink with the external parameters*. Similarly, in the cloud infrastructure, elasticity can be defined as the ability to automatically provision additional resources to meet the high demand and reducing the extended number of resources when the demand lowers.

Unlike a public cloud, generally, traditional data centers do not have on-demand scalability and elasticity. The following sections compare *traditional data center* and *cloud infrastructure resourcing*.

Traditional data center resourcing

As shown in the following *Figure 2.8*, in traditional data centers, there may be situations when provisioned infrastructure capacity is either more than what is needed or less than required. When the capacity is more than what is required, it's a waste of CapEx and when it is less than required, it would result in throttling performance:

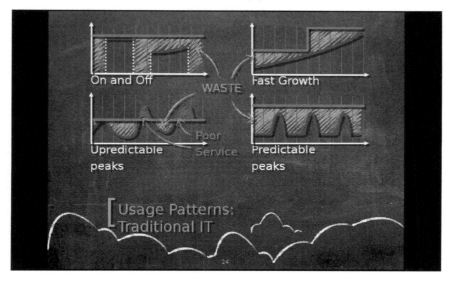

Figure 2.8: Traditional data center workload actual versus provisioned capacity

Image source: https://www.slideshare.net/AmazonWebServices/aws-101-cloud-computing-seminar-2012/12-On_and_Off_WASTE_Fast

Cloud infrastructure resourcing

In contrast to traditional data centers, cloud infrastructure can be designed with dynamic scalability and elasticity based on actual workload. As shown in the following *Figure 2.9*, such flexibility almost nullifies the wastage of resources or performance throttling. Until the time *soft limit* is reached, cloud infrastructure can keep scaling out and scaling down based on actual workload.

To achieve such flexibility, cloud infrastructure has to be designed and automatically provisioned in line with such requirements using various services offered by respective cloud service providers:

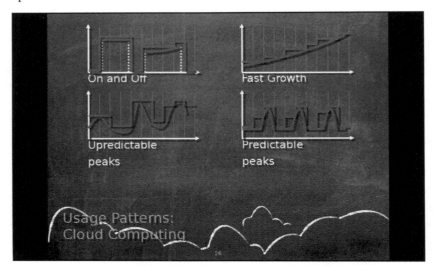

Figure 2.9: Cloud infrastructure actual workload versus provisioned capacity

Image source: https://www.slideshare.net/AmazonWebServices/aws-101-cloud-computing-seminar-2012/12-On_and_Off_WASTE_Fast

Comparing AWS cloud and on-premises data centers

Whenever an organization thinks of migrating their infrastructure over to a public cloud, the first question that strikes the organization is cost. AWS provides major advantages over on-premise environments as there is no upfront cost of using AWS. Thus, there is no CapEx requirement as AWS works on OpEx. That means a customer pays only on a monthly basis based on actual consumption of AWS resources.

The following table differentiates cost on various counts between AWS and on-premise environments:

Pricing model	One time upfront cost		Monthly cost	
	Public cloud	On-premise DC	Public cloud	On-premise DC
Server hardware	0	$$	$$	0
Network hardware	0	$$	0	0
Hardware maintenance	0	$$	0	$
Software OS	0	$$	$	0
Power and cooling	0	$$	$	$
Data center space	0	$$	0	0
Administration	0	$$	0	$$$
Storage	0	$$	$$	0
Network bandwidth	0	$	$	$
Resource management software	0	0	$	$
24x7 support	0	0	$	$

Cost comparison example is based on some assumptions

Total Cost of Ownership (TCO) versus Return on Investment (ROI)

There is no doubt that public cloud computing has many advantages over traditional data center concepts, such as it provides a cutting-edge, secure, and robust platform to host an organization's IT infrastructure. Surely it impacts costs by turning CapEx into OpEx. However, when making an investment in any technology or service, it is important for a business to understand two key aspects, that is, ROI and TCO. Both of these involve careful and critical analysis. It is very important to find the lowest cost in the long run rather than just the lowest initial cost.

Deriving TCO not only involves purchase cost and maintenance cost, but it also involves hidden costs such as operating cost, setup cost, change or reconfiguration cost, upgrade cost, security cost, infrastructure support cost, insurance cost, electricity cost, depreciation, tax savings, and environmental impact.

> AWS provides an online TCO calculator at `https://awstcocalculator.com`.

RoI can be derived using a mathematical formula. Primarily, it can be used to evaluate investments and decide how well a particular investment can perform compared to others. In terms of IT, usually an enterprise's top-level management or CIO performs such a comparison between owning a data center and using a public cloud.

> AWS also provides a cost calculator to find monthly estimated expenses at `https://calculator.s3.amazonaws.com/index.html`.

Creating a new AWS account

Creating a new account at AWS to start using cloud services is easy just like opening a new email account. The steps to create an AWS account are as follows:

> The AWS interface may change from time-to-time.

1. In a web browser, open the following URL: `https://aws.amazon.com/`.
2. Click **Create an AWS Account**, as shown in the following *Figure 2.10*:

Figure 2.10: Create a new AWS account

3. First, select **I am a new user.**, provide an **E-mail or mobile number:** of an authorized person to open a new account, and finally click on **Sign in using our secure server** as follows:

Figure 2.11: Sign in new AWS account

4. Enter **Login Credentials** such as name, email address, and password and finally click on **Create account** as follows:

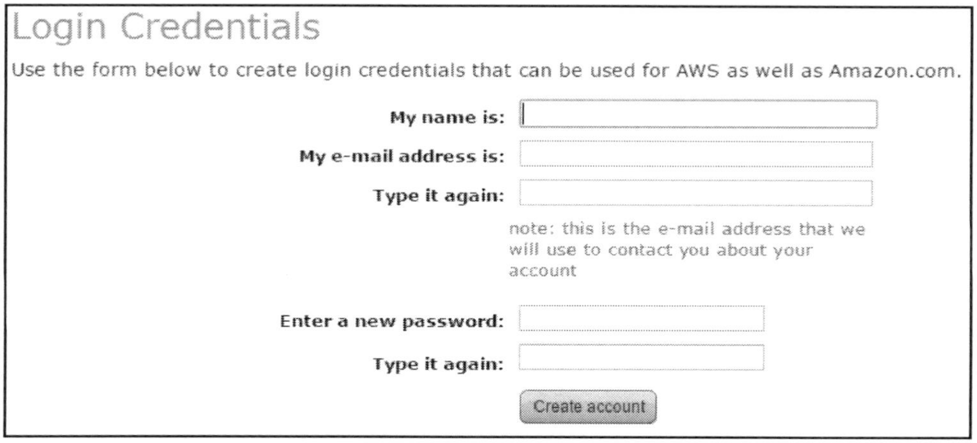

Figure 2.12: Login credentials

5. Provide **Contact Information** as follows:

As per the actual usage, select a category **Company Account** or **Personal Account**. Please provide the appropriate **Captcha** and accept the agreement after understanding.

Figure 2.13: Contact details

When the country selected is **India,** later it cannot be changed. If you select any other country, it can be changed later. This restriction is specific to India.

6. Provide payment and PAN card details, as follows:

In case of a credit/debit card not being handy, than it can be skipped during this wizard and it can be provided later on. Also, PAN card details are optional.

Figure 2.14: Payment information

When card details are provided, based on the card type, you may be asked to fill in a credit/debit card PIN to complete the transaction. To verify card details, INR 2.00 may be deducted from your account. Later, it will be adjusted to your usage (that is, monthly billing).

7. Provide appropriate contact details and verify the captcha image. The AWS automated system will make a verification call. On screen, it will display a four-digit PIN that you need to provide when you receive an automated verification call. The following *Figure 2.15* shows a similar verification screen:

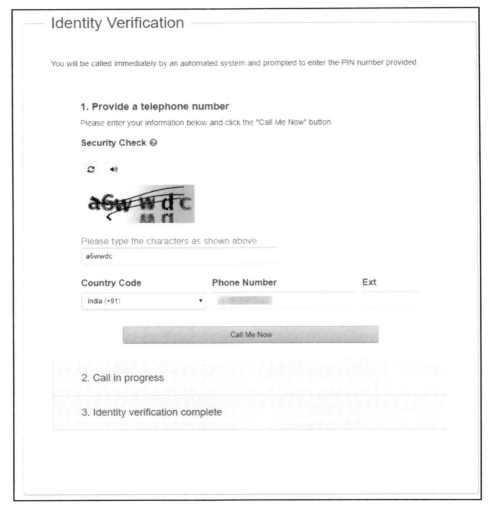

Figure 2.15: Identity verification

8. Finally, select **Support Plan**, as shown in the following *Figure 2.16*:

Figure 2.16: Support plan

Based on the plan selected, charges are applied to the monthly billing.

9. Finally, a new AWS account creation is done and a welcome email is sent to the authorized person's email address.

Deleting an AWS account

The way we created an AWS account, similarly, an AWS account can be deleted easily. Once logged in to the AWS account using the root user, click on the right-hand side drop-down menu. Usually, it is marked with the name given at the time of creating an AWS account. Under that, select **My Account**. It may open **My Account Dashboard** in a new tab. At the bottom of the dashboard, select the checkbox under **Close Account** and finally click **Close Account** as follows:

▾ Close Account

☑ I understand that by clicking this checkbox, I am willing to close my AWS account. Monthly usage of certain AWS services is calculated and billed at the beginning of the following month. If you have used these types of services this month, then at the beginning of next month you will receive a bill for usage that occurred prior to termination of your account. If you own a Reserved Instance for which you have elected to pay in monthly installments, when your account is closed you will continue to be billed your monthly recurring payment until the Reserved Instance is sold on the Reserved Instance Marketplace or it expires.

Close Account

Figure 2.17: Deleting AWS account confirmation

 For the current month, billing may be completed at the end of the month. All the AWS resources and data will be wiped out. Once the account is closed, there will be no mechanism to undo and/or get the data back. It is highly recommended to back up important data at a secured and safe place before closing the AWS account.

AWS free tier

Opening a new AWS account comes along with a limited free tier capacity for 12 months, mostly on all services with some limitations on usage. The main purpose of the free tier is to enable users to have hands-on experience and build their confidence. The latest AWS free tier details can be obtained from the following URL: `https://aws.amazon.com/free/`.

If AWS resource consumption exceeds the limit of the free tier, actual charges are applicable, which are billed in a monthly cycle. It is highly recommended to closely monitor running resources on the AWS cloud all the time.

Root user versus non-root user

The email address and passwords that are used to create an AWS account are called the **root user**. This user has the highest privileges. It is highly recommended and also best practice to log in with the root user and then create appropriate IAM users for day-to-day activities (that is, for database administrator, system administrator) and so on. The root user can log in to the AWS account using the following URL: `https://console.aws.amazon.com/console/home`.

Provide a valid username and password created in earlier steps (that is creating a new AWS account).

If you are not able to memorize the preceding URL, go to `https://aws.amazon.com` and select **My Account** than **AWS Management Console**. This way also, it will bring up the same login screen as follows:

Figure 2.18: AWS account

For a non-root user login, individual users are created with the help of the IAM service to perform day-to-day infrastructure activities. To obtain a URL to log in using an IAM user, it is essential to log in once with the root credentials. Go to the IAM dashboard and it will give IAM users a sign in link: `https://123456789012.signin.aws.amazon.com/console/`.

In the preceding URL, the first 12 characters represent an AWS account number and it varies from AWS account to account.

AWS dashboard

Having a good understanding of the AWS dashboard is essential to perform day-to-day activities. There are a number of components of the AWS dashboard, as shown in the following *Figure 2.19*. The AWS dashboard layout may change from time-to-time. The following *Figure 2.19* is given for an overview here:

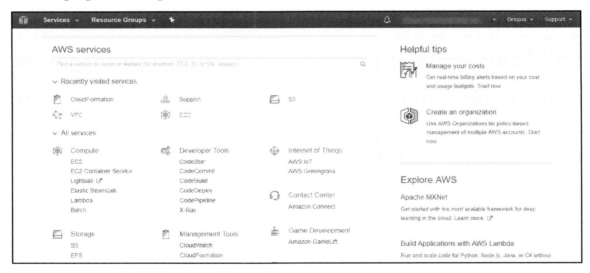

Figure 2.19: AWS web console

Components of the AWS dashboard

As you can see in the preceding screenshot, there are a number of components on the AWS dashboard. The following list gives you an overview of these components:

- ⬚: This icon represents console home. Clicking on this, you can go to dashboard home:

- **Services** ˅: This drop-down lists a number of AWS services. Clicking on individual service takes you to the specific service console.

- **Resource Groups** ˅: You can segregate various services in resource groups. Resource groups provide you a way to quickly group and access frequently used services based on your requirement:

- 📌: Frequently accessed services can be dragged and pinned at the top bar. It can be toggled between **Icon** only, **Text** only, and **icon with text**.

- 🔔: Shows all the alerts and errors from AWS. Any planned maintenance from AWS is also highlighted in advance:

- **Name** ˅: This is a drop-down menu to access **My Account**, **My Billing Dashboard**, **My Security** credentials, and **Sign Out** options.

- **N. Virginia** ˅: Based on your region, you may see the region name here and in case you need to change the region, you can select it from the drop-down menu. Most of the services are region-specific, but a few services are global, such as AWS dashboard, IAM, and a few others.

> The region drop-down menu by default doesn't show Government Cloud and China Region.

- A support drop-down menu gives options to go to **Support Center**, **Forums**, **Documentation**, **Training**, and other resources.
- A search bar is available to quickly find AWS services; sometimes it may be time-consuming to find the desired AWS services from the long list of various services.

On your dashboard, recently accessed AWS services appear at the top based on your usage of these services.

It is suggested to explore every corner of the AWS dashboard; it provides links to various solutions, tutorials, and more useful information.

Core AWS services

 Some of the AWS services are fully managed. This means the infrastructure and other resources required to provide such services are fully managed by AWS. You can use these services without worrying about infrastructure, configuration, or any other resources. With managed services options, users get robust and reliable services without any overhead of service maintenance.

Services are divided in various groups based on their use. The following table describes a number of services provided by AWS with their purpose. As AWS continuously evolves its service catalog, there may be periodic additions to this list:

Group	AWS service	Purpose
Compute	**Elastic Cloud Compute (EC2)**	Provides scalable compute capacity (virtual servers).
	EC2 Container Service	Highly scalable and high performance container management service. Supports Docker and runs on a managed cluster of EC2 instances.
	Lightsail	Provides template based computing. It is also called **Virtual Private Servers** (**VPS**). It makes it possible to quickly launch virtual machines from templates rather than selecting individual components in EC2.
	Elastic Beanstalk	Developers can quickly deploy and manage applications in the AWS cloud. Developers just have to upload their application and the rest is taken care of by Elastic Beanstalk.

	Lambda	Allows us to run code without actually spinning servers. Such code can be triggered on certain events in other AWS services such as S3, SNS, DynamoDB, Kinesis Stream, and many other AWS services.
	Batch	Makes running any number of batch processing for developers, scientists, and engineers on AWS cloud.
Storage	**Simple Storage Service (S3)**	Provides highly-scalable, reliable, and low-latency object storage.
	Elastic File System	Fully managed, scalable, and sharable storage among thousands of EC2 instances.
	Glacier	Secure, durable, and extremely low-cost solutions for backup and archiving.
	Storage Gateway	Seamlessly connect on-premises applications or services with the AWS cloud storage.
Database	**Relational Database Service (RDS)**	Managed database service. Supports Amazon Aurora, MySQL, MariaDB, Oracle, SQL Server, and PostgreSQL database engines.
	DynamoDB	Fast and flexible NoSQL database service. Provides predictable performance.
	ElastiCache	Makes it easy to deploy Memcached or Redis protocol compliant server nodes in the cloud. Primarily, it improves application performance by storing frequently accessed information into memory.
	RedShift	Fully managed petabyte-scalable columnar data warehousing service. Also provides ODBC and JDBC connectivity and SQL-based retrieval.
Networking and Content Delivery	**Virtual Private Cloud (VPC)**	Logically isolates networks. Allows us to define IP range selection, subnet creation, configuring route, and network gateways.
	CloudFront	Using edge locations, contents are distributed to provide low-latency and high data transfer speed across the globe.

	Direct Connect	It provides alternatives to bypass the internet and uses dedicated networks to connect private data centers and the AWS cloud.
	Route 53	Highly available and scalable global DNS service.
Migration	**Database Migration Service (DMS)**	Cross schema conversion tools such as Oracle PL/SQL to SQL Server.
	Server Migration	Enables VMware VM migration to AWS EC2.
	Snowball	Accelerates TBs of data transportation between data centers and AWS securely. Available in two sizes, 50 TB and 80 TB.
	Snowmobile	Makes possible exabytes of data transfer. Possible to transfer up to 100 PB per Snowmobile. Comes in a 45-foot long rugged shipping container.
Developer tools	CodeCommit	Provides scalable and managed private Git repository. Anything from code to binaries can be stored.
	CodeBuild	Full managed build service. Performs compiling source code, testing and makes them ready to deploy.
	CodeDeploy	Automated code deployment to any instance (that is EC2 or on-premises).
	CodePipeline	CodePipeline is an AWS product that automates the software deployment process, allowing a developer to quickly model, visualize, and deliver code for new features and updates. This method is called continuous delivery.
Management tools	CloudWatch	Can be configured to monitor AWS resources. It can collect metrics and logs to monitor and generate alerts.
	CloudFormation	Automates and simplifies the repeated infrastructure tasks such as creating repeatedly the same infrastructure in the same or different AZ or region.

	CloudTrail	Records each AWS API call and stores log files into an S3 bucket.
	Config	Provides AWS resource inventory, configuration history, and changes notifications to enable security and governance.
	OpsWorks	AWS OpsWorks is a configuration management service that uses Chef, an automation platform that treats server configurations as code. OpsWorks uses Chef to automate how servers are configured, deployed, and managed across your Amazon EC2 instances or on-premises compute environments.
	Service catalog	AWS service catalog allows organizations to centrally manage commonly deployed IT services, and helps organizations achieve consistent governance and meet compliance requirements, while enabling users to quickly deploy only the approved IT services they need with the constraints your organization sets.
	Trusted advisor	Helps to reduce monthly billing, and increase performance and security.
	Application discovery service	Quickly and reliably finds out an application's dependencies and performance profile, running on-premises data centers.
Security, Identity & Compliance	**Identity Access and Management (IAM)**	Allows us to create and manage groups and users to grant them required permissions to perform day-to-day infra tasks.
	Inspector	Automated security assessment service to test the security state of applications hosted on EC2.
	Certificate Manager	Manages SSL/TLS certificates. Also makes it easy to deploy them across various AWS services.
	Directory Service	It is an AWS Directory service for Microsoft Active directory. Makes it easy to deploy directory-aware workloads on AWS resources to use and manage AD in the AWS cloud.

	Web Application Firewall (WAF)	By configuring rules to allow, block, or just monitor web requests, protects web applications from external attack.
	Shield	Managed service to protect web applications against DDoS attacks running on AWS.
Analytics	Athena	Interactive query service to analyze data in Amazon S3 using SQL.
	Elastic Map Reduce (EMR)	Based on the Hadoop framework, it provides easy and cost-effective big data solutions.
	CloudSearch	Fully managed and scalable textual search solutions for websites or applications.
	Elasticsearch	Managed services make it easy to deploy, operate, and scale Elasticsearch clusters in the AWS cloud.
	Kinesis	Makes it possible to work on live streams of data to load and analyze with AWS services.
	Data Pipeline	Enables data movement and data processing within AWS and also between on-premises and the AWS cloud.
	QuickSight	Fast, easy-to-use, and cloud-powered business analytics service to build data visualization and ad hoc analysis.
Artificial Intelligence	Lex	Provides a platform to build text and voice-based interfaces, having high-quality speech recognition and language understanding capabilities. Powered by the Alexa engine.
	Polly	Provides a voice to the application, to speak. It basically converts text into speech.
	Rekognition	Fully managed image recognition service powered by deep learning.
	Machine Learning	Allows us to build algorithm-based predictive applications, including fraud detection, demand forecasting, and click prediction.
Internet of Things (IoT)	AWS IoT	Platform to connect devices and sensors to cloud easily and securely.

Game development	GameLift	Fully managed service to deploy, operate, and scale session-based multiplayer game servers in the cloud.
Mobile services	Mobile Hub	Provides a platform to build, test, and monitor mobile app usage.
	Cognito	Provides sign-up and authentication to web and mobile apps. Also provides synchronization of data between various devices (that is, mobile, tablet, and laptop).
	Device Farm	Enables mobile application (that is, Android and iPhone) testing parallel on hundreds of real devices in the AWS cloud.
	Mobile Analytics	Can be used to analyze and visualize mobile application usage. Compared to other such analytical tools, it delivers reports within 60 minutes of receiving data while other tools take a long time.
	Pinpoint	Specifically designed to run precise campaigns for mobile users engagement. Pinpoint observes users interaction with the mobile application and determines what message at what time to send them.
Application services	Step functions	Managed service, coordinates the components of distributed applications and microservices using visual workflows.
	Simple Workflow (SWF)	Coordinates tasks (that is, scheduling tasks and executing dependent processes) across distributed application components.
	API Gateway	Enables developers to publish, monitor, and maintain APIs in a secure and scalable manner.
	Elastic Transcoder	Allows developers to transcode (that is, convert) video and audio files from one to another format using APIs.

Messaging	**Simple Queue Service (SQS)**	Provides a robust and secured message queue mechanism to store and schedule process messages.
	Simple Notification Service (SNS)	Notifies real-time events (that is, publishes messages) to the intended recipients. It can also provide events to trigger other AWS services.
	Simple Email Service (SES)	Cost-effective and scalable solutions for email campaigning.
Business productivity	WorkDocs	Managed and secured enterprise storage solution. Enterprise grade solution to share files, managing multiple versions and sharing with others for feedback. Allows to control access.
	WorkMail	Managed business emails, contacts, and calendar. Allows seamless access from mobile devices, web browsers, or Microsoft Outlook.
Desktop & App Streaming	WorkSpaces	Managed desktop computing. End users can connect to high-end desktops in the cloud using thin clients. Usually, EC2 is used to host servers not desktops.
	AppStream 2.0	Enables Windows application streaming by running on the AWS cloud. It's an enterprise application streaming service for Windows application on AWS cloud.

AWS services

Shared security responsibility model

Before developing, designing, and implementing cloud solutions, it is important to understand the security responsibility shared between AWS and the customers who consume these services. The following *Figure 2.20* distinguishes the responsibilities of AWS as a cloud service provider and the customers who consume these services:

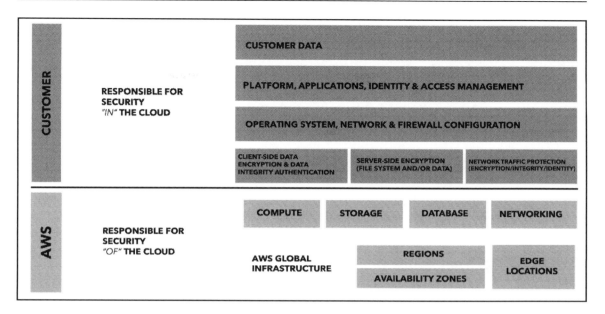

Figure 2.20: Reference URL: https://aws.amazon.com/compliance/shared-responsibility-model/

AWS cloud shared responsibility between service providers and customers

Amazon promises that security is its highest priority as a public cloud service provider. AWS is committed to providing consistent, robust, and secured AWS public cloud services to their customers. Amazon achieves this by securing the foundation services, that is, compute, storage, database, and networking, and global infrastructure such as regions, AZs, and edge locations. Customers have to manage the security of their data, operating systems, application platforms, applications, network, system or any customer-specific services deployed on AWS by them using IaaS. AWS provides various services such as **AWS Inspector**, **CloudWatch**, **IAM**, **Trusted Advisor**, and **CloudTrail** to manage the security in an automated way such that users need not spend much time on routine security and audit tasks. You can use these services as a building block of your environment on AWS.

In other words, AWS is responsible for providing security of the AWS cloud and the customer is responsible for the security of the resources deployed within the cloud. In case of managed services (that is, DynamoDB, RDS, Redshift, and so on), AWS is responsible for handling the basic security tasks of the underlying AWS resources and also at OS level.

To match an organization's IT compliance requirement, AWS also provides third-party audit reports to ensure that the AWS cloud fulfills all the essential compliance needs. You can refer to `https://aws.amazon.com/compliance` for more details.

Some of the compliances followed by AWS are given here:

- **IT security compliances:**
    - SOC 1/SSAE 16/ISAE 3402 (formerly SAS 70)
    - SOC 2
    - SOC 3
    - FISMA, DIACAP, and FedRAMP
    - DOD CSM Levels 1-5
    - PCI DSS Level 1
    - ISO 9001 / ISO 27001
    - ITAR
    - FIPS 140-2
    - MTCS Level 3
- **Industry compliances:**
    - Criminal Justice Information Services (CJIS)
    - Cloud Security Alliance (CSA)
    - Family Educational Rights and Privacy Act (FERPA)
    - Health Insurance Portability and Accountability Act (HIPAA)
    - Motion Picture Association of America (MPAA)

The AWS network provides protection against traditional network security problems (that is, DDoS and MITM attacks, IP spoofing, and port scanning).

Remember, you need to take prior approval from AWS to perform penetration testing in your AWS account, otherwise AWS understands such testing as malicious attacks and your AWS account may be blocked.

AWS also ensures that when **Elastic Block Store** (**EBS**) volumes are deleted from one account, internal wiping takes place before it is reused for another AWS account. Wiping is done as per the industry standards (that is, DoD 5220.22-M or NIST 800-88). It is also possible to encrypt sensitive data on EBS volumes. AWS uses the AES-256 algorithm.

 Detailed understanding of shared responsibility model can be obtained from `https://d0.awsstatic.com/whitepapers/aws-security-whitepaper.pdf`.

AWS soft limits

For every AWS account, region-based limits are enabled for each of the AWS services. Such limits restricts an AWS account to provision limited numbers of resources in specific AWS service. For example, a news AWS account can provision around 20 EC2 instances. This limits may vary from resource types and respective AWS service. Some of these limits are soft limits and you can raise a support request to AWS for revising this limit in your AWS account.

AWS Trusted Advisor displays account usage and limits for each specific service region.

Authorized IAM users or root accounts can place a request with AWS support to increase such service limits.

Here's how you can request a change in service limit:

1. Log in to your AWS account, on the top right-hand side corner click on the **Support** drop-down menu and select **Support Center**.
2. Click **Create Case** and select **Service Limit Increase**.
3. Select the AWS service whose limit is to be increased in the **Limit Type** drop-down menu.

When any resource's soft limit is reached, no new resources can be provisioned until the soft limit has been increased from the AWS end. For example, if your soft limit in North Virginia is 20, EC2 instances then spinning up the 21st instance would result in an error.

Disaster recovery with AWS

For any enterprise, unplanned downtime to a business can have a devastating impact not only on ongoing business but also on overall enterprise. Any catastrophe or disaster can bring a city or a region to a standstill and can impact businesses for a prolonged period. It is critical for organizations to plan for such disasters that can halt their business. AWS provides a number of services and features that can be used to overcome such unplanned downtime arising out of natural disasters or human error.

Disaster Recovery (DR) is the process of designing an architecture that is able to recover from any disaster situation within a stipulated time. The cost of DR planning is inversely proportional to the time required to recover the infrastructure. Traditionally, in the case of private data center, it may be required to create similar data centers at any distant and safe place. It also requires huge upfront investment, constant staff training, and maintenance. On the other hand, by hosting infrastructure on AWS, it can be easier to plan for DR setup in multiple regions or AZs. Resources in such additional regions or AZs can be automatically scaled up or down as per actual workload and you pay only for what is actually used. One of the best aspects of AWS is *you can have a wide range of region selection to host DR infrastructure.*

Before DR planning begins, there are two very critical aspects of a DR plan that we need to understand:

- **Recovery Time Objective (RTO)**: This defines the time within which business processes should be recovered from downtime. The maximum time a business process can sustain a down condition depends upon the criticality of the process. Generally, RTO is defined separately for each business process and related environment. For example, let's consider the RTO of a business process is 3 hours. In this case, if disaster occurs, businesses can afford downtime of maximum 3 hours within which the environment should be recovered.
- **Recovery Point Objective (RPO)**: This defines the acceptable amount of data loss, measured in time. For example, let's consider that the RPO of a business process is 1 hour. In this case, if disaster occurs at 2:00 P.M. then all the stored data should be available at least until 1:00 PM. Thus, a business can afford to lose 1 hour's data in case of any disaster.

The best way to define RTO is to understand the financial impact to the business when the system is not available, and similarly the best way to define RPO is to understand the financial impact on the business when business data is not available for a specific time frame. By considering these aspects along with technical feasibility and cost of setting up DR, one can understand and define the RTO and RPO of a business process.

In the case of having a traditional data center, hosting a DR site usually involves duplication of the same type of data center at distant and safe site. It also involves huge upfront CapEx. On the other hand, by hosting IT infrastructure in AWS, it is possible only to go for a *pay as you go* model. AWS services and concepts such as Region, AZs, EC2, DNS - Route 53, Networking Service (VPC), Elastic Load Balancing, Auto Scaling, CloudFormation, and many others can help in designing the DR plan.

The following *Figure 2.21* shows the various DR reference models using AWS services:

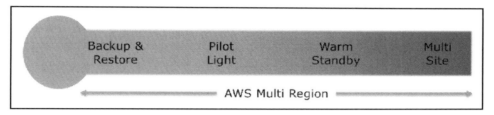

Figure 2.21: AWS Multi Region

Reference URL: https://d0.awsstatic.com/whitepapers/aws-disaster-recovery.pdf

The DR approach can be broadly categorized in four models:

- Backup and restore
- Pilot light
- Warm standby
- Multi-site

Out of the four models described in the preceding *Figure 2.21*, Backup and restore is the most economical model, but it may take more time in recovery. If you go from left to right in the preceding figure, time to recovery decreases, but at the same time, cost to recover increases. The same way, if you go from right to left as given in the preceding figure, time to recovery increases and cost to recover decreases. Let's understand these DR models in subsequent sections.

Backup and restore

This approach of DR involves periodically backing up the critical data and keeping it at a safe and secured place for later use. In case of any disaster, the backed-up data can be restored as needed.

Let's consider a traditional data center approach to understand the backup and restore DR model. In this approach, data is periodically backed up on tape drives and sent offsite. In case of any disaster in DC, one needs to bring the backup tapes from an offsite location to wherever restoration takes place. It takes longer to restore the data from tape drives as tape drives perform a sequential read of data. Usually, this type of DR mechanism is obsolete in a modern fast paced enterprise.

For a similar Backup and Restore approach, AWS provides a number of services such as S3 and Glacier services. Transferring data to and from S3 and Glacier is much faster, safer, and economical compared to the tape drives. S3 can be compared to an offline object storage, whereas Glacier can be compared to an economical tape drives used for archiving purposes. S3 provides instant access to your data, whereas the comparatively cheaper option Glacier may take around 3 to 4 hours to restore archived data. AWS also provides a service called **Import/Export,** which offers physical data storage devices that can be used to perform large data transfer directly to AWS. There are other options as well for importing/exporting a large amount of data on AWS such as **Snowball** or **Snowmobile**.

AWS Snowball is a service that accelerates transferring large amounts of data into and out of AWS using physical storage appliances, bypassing the internet.

AWS Snowmobile is an exabyte-scale data transfer service used to move extremely large amounts of data to AWS. You can transfer up to 100 PB per Snowmobile, a 45-foot long ruggedized shipping container, pulled by a semi-trailer truck.

AWS also provides a service called Storage Gateway. It directly connects a physical data center to AWS storage services. Using Storage Gateway, organizations can directly store data to S3 or Glacier as a part of their DR strategy. Storage Gateway is fast, economical, and robust.

The following *Figure 2.22* shows an example configuration to achieve a backup and restore DR setup scenario on AWS and physical data center:

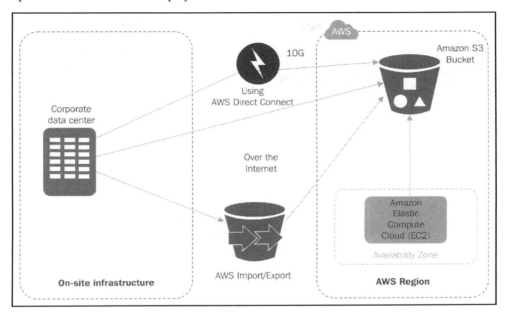

Figure 2.22: Using AWS services to design backup and restore DR setup

Reference URL: https://d0.awsstatic.com/whitepapers/aws-disaster-recovery.pdf

Pilot light

This model can be easily explained by the example of a gas heater, where a small flame is always ignited and can be quickly ignited to a larger flame in a boiler to heat up an entire house. The term *pilot light* is derived from the same concept.

In this DR scenario, the minimal DR version with the most critical components of the environment is always kept running in parallel to the production environment. This can be explained through a couple of examples:

- Primary site runs in on-premise DC and a DR setup with minimal critical resources is kept running in the cloud. In case of any issue in the data center, other required resources can be provisioned in the cloud infrastructure and it can start serving the traffic after failover to the DR setup.

- Primary site runs on AWS in one region and a DR setup with minimal critical resources is kept running in another region on AWS. In case of any issue in one AWS region, other required resources can be provisioned in cloud infrastructure in another region to match the primary environment setup and it can start serving the traffic after failover to the DR setup.

When an enterprise's IT is running on a traditional data center, it is also possible to shift only critical applications, load to the cloud, and run the rest of the infrastructure in traditional fashion. The following *Figure 2.23* and *Figure 2.24* shows how this model works in normal conditions and failover conditions, respectively:

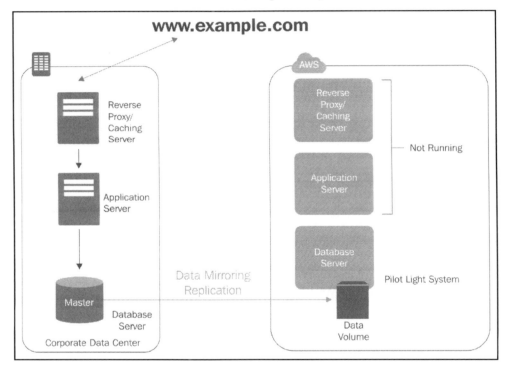

Figure 2.23: Applications running under normal situation

Reference URL: https://d0.awsstatic.com/whitepapers/aws-disaster-recovery.pdf

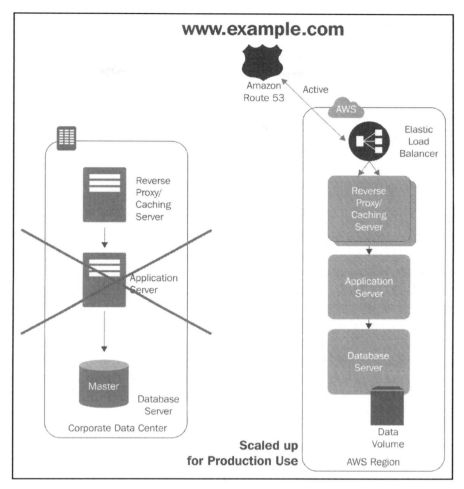

Figure 2.24: Earlier infrastructure under failover conditions

Reference URL: https://d0.awsstatic.com/whitepapers/aws-disaster-recovery.pdf

With the help of the *Figure 2.24* and *Figure 2.25*, we can clearly understand that in the event of any disaster at the primary site (that is, data center or cloud-based) traffic is automatically diverted to the secondary site. This is also called a *failover scenario*. Thus users experience consistent performance rather than experiencing down time on the application. Compared to the Backup and restore model, the pilot light model is much faster. It may require a few manual steps to perform or can be automated with the help of some automation process using **DevOps**.

Warm standby

In this DR scenario, a scaled-down and fully functional environment is always running in the cloud. It extends the pilot light DR model. In case of the pilot light model, one needs to create additional instances or resources to match the size of the primary environment. In contrast to pilot light, Warm Standby keeps a fully functional DR setup with a minimum fleet of instances with the minimum possible size of instances. In the event of any disaster, the DR setup is scaled up to match the primary site and traffic is failed over to the DR setup. Since fully functional infrastructure always runs in the warm standby approach, it further reduces required recovery time.

The following *Figure 2.25* and *Figure 2.26* explain the concepts of primary and secondary sites under a warm standby DR model. It explains how the load is transferred to secondary site when primary fails:

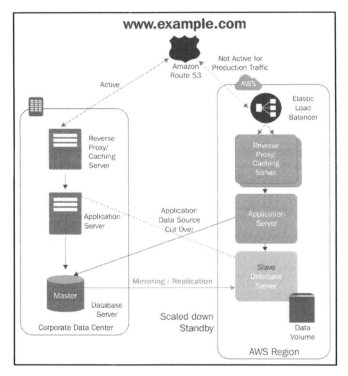

Figure 2.25: End users are accessing a primary site under normal conditions

Reference URL: https://d0.awsstatic.com/whitepapers/aws-disaster-recovery.pdf

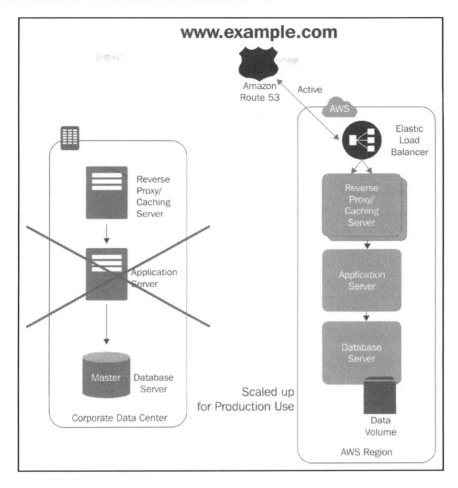

Figure 2.26: End users are diverted to a secondary site under warm standby DR model

Reference URL: https://d0.awsstatic.com/whitepapers/aws-disaster-recovery.pdf

Multi-site

In a Multi-site DR model, same size infrastructure is always in sync and running at multiple locations. These multiple locations can be between a physical data center and AWS or between various AWS regions. In either case, when a primary site fails, the total workload is transferred to the secondary site. In some practices, the secondary site keeps handling partial traffic in parallel to the production environment. Such ratio can vary from 50-50 to 80-20 between primary and secondary sites.

In multi-site models, resources are always synchronized across each facility (that is, primary and secondary sites). Compared to all previous DR models, the multi-site option provides least downtime (that is, virtually none), but it is a little expensive. Since AWS follows the *pay as you go* model for actual usage, it doesn't cost much compared to the loss that can occur to the enterprise in absence of primary site failure. The following *Figure 2.27* and *Figure 2.28* explain how multi-site DR configuration actually works:

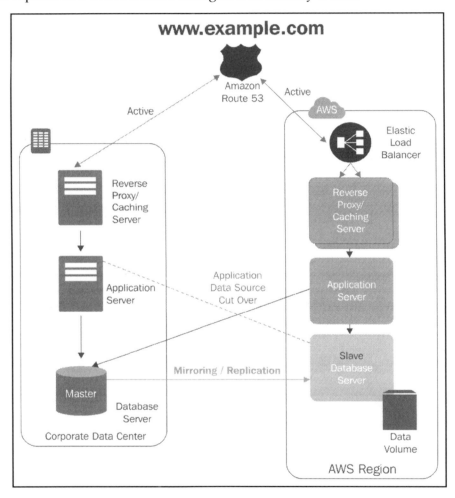

Figure 2.27: End users accesses primary and secondary sites in parallel under normal circumstances

Reference URL: https://d0.awsstatic.com/whitepapers/aws-disaster-recovery.pdf

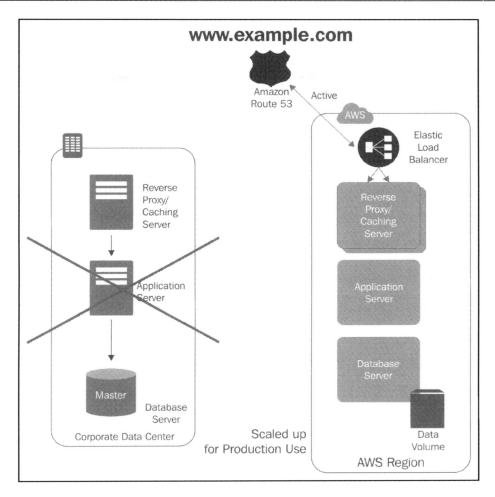

Figure 2.28: Whole workload is transferred to a secondary site in case the primary site fails

Reference URL: https://d0.awsstatic.com/whitepapers/aws-disaster-recovery.pdf

3
Getting Familiar with Identity and Access Management

Any organization using IT services may have a number of resources, processes, environments, projects, and operational activities. All the organizational activities are carried out by various departments. There is always a clear distinction in who needs to do what. Infrastructure and operational activities are performed by a specific set of personnel in the organization. Similarly, there may be a development team, testing team, projects team, finance team, security team, and other relevant teams in the organization that need to perform specific tasks in the organization.

As there are various teams to perform different activities in the organization, similarly there is a clear set of responsibilities and accountability for each of the individuals in a team. A developer may not need to access testing resources. In the same line, a testing resource may not need access to production environments. On the other hand, a system administrator may need to access all the servers, but may not need to access security compliance hardware.

Based on the preceding examples, we can understand that an organization has complex access and security requirements. Addressing an organization's access and security requirement is a very critical task. AWS provides a robust service to fulfill this requirement that is called the IAM service.

Here's how we can define IAM: AWS IAM is a global service that is specifically designed to create and manage users, groups, roles, and policies for securely controlling access to various AWS resources. You use IAM to control who can use your AWS resources (authentication) and what resources they can use and in what ways (authorization).

Understanding AWS root user

Creating an AWS account also creates a root user. The email and password supplied at the time of creating the AWS account becomes the username and password for the root user. This combination of email address and password is called **root account credentials.**

The root account that is the root user has complete, unrestricted access to all resources including billing information on the account. This is a supreme user and its permission cannot be altered by any other user on the account.

Since the root account has unrestricted access to all the resources on the account, it is highly recommended that you avoid using the root account for day to day activities. On a newly created AWS account, it is recommended that you create individual IAM users based on the organizational need and assign them required permissions. These non-root user accounts should be used for day-to-day activities.

 It is best practice not to share individual credentials with other users, especially root credentials, as they give unrestricted access within an AWS account.

Elements of IAM

It is essential to understand a few basic IAM terminologies, to effectively manage real-life organizational users and their permissions to access AWS resources as per their roles and responsibilities. The following list briefly describes these terminologies and subsequently goes into the detail of each of the elements of IAM:

- **User**: A user is a person or an application that requires access to various AWS resources to perform designated tasks. A user can access AWS resources with either a username and password or with an access key and secret key.
- **Access key**: An access key is a 20-character alphanumeric key that acts as a user ID.

- **Secret key**: A secret key is a 40-character alphanumeric key that acts as a password or secret key. The access key and secret key are used together for initiating API, SDK, and CLI authentication.
- **Password policy**: Password policy specifies the complexity requirement of a password and defines the mandatory rotation period for a password associated with IAM users.
- **Multi-Factor Authentication (MFA)**: It is an extra layer of security protection for user authentication that requires users to enter a six-digit token on top of the username and password.
- **Group**: A group is a collection of IAM users.
- **Role**: A role is an IAM entity that constitutes one or more IAM policies defining resource permissions. A role enables access to perform specific operations mentioned in the respective policies associated with the role.
- **Policy**: A policy is a document written in JSON format that formally states one or more permissions as per the IAM policy standards.

Let us now understand all these terminologies in detail and their significance in IAM.

Users

AWS IAM users can be created for any organizational entity (actual end users such as a person or an application). As per their roles and responsibility in the organization, these users need to access AWS resources to perform their day-to-day tasks. By asking a question *Who is that user?* we will get an idea whether that entity is a user or an application.

Usually, an individual user is authenticated by username and password. Similarly, programmatic access (that is SDKs and CLIs, also known as applications) are authenticated using an access key and secret key. Individual users can also use an access key and secret key by configuring them on EC2 instances or physical computers to execute AWS CLI commands.

It is best practice to identify organizational entity and create respective IAM users with credentials to give them access to the AWS platform. Every user, whether it is an individual or an application, must provide appropriate credentials for authentication. Only after a successful authentication, a user can access AWS resources such as AWS dashboard, API, or CLI or any other AWS service.

Logical representation of organizational users can be explained with the help of the following *Figure 3.1*:

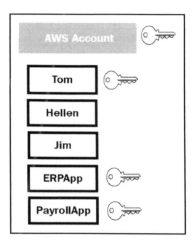

Figure 3.1: Conceptual understanding of IAM users in AWS accounts

As shown in the preceding figure, various users are created in AWS accounts for individuals or applications. Let's suppose that Tom is a system administrator, Helen is a network administrator, and Jim is a database administrator. Best practice is to grant minimum required privileges to each user based on what their role is expected to be. A system administrator may need access on all the infrastructure, a network administrator may need access to all network services and resources. Similarly, a database administrator may need access only to databases.

On the other side, applications such as ERP and payroll application may also need to access required AWS resources. Applications hosted on EC2 may need to access a hosted database on RDS. For all such applications, there may be a user ID with an access key and secret key that an application can use to access respective resources on AWS.

Permissions can be granted to applications using an AWS role as well. In subsequent sections, we will see how authentication works with AWS roles.

The access key and secret key are not generated for all users as we have seen in the previous diagram. It is only generated for the users who need to access AWS resources using API, SDKs, and CLIs. For accessing services using an AWS console, one can use a username and password.

Access key and secret key

An access key and secret key are in a pair. An Access key is a 20-digit key and a secret key is a 40-digit key. Only corresponding keys work with each other for authentication. These keys are used along with AWS SDK, CLI, REST, or Query APIs. As the name suggests, a secret key is meant to be kept secret and protected. Best practice is not to hardcode an access key and a secret key in application coding. If these keys are hardcoded and not removed before sharing AMI or EBS snapshot with others, it may pose a security risk.

An access key and a secret key are generated only once. Either at the time of creating a user or later, as and when required manually. At the time of generating an access key and a secret key, AWS gives an option to download them in CSV format. Once it is created, you need to download and keep it securely. AWS does not provide any mechanism to retrieve an access key and a secret key if these keys are lost. The only solution is to delete old keys and regenerate new keys. As a result, you will need to edit earlier key pair with a regenerated new key pair for applications to work smoothly. A maximum two sets of access keys and secret keys can be attached with any IAM user.

An access key and secret key look like this:

Access key: AKIAJ4B7SOIHQBQUXXXX

Secret key: oSpG3je8kYS1XpMDRG8kpo1awLizvnv1GaNBXXXX

It is best practice to periodically rotate access keys and secret keys for security purposes. It is also recommended practice to periodically remove unutilized and unwanted access keys and secret keys from an AWS account.

Password policy

Password policy specifies the complexity requirement of a password and defines a mandatory rotation period for a password associated with IAM users.

While creating an IAM user, an IAM administrator can provide a reasonably strong password on behalf of the user. Optionally, an IAM administrator can also configure a user to change the respective user password when the user logs in for the first time to AWS. Password policy can be configured from **Account settings** within the IAM dashboard. As per the organization's compliance requirement, password complexity can be configured by choosing one or more options as shown in the following *Figure 3.2*:

Minimum password length:	6

☐ Require at least one uppercase letter ❶

☐ Require at least one lowercase letter ❶

☐ Require at least one number ❶

☐ Require at least one non-alphanumeric character ❶

☑ Allow users to change their own password ❶

☐ Enable password expiration ❶

Password expiration period (in days):

☐ Prevent password reuse ❶

Number of passwords to remember:

☐ Password expiration requires administrator reset ❶

Apply password policy   **Delete password policy**

Figure 3.2: Password policy options

It is important to note that password policy only affects the user password. It does not affect in any way the access key and secret key. As a result of password policy, a user password may expire after the configured number of days, but the access key and secret key does not expire. When a password expires, user cannot log in to the AWS console, but API calls work fine using an access key and a secret key.

Change in password policy comes into effect for all the new users, but for all existing users, it comes into effect whenever their respective password is changed. It does not apply to the existing user password until it is updated.

Multi-Factor Authentication (MFA)

MFA is an extra layer of security protection for user authentication that requires users to enter a six-digit token on top of the username and password. MFA can be enabled for individual IAM users. It is a best practice to enable MFA for all users. It adds an extra layer of protection on top of the username and password. Once it is enabled, the user needs to enter unique six-digit authentication code from an approved authentication source (that is hardware or software based) or an SMS text message while accessing the AWS Management Console.

MFA can be enabled for both types of users: an individual console login as well as an application's programmatic calls to the AWS. It can be also enabled for the root user.

MFA can be enabled in one of the following ways:

- Security token with hardware or software
- SMS text message-based

Security token-based MFA

When it comes to security token-based MFA, there are two options available, hardware based or software/virtual (that is, mobile application based). Hardware based security tokens can be purchased from an authorized vendor and a virtual security token application can be installed on smart phones. A hardware-based MFA token device may look something like this:

Figure 3.3: Hardware MFA device for RSA token

For enabling MFA tokens on an IAM user, MFA hardware or software applications need to be registered with an IAM user. Once it is registered with either a hardware device or software application, it keeps generating six-digit numeric code based on time synchronization one-time password algorithm. It appears for 30 seconds and keeps changing. Enabling MFA increases a security layer. If username and password falls into an unauthorized person's hands, still the person cannot misuse it without an MFA token. MFA token keeps rotating the token and it's generated only through an synchronized MFA device for that particular IAM user.

Steps for enabling a virtual MFA device for a user

The following steps describe how to enable MFA for a user:

1. Log in to the AWS console.
2. Go to the IAM dashboard.
3. Select **Users** from the left pane and click on a user as shown in the following *Figure 3.4*:

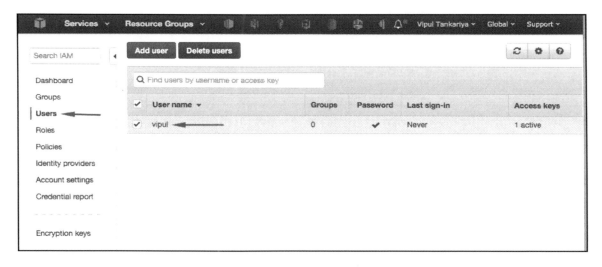

Figure 3.4: User selection for enabling virtual MFA

4. Select the **Security credentials** tab as shown in the following *Figure 3.5*:

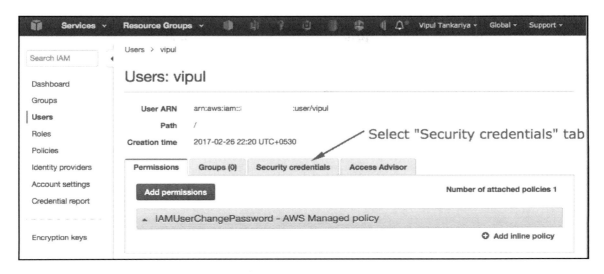

Figure 3.5: Enabling MFA - Security credentials - tab selection

5. Click on the edit button to edit **Assigned MFA device** as shown in the following *Figure 3.6*:

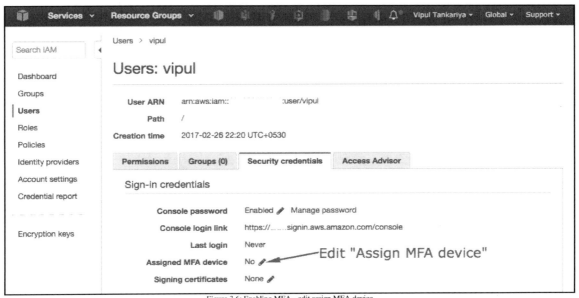

Figure 3.6: Enabling MFA - edit assign MFA device

6. Select **A virtual MFA device** and click on the **Next Step** button:

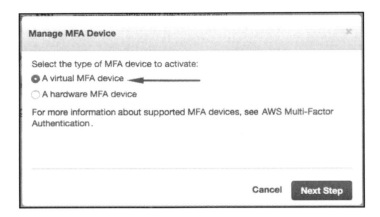

Figure 3.7: Enabling MFA - select a virtual MFA device

7. From the subsequent screen, click on the link **here** as shown in the following *Figure 3.8*. It provides a list of AWS MFA compatible apps, supported for various mobile platforms. If you have already installed the **Virtual MFA Applications**, you can click on **Next Step** and proceed to step 9.

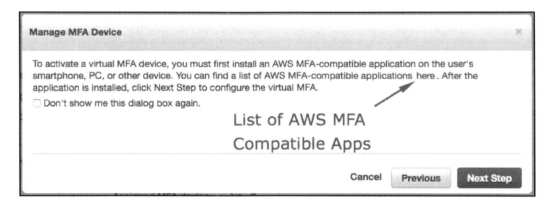

Figure 3.8: Enabling MFA - Select a virtual MFA device

8. You can download the **Virtual MFA Applications** from your respective device application store. Supported applications for various platforms are indicated in the following *Figure 3.9*. You can close this information window to go back to the previous screen as indicated in the preceding *Figure 3.8* and click on **Next Step**.

Virtual MFA Applications	
Applications for your smartphone can be installed from the application store that is specific to your phone type. The following table lists some applications for different smartphone types.	
Android	Google Authenticator; Authy 2-Factor Authentication
iPhone	Google Authenticator; Authy 2-Factor Authentication
Windows Phone	Authenticator
Blackberry	Google Authenticator

Figure 3.9: Enabling MFA - Virtual MFA Applications

9. Determine whether the MFA app supports QR codes, and then do one of the following:

- Use your mobile app for scanning the QR code. Depending up on the application that you use, you may have to choose camera icon or some similar option. Subsequently, you need to use the device camera for scanning the code.
- In the **Manage MFA Device** wizard, choose **Show secret key for manual configuration**, and then type the secret configuration key into your MFA application.

When you are finished, the virtual MFA device starts generating one-time passwords.

Figure 3.10: Enabling MFA - entering authentication codes

10. As shown in the *Figure 3.10*, you need to type one-time password in the **Authentication Code 1** box. You can use the one-time password given in the virtual MFA device. Before you can enter second one-time password in the **Authentication Code 2** box, you need to wait for approximately 30 seconds. After a wait period, device generates another one-time password. You can use the fresh one-time password again and enter it into the **Authentication Code 2** box. Subsequently, you can choose **Activate Virtual MFA**.

Now your virtual MFA device is ready for use. When a user for whom the MFA token is enabled, tries to log in to the AWS console, AWS poses an MFA token challenge after authenticating a user with a valid user ID and password.

SMS text message–based MFA

To enable SMS text message-based MFA, you need to configure IAM user with the user's phone number to receive SMS messages. When a user tries to log in by providing a valid username and password, it asks for the six-digit numeric code sent from AWS to the user's mobile number as an SMS. This MFA mechanism can be used only for IAM users and not for the root user. Also, at present SMS-based MFA can be used only for signing in to an AWS Management Console. It cannot be used with API or CLI calls.

Creating an AWS IAM user using the AWS dashboard

The steps for creating an AWS IAM user using AWS dashboard are discussed as follows:

1. Log in to the AWS Management Console with the appropriate credentials. The IAM user must have sufficient privileges to create IAM resources (that is, user, group, policy, and so on). In the case of a fresh AWS account, you need to log in with the root credentials. It will take the user to the AWS dashboard.
2. Select **IAM** under **Security, Identity & Compliance** group from the AWS dashboard. It will take the user to the IAM dashboard.

3. Select **Users** and click **Add user**. It displays the following screen:

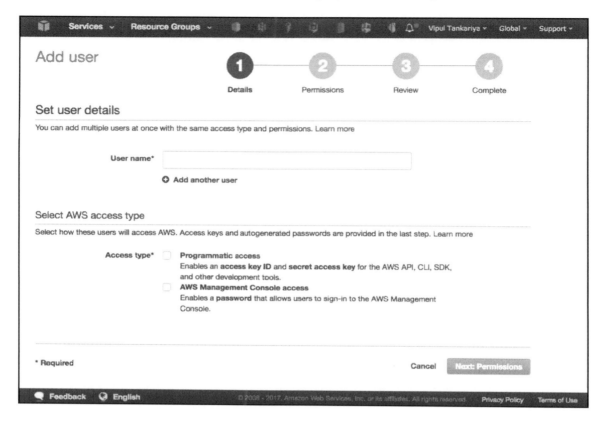

Figure 3.11: IAM - Add user screen

4. Provide a meaningful and relevant **User name** to resemble a real world entity. It will help to easily identify correct user when performing day-to-day maintenance activity. A valid username can have only alphanumeric characters or _+=,.@- symbols. It is also possible to add multiple users (max 10 users) at the same time by clicking on the **Add another user** link given next to the **User name** textbox, as shown in the preceding *Figure 3.11*.

5. After entering the username, you must select **Access type.** You need to select at least one option. It is also possible to select both the options. Usually **Programmatic access** is preferred for authentication through an access key and a secret key while using APIs, SDKs, and CLI. For individual users, ideally **AWS Management Console access** is selected. If you select **Programmatic access**, you can proceed to step 7. If you select **AWS Management Console access**, it displays more options in the same screen as shown in the following *Figure 3.12*:

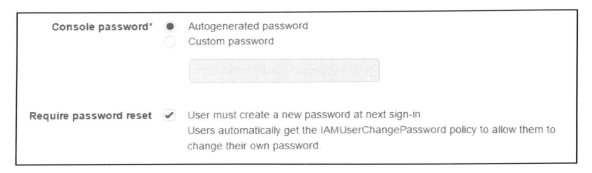

Figure 3.12: Password configuration options while creating an IAM user

6. If you select **AWS Management Console access type**, it allows you to configure **Autogenerated password** or **Custom password** for the user. Also, the IAM administrator can force a user to reset the password on the next login by selecting options for the same as shown in the preceding figure. After selecting the required options, select the **Next: Permission** button.

7. You can now see the screen with three options to assign permissions to the user, as shown in the following *Figure 3.13*. You can create a group and add the user to a new group or you can add the user to an existing group. It is recommended that you add a user to any group for better user management and access control; however, it is not mandatory. A user can be added to any group in the future without any requirement:

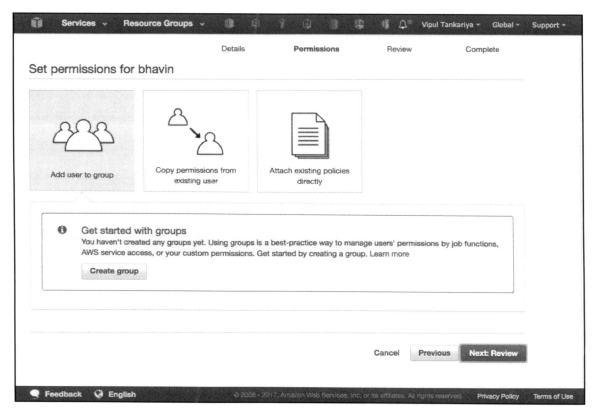

Figure 3.13: IAM - Add user permissions

8. The next step is to assign permissions to the newly created user. For assigning permissions to the user, you can either **Copy permissions from existing user** or **Attach existing policies directly** as shown in the preceding *Figure 3.13*. By default, newly created users do not have any privileges in the AWS platform, until and unless appropriate policy is attached to the user ID. Any permissions you grant to a user can be modified at a later stage. After adding the user to an appropriate group or policy, you can click on the **Next: Review** button.

9. Verify the details when the final review page appears. If any ambiguity is there, you can perform modifications by going to the previous pages. It is also possible to modify the user's property after it is created. In worst-case scenarios, an existing user can be deleted and recreated.

10. Finally, click on **Create** to create an IAM user.

Introduction to AWS CLI

Before you start using AWS CLI, it is essential to set up a CLI environment. For setting up CLI environment, you need to install the AWS CLI utility based on your system's operating system where you want to set up the CLI. For Windows, you can install it with MSI installer, for Unix/Mac you can install it with a bundled installer or `pip`.

Installing AWS CLI

AWS CLI installation on the Windows operating system is very easy using a step-by-step wizard with MSI installer. This section describes how to install AWS CLI on Linux and Mac. On Linux and Mac, AWS CLI can be installed using `pip`, a package manager for Python. The minimum requirement to install AWS CLI is to have `pip` package manager, Python 2.6.5+ or Python 3.3+. Once `pip` package manager is installed, AWS CLI can be installed using the following command:

```
$ pip install --upgrade --user awscli
```

 Based on the OS, specific methods can be used to install Python pip package manager. In this example, all the commands are related to RHEL/CentOS.

The functionality of the AWS CLI utility is periodically updated by AWS to support the command line for recently added services and features. To update the installed AWS CLI again the same command can be used:

```
$ pip install --upgrade --user awscli
```

You can use the following command to uninstall AWS CLI:

```
$ pip uninstall awscli
```

To make sure awscli is properly installed and to check the version, the following command can be used:

```
$ aws --version
```

It may display the following, or appropriate version information installed on your system:

```
aws-cli/1.11.55 Python/2.7.12 Linux/4.4.41-36.55.amzn1.x86_64
botocore/1.5.18
$ pip install --upgrade --user awscli
```

Getting a AWS user access key and secret key

We will now discuss the steps for getting a AWS user access key and secret key.

1. Log in to the AWS Management Console with the appropriate credentials. An IAM user must have sufficient privileges to create IAM resources (that is, user, group, policy, and so on).
2. Select **IAM** under the **Security, Identity & Compliance** group from AWS dashboard. It will take you to an IAM dashboard.
3. Select **Users**, select the intended user to an generate access key and secret key.
4. Go to the **Security credentials** tab.
5. Click **Create access key** to generate access key and secret key pair.
6. You need to ensure that the keys are stored safely as AWS does not allow you to download these keys again.
7. Finally, click **Close**.

Configuring AWS CLI

After installing AWS CLI and obtaining the access key and secret key, we need to configure the CLI before we can start using it.

AWS CLI uses the local machine date and time as a signature while making calls to AWS. It is important to make sure that machine's date and time are set correctly; otherwise AWS rejects any CLI request.

To configure AWS CLI, the following command can be used:

```
$ aws configureAWS Access Key ID [None]: AKIAJ4B7SOIHQBQUXXXXAWS Secret
Access Key [None]: oSpG3je8kYS1XpMDRG8kpo1awLizvnv1GaNBXXXXDefault region
name [None]: us-east-2Default output format [None]: ENTER
```

It will ask for four inputs: `Access Key ID`, `Secret Access Key`, `Default region name` where it should request the command, and `Default output format`. Output format can be JSON, table, or text format. If the output format is not defined, the default output format will be JSON.

AWS CLI syntax

AWS CLI supports commands for almost all AWS services. All the commands should be preceded with `aws` as described in the following syntax:

```
aws <top level command> <subcommands> <parameters>
```

Top level commands indicate the AWS service name such as `ec2`, `s3`, `iam`, and so on, while subcommands are AWS service-specific.

Getting AWS CLI help

It is possible to get detailed help for any of the `aws` top or sub level commands just by placing help at the end of the command, as shown in the following example:

```
$ aws help
$ aws iam help
```

Creating an IAM user using AWS CLI

The AWS CLI `create-user` subcommand with the `iam` top command can be used to create a new IAM user. The following AWS CLI command shows how to get more details about subcommands:

```
$ aws iam create-user help
```

A new IAM user can be created using the following command. Essential parameter is `--user-name`:

```
$ aws iam create-user --user-name Jack
```

Group

In an organization, several people work in different departments (that is, sales, purchase, IT, and so on). Usually, only members from the IT department need to access AWS resources. But it depends on the nature of organization and its organizational hierarchy. In each department, there can be subdepartments (that is, in IT there can be many branches such as development, testing, operations, quality, security, and network). Each subdepartment may have several people working in it. An organizational hierarchical structure looks something like the following *Figure 3.14*:

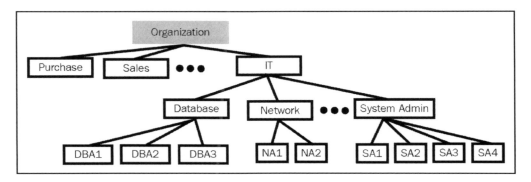

Figure 3.14: Logical representations of organizational entities

It is easy to manage privileges for a few users individually, but it becomes increasingly difficult to manage these users separately as the user base increases. Most of the time, when users belong to the same department with same or similar roles and responsibilities, their privileges requirement may also be the same. In such scenarios, it is recommended that you divide the users into logical groups and assign privileges to a single group instead of individual users. A similar concept is used in an IAM group.

In simple terms, *An IAM group is a collection of IAM users.* A group lets you add, change, or remove permissions for multiple users altogether.

Assign privileges (that is policies) to a group rather than handling privileges at an individual user level. Some users who are part of a group may require extra privileges to perform advance tasks. For such users, separate policies can be attached at user level. When multiple policies are attached to any user or a group, such users or group get a union of all the permissions from the attached policies. User and group management of a small company is illustrated in the following *Figure 3.15*:

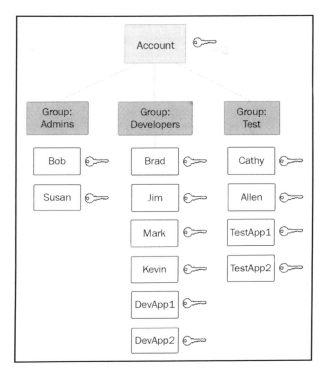

Figure 3.15: Logical representation of group and user in small enterprise

Source: IAM manual

As we have seen so far, groups are primarily used to assign specific permissions to a set of users. When any user is added to a group, the user automatically inherits all the permissions granted to that group.

Whenever a new employee joins an organization, the process of onboarding and granting permissions to that employee becomes very easy if the organization follows the concept of user groups. Just by creating an IAM user and adding that user as a member of a group, the user automatically inherits all the privileges assigned to that IAM group. When the same employee either changes department within the organization or leaves the organization, managing the employee's privileges becomes easier just by removing the user from the respective group.

Important characteristics of an IAM group:

- Any group can have many users, and a user can be a member of multiple groups.
- Groups can't be nested (that is group within group); they can contain only users, not other groups.
- By default, users are not part of any group. As and when required, you need to explicitly add them to required groups.
- There is a soft limit of a maximum 100 IAM groups and 5000 users. If more users are required, it is advisable to use the identity federation service to create temporary security credentials.

Creating a new IAM group

The steps for creating IAM group are discussed as follows:

1. Log in to the AWS Management Console with the appropriate credentials. An IAM user must have sufficient privileges to create IAM resources (that is, user, group, policy, and so on).
2. Select **IAM** under **Security, Identity & Compliance** group from AWS dashboard. It will take you to an IAM dashboard.
3. Select **Groups** and click **Create New Group**.
4. Provide a meaningful group name. Group name can have a maximum of 128 characters. Click **Next Step**.
5. Attach the required IAM policies to the IAM Group. When policies attached to a group are modified, all the existing and future members of the group inherit the updated privileges. It is always a best practice to grant minimum privileges to a user or a group.
6. At this stage, review group creation. If everything is fine, click on **Create Group**.

Creating IAM group using CLI

A new IAM group can be created using the following command; essential parameter is `--group-name`:

```
$ aws iam create-group --group-name Developers
```

Adding existing users to a group

The following steps describe how to add an existing user to one or more groups:

1. Log in to the AWS Management Console with the appropriate credentials. An IAM user must have sufficient privileges to create IAM resources (that is user, group, policy, and so on).
2. Select **IAM** under **Security, Identity & Compliance** group from AWS dashboard. It will take the user to an IAM dashboard.
3. Select **existing user** from **Users**.
4. Select the **Groups** tab.
5. Click **Add user to groups**.
6. List of existing groups appear. Select the appropriate group. It is possible to select one or more number of groups. One user can be a member of one or more groups and can inherits all the permissions from the respective groups.
7. Finally, click on **Add to Groups**.

IAM role

An IAM role is an AWS Identity. Every IAM role has its own permission policy, that defines what that role can do and what it cannot do. It is like an IAM user without password or an access key and a secret key. An IAM policy can be associated with an IAM user or group, whereas an IAM role cannot be associated with a user or a group. It can be assumed by a user, application, or service to delegate access to an AWS resource within the same or another account. It dynamically generates a temporary access key and secret key, that can be assumed by an entity for authentication. Once a role is assumed, an entity can make API calls to AWS services permitted to the role assumed by the entity.

For example, a role can be assigned to an EC2 instance with permission to access DynamoDB and RDS Database. An application hosted on the EC2 can assume the role and make API calls to access DynamoDB or database on RDS.

Similarly, if you want to allow your web or mobile application to access AWS resources, but you don't want to hardcode an access key and secret key in the application code, an IAM role can come to the rescue. IAM roles can also be used to provide federated access to AWS services using Microsoft **Active Directory (AD)**, LDAP or similar identity providers. In the subsequent sections, we will get into the details of these aspects.

In nutshell, AWS resource permissions in the form of IAM policies are attached to the IAM roles rather than being attached to the IAM users or groups. IAM roles can be assumed by:

- An IAM user in the same AWS account
- An IAM user in a different AWS account
- AWS web services (for example, EC2)
- External user authentication software that uses an external **identity provider (IdP)**, compatible with **Security Assertion Markup Language (SAML)** 2.0 or **OpenID Connect (OIDC)** or custom identity broker

Let's start with understanding some of the important terminologies with respect to IAM role. These terminologies are:

- Delegation
- Federation
- Policy
- Principal
- Cross-account access

Each of the preceding concepts are explained individually in the subsequent passage.

Delegation: Delegation is a way to extend an entity's permission on AWS resources, to other users or applications, allowing them to perform certain operations on the resources. It involves creating a trust between the account where the AWS resources are hosted and the account that contains the user that needs to access these resources.

The source account where the AWS resources are available is called a trusting account and the account from where the user wants to access those source resources is called a trusted account.

Trusting (source) and trusted (destination) accounts can be:

- The same AWS account
- Two different accounts managed by the same organization
- Two different accounts managed by different organizations

To delegate permission, you need to attach two policies to the IAM role. One policy defines the permissions to be given and another is a trust policy that defines trusted accounts that are allowed to grant its user permission to assume the role.

Federation: Identity federation is a mechanism through which applications can use external IdPs for authenticating users rather than writing custom sign-in code for authenticating the users. These external IdPs include Amazon, Facebook, Google, or any IdP that is compatible with OIDC, MS AD, or LDAP that supports SAML 2.0 to configure token-based authentication mechanisms between external IdPs and AWS-hosted applications. Web identity federation is further elaborated in one of the subsequent sections with more detail.

Policy: Policy is a JSON formatted document and written as per IAM policy notation. It defines the permissions to be granted to an IAM role. Policies can also be written for attaching it to IAM users and groups.

Principal: It is an element that is generally used in a policy to denote a user (IAM user, federated user, or assumed role user), AWS account, AWS service, or other principal entity that is allowed or denied access to a resource. Specified users are allowed or denied access to perform actions on AWS resources.

Cross-account access: When AWS resources existing in one account are being accessed from another account based on a trust relationship, it is called cross-account access. IAM roles are a primary way to grant cross-account access.

As we have gone through various elements of IAM role, let's understand how to create a role.

Creating roles for AWS service

To create a role for an AWS service, follow the steps which are discussed as follows:

1. Log in to the AWS Management Console with the appropriate credentials. An IAM user must have sufficient privileges to create IAM resources (that is, user, group, policy, and so on).
2. Select **IAM** under **Security, Identity & Compliance** group from the AWS dashboard. It will take the user to an IAM dashboard.
3. Select **Roles** from an IAM dashboard.

4. Select **Create New Role** as shown in the following *Figure 3.16*:

Figure 3.16: IAM - Create New Role

5. Give a meaningful role name with a maximum of 64 characters shown as in *Figure 3.17*:

Figure 3.17: IAM - Role Name

6. Select role type as **AWS Service Roles** as given in the following *Figure 3.18*:

- **AWS Service Roles** is assigned to AWS resource such as EC2, RDS, Redshift, and so on. It grants them privileges to perform various operations on required AWS services based on permissions granted on the role.
- **Role for Cross-Account Access** is used for establishing a trust relationship between multiple AWS accounts.
- **Role for Identity Provider Access** is used by external IdPs for federated authentication.

7. Subsequent steps appear based on the selection in the previous step. Since we are here exploring the role for AWS service (EC2), select **AWS Service Roles** and click on **Select** against **Amazon EC2** which is shown as follows:

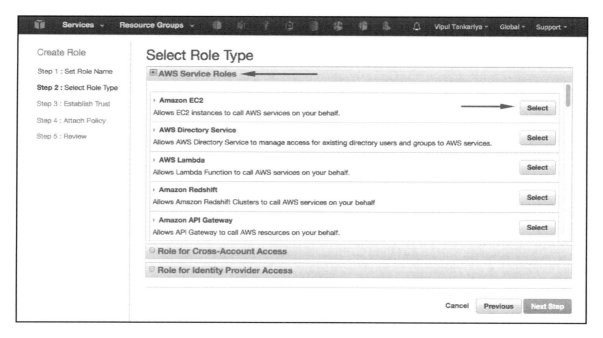

Figure 3.18: IAM role - Select Role Type

8. **Attach Policy**, as per the permissions required by the application hosted on EC2. The policy may contain permissions for accessing S3 bucket, RDS, DynamoDB table, or any other AWS services as per the application needs. Policies can be selected from the screen as shown in the following *Figure 3.19*:

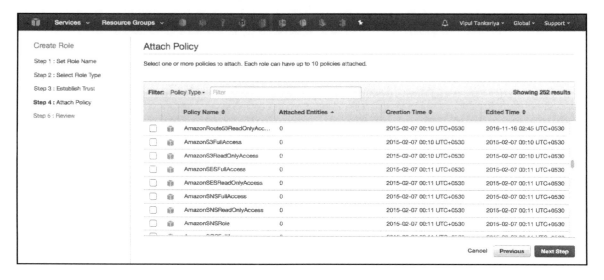

Figure 3.19: Create IAM role - Attach Policy

9. Finally **Review** and click on **Create Role** as shown in the following figure. This is the concluding step in creating an IAM role for an AWS service. You can assign this role to an EC2 instance while launching a new instance.

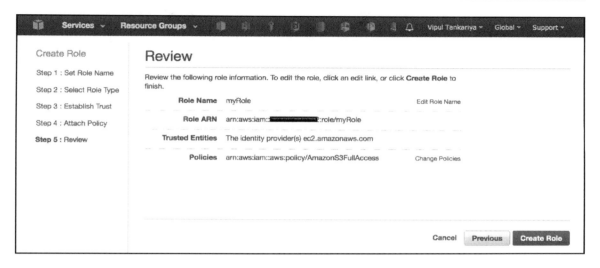

Figure 3.20: Create IAM role - Review

Creating IAM role using AWS CLI

A new IAM role can be created using the following command; essential parameters are `--role-name` and `--assume-role-policy-document`, that define JSON-documented policy:

```
$ aws iam create-role --role-name Test-Role --assume-role-policy-document
file://Test-Role-Trust-Policy.json
```

Policy

A policy is a document that formally states one or more permissions. Basically, policies are written to explicitly allow or deny permissions to access one or more AWS resources. Policies can be associated with one or more IAM users, groups, roles or resources, based on their type. Broadly, IAM policies can be classified as:

- Managed policies
    - AWS managed policies
    - Customer managed policies
- Inline policies
- Resource-based policies

Managed policies

Built-in policies that are managed by AWS or policies that are created and managed by customers are called managed policies. These policies can be attached to multiple users, groups, and roles. Managed policies cannot be attached to resources. Managed policies are further classified as:

- **AWS managed policies:** As the name suggests, there are built-in policies that are created and managed by AWS. They are also updated from time to time and updates are automatically applied to the attached IAM principal entities.
- **Customer managed policies:** Policies that are created and managed by customers in their AWS account are called customer managed policies. These policies can be updated by customers as and when required. Effects of such changes are applied immediately to the principal entities to which the policies are attached.

The main difference between these two policy types is: AWS managed policies are generic while customer managed policies are precise to actual permission requirements. The similarity between an AWS managed and a customer managed policy is that, amendment to the policy doesn't overwrite it, IAM creates a new version of the managed policy every time it is updated. Managed policy can have up to five versions. Beyond that it is required to delete one or more of the existing versions.

Inline policies

Inline policies are also customer managed policies. But these policies have a one-to-one relation between policies and principal resources. These policies are created and managed to directly attach only with a single user, group, or role. Such policies are useful to make sure that permissions in a policy are precisely granted as per the organizational requirement. Such policies are also automatically deleted when underlined resource is deleted using an AWS Management Console. In contrast to the customer managed policies, changes are immediately applied to the principal resources where policies are attached.

Resource-based policies

Resource-based policies are also inline policy type as they are written in-line for attaching it to a particular resource. All AWS services do not support resource-based policies. At present only S3 bucket, SNS topic, Amazon glacier Vaults, AWS Opsworks stacks, AWS Lambda functions, and SQS queue supports resource-based policies.

Now that we understand what are different types of polices, let's understand how to write a policy. Every policy is JSON-formatted and carries at least one statement. Usually, a policy consists of multiple statements to grant permission on different sets of resources. The following is an example of a basic customer managed policy:

```
{
  "Version": "2012-10-17",
  "Statement": {
    "Effect": "Allow",
    "Action": "s3:*",
    "Resource":
    "arn:aws:s3:::example_bucket"
  }
}
```

 Amazon Resource Name (ARN) is a unique identifier for each of the AWS resources. It is used in IAM policies, API calls, and wherever it's required to identify AWS resources unambiguously. An basic example of ARN is as follows:

```
arn:partition:service:region:account-id:resource
arn:partition:service:region:account-id:resourcetype/resource
arn:partition:service:region:account-id:resourcetype:resource
```

where:

`partition`: This specifies which AWS partition the AWS resource belongs to. Various AWS partitions are as follows:

`aws`: public AWS partition

`aws-cn`: AWS China

`aws-us-gov`: AWS GovCloud

`service`: Specified AWS service name (that is, EC2, S3, IAM, and so on)

`region`: Specifies the AWS region where the resource resides. As some of the AWS services are global such as IAM, the ARN for such resources doesn't have a region.

`account ID`: Specifies 12-digit AWS account number.

`resource, resourcetype:resource or resourcetype/resource`: This part of ARN varies from AWS service to service, as some of the services allow paths for resource names (that is, slash (/) or colon (:)).

Examples for some of the ARN are as follows:

ARN for EC2 resource:

```
arn:aws:ec2:us-east-1:123456789012:dedicated-host/h-12345678
```

ARN for IAM role:

```
arn:aws:iam::123456789012:role/application_abc/component_xyz/S3Access
```

The preceding customer managed policy allows us to perform any possible operations on S3 `example_bucket`. By attaching this policy to the IAM entity (user, group or role), it gets permission to read, write, delete, or any possible operations on the specified S3 bucket. Various elements of IAM policy are explained as follows:

Version: This element specifies the IAM policy language version.

 Latest and current version is 2012-10-17. It should be used for all the policies (that is, managed or resource-based policy). For inline policies, version element can be 2008-10-17, but it is highly recommended to keep 2012-10-17.

Effect: This defines whether the specified list of actions in `Action` elements on specified resources specified in `Resource` elements are allowed or denied. By default, every service and resource is denied the access. Usually, policies are written to allow resource access.

Actions: This defines a list of actions. Each AWS service has got its own set of actions. As per the policy written for the resource, this list of actions varies.

Resources: This section specifies the list of resources on which the preceding specified list of actions are allowed.

The major difference between a managed policy and a resource-based policy is a *resource-based policy specifies who has access to the resource (principal) and list of permitted actions*, whereas in a managed policies only list of actions is specified, not the principal entity. An IAM resource-based policy can also be generated with the help of the AWS policy generator. The URL for the AWS policy generator is `https://awspolicygen.s3.amazonaws.com/policygen.html`.

Example of resource-based policy

The following example describes a resource-based policy. The S3 bucket policy in account A might look like the following policy. In this example, account A's S3 bucket is named `mybucket`, and account B's account number is 111122223333. It does not specify any individual users or groups in account B, only the account itself:

```
{
  "Version": "2012-10-17",
  "Statement": {
    "Sid": "AccountBAccess1",
    "Effect": "Allow",
    "Principal": {"AWS": "111122223333"},
    "Action": "s3:*",
    "Resource": [
      "arn:aws:s3:::mybucket",
      "arn:aws:s3:::mybucket/*"
    ]
  }
}
```

To implement this policy, account B uses IAM to attach it to the appropriate user (or group) in account B:

```
{
  "Version": "2012-10-17",
  "Statement": {
    "Effect": "Allow",
    "Action": "s3:List*",
    "Resource": [
      "arn:aws:s3:::mybucket",
      "arn:aws:s3:::mybucket/*"
    ]
  }
}
```

IAM policy simulator

Writing IAM policy can be a lengthy and error prone process. There can be a few human or logical errors while writing a policy. It can be a very time consuming and tedious process to find and rectify such policy errors. An IAM policy simulator provides a platform to simulate and test the policies before using them in an AWS account. Using the IAM policy simulator, an existing AWS or custom managed policy can be copied and modified as per the requirement. It makes writing new policies easier. The IAM policy simulator uses the same engine as used in an AWS account to evaluate policies. The only difference is, the IAM policy simulator is safe to test as it doesn't make actual AWS service requests, and rather it just simulates them. The policy simulator can be accessed from the URL: `https://policysim.aws.amazon.com`.

Active Directory Federation Service (ADFS)

As you have seen in this chapter so far, you can access AWS resources either using an IAM user ID and password or using an access key and secret key combination. Let us consider a scenario in which a user uses IAM credentials to access AWS resources and an AD user ID and password to access resources hosted within the on-premise environment. In such a scenario, in an organization where there are a number of users, it becomes increasingly difficult to maintain credentials in multiple systems. Users and operations teams, not only have to maintain user detail on their organization's identity provider, but also on IAM. To cater to such scenarios, IAM also supports identity federation for delegated access to the AWS Management Console or AWS APIs. With identity federation, external identities such as federated users are granted secure access to resources in your AWS account without having to create IAM users. Active Directory Federation is one such method through which you can access your AWS resources with your organization's AD services.

Let's take a look at a couple of scenarios on what you can do with ADFS with AWS:

- You can access the AWS Management Console by authenticating against your organization's AD instead of using your IAM credentials. Once authenticated against the AD, AWS generates temporary credentials for the user and allows access on the AWS console.
- You can access a web application hosted on AWS by authenticating against your organization's AD. Once authenticated against AD, it provides **Single Sign-On (SSO)** that provides users with seamless access to applications without re-prompting for credentials after initial authentication.

Such a setup that can authenticate as an identity provider and communicate with AWS is achieved using Windows AD, ADFS, and SAML. Let's understand these terms before getting into configuration details for such a setup.

Windows AD is a database that keeps track of all the user accounts and passwords in your organization.

ADFS is part of Windows AD services in the form of a web service that provides a token-based SSO service for accessing systems and applications located across organizational boundaries

SAML is an XML-based, open-standard data format for exchanging authentication and authorization data between an IdP and a service provider.

Integration between ADFS and AWS console

Now we know the terminologies around enabling ADFS with AWS, let's take a look at how ADFS authentication works to access the AWS console:

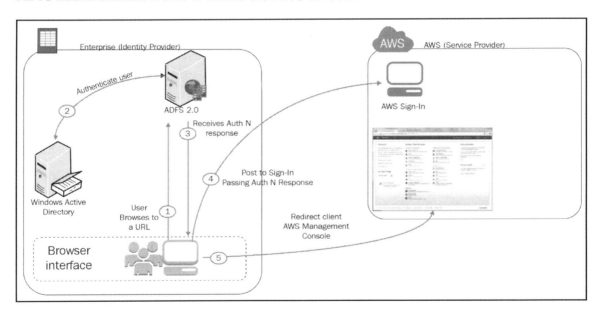

Figure 3.21

As indicated in the preceding *Figure 3.21*, accessing AWS console using ADFS is a five-step process. These steps are described here:

1. A user initiates a request to an ADFS web URL in an internet browser. This URL may look something like `https://HostName/adfs/ls/IdpInitiatedSignOn.aspx`. When you enable an ADFS role on a Windows instance, it creates a virtual directory named `adfs` in your default site. The sign-on page is automatically created under the `adfs` virtual directory. This page provides an interface to enter a user ID and password to authenticate against the site.

2. When a user submits the credentials, ADFS authenticates the user against Windows AD.

3. In the third step, the user browser receives a SAML assertion in the form of an authentication response from ADFS.

4. A user browser posts the SAML assertion to the AWS sign-in endpoint for SAML (`https://signin.aws.amazon.com/saml`). Behind the scenes, sign-in uses the AssumeRoleWithSAML API to request temporary security credentials and then constructs a sign-in URL for the AWS Management Console.

5. A user browser receives the sign-in URL and is redirected to the console.

The preceding details are sufficient to understand the ADFS as far as the scope of the exam is concerned. If you need more details around setting up and configuring ADFS with an AWS console, you can refer to the AWS URL `https://aws.amazon.com/blogs/security/enabling-federation-to-aws-using-windows-active-directory-adfs-and-saml-2-0/`.

Web identity federation

When you create a web application or a mobile application, creating a user repository and authenticating the users against the repository is one of the core tasks of the application development lifecycle.

If you are creating a mobile application and that mobile application needs access to AWS resources such as S3 and DynamoDB, how would you enable the application to access these AWS resources? One way is to use an access key and a secret key in the application that provides access to S3 and DynamoDB. However, the application would work with such an approach, but it is not recommended to embed or distribute long term AWS credentials to an app that a user downloads to a device. Even if these credentials are stored in an encrypted format on the device, it would pose a security risk.

In such a scenario, AWS recommends using web identity federation. Using web identity federation, applications can request temporary security credentials dynamically when required. The credentials are generated based on an AWS role that carries permissions to perform only required operations on specific AWS resources as permitted in the role.

Web identity federation enables you to use many well-known identity providers such as Amazon, Facebook, Google, LinkedIn, or any other OIDC compatible IdP for authenticating users. You don't need to create your own custom sign-in code or manage own user identities. The application can authenticate a user against such IdP. If a user is authenticated, the application receives an authentication token. This token is exchanged in AWS for temporary security credentials. Since these temporary security credentials are based on an AWS role, the token carries permission only to perform specific tasks mentioned in the role permissions. Using web identity federation, you don't have to embed or distribute credentials with applications that keeps your AWS account secure.

The following *Figure 3.22* shows a sample workflow using web identity federation:

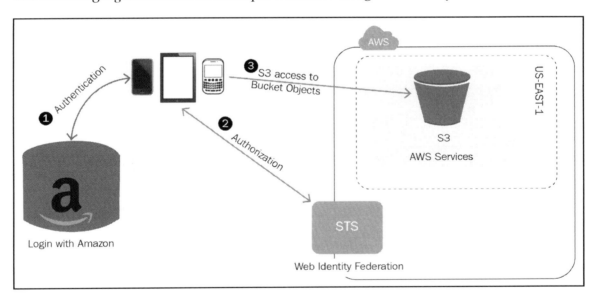

Figure 3.22: Workflow using web identity federation

1. As shown in the preceding figure, when a user loads the application, the application prompts the user for authentication using the login with Amazon SDK. The app authenticates the user and receives a token from Amazon.

2. Next, the user needs to be authorized to access resources in your AWS account. The app makes an unsigned `AssumeRoleWithWebIdentity` request to STS, passing the token from the previous step. **Security Token Service (STS)** verifies the authenticity of the token; if the token is valid, STS returns a set of temporary security credentials to the app. By default, the credentials can be used for one hour.

3. Finally, the app uses the temporary security credentials to make signed requests for resources in your S3 bucket. Because the roles access policy used variables that reference the app ID and the user ID, the temporary security credentials are scoped to that end user and will prevent them from accessing objects owned by other users.

AWS recommends using Amazon Cognito with web identity federation instead of writing your custom code for authentication. Amazon Cognito lets you easily add user sign-up and sign-in to your mobile and web apps. With Amazon Cognito, you also have the options to authenticate users through social IdP such as Facebook, Twitter, or Amazon, with SAML identity solutions, or by using your own identity system.

The following *Figure 3.23* shows a sample workflow using web identity federation with Cognito:

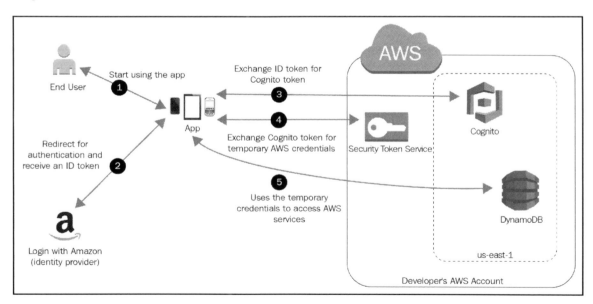

Figure 3.23: Workflow using web identity federation with Cognito

1. As you can see in the preceding figure, an end user starts your app on a mobile device. The application prompts the user to sign-in.
2. When a user enters the credentials, and submits the authentication request, the application redirects it to a *Login with Amazon*, third-party IdP for verifying the credentials. If the user is authenticated, it receives an authentication token.
3. The application forwards the authentication token to Cognito using Cognito APIs and exchanges the authentication token for a Cognito token.
4. The application passes the Cognito token to AWS STS to request temporary security credentials. AWS STS provides temporary security credentials.
5. The temporary security credentials can be used by the app to access any AWS resources required by the app to operate. The role associated with the temporary security credentials and its assigned policies determines what can be accessed.

STS

STS is a web service that enables an application to dynamically generate *temporary security credentials* with restricted permissions based on an IAM Role. This temporary credential can be generated either for an IAM user or for a federated user as we have seen in the previous section for web identity federation.

Temporary security credentials generated using AWS STS for a trusted user can control access to your AWS resources. Temporary security credentials and the long-term access key credentials used by IAM users work almost similarly except for a few differences:

- Temporary security credentials, as the name suggests, are for short term use only. These credentials expire after a specific time.
- Temporary security credentials can be configured to expire within a few minutes to several hours.
- After the credentials expire, AWS does not recognize them. Any kind of access from API requests made with expired credentials is not allowed.
- Temporary security credentials are not stored with the user, but are generated dynamically.
- They are provided to the user or application based on the request.
- The application or user should request new credentials before they expire.
- When (or even before) the temporary security credentials expire, the user can request new credentials, as long as the user requesting them still has permissions to do so.

These differences lead to the following advantages for using temporary credentials:

- You do not have to distribute or embed long-term AWS security credentials with an application.
- You can provide access to your AWS resources to users without having to define an AWS identity for them. Temporary credentials are the basis for roles and identity federation.
- The temporary security credentials have a limited lifetime, so you do not have to rotate them or explicitly revoke them when they're no longer needed. After temporary security credentials expire, they cannot be reused. You can specify how long the credentials are valid, up to a maximum limit.

AWS STS and AWS regions

Temporary security credentials are generated by AWS STS. By default, AWS STS is a global service with a single endpoint at `https://sts.amazonaws.com`. However, you can also choose to make AWS STS API calls to endpoints in any other supported region. This can reduce latency (server lag) by sending the requests to servers in a region that is geographically closer to you. No matter which region your credentials come from, they work globally.

Using temporary credentials in Amazon EC2 instances

If you want to run AWS CLI commands or code inside an EC2 instance, the recommended way to get credentials is to use roles for Amazon EC2. You create an IAM role that specifies the permissions that you want to grant to applications that run on the EC2 instances. When you launch the instance, you associate the role with the instance.

Applications, AWS CLI, and tools for Windows PowerShell commands that run on the instance can then get automatic temporary security credentials from the instance metadata. You do not have to explicitly get the temporary security credentials—the AWS SDKs, AWS CLI, and tools for Windows PowerShell automatically get the credentials from the EC2 instance metadata service and use them. The temporary credentials have the permissions that you define for the role that is associated with the instance.

Using temporary security credentials with the AWS SDKs

To use temporary security credentials in code, you programmatically call an AWS STS API such as `AssumeRole`, extract the resulting credentials and session token, and then use those values as credentials for subsequent calls to AWS. The following example shows pseudo code for how to use temporary security credentials if you're using an AWS SDK:

```
assumeRoleResult = AssumeRole(role-arn);
tempCredentials = new SessionAWSCredentials(
    assumeRoleResult.AccessKeyId,
    assumeRoleResult.SecretAccessKey,
    assumeRoleResult.SessionToken);
s3Request = CreateAmazonS3Client(tempCredentials);
```

IAM best practices

The security of your AWS resources can be maintained by following these best practices:

- Never share credentials (that is, password or access key and secret key). Specifically, sharing root user credentials can pose a very serious security threat as it carries the highest level of access in relevant AWS account.
- Never use the root account for day-to-day tasks. Create individual IAM users for designated roles and responsibilities.
- Until and unless it is essential, do not create an access key and a secret key. Also, keep rotating the password and keys periodically.
- It is not best practice to hardcode access key and secret key in any program or application.
- Keep your access key and secret key secured such that it does not fall into hands of any unauthorized person. A secret key is only generated once paired with a relevant access key. If a secret key is lost then there is no mechanism in AWS to retrieve it. You need to discard the existing key and regenerate it. When a secret key is lost and discarded, the user must update the new key pair in the application, API, SDKs, CLI, and wherever the old key pair is used. Updating the new key pair ensures smooth functioning of relevant applications, programs, or services.

- Periodically remove unused IAM accounts and access keys and secret keys.
- Implement a reasonably strong password policy to avoid compromising user passwords. Password policy can be configured from **Account settings** in the IAM dashboard.
- Implement MFA for all users and possible SDKs.
- Always grant least privilege to the users. Only grant required and essential permissions to perform their day-to-day tasks. While inspecting privileges for user, group, role, and policy, accessing the **Advisor** tab from the IAM dashboard can help.
- To grant permissions, use group rather than applying the permissions at user level. Group makes it easier to manage permissions. If a user requires extra permissions, a separate policy can be attached to a specific IAM user based on needs.
- Periodically audit existing users, groups, policies, and roles. Remove unwanted privileges from policies. Remove unused users, groups, and roles.
- To provide credentials to an application running on EC2, create an IAM role and attach it to an EC2 instance. Roles don't have a username and password or an access key and secret key. Temporary credentials are dynamically generated for roles and such temporary credentials are automatically rotated.
- Apply policy conditions for an extra layer of security. For example, conditions can be specified for an allowed range of IP addresses.
- Monitor AWS account activity (that is, creation, deletion, accessing, and modifying resources) using various AWS services such as Amazon CloudTrail, Amazon Cloudwatch, and AWS Config.
- It is suggested that you customize IAM user sign-in link with an easy to remember name as it is used by AWS IAM users to log in to AWS. Sign-in link contains 12-digit account number in the URL, which may be difficult for a user to remember. It can be customized with a meaningful and unique name.

Exam tips

The following points discuss about exam tips of AWS IAM:

- AWS IAM service is a global service. It means it is not region specific. IAM entities such as users, groups, roles, and policies are the same across all the regions. Once they are created, they are same for all the AWS regions.
- By default, newly created IAM users do not have any privileges to perform any tasks on AWS accounts. Users must be granted permissions to access any service or perform any operation in AWS. User permissions are granted by either adding the user to a group with required permissions or by directly attaching an access policy to a user.
- IAM users can be a member of any IAM group, but an IAM group cannot be a member of any IAM group. In other words, an IAM group cannot be a nested.
- One user can be part of multiple policies and multiple policies can be attached to a single user.
- An IAM user password is used for an AWS dashboard login and an access key and secret key pair is used for API, CLI, and SDKs authentication. However, vice-a-versa is not possible.
- By default, for any IAM users, groups, or roles, permission to access any AWS resource is denied, until and unless explicitly allowed in IAM policies. When multiple IAM policies are attached to an IAM entity, explicitly denied access to any AWS resource overrides explicit allowed. For example, if a user is granted permission to access an S3 bucket in one policy and the same user is explicitly denied permission to access that S3 bucket, that user cannot access the specified S3 bucket as explicit deny overrides explicit allow permissions.
- Configuring or re-configuring password policy does not impact existing user password. Password policy comes into effect, only when a new user is created or when an existing user updates the password.

- It is important to remember that IAM policies are JSON documents, written as per the IAM policy standards. By default, access to AWS resources is denied, so usually IAM policies are written to grant permission to any user, group, or service.
- It is very important to understand policy structure (that is, effect, action, and resource), how to write policy, and interpret it.
- Understand IAM elements such as users, groups, and roles. As we know, users are end users, groups are a bunch of logically similar users, and roles are IAM entities that can be assumed by AWS resources and federated users. Roles can also be assigned to application or program resources such as EC2 or Lambda. An attached role has its own policy based on that permission is granted to access various AWS resources.
- IAM roles don't have permanent credentials. As and when roles are assumed, a temporary access key and secret key is dynamically generated and automatically rotated.
- IAM roles can be of three types:
    - IAM roles for AWS resources (EC2 and Lambda)
    - IAM roles for cross-accounts (granting permissions to IAM users across AWS accounts)
    - IAM roles for federated identity
- Before running AWS CLI, it is important to install and configure a default access key, secret key, region, and output format. Default output format is JSON.

4

Virtual Private Cloud

Before we understand what VPC is, let us understand what a computer network is. In very simple terms, when two or more computers are interconnected for sharing resources and communicating between each other, it is called a computer network.

When we talk about interconnected computers in an organization, there are some distinct requirements on usage of these computers:

- Some computers are restricted to be accessed from within the organization
- Some computers are required to be accessed from within the organization as well as from outside of it

Based on the usage of the resources in a network, the network is subdivided into a number of segments. For example, the resources, that are required to be accessed from within the organization, are kept in a private segment of the network.

Similarly, the resources, which are required to be accessed from within the organization as well as from outside of it, are kept in a public segment of the network.

The segment that logically isolates the resources in a network is called a subnet. In an organization, a network may be subdivided into multiple subnets based on the need of the organization. In other words, there may be more than one public or private subnets in a network.

Resources in a network need to communicate with one another, hence they need to have a unique identity through which these resources can be distinctly identified and communication can be initiated between them. Such identity for resources in a network is called an IP address.

So far, we have understood networks in simple terms. Let us revisit our understanding about networks in a few simple points:

- When two or more computers are interconnected for communication between each other, it is called a network
- Resources in a network need to communicate with each other based on requirement
- Resources in a network are subdivided into logical segments called *subnets*
- Resources in a private subnet are accessible within the network or organization
- Resources in a public subnet are accessible from outside the organization as well
- We have also seen that resources in a network are logically isolated in subnets

AWS VPC

As we now have a basic understanding of what a computer network is, let us understand what AWS VPC is. A VPC is similar to a computer network that we can create in an on premise data center. The way we create dedicated and private networks within an organization, where computers in a network share the network devices such as router, switches, and so on, we can create a VPC the same way, when we create a new account in AWS. VPC makes it possible to shape similar network infrastructure as we can shape it in our own data center. The difference is, it is a virtual environment within a public cloud wherein the virtual network is logically isolated from other similar networks within the public cloud.

This chapter covers the following VPC components. Each of these components are described in subsequent pages of the chapter:
VPC networking components
Elastic Network Interface (ENI)
Route table
IGW
Egress-only IGW
NAT
DHCP option sets
DNS
VPC peering
VPC endpoint
ClassicLink

Unlike a traditional data center, a VPC can be created on demand without buying any hardware. You just need to create an AWS account and you are ready to get started.

Let us understand VPC with some visualization. As we have seen in the previous chapters, AWS has multiple regions. At present while writing this book, there are 16 AWS regions, out of that, three random regions are illustrated in the following *Figure 4.1* for visualizing the regions. We will see in subsequent diagrams how a VPC looks within a region.

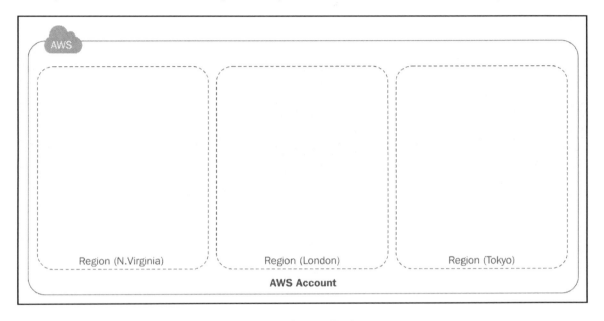

Figure 4.1: AWS account with regions

Every AWS region has two or more AZs. In the next *Figure 4.2*, we have considered one region to visualize multiple AZ and how a VPC spans within a region and across multiple AZs.

Each AWS account can access multiple regions and each region has two or more AZs. A VPC can be created in any region and can span to multiple AZs. A VPC's scope is limited to a single region, however, it can span across multiple AZs. To explain this concept, the following *Figure 4.2* represents an AWS account, one region out of multiple AWS Regions, Default VPC with **Classless Inter-Domain Routing (CIDR)** (172.31.0.0/16), and two AZs.

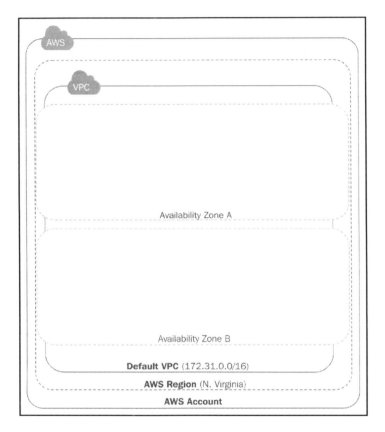

Figure 4.2: VPC visualization in a region with multiple AZs

Within one AWS account, several networks may exist (such as 10.0.0.0/16 and 10.1.0.0/16). For example, an organization can work on several different projects at the same time, and for each of the projects they can create individual networks VPC to isolate traffic and AWS resources. Each VPC spans across a region, in which it is created. An organization may also create multiple VPCs for each of the regions where their offices are located.

When you create a VPC, you need to specify an IP range for that VPC. This IP range is called CIDR, for example, `10.0.0.0/16`. CIDR is a set of IP standards that is used to create a unique identity for a network. It defines a set of IPs that can be allocated to resources within a network. You can look at RFC 4632 standards in the URL `https://tools.ietf.org/html/rfc4632` for more information on CIDR.

Now, let us understand what a subnet inside a network is with respect to a VPC.

Subnet

Subnet is a short form of **subnetwork**. As we have seen in the beginning section of the chapter, a network is sub-divided into multiple logical parts for controlling access to individual logical subparts of the network. When we create a subnet, we need to specify a unique CIDR block for the subnet. This CIDR block has to be a subset of the VPC CIDR block. Each subnet must reside entirely within a single AZ as a subnet cannot span in multiple AZs.

Subnets are categorized as public and private subnets based on their security profile or in other words based on its route table. We will now discuss different types of subnets.

Private subnet

A private subnet is a subset of a network wherein resources within a subnet are isolated and restricted for access from within the VPC. Any incoming traffic from the internet cannot directly access the resources within a private subnet. Similarly, outgoing traffic from a private subnet cannot directly access the internet. Outgoing traffic to the internet is either restricted or it is routed through a **Network Address Translator** (**NAT**). We will learn more about NAT in subsequent sections of the chapter.

Resources in a private subnet are assigned a private IP, that is accessible only from within the VPC. A route table defines the routing of the traffic to and from the subnet and ultimately determines whether a subnet is a private or a public subnet based on whether it has a direct route to **Internet gateway** (**IGW**) or not. This chapter discusses more on IGW in subsequent sections.

Public subnet

A public subnet is a subset of a network wherein resources within a subnet are isolated and can be accessed from within the VPC as well as from the internet. Any incoming traffic can directly access the resources located in a public subnet. Resources in a public subnet are assigned a public IP, that is accessible from the internet. Similarly, traffic originated from a public subnet can directly access the internet. Unlike a private subnet, traffic going out from a public subnet is not routed to a NAT, but directly routed to IGW. Such routing makes it possible for the resources to directly access the internet from a public subnet.

The following *Figure 4.3* describes how public and private subnets are segregated within a VPC:

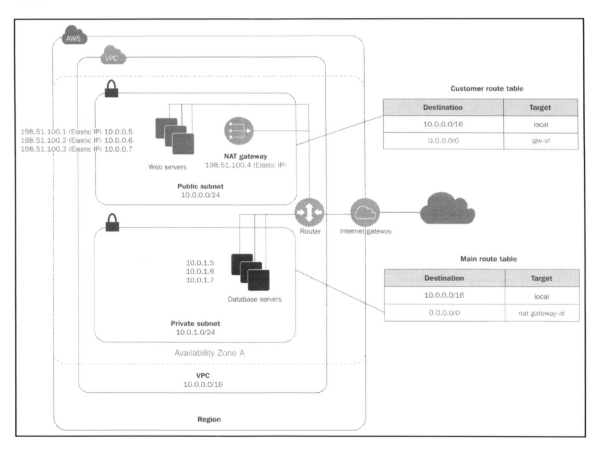

Figure 4.3: VPC with public and private subnets

As you can see in the preceding *Figure 4.3*, VPC CIDR is `10.0.0.0/16` and there are two subnets, one each for public and private resources. Both the subnets have their own CIDR. The main differentiator is the route table. As you can see in the route table, for destination `0.0.0.0/0`, the target in the private subnet is a NAT gateway ID and the target for the public subnet is IGW ID. CIDR `0.0.0.0/0` denotes any traffic over the internet.

IP addressing

When an EC2 instance is launched, it carries an IP address and IPv4 DNS hostname. The IP address and DNS hostname varies depending upon whether the instance is launched in an EC2-Classic platform or a VPC. When an instance is launched in Amazon VPC, it supports both IPv4 and IPv6 addresses. EC2-Classic platform supports only IPv4, it does not support IPv6.

By default, Amazon uses IPv4 addressing for the instance and VPC CIDR. This is the default behavior of EC2 instances and VPC. Alternatively, a user can assign IPv6 addressing protocol to VPC and subnets that would subsequently allow you to assign IPv6 addresses to instances in a VPC.

Private IP

As we have seen in earlier sections, a private IP address cannot be reached over the internet. Private IP addresses can be used for communication between the instances within the same network. When an instance is launched, Amazon uses **Dynamic Host Configuration Protocol (DHCP)** to assign a private IP address to the instance. Apart from a private IP address, an instance is also assigned an internal DNS hostname that ultimately resolves to a private IPv4 address of the instance.

Here is an example of an internal DNS hostname: `ip-10-5-200-21.ec2.internal`. This DNS name can be used for communication between instances within the same network, but it cannot be resolved outside of the network or over the internet since it is a private DNS address.

When an instance is launched in a VPC, it is assigned a primary private IP address. This IP address is automatically selected from the IPv4 range of the subnet. Alternatively, you can also specify a custom IP address out of the IPv4 CIDR range of the subnet. If you specify a custom IP, that IP must not be already in use by any other instance. A primary IP address is assigned to a default Ethernet interface. This default Ethernet interface is named as **eth0**. A primary IP address cannot be changed once an instance is launched. You can also assign a secondary IP address to an instance. Unlike a primary IP address, a secondary IP address can be changed and assigned to other instances.

EC2 instances launched in VPC retain their IP addresses even if the instances are stopped or restarted. The IP address is released only when the instance is terminated. Instances in EC2-Classic release their IP address as soon as they are stopped or terminated. If an instance in EC2-Classic is restarted, it is assigned a new IPv4 address.

Public IP

Unlike a private IP address, a public IP address can be reached over the internet. Public IP addresses can be used for communication over the internet. When an instance is assigned a public IP address, it also receives an external DNS hostname.

Here is an example of an external DNS hostname: `ip-XXX-XXX-XXX-XXX.compute-1.amazonaws.com`, where `XXX-XXX-XXX-XXX` indicates public IP address of the instance.

This public DNS name can be used for communication between instances within the same network or outside of the network over the internet. When this external hostname is used within the network, it is resolved to a private IP address of the instance. If this external DNS name is used outside the network then it resolves to a public IP address. This public IP address is mapped to a primary private IP address using NAT.

In an EC2-Classic platform, when an instance is launched, it is automatically assigned a public IP from the public IPv4 address pool. Instances launched in an EC2-Classic platform must have a public IP . This is the default behavior of the EC2-Classic platform and it cannot be changed.

When an instance is launched in a VPC subnet, there is a subnet attribute that determines if an instance launched in the subnet automatically gets a public IP or not. Public IPs for VPC instances are assigned from the EC2-VPC public IPv4 address pool. Amazon automatically assigns a public IP to an instance launched in a default VPC, whereas instances in a non-default VPC do not get a public IP automatically. This behavior can be controlled using the VPC subnet settings.

Here's how you can control public IPv4 addressing attributes for a VPC subnet:

1. Go to the VPC console through the dashboard or browse the URL `https://console.aws.amazon.com/vpc/`.
2. From the VPC console go to **Subnets**.
3. Select a subnet from the list of subnets in your VPC and choose **Subnet Actions**.
4. Select **Modify auto-assign IP settings**.
5. Select the **Enable auto-assign public IPv4 address** checkbox.
6. When this checkbox is selected, it assigns a public IPv4 address every time an instance is launched in the selected subnet. You can select or clear this checkbox based on the requirement and then save the settings.

You can override this behavior while launching an instance in a VPC subnet. Amazon provides an option to choose whether you want to auto assign a public IP to the instance or not while launching an EC2 instance.

After an instance is launched, one cannot assign or release a public IP address manually to an instance. Amazon releases the public IP when an instance is stopped or terminated. When the same instance is stopped and restarted, it automatically gets a new public IP address. Again, you cannot control this behavior. If you want to use a persistent IP address or need to manually assign/release the IP address, you need to use **Elastic IP address**.

When you assign an Elastic IP address to the primary Ethernet interface, Amazon automatically releases the public IP address of the instance. An Elastic IP address is equivalent to a public IP address, that can be controlled by users.

Elastic IP address

An Elastic IP address is a public IPv4 address that can be allocated to an AWS account. An Elastic IP can be assigned or released from an instance as needed. Once an Elastic IP is allocated, it remains in the account until it is explicitly released from the account. As far as the usage of an Elastic IP is concerned, it is similar to a public IP specified in the previous point. Here's some of the important aspects of an Elastic IP:

- For using an Elastic IP, first you need to allocate it in your account. Once an Elastic IP is allocated, you can assign it to an EC2 instance or a network interface.
- If an Elastic IP is associated with a primary network interface of an instance, Amazon automatically releases the public IP address associated with the instance or interface. An instance with a primary network interface cannot have an Elastic IP as well as a public IP at the same time.
- You can associate an Elastic IP to an EC2 instance and disassociate it as needed. Once the Elastic IP is disassociated from the instance, the same IP can be associated to any other instance.
- If you disassociate an Elastic IP from an instance, it remains in the account until you explicitly release it from the account.
- If an Elastic IP is not associated to an instance, Amazon charges the account on an hourly basis for that IP. Amazon also charges if an Elastic IP is associated to a stopped instance. In short, Amazon charges small fees for any unutilized Elastic IP address to ensure efficient usage of Elastic IPs. There is no charge for one Elastic IP address if it is associated with a running instance. If there are more than one Elastic IP addresses associated with an instance, you are charged for additional Elastic IP addresses.
- An Elastic IP is associated with a specific region. You cannot use the same Elastic IP in different regions.
- When an Elastic IP is associated with a primary network interface of an instance, its public IPv4 address is released and its public DNS hostname is updated to reflect the Elastic IP address.
- When a public DNS hostname is accessed from outside the VPC or network, it resolves to a public IP or Elastic IP of the instance. If a public DNS hostname is accessed from within the VPC or network, it resolves to a private IP of the instance.

Creating a VPC

By default, when you create an AWS account, Amazon automatically provisions a default VPC for you. You can customize the default VPC based on your needs. You can add more subnets, remove any existing subnet, change default route table, attach network gateways, or change the **Network Access Control List (NACL)** as per the requirement.

You can configure the default VPC and use it as needed or you can create additional VPCs using either VPC wizard or create custom VPCs manually. VPC wizard provides four predefined categories of VPCs, which can help you quickly build the VPCs.

The wizard provides the following four types of VPCs:

- VPC with a single public subnet
- VPC with public and private subnets
- VPC with public and private subnets and hardware VPN access
- VPC with private subnet only and hardware VPN access

Let's understand each of these VPC types and the steps involved in creating the respective VPCs.

VPC with a single public subnet

For creating a VPC with a single public subnet using a wizard, follow these steps:

1. Browse `https://console.aws.amazon.com/vpc` or select **VPC** from the AWS dashboard. It brings up the VPC dashboard as follows:

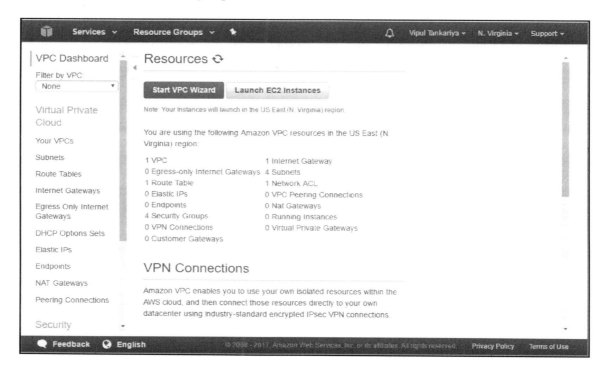

Figure 4.4: VPC dashboard

2. Ensure that you have selected the right region where you want to create the VPC. Region can be selected from the top right corner of the screen like **N.Virginia** is selected in the preceding figure.

3. Click on the **Start VPC Wizard** button, and the following *Figure 4.5* will appear:

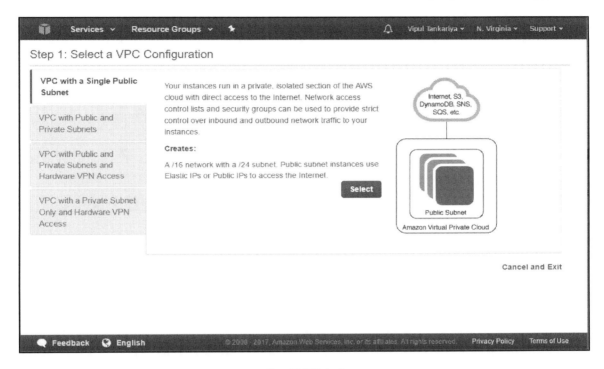

Figure 4.5: VPC wizard

4. Click on the **Select** button. It will give you the following *Figure 4.6*:

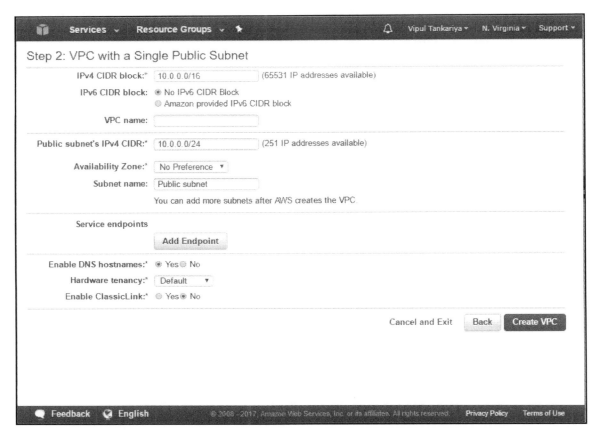

Figure 4.6: VPC wizard

5. Provide an **IPv4 CIDR block**. The default is 10.0.0.0/16, which provides 65531 IPs in the VPC. This is the maximum size of VPC you can create in AWS by using the /16 CIDR range. The following table shows the IP range for CIDR 10.0.0.0/16. If you are not familiar with how to calculate the CIDR range, you can visit sites like http://ipaddressguide.com/cidr and play around with the CIDR calculator. As you can see in the following table, the total hosts or IP address range in this CIDR is 65536, however, only 65531 IPs are usable. Amazon reserves five IPs in any subnet for various purposes shown as follows:

CIDR range	10.0.0.0/16
Netmask	255.255.0.0
Wildcard bits	0.0.255.255
First IP	10.0.0.0
Last IP	10.0.255.255
Total IPs	65536

Details of the reserved IPs are given in the following table. From the following table, it is understandable that whenever you create any subnet, the respective five IPs in that subnet are reserved by AWS, that is, x.x.x.0, x.x.x.1, x.x.x.2, x.x.x.3, and x.x.x.255.

10.0.0.0	**Network address**
10.0.0.1	Reserved for VPC router
10.0.0.2	Reserved for DNS server
10.0.0.3	Reserved for future use
10.0.0.255	Network broadcast address

AWS reserved IPs in the VPC

6. You can keep **No IPv6 CIDR** block selected or select **Amazon provided IPv6 CIDR block** if your VPC needs IPv6 addresses as well. For ease of understanding, keep **No IPv6 CIDR** block as selected.
7. Enter the VPC name as required again in the **VPC name** field. VPC name can have a maximum of 256 characters.
8. Specify the public subnet's CIDR range. The default is 10.0.0.0/24. This CIDR range spans to 256 IPs, out of which five IPs are reserved as described in point 5, leaving reserved IPs aside; it gives you 251 usable IPs in the subnet.
9. You can choose to specify any specific AZ for the subnet or keep **No Preference** as selected against the **Availability Zone** field.
10. Enter any subnet name against the **Subnet name** field. A subnet name can have a maximum of 256 characters. You can add more subnets after the VPC is created.

11. You can add **Service endpoints** by clicking on the **Add Endpoint** button. With service endpoints, you can directly access respective service from within the VPC. Currently, this feature supports the S3 endpoint. Adding an S3 endpoint to VPC allows direct access from VPC to S3. If an S3 endpoint is not added, any request to S3 goes through IGW. That means your data or traffic goes through the internet for any interaction with S3 service. Adding an S3 endpoint routes the traffic directly to S3 and keeps the communication within the VPC network. For now, do not add any endpoint for ease of understanding.

12. Keep **Enable DNS hostnames** selected as **Yes**. When the DNS hostnames attribute is enabled in a VPC, any EC2 instance provisioned in the VPC is automatically assigned a DNS hostname.

13. In the next step, you need to select **Hardware tenancy**. You can select either **Default** tenancy or **Dedicated** tenancy. **Default** tenancy specifies that a single physical AWS machine may run instances provisioned by multiple AWS customers. If you select **Dedicated** tenancy, it ensures that EC2 instances launched in this VPC are launched on a dedicated hardware. Tenancy of a VPC cannot be changed after a VPC is created. **Dedicated** tenancy costs more than **Default** tenancy. Select this option considering the requirement.

14. **Enable ClassicLink** option allows a VPC to communicate with the EC2 instances launched in EC2-Classic. Without this option enabled, resources in the VPC need to use a public IP address of the EC2-Classic instance or tunneling for communication. If you have any resources in EC2-Classic, you can choose **Yes** to enable the ClassicLink, or else you can keep **No** as selected.

15. Click on the **Create VPC** button to create the VPC. This final step pops up a small progress bar while the system creates your VPC. Once the progress completes 100%, it shows the newly created VPC in the **Your VPCs** list from the VPC dashboard:

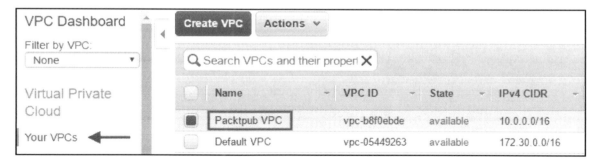

Figure 4.7: Your VPCs in VPC dashboard

The previously mentioned points for creating a VPC, generates a VPC with a single public subnet. The following *Figure 4.8* shows the architecture diagram of the VPC:

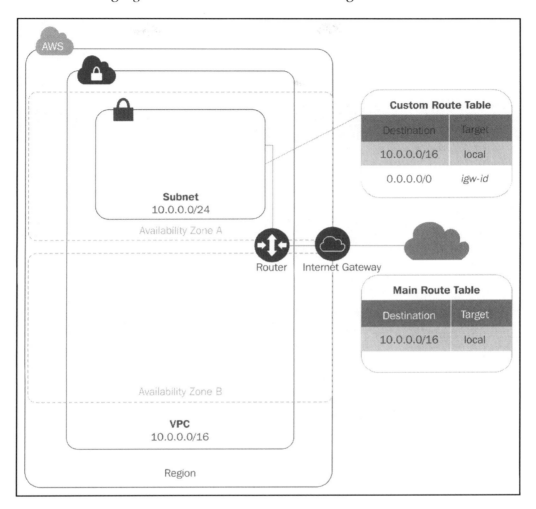

Figure 4.8: Architecture diagram - VPC with single public subnet

The wizard creates a VPC with the following list of features:

- It creates a VPC with `10.0.0.0/16` CIDR block and 65536 IPv4 addresses.
- Associates IGW to the VPC.

- It also creates a public subnet with `10.0.0.0/24` CIDR range. It encompasses 256 IPv4 addresses. As elaborated earlier, Amazon reserves five IPs out of the subnet, which leaves 251 usable IPv4 addresses.
- It creates a custom route table and attaches it to the subnet. This route table enables traffic between the subnet and IGW.

VPC with private and public subnets

Steps for creating a VPC with private and public subnets are almost identical to VPC with a single public subnet except the wizard offers to create private subnets and it also offers to attach a NAT gateway for routing traffic from private subnets to the internet.

For creating a VPC with single, private, and public subnets using wizard, follow these steps:

1. Browse `https://console.aws.amazon.com/vpc` or select **VPC** from the AWS dashboard.
2. Ensure that you have selected the right region where you want to create the VPC and click on **Start VPC Wizard.**
3. From the subsequent screen, select **VPC with Public and Private Subnets** as shown and click on the **Select** button:

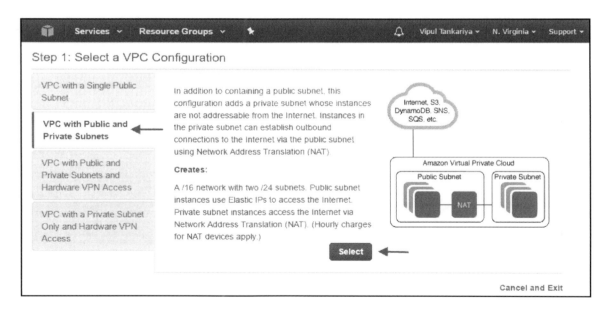

Figure 4.9: VPC wizard for VPC with public and private subnets

4. On the subsequent screen, you can see that the wizard is almost identical to the wizard for creating a VPC with single public subnet. This wizard offers to create private subnets and it also offers to attach a NAT gateway for routing traffic from private subnets to the internet:

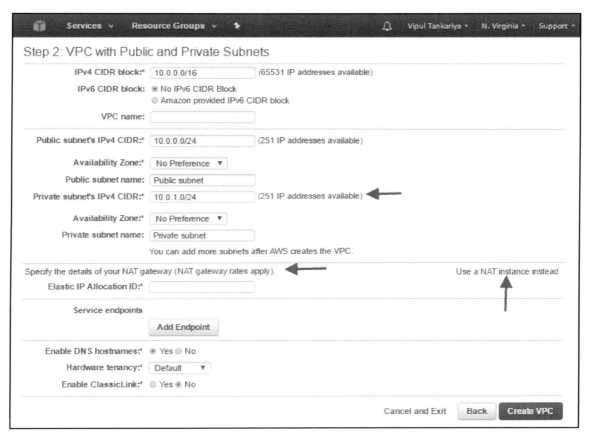

Figure 4.10: VPC wizard - NAT and private subnet detail

5. Specify details in all the fields as required including **Elastic IP Allocation ID** in the **Specify the details of your NAT gateway** section. You can allocate a new Elastic IP address and obtain its allocation ID from the listing of **EC2 dashboard | Elastic IPs**.

6. Click on the **Create VPC** button after providing all the required details on the screen. It creates a VPC with private and public subnets.

The following *Figure 4.11* shows the architecture diagram of the newly created VPC:

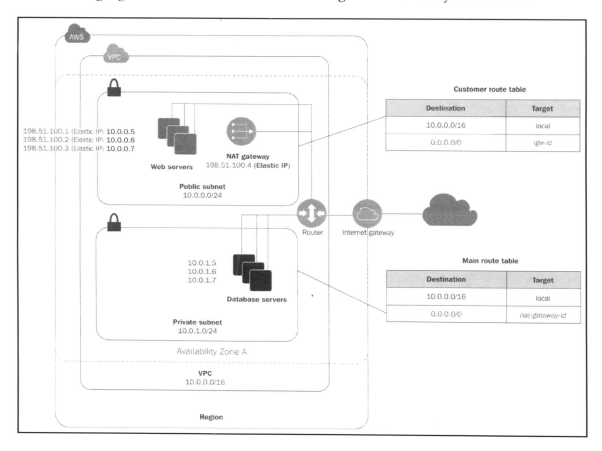

Figure 4.11: Architecture diagram - VPC with private and public subnets

Here are the details of the VPC created using the wizard:

- It creates a VPC with /16 CIDR range and 65,536 IPv4 addresses.
- It also creates a public subnet with /24 IPv4 CIDR range and 256 IPv4 addresses. Since this is a public subnet, it also creates a route table entry with route to IGW.
- It creates a private subnet with /24 IPv4 CIDR range and 256 private IPv4 addresses.

- It also adds an IGW and connects the VPC to the internet as well as other AWS services.
- It creates a NAT gateway with an Elastic IPv4 address supplied during the wizard. This allows instances in the private subnet to communicate over the internet through the NAT gateway.
- It adds a custom route table and associates it with the public subnet. This route table enables the instances in the public subnet to communicate with each other and over the internet through IGW.

VPC with public and private subnets and hardware VPN access

Steps for creating a VPC with private and public subnets and hardware VPN access are almost identical to the previous wizard except for an additional screen that requires details for creating hardware VPN access. For ease of use and better understanding, only the last part of the wizard is elaborated here.

The steps in brief are discussed as follows:

1. Browse `https://console.aws.amazon.com/vpc` or select **VPC** from the AWS dashboard.
2. Ensure that you have selected the right region where you want to create the VPC and click on **Start VPC Wizard.**
3. From the subsequent screen, select **VPC with Public and Private Subnets and Hardware VPN Access** and click on the **Select** button.
4. Fill all the fields in the subsequent screen, which are identical to what we have gone through in the previous wizard.

5. After filling all the fields, click on the **Next** button. It will bring up the following *Figure 4.12*:

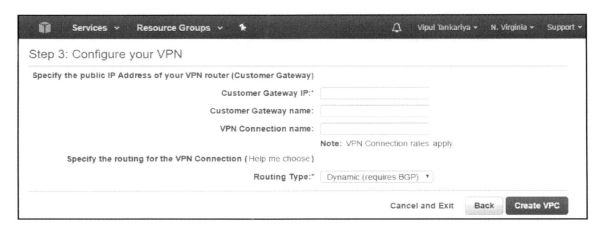

Figure 4.12: Create VPC wizard - Configure your VPN

6. Specify **Customer Gateway IP:** It is an IP address of the anchor from on-premise or target location where we need to establish a VPN tunnel from our AWS VPC. The anchor can be a hardware or software appliance or router.

7. Provide **Customer Gateway name:** This is optional but recommended for easily identifying the customer gateway.

8. Provide **VPN Connection name:** This is also optional but it is recommended to give a name to this connection.

9. Select **Routing Type:** There are two route types, dynamic and static. If you select static routing, it requires you to manually enter the IP prefix for your network while creating the VPN connection. When you select dynamic routing, the IP prefix is advertised automatically to the VPN gateway using **Border Gateway Protocol (BGP)**. Ensure that your target appliance supports BGP if you select **Dynamic (requires BGP).**

10. Click on the **Create VPC** button after providing all the required details on the screen. It creates a VPC with private and public subnets and hardware VPN access.

For establishing a VPN connection between a VPC and a target network, an administrator on the target network needs to configure the anchor appliance at the target. This is generally not required for a developer to understand. Also, it is out of the scope of the *AWS Certified Developer - Associate exam*. If you're interested in knowing more about how a network administrator needs to configure the target anchor appliance for VPN connectivity, you can refer to the following URL: `http://docs.aws.amazon.com/AmazonVPC/latest/NetworkAdminGuide/Welcome.html`.

The following *Figure 4.13* shows the architecture diagram of the newly created VPC:

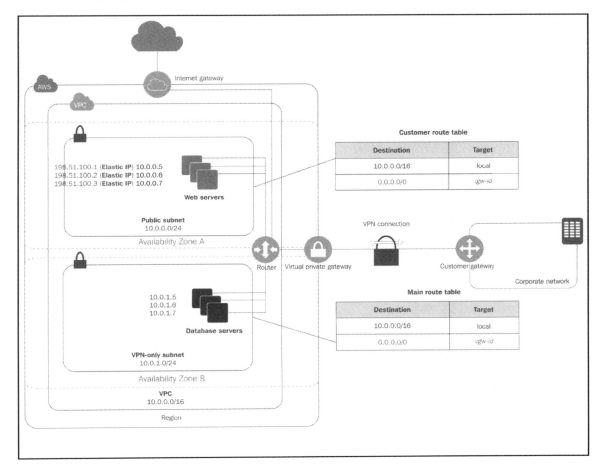

Figure 4.13: VPC with private and public subnets and VPN access

The following points describe the VPC created using the wizard:

- It creates a VPC with a size /16 IPv4 CIDR range with 65,536 private IPv4 addresses.
- It creates a public subnet /24 IPv4 CIDR block and 256 private IPv4 addresses.
- It creates a VPN-only subnet with IPv4 CIDR block of size /24 and 256 private IPv4 addresses.
- It also creates an IGW that connects the VPC to the internet and other AWS services.
- It also creates a VPN connection between the VPC and target network. The VPN connection needs a **Virtual Private Gateway (VGW)** that points to the VPC endpoint on AWS and a **Customer Gateway (CGW)** that points to the target network endpoint.
- It creates a NAT gateway with an Elastic IPv4 address supplied during the wizard. This allows instances in a private subnet to communicate over the internet through the NAT gateway.
- It adds a custom route table and associates it with the public subnet. This route table enables the instances in the public subnet to communicate with each other and over the internet through IGW.
- It also creates a route for routing the traffic to a VPN connection that is ultimately routed to CGW. This entry enables the instances in VPC to communicate with resources on the target network.

VPC with private subnet only and hardware VPN access

Steps for creating a VPC with a private subnet only and hardware VPN access are almost identical to previous wizards except one change wherein no public subnets are created in this wizard. This wizard creates a VPN connection between the VPC and target network over an IPsec VPN tunnel. There is no IGW for any communication with the internet. This scenario is recommended for extending a target or an on-premise network to AWS VPC for a secure communication without exposing it to the internet.

The steps in brief for creating a VPC with a private subnet only and hardware VPN access are as follows:

1. Browse `https://console.aws.amazon.com/vpc` or select **VPC** from the AWS dashboard.
2. Ensure that you have selected the right region where you want to create the VPC and click on **Start VPC Wizard**.
3. From the subsequent screen, select **VPC with Private Subnets Only and Hardware VPN Access** and click on the **Select** button.
4. Fill all the fields in the subsequent screen, which are identical to what we have gone through in the previous wizard.
5. After filling all the fields, click on the **Next** button. It will bring the screen that we saw in the previous wizard.
6. Specify **Customer Gateway IP:** It is an IP address of the anchor from an on-premise or target location where we need to establish a VPN tunnel from our AWS VPC. The anchor can be a hardware or software appliance or router.
7. Provide **Customer Gateway name:** This is optional but recommended for easily identifying the customer gateway.
8. Provide **VPN Connection name**. This is also optional, but it is recommended to give a name to this connection.
9. Select **Routing Type:** There are two route types, dynamic and static. If you select static routing, it requires you to manually enter the IP prefix for your network while creating the VPN connection. When you select dynamic routing, the IP prefix is advertised automatically to the VPN gateway using BGP. Ensure that your target appliance supports BGP if you select **Dynamic (requires BGP)**.
10. Click on the **Create VPC** button after providing all the required details on the screen. It creates a VPC with private subnet only and hardware VPN access.

For establishing a VPN connection between a VPC and the target network, an administrator on the target network needs to configure the anchor appliance at the target. This is generally not required for a developer to understand. Also, it is out of the scope of the *AWS Certified Developer - Associate exam*. If you're interested in knowing more about how a network administrator needs to configure the target anchor appliance for VPN connectivity, you can refer to the following URL:
`http://docs.aws.amazon.com/AmazonVPC/latest/NetworkAdminGuide/Welcome.html`

The following *Figure 4.14* shows VPC created for a private subnet only with hardware VPN access:

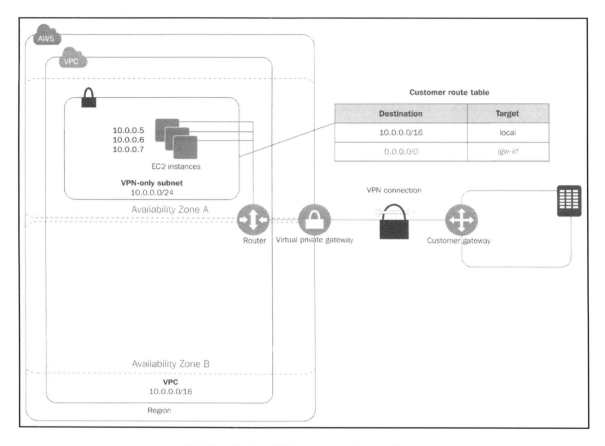

Figure 4.14: Architecture - VPC with private only and hardware VPN access

The architecture created using this wizard includes the following:

- It creates a VPC with /16 CIDR range and 65,536 private IP addresses.
- It creates a VPN-only subnet with /24 CIDR range and 256 private IP addresses.
- It creates a VPN connection between your VPC and target network. The VPN connection includes a VGW pointing to the VPC and a CGW that points to the anchor appliance on the target network.
- It creates a custom route table associated to the subnet. The route table contains route entries for communication between instances within the VPC and also an entry for communication with other resources on the target network.

Security

While creating a VPC, security is one of the most critical aspects of the VPN of an organization. As AWS states in many of its official communication, security of the customer network is one of its highest priorities. Keeping the security on top of the AWS charter, Amazon provides two features for taking care of network security and one feature for monitoring the network.

Security group and NACL are for network security and **Flow logs** is for network monitoring. Security groups act as an EC2 instance level firewall, whereas NACL acts as a subnet level firewall. Flow logs provide insight on network traffic. In the following sections in this chapter, these features will be described in detail.

To start with, let's take a high level overview of the difference between Security group and NACL. The layers of communication as shown in the following *Figure 4.15* helps to understand the significance of Security group and NACL in a VPC.

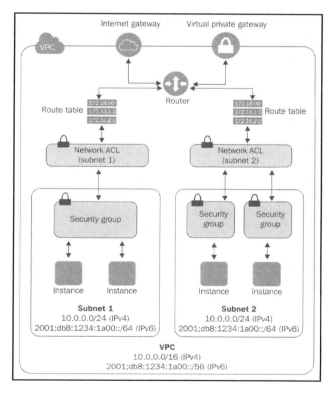

Figure 4.15: Security group and NACL
Reference URL: https://docs.aws.amazon.com/AmazonVPC/latest/UserGuide/VPC_Security.html

Security group

A security group can be described as a virtual firewall that controls any traffic coming in or going out of the instances associated with the security group. When an EC2 instance is launched, that instance is associated with one or more security groups. Each of the security groups contains rules to allow traffic to or from its associated instances.

A security group can have multiple rules for inbound and outbound traffic. Inbound and outbound traffic is also called ingress and egress traffic, respectively. Security groups can be attached to an EC2 instance to restrict unsolicited traffic. Each security group can be attached to multiple EC2 instances. It is best practice to create an application specific security group and attach it to one or more EC2 instances hosting the same application, use AWS to modify the security group and fine tune it as per the changing business need from time to time. As and when required, you can allow or block communication on certain protocols, ports, and source IPs, without disturbing communication for other applications. In general, security group rules are implemented as per the hosted application's communication requirement for protocol, ports, and source IPs, on relevant EC2 instances.

To meet an organization's advanced security needs, third-party EC2-based firewall applications can be deployed in an AWS account on top of the security groups attached to EC2 instances. While launching an EC2 instance in a VPC, if a security group is not attached explicitly, then a default security group of the VPC is automatically attached to the EC2 instance. Security groups attached to an EC2 instance can be changed at any time based on the need.

With the help of CIDR notation, a source IP can be fixed to the particular IP, such as 10.108.20.107/32. Also, any source IP can be allowed by 0.0.0.0/0 CIDR notation. It is best practice to allow ingress communication from a specified source IP rather than allowing it from everywhere, until and unless project specific requirement is there. For example, communication on HTTP (port 80) or HTTPS (443) should be allowed from anywhere, but for SSH (22) and RDP (3389) it should be allowed only from trusted source IP(s). Also, a security group ID can be specified as a source IP, to allow communication from all the instances that are attached to that security group. For example, in case of Auto Scaling, number of EC2 instances (that is, a hosted web application) and their IP address keep changing. In such situations, it is best practice to attach a security group to such EC2 instances with the help of an Auto Scaling template and place a security group ID as a source IP in another security group. This other security group may be attached to the EC2 instance hosted with a database.

A security group attached to an EC2 instance should have at least one rule to allow SSH (22) or RDP (3389) to log in and perform maintenance activities from the trusted IP source.

Some important points about security groups are listed in the following list:

- Each security group can have a maximum of 50 separate rules for inbound and outbound.
- One security group can be attached to more than one EC2 instance.
- At any given time, a maximum of five security groups can be attached to a network interface.
- When multiple security groups are attached to a single network interface, virtually rules from each security group are aggregated as one rule and evaluated for any inbound or outbound traffic request.
- In the case where multiple rules for the same protocol and ports are given for an EC2 instance, in such situations most permissive rules are applied. For example, one rule allows communication on protocol TCP port 22 (that is, SSH) from 10.108.123.65 and another rule allows communication on protocol TCP port 22 from everywhere 0.0.0.0. In that situation, communication from everywhere is allowed.
- As soon as any modification in security group rules is saved, it immediately gets applied to all associated EC2 instances.
- By default, when a security group is created, it allows all outgoing communication and blocks all incoming communication.
- In a security group, each rule is defined only to allow communication. There is no provision in a security group to create a rule for explicitly denying any traffic. Security group allows incoming traffic from all the ports and protocols defined in the rules. All other traffic is implicitly denied. This way, it eliminates the need for any explicit deny rule.
- Security groups are stateful. That means, any traffic allowed on a specific inbound port and protocol are automatically allowed for outbound traffic on the same port and protocol. You don't need to create outbound traffic rules for port and protocol described in inbound rules.
- Instances associated with the same security group cannot communicate with each other unless there is a rule placed in any security group associated with these instances, that allows communication between these instances.

Network ACLs

NACL acts as a virtual firewall at subnet level. It is an optional layer of security. Every VPC has default NACL. Creating VPC automatically creates a default NACL. Every subnet, whether it is private or public in a VPC, must be associated to one NACL. By default, NACL blocks all inbound and outbound IPv4 traffic. At any given time NACL rules can be modified and be put into immediate effect as they are saved. In the same VPC, different subnets can be associated with different NACL.

Some important points about NACL:

- Each subnet in a VPC must be associated with at least one NACL. At the time of creating subnet, if it is not explicitly associated with any NACL then it automatically gets associated with the default NACL.
- One NACL can be associated with one or more subnets, however, at any given time only one NACL can be associated to a subnet.
- NACL rules are evaluated based on its rule numbers. It evaluates the rule starting from lowest number to highest number. Highest number can be 32766. It is best practice to create rules with the sequence numbers having increments of 10, 50, or 100. It gives freedom to insert rules in-between, if required in the future.
- Separate rules to allow or deny, can be created for inbound and outbound.
- Unlike security groups, NACL rules are stateless. That means, if a port is open for allowing inbound traffic, it does not automatically allow outbound traffic on that port. Similarly, if a port is allowed for outbound traffic, it does not automatically allow inbound traffic on that port. Rules for inbound and outbound traffic have to be defined separately.
- Default NACL for any VPC contains a rule, numbered as * in inbound and outbound. This rule appears and executes at the last. While evaluating a traffic request, if any of the rules do not match whether to *allow* or *block* the network traffic, it blocks that traffic. This is the default behavior of NACL and it cannot be changed.
- Adding more rules to any NACL may bring network performance implications. Add NACL rules carefully.

Security group versus NACL

We will now compare a security group with NACL.

Security Group	NACL
It is stateful, which means opening any inbound traffic on a port/protocol automatically allows outbound traffic on that port and protocol.	It is stateless, which means you need to explicitly define inbound and outbound traffic rules. It does not allow inbound traffic for a rule defined for outbound traffic and vice versa.
Acts as a firewall at EC2 level. You need to associate a security group with one or more EC2 instances.	Acts as a firewall at subnet level. NACL rules get applied to all EC2 instances within the related subnet.
By default all incoming requests are denied and all outgoing requests are allowed.	By default, all incoming and outgoing requests are denied.
Rules do not execute in a sequence.	Rules execute in a sequence, as they are numbered.
Up to five security groups can be attached to a network interface.	Only one NACL can be attached to a subnet.

Flow logs

Flow logs is a feature that enables you to track incoming and outgoing traffic from a VPC's network interfaces. Flow logs can be enabled on a network interface, subnet, or VPC. Flow logs makes it possible to audit network traffic. It contains information about source and destination IP address, port, the IANA protocol number, and much more details for allowed and denied traffic based on the security groups and NACL. It stores data in CloudWatch logs. It is also possible to create alarms, which notify you on occurrence of certain network traffic. Once a flow log is enabled on the AWS resources, it may take a little while to start collecting the data and appearing on CloudWatch Logs. It does not capture real-time log streams for the network interfaces. Flow logs help in fault diagnostics and traffic monitoring.

Flow logs for each network interface get stored in a separate log stream. It is possible to create multiple flow logs publishing data to the same log group in CloudWatch Logs. For the same network interface, there could be a separate flow log just to capture rejected or accepted traffic. In such situations, flow logs are automatically combined as one log stream for the same network interface appearing multiple times in a log group.

Flow logs can be enabled for the network interfaces, which are either created for custom AWS resources such as EC2 instance or AWS services such as Elastic Load Balancing, ElasticCache, RDS, and so on. Once a flow log is enabled at subnet or VPC level, adding a new instance in that subnet or VPC automatically starts collecting the flow logs for newly created network interfaces on that EC2 instance.

Once diagnostic or network audit has been done, any time flow logs can be deleted. Deleting flow log does not delete existing flow log records or log streams. It just disables flow log service and stops collecting new logs for respective resources such as network interface, subnet, or VPC. Existing log streams can be deleted from the CloudWatch log console.

Limitations of flow logs are as follows:

- It cannot be enabled for a VPC that is peered with a VPC in another AWS account. It can only be enabled when both the peered VPCs are in the same AWS account.
- It is not possible to tag a flow log.
- Once a flow log is created, it is not possible to modify its configuration. You need to delete existing flow log and create a new one.
- In case any network interface has multiple IPv4 addresses, then in a flow log, traffic sent to a secondary IP displays the primary private IPv4 address in the destination IP address field.
- It captures traffic for custom created DNS servers in the VPC, but does not capture traffic for an Amazon DNS server and DHCP traffic.
- It does not capture traffic generated by Microsoft Windows instances for Amazon Windows license activation.
- It does not capture traffic for instance metadata, to and from 169.254.169.254. This is a dynamically generated link-local address that is used by the instance for collecting its instance metadata.
- It does not capture traffic to the reserved IP address for the default VPC router.

 Creating a flow log must be associated with an IAM role having sufficient permissions to publish flow logs to the specified log group in CloudWatch logs. Also an IAM role must have a trust relationship, that should allow the flow log service to assume the role.

Controlling access

While designing the architecture of a VPC, it is recommended you use at least a privilege policy. Access to various resources and services in the VPC should be granted to individuals based on their role. There may be a number of roles in an organization such as network administrator, developer, database administrator, tester, and so on. All these individuals with different roles should have access to specific resources and services as their organizational role demands. AWS IAM makes it possible to define different access policies for various users rather than giving full control to all of them. By defining access policies, we can restrict the users to using specific APIs and take limited actions against various AWS services.

The following is an example of an access policy for a network administrator. This policy grants an administrator the access to create and manage the VPC:

```
{
   "Version": "2012-10-17",
   "Statement":[{
   "Effect":"Allow",
   "Action":["ec2:*Vpc*",
        "ec2:*Subnet*",
        "ec2:*Gateway*",
        "ec2:*Vpn*",
        "ec2:*Route*",
        "ec2:*Address*",
        "ec2:*SecurityGroup*",
        "ec2:*NetworkAcl*",
        "ec2:*DhcpOptions*",
        "ec2:RunInstances",
        "ec2:StopInstances",
        "ec2:StartInstances",
        "ec2:TerminateInstances",
        "ec2:Describe*"],
   "Resource":"*"
   }
  ]
  }
```

The following is an example of a read-only policy. A user with this policy can list all VPCs and various resources associated with the VPC:

```
{
   "Version": "2012-10-17",
   "Statement":[{
   "Effect":"Allow",
   "Action":["ec2:DescribeVpcs",
```

```
            "ec2:DescribeSubnets",
            "ec2:DescribeInternetGateways",
            "ec2:DescribeEgressOnlyInternetGateways",
            "ec2:DescribeVpcEndpoints",
            "ec2:DescribeNatGateways",
            "ec2:DescribeCustomerGateways",
            "ec2:DescribeVpnGateways",
            "ec2:DescribeVpnConnections",
            "ec2:DescribeRouteTables",
            "ec2:DescribeAddresses",
            "ec2:DescribeSecurityGroups",
            "ec2:DescribeNetworkAcls",
            "ec2:DescribeDhcpOptions",
            "ec2:DescribeTags",
            "ec2:DescribeInstances"],
      "Resource":"*"
      }
    ]
}
```

Similarly, you can create more such policies based on the need and assign it to specific users for controlling access to the VPC.

VPC networking components

A VPC network consists of certain components, we will now look at these components in brief:

ENI

ENI is a virtual network interface. It is a communication hub for an EC2 instance, that enables network communication on an instance. An EC2 instance can have one or more network interfaces. When any EC2 instance is created inside a VPC, by default, a network interface is also created and attached to it. The default network interface created while launching an instance is called a primary network interface of the instance. This primary network interface also gets one primary IPv4 address from the subnet's available IP range. You cannot detach a primary network interface from an EC2 instance and attach to another. However, you cannot detach a primary network interface, AWS allows us to create additional network interfaces that can be attached to the EC2 instance. Additional network interfaces are also called secondary network interfaces. Secondary network interfaces can be detached from one EC2 instance and attached to another EC2 instance. During this transition from one EC2 instance to another, its attributes remain intact.

A network interface can have the following attributes:

- Usually, default network interface (that is, a primary network interface) is referred to as **eth0**.
- One primary private IPv4 address is automatically associated with it from the available range of IPs in its respective subnet.
- One Elastic IPv4 address per private IPv4 address can be attached to a network interface. Similarly, one public IPv4 address can be auto assigned to a primary private IPv4 address.
- One or more IPv6 address can be attached to an ENI.
- One or more security groups can be attached to a single network interface. Currently, AWS allows a maximum of five security groups with a single network interface.
- A **Media Access Control (MAC)** address is associated with each network interface.
- For easy identification, you can also specify a description of each network interface.
- A number of network interfaces and secondary private IPs to an ENI depends upon the EC2 instance type. In general, the bigger the instance type, the more network interfaces and the more secondary private IPs can be attached to it.
- You can attach multiple network interfaces to an instance for creating a management network or for implementing network and security appliances in a VPC.

Route table

A route table is a set of rules that determines how the network traffic is routed. The set of rules is also called routes. Routes determine how data packets travelling over an IP network are directed. A route table is a very important VPC resource for controlling the flow of network traffic.

For every VPC there should be a main route table. While creating a custom VPC automatically a main route table is also created. Each subnet in the VPC must be associated with a route table, that controls routing for it. A subnet can be associated only with one route table while a route table can be associated with many subnets. While creating a subnet, if explicitly it is not associated with any route table, then it is associated with a VPC's main route table. The main route table controls the network traffic for all the subnets, which are explicitly not attached to any route tables. A route table attached to subnets and its respective route entries can be changed any time as per requirement.

It is recommended you create a custom route table rather than directly making permanent changes in a VPC's default route table. Even if it is required to change the default route table, it is best practice to perform tests in a custom route table before updating the default route table. Once results are satisfactory and not disrupting network communication then the change can be applied to a VPC's default route table.

Some important points about route tables:

- Every VPC has an implicit router.
- Every VPC has a main route table. It cannot be deleted, but it can be complemented with other additional route tables. Also, route entries in a main route table can be changed.
- Each route entry in a route table specifies a destination CIDR and a target. A target indicates that traffic for this specific CIDR block should be routed through this specific VPC resource such as IGW, VGW, a NAT device, a peering connection, or a VPC endpoint. For example, internet traffic (0.0.0.0/0) should be routed through internet gateway (igw-id).
- Every route table contains one route entry to communicate within the VPC over IPv4. It allows communication from one subnet to another subnet. For example, communication between web or application servers deployed in a public subnet and DB servers or RDS hosted in a private subnet.
- Currently, AWS allows a hard limit of 200 route tables per VPC and a maximum of 50 routes per table.

Selection of the optimum route for network traffic is done based on the longest prefix match. In other words, the most specific routes that match the network traffic. It is explained in the following example route table:

Destination	Target	Description
172.168.0.0/16	local	Network traffic for IPv4 address range 172.168.0.0/16, destination will be routed only within the VPC.
0.0.0.0/0	igw-abcd1236	Network traffic for internet IPv4 address 0.0.0.0/0 to be routed to the internet gateway (igw-abcd1236).
172.31.0.0/16	pcx-1234abcd	Network traffic for IPv4 address 172.31.0.0/16 points to a peering connection (pcx-1234abcd).

In case route entries for VPN connection or AWS Direct Connect overlap with local routes for VPC, local routes are given priority.

IGW

An IGW is a virtual router in a VPC and an important stopping point for data on its way to and from the internet. IGW makes it possible for EC2 instances to communicate to the internet. As a result, we can take a remote access (that is, RDP or SSH) of the EC2 instance available in public subnets. By deploying NAT instances in a public subnet, it can also provide internet connection to the EC2 instance in a private subnet. In subsequent topics, we will see NAT in more detail. A NAT instance prevents unsolicited access from the internet to the instances in a private subnet. IGW is highly available, redundant, and horizontally scaled in nature. It ensures that there is no bandwidth constraints and no availability risk.

The following points are critical for enabling internet access in a VPC subnet:

- VPC must be attached to an IGW
- All public route tables must point to IGW
- Instances in a subnet need to have globally unique IP address, be it an IPv4 address, Elastic IP address, or IPv6 address
- NACL and security groups should allow the traffic to and from the internet

The following *Figure 4.16* illustrates how traffic from public subnet 1 (10.0.0.0/24) is routed to the internet. A custom route table entry for internet traffic (0.0.0.0/0) pointing to igw-id enables the subnet to access internet.

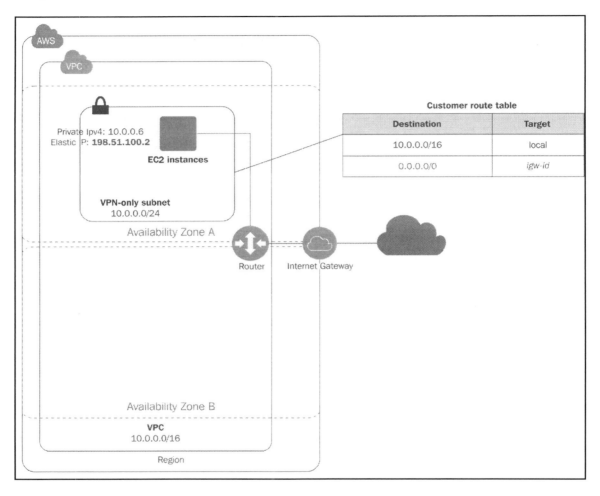

Figure 4.16: Internet gateway

Egress-only IGW

As with IGW, egress-only IGW is also highly available, redundant, and horizontally scaled. It only works with IPv6; it doesn't work with IPv4 addresses. For IPv4 network traffic, you can use a NAT gateway instead of egress-only internet traffic.

Egress-only IGW ensures that EC2 instances can communicate with the internet, however, these instances are not directly accessible from the internet. The main purpose of egress-only IGW is to secure the subnet against internet traffic and at the same time enable the instances in a subnet to access the internet.

For enabling egress-only internet traffic, you need to create an egress-only IGW in VPC and add a route to the route table pointing all IPv6 traffic to (::/0) to the egress-only IGW. It is a stateful VPC resource. NACL can be used to control network traffic for egress-only IGW.

NAT

NAT can be defined as a virtual router or a gateway in a VPC, that enables instances in a private subnet to interact with the internet. It's an important stopping point for data on its way from private subnets to the internet without directly exposing the instances to the internet. It acts as a firewall, dynamically assigns a temporary public address to an instance, and routes the traffic between the requesting instances and the internet.

There are two types of NAT devices:

- NAT gateway: It is the gateway service provided and managed by AWS
- NAT instance: It is a custom-provisioned EC2 instance hosting NAT services

These NAT devices only support IPv4 network traffic. EC2 instances in a private subnet do not have a public or an Elastic IP and a subnet's route table does not have route entry to send traffic directly to the internet through IGW. The NAT device acts as an intermediate point between instances and IGW. It receives traffic from an EC2 instance residing in a private subnet and before forwarding the traffic to the internet, it replaces the *reply-to* IPv4 address with its own public or Elastic IP address. When a reply is received from internet, again it changes the *reply-to* address from its IP address to the EC2 instance private IP address.

NAT devices do not support IPv6 traffic. If you need to use an IPv6 address for an EC2 instance, you can use egress-only IGW instead of NAT restricting unsolicited connection requests from the internet.

In an enterprise's AWS cloud infrastructure, either a NAT gateway or a NAT instance is deployed in a public subnet. NAT instance can have a public or Elastic IP, whereas the NAT gateway requires an Elastic IP. To route traffic from private subnet to internet, there should be a route entry in a private subnet's route table, pointing internet traffic to the NAT instance or NAT gateway.

A NAT gateway is provisioned in a public subnet of an AZ in a VPC. Multiple private subnets in a single AZ can use the same NAT Gateway. In case an AZ fails, NAT gateway residing in that AZ fails and all the subnets using the NAT gateway cannot reach the internet. It is advisable to create a NAT gateway in multiple AZ for failover.

Unlike a NAT gateway, there is an additional setting when you create a NAT instance. To facilitate internet requests, you need to disable the source and destination check on the NAT instance. By default, before sending traffic to the internet, every EC2 instance checks that its public address is in the source or destination address. But in case of a NAT instance, it sends and receives traffic on behalf of EC2 instances residing in a private subnet. In this scenario, if the source/destination check is not disabled on the NAT instance, it cannot serve the requests from other EC2 instances. If you ever find that EC2 instances in your private subnet are not able to connect to the internet, do check if the source/destination check on NAT EC2 instance is disabled.

The following are the steps to disable the source and destination check on a NAT instance:

1. Log in to the AWS web console using the appropriate credentials.
2. Navigate to the EC2 dashboard.
3. In the left-hand navigation pane, select **Instances**.
4. On the right-hand side, upper pane, from the list of EC2 instances select the **NAT instance**.
5. From the top toolbar select **Actions** or right-click on the selected instance. Select **Networking** and then **Change Source/Dest**. Check from the available options.
6. The subsequent dialogue box gives provision to enable or disable the Source/Destination check.

Characteristics of a NAT gateway:

- A NAT gateway supports burstable bandwidth up to 10 GBps. Higher than 10 GBps bandwidth can also be achieved by deploying AWS resources into multiple subnets and creating a NAT gateway for individual subnets.
- A NAT gateway supports TCP, UDP, and ICMP protocols.

- Creating a NAT gateway automatically creates a network interface and allocates a private IP from the subnet's address range. One Elastic IP address has to be also attached. Once a NAT gateway is deleted, the attached Elastic IP gets released from the NAT gateway, but remains reserved in the AWS account.

The following *Figure 4.17* helps us to understand a NAT gateway:

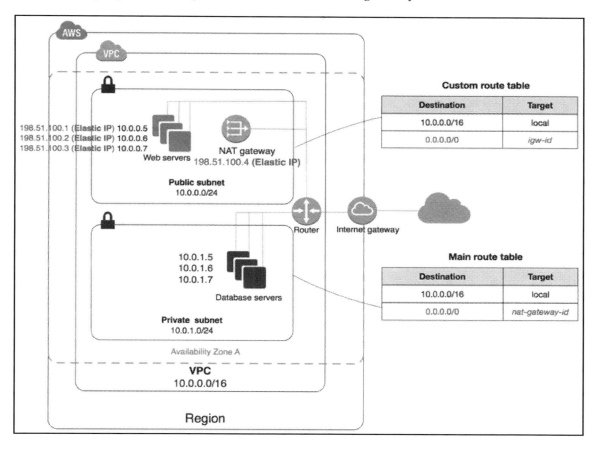

Figure 4.17: NAT gateway architecture

Reference URL: https://docs.aws.amazon.com/AmazonVPC/latest/UserGuide/vpc-nat-gateway.html

As you can observe from the preceding *Figure 4.17*, `10.0.1.0/24` is a private subnet. A route table entry is added to the main route table with `0.0.0.0/0` as the destination is routed to `nat-gateway-id`. Unlike private subnets, the public subnet's route table has `igw-id` as the target for internet traffic. This means the private subnet routes the internet traffic to a NAT gateway and the public subnet routes the traffic directly to IGW.

Comparison of NAT instances and NAT gateways

It is highly recommended you use a NAT gateway rather than a NAT instance as it provides better availability and higher bandwidth compared to a NAT instance. If you opt for a NAT instance, bandwidth depends on the EC2 instance type. Also, you have to design a custom failover logic for NAT instances unlike a NAT gateway. A NAT gateway is managed by AWS and does not require you to perform maintenance activity. A NAT gateway being a managed service, Amazon takes care of maintenance activities. Amazon optimizes NAT gateways for performance and cost effectiveness.

The following troubleshooting steps may help in certain situations where some instances in a VPC are unable to route traffic though a NAT instance:

- Ensure that there is a route entry in the route table of each private subnet for routing internet traffic to `nat-gateway-id`.
- Ensure that the source/destination check is disabled on NAT instance.
- If some instances from a private subnet are able to access internet and some instances are not, it may be because of the NAT instance's network bandwidth limitation. Ensure that the NAT instance type provides expected bandwidth required to serve the traffic. You may need to change the instance type for better network bandwidth.

 It is recommended you use NAT gateway over NAT instance. An existing AWS cloud infrastructure having a NAT instance can easily migrate to a NAT gateway by creating a NAT gateway and changing the route table entries to point to `nat-gateway-id`.

DHCP option sets

DHCP is a network protocol, that dynamically assigns IP addresses to instances in a VPC from the respective subnet's CIDR block. It also passes configuration information such as domain name, **Domain Name Server (DNS)**, NTP server, and so on. This configuration information is called a DHCP option set. A DHCP option set is very essential for any newly created EC2 instance in a VPC. Every VPC has one DHCP option set. When creating a custom VPC, it automatically associates a default DHCP option set for the VPC. Once DHCP option set is created, its parameters cannot be modified. You need to create new DHCP option set and associate it with the VPC. If you do not want to automatically assign configuration to a VPC, no DHCP option set can also be configured. As soon as the DHCP option set changes for any VPC, existing and new EC2 instances start using new DHCP option sets. Changing the DHCP option set does not require restarting EC2 instances. A DHCP option set allows configuring of the following parameters:

DHCP Option Name	Description
domain-name	Domain names are very useful in various networking and application-specific naming and addressing purposes. Usually, an organization's name or abbreviated name is used as a high-level domain name. By default, an Amazon-provided DNS is `ec2.internal` for the us-east-1 (N. Virginia) and in other regions `region.compute.internal`. For example, in the Tokyo region, it is `ap-northeast-1.compute.internal`.
domain-name-servers	It is also referred to as a DNS. It can be either an Amazon-provided DNS or a maximum of four IP addresses of a custom DNS separated by commas. It is essential to have a custom DNS when you want to use custom domain names for instances in a VPC.
netbios-name-servers	**Network Basic Input/Output (NetBIOS)** is a legacy networking protocol. A NetBIOS name server is required, in case an enterprise runs some legacy applications requiring WINS. A maximum of up to four comma separated IPv4 addresses can be specified for the NetBIOS server.

`ntp-servers`	A **Network Time Protocol (NTP)** is used to synchronize the clocks of computers to some time reference. In an organization, it is essential to have all the computers using the same clock settings. Having the same clock on all computers, not only helps for log auditing and understanding events sequence, but also fulfils a base requirement to run many enterprise-grade applications. You can specify a maximum of up to four NTP server's IPv4 addresses, separated by commas.
`netbios-node-type`	It is a method that computers use to resolve a NetBIOS name into an IP address. In general, a node type can be any of the following types: 1 - It is for broadcast node, also called B-node. 2 - It is for peer-to-peer node, also called P-node. 4 - It is for mixed node, combination of B and P nodes, but by default functions as B-node. 8 - It is for hybrid node, combination of P-node and B-node, but by default functions as P-node. It is recommended you use value 2 (peer-to-peer) as value 1, 4, and 8 with broadcast and multicast are not currently supported.

DNS

Usually, DNS and DHCP work together to translate a domain name to an IP address and vice versa. It also provides configuration information to instances within the network. Every EC2 instance in a VPC requires a unique DNS name. A DNS name is a combination of hostname and domain name. For any instance, to communicate over the internet, it requires a public IP and it requires a private IP to communicate within a local network.

When launching a new EC2 instance inside a default VPC, by default, it gets a private and public DNS hostname corresponding to private and public IPv4 addresses. However, when an EC2 instance is launched in a custom VPC, by default it gets only a private DNS hostname and a corresponding IPv4 address. An internal DNS (private Amazon-provided DNS) provides a DNS hostname to the EC2 instances in the form of `ip-<private-ipv4-address>.ec2.internal` in N. Virginia (us-east-1) and `ip-<private-ipv4-address>.region.compute.internal` for other regions. A public DNS (external Amazon-provided DNS) hostname `ec2-public-ipv4-address.compute-1.amazonaws.com` in N. Virginia (us-east-1) and `ec2-public-ipv4-address.region.amazonaws.com` for other regions.

For a custom VPC, the behavior of a DNS can be modified with the help of the following parameters:

Attribute	Description
enableDnsHostnames	A parameter value can be true or false. When it is true an EC2 instance in the VPC gets public DNS hostnames. When this parameter is true, it also requires enableDnsSupport attribute to true.
enableDnsSupport	A parameter value can be true or false. It indicates whether DNS resolution (host to an IPv4 address and vice-a-versa) is supported or not. If it is set to false, it does not resolve public hostnames to an IPv4 address.

By default, in a default VPC both of the preceding parameters are set to true. However, in the case of a custom VPC, only the enableDnsSupport parameter is, by default, set to true. When both of the preceding parameters are set to true then an EC2 instance gets a public DNS hostname and it can resolve an Amazon-provided private DNS hostname. When both parameters are set to false, the instance does not get a public DNS hostname, the Amazon-provided private DNS server cannot resolve the private hostname to IP, and the EC2 instance gets a custom private DNS hostname if the custom domain name is specified in a DHCP option set.

As of writing this book, AWS VPC does not provide DNS for IPv6 addresses.

VPC peering

VPC peering is a way to connect two different VPCs within the same region for routing traffic between them using IPv4 or IPv6 addresses. Once a VPC peering connection is established between two VPCs, instances in either of these VPCs can communicate with each other as they communicate with local instances within the same VPC.

By default, network traffic either flows within the same VPC or to and from the internet, but it does not route to other VPCs. If there is a need to route traffic between two VPCs, a VPC peering connection can be established. VPC peering can be used between two VPCs within the same region irrespective of whether they belong to the same AWS account or a different AWS account. Communication among peered VPCs takes place through routing. Network traffic does not flow through any separate VPC resources such as gateway or VPN connections.

We will follow the following steps to enable VPC peering:

- The owner of VPC1 initiates a peering request for VPC2
- VPC1 and VPC2 can belong to the same AWS account or to a different account
- Both the VPCs can belong to the same or different owner
- Both the VPCs cannot have a CIDR block that overlaps with each other
- The VPC2 owner accepts the peering request
- For enabling traffic between the two VPCs, both the VPCs need to add a router entry in their respective route tables pointing to the IP address range of peering VPCs
- Update security groups of each VPCs, where required, for enabling the traffic from peering VPC
- If there is a need to resolve DNS hostnames from peering VPCs, you need to enable DNS hostname resolution in the respective VPC configuration
- By default, when instances in both sides of the VPC peering connection refers to each other using a public DNS name, it resolves to a public IP address of the target instances

VPC endpoint

Generally, AWS services are different entities and do not allow direct communication with each other without going through either IGW, NAT gateway/instance, VPN connection, or AWS Direct Connect. VPC endpoint is an AWS service, that enables you to create a private connection between different AWS services without going through the previously mentioned communication gateways.

Let's understand this scenario with some examples. In an enterprise infrastructure, an EC2 instance residing in a private subnet often requires to communicate with resources in other AWS services. For example, storing and retrieving objects in S3. Before the launch of VPC endpoint, you need to deploy a NAT device in a public subnet with an Elastic IP and route entry in the private subnet's route table. Such communication used to take place through the internet. Now with the help of VPC endpoint, there is no need to route traffic through the internet. It routes the traffic within the AWS infrastructure. VPC endpoint is highly available, horizontally scaled, redundant, and easy to configure. It does not use any other VPC resources such as VPN connection, NAT devices, or Direct Connect for communication. It simply works using basic VPC components. There are no additional charges for using VPC endpoints. Only standard charges for resource usage and data transfer apply.

When creating a VPC endpoint, you need to define a source VPC and target AWS service. At the same time, custom policy can be applied to fine-grain the access in a targeted AWS service. Enabling a VPC endpoint automatically identifies associated route tables with the source VPC and also automatically adds a route to each of the route tables. In route entry, destination specifies the prefix list ID of the service (pl-xxxxxxxx), that represents the range of public IPv4 addresses used by the service. It indicates a target with the endpoint ID (vpce-xxxxxxxx). As a result, automatically all the EC2 instances in all the subnets using any of the route table associated with VPC starts using this route to communicate with specific AWS services.

VPC endpoints limitations are as follows:

- It is not possible to tag VPC endpoints.
- It is not possible to transfer a VPC endpoint from one VPC to another VPC. You need to create new VPC endpoints for the desired AWS services in a related VPC and delete old unwanted VPC endpoints.
- VPC endpoints support only within the same region. Source VPC and target resources of AWS services both must be in the same region.
- VPC endpoint connections just work within VPC. It does not work with the VPN, VPC peering and Direct Connect, or Classiclink connection.
- In order to use a VPC endpoint, it is essential to enable a DNS resolution in a VPC whether using custom or Amazon-provided DNS servers.
- VPC endpoints prefix list IDs cannot be used in NACL's outbound rule to allow or deny network traffic.

ClassicLink

Since 2013-12-04, AWS supports EC2-VPC only. But before that it was possible to create EC2-Classic. EC2-Classic and EC2-VPC both are totally different in many ways. ClassicLink is the only way to make communication possible between them within the same region. Enabling the ClassicLink option allows a VPC to communicate with the EC2 instances launched in EC2-Classic. Without this option enabled, resources in the VPC need to use the public IP address of the EC2-Classic instance or tunneling for communication. If you have any resources in EC2-Classic that require direct communication with VPC resources, ClassicLink can help.

Enabling ClassicLink allows you to use VPC security groups on the EC2-Classic instances and in turn, it enables communication between instances in EC2-Classic and VPC using private IPv4 addresses. It is available in all AWS accounts, that support EC2-Classic instances. There is no additional charge for using ClassicLink, however, standard data transfer charges apply.

VPC best practices

The list summarizing VPC best practices are as follows:

- Before starting designing and implementing AWS VPC, it is essential to understand present and future needs. It is recommended you plan your VPC architecture, considering the minimum requirement for the next two years. Once infrastructure is created on a VPC, making any changes in VPC requires re-designing and recreating infrastructure. Lateral changes in the design and infrastructure can be very time consuming and expensive.
- It is suggested you use CIDR range as per the RFC 1918. Also, make sure that a sufficient number of IP addresses are available in each subnet to match with present and future needs. Also, ensure that the CIDR range in AWS does not conflict with the CIDR range used in any other data center or VPC where you may have to establish a VPN or Direct Connect connection.

- Remember, AWS reserves five IP address for internal purposes. The first four and the last one are in an IP range.
- Create subnets to isolate resources as per the project requirement,(that is, DMZ/Proxy, ELB, web applications, database, and so on). For example, a public subnet to host internet-facing resources and a private subnet for databases that do accept web requests.
- Create multiple subnets (that is, public or private) in multiple AZs to host multi AZ infrastructure and avoid single point of failure. By default, each subnet can communicate with each other in the same VPC.
- Make sure that only required ports and protocols from trusted sources are allowed to access AWS resources using security groups and NACL.
- Create individual security groups for each resource or the same type of resources. For example, create a single security group for web servers.
- Make sure unwanted outgoing ports are not open in security groups. For example, a security group for a web application does not need to open incoming mail server ports.
- Control access to AWS VPC services using appropriate user segregation, groups, and policies.
- Use NACL wisely. More rules at NACL may bring performance implications to overall networks.
- While adding rules to the NACL, number each rule in increments of 10, 50, or 100. It gives flexibility to add rules in-between, when required.
- Preferably, use a NAT gateway over a NAT instance. A NAT gateway provides redundancy and better network bandwidth.
- Rather than modifying a default route table and NACL, create a custom route table. By default, route table is used for newly created subnets.
- Use Elastic IPs wisely. Unused Elastic IPs and IPs attached to stopped EC2 instances may incur charges to the AWS account.
- It is essential to disable the source/destination check when a NAT instance is configured.

- Use a bastion host to access private machines hosted in a private network in a VPC.
- Enable VPC flow logs for audit purposes. Studying flow logs time to time highlights unauthorized attempts to access the resources.
- Never create security group rules allowing 0.0.0.0/0 unless it is unavoidable. It is highly recommended you create customized security groups for each resource or group of resources.
- It is recommended not to allow UDP/ICMP ports for private instances in security groups.
- While defining a security group, use a target security group ID instead of using an IP address for restricting the access instead of using CIDR as target. Such approaches ensure that your environment security is not compromised or mismanaged, even if IP addresses change.
- VPC peering can be used to make communication between VPCs within the same account, different AWS accounts, or any two VPCs within the same region.

5

Getting Started with Elastic Compute Cloud

In the last decade of the 20th century, the world started rapidly moving towards computerization. Now, while we are nearing the end of the second decade in the 21st century, the word compute has become a necessity in almost every walk of our life. Be it mobiles, phablets, tablets, laptops, desktops, high-end servers, cars, GPS systems, toys, digital advertisement boards, point of sale terminals, or a number IoT devices, they all use compute power. When computing has such a deep impact in our life, how can any organization stay away from it? For any enterprise, of any scale, computers are one of the essential IT resources. They provide a mechanism to host and run business applications.

Introduction to EC2

The technology is evolving, demand is increasing, competition is increasing and organizations are continuously coming up with innovative solutions to serve their customers. This entire ecosystem is dependent on computing power. It has become very critical for organizations to arrange highly available and reliable computing resources to run their businesses. Amazon's EC2 is a compute service that provides an on-demand and scalable computing service on the cloud. It eliminates the need for upfront investment on hardware with the *pay as you go* model. With such flexibility in provisioning computing resources, it makes it possible to develop and deploy applications faster. You can provision as many EC2 instances as you want, be it a single instance or tens or hundreds or thousands of servers based on your need. You pay only for what you use. If you do not require the provisioned instances, you can terminate them at will. You can scale up your fleet of servers or scale them down, based on what your business demands. You can configure security, manage networking, add or remove storage as your business demands.

Some of the important aspects of EC2 are:

- Amazon EC2 is a virtualized environment on the cloud.
- A provisioned EC2 resource is called an instance.
- You can create new instances based on AMI.
- AMIs are preconfigured templates, which include base operating systems and any additional software in a single package.
- It provides various combinations of CPU, memory, storage and networking capacity for provisioning instances. These combinations are called instance types.
- It provides a highly secured mechanism to log in to your instances using key pairs. A key pair is a combination of private and public keys. When an instance is provisioned, a public key resides on the EC2 instance and a private key is provided to the user who provisions the server. A key pair is used for login to an instance associated with the key pair.
- Amazon provides temporary as well as persistent storage for your EC2 instances.
- Temporary storage is also called instance store.
- Data on an instance store vanishes when the instances are stopped or restarted.
- Amazon also provides persistent storage volumes on EC2, which is called EBS.
- Amazon provides multiple physical locations for provisioning EC2 instances known as AZs.
- It provides firewall to your instances using security groups.
- Security groups can control what port, protocol, and source IPs can access your instance.
- It provides a static IPv4 address for your instances, which is called Elastic IP address.
- It allows you to assign metadata to your instances known as tags. Tags can be used to identify an instance. A tag can be a name, environment, department, cost center, and so on
- EC2 instances are created in an isolated virtual environment and can be associated to a VPC.

This chapter gradually touches upon all the critical points of EC2 in subsequent pages.

Pricing for EC2

If you just want to get started working with EC2 and learn, Amazon provides EC2 in free tier. It offers a `t2.micro` instance type to run for up to 750 hours per month. You can use Amazon free tier for 12 months from the date of opening a new account. These 750 hours can be utilized either by one instance for 30 days 24 x 7 or running 10 instances for 15 hours as you need.

When using instance types other than free tier, charges apply on a per hour basis and charges vary based on instance type, region, and payment option. A small instance type, with less number of vCPU and memory, costs less compared to an instance type having more vCPUs and memory.

Amazon charges EC2 instances on a per hour basis and actual EC2 pricing depends on instances type, size, and payment model. There are four ways to pay for Amazon EC2 instances which are discussed as follows:

- **On-Demand**: By default, EC2 hourly charges are applied at the On-Demand rate. In this mode, compute (CPU and memory) is used as and when required. There is no need to have any long-term commitment. Compute capacity can be increased or decreased on the fly, to meet the business needs.

   When to use On-Demand instances:

   - Usually this payment mode is suitable when you create new infrastructure in a cloud and are not sure what instance type and number of instances are required
   - You can even use On-Demand instances for carrying out tests
   - When low-cost and flexible compute is required without any upfront payment or long-term commitment
   - You can use On-Demand instances for short term applications with unpredictable workload

Things to remember while using On-Demand pricing:

- On-Demand instances are charged on an hourly basis
- It is the costliest pricing option available in AWS
- When an instance is stopped, partial EC2 hours are rounded up for billing and you pay for a full hour
- On-Demand instances can be launched through AWS Management Console
- You can launch up to 20 instances at a time using the RunInstance API

- **Spot instances**: It allows us to bid for a spare Amazon EC2 compute capacity. Usually, these computes can be up to 90% cheaper than On-Demand instances. It requires you to bid and it specifies the maximum price you want to pay per instance along with instance type and AZ. You get your spot instance, based on availability and current spot pricing in the specified AZ. The prices for instance types vary on the basis of availability of spare capacity in the specified AZ. In other words, it's all about the supply and demand ratio of spare capacity. As the demand for a specific instance type in spot instance increases, spot instance prices also increase. When the current spot instance price goes above your bid price, AWS terminates your spot instance. Before terminating EC2 spot instances, AWS gives a notification, two minutes prior to termination.

When to use spot instances:

- When you need cheap resources for a temporary purpose
- When your application runtime is flexible and application workload can be interrupted
- When you need a large amount of additional computing capacity

Things to remember while using spot instances:

- If a spot instance is terminated by AWS before completing an hour, you are not charged for that hour.
- If you terminate a spot instance in between an hour, you're charged for that incomplete hour.
- Spot instances cannot be stopped and restarted. If a spot instance is stopped, it gets terminated.

- **Reserved Instances**: This provides significant discount on the On-Demand per hour prices. You can Reserve Instance for a one or three year duration for your predictable resource demand. It offers three types of reservation request: **All Upfront**, **Partial Upfront**, and **No Upfront** payment options. With the all Upfront payment option, you can save up to 75% in comparison to On-Demand pricing. In the Partial Upfront method, a partial amount of total billing is paid upfront and the remaining amount is paid on a monthly basis. The third option for reservation is with No Upfront cost wherein you pay only on monthly basis for your Reserved Instances. Even with No Upfront reservation, you can save around 35% to 40% of cost in comparison to On-Demand pricing.

When to use Reserved Instances:

- When you need to run a predictable and consistent workflow for a long period
- All applications require steady state infrastructure
- Users or organizations who can commit to a one or three year duration

Things to remember about Reserved Instances:

- When you reserve an EC2 instance, you reserve an instance type and not a specific instance. Discounted prices are automatically applied on a monthly bill basis on an instance type usage in the account.
- EC2 instances can be reserved at the AZ or at the region. Reserved Instance at the region level gives flexibility to select an instance type and AZ.
- Payment mode (that is, All Upfront, Partial Upfront, or No Upfront) and term (one year or three years) can be selected. It is recommended to reserve for a year only, as AWS periodically reduces resource pricing.

- **Dedicated Hosts**: In a normal scenario, when you launch an EC2 instance, it is provisioned in a virtual environment hosted on shared hardware. Though each instance has its own dedicated resources, it shares the hardware platform with other accounts. When using Dedicated Hosts, EC2 instances from the same AWS account are physically isolated on Dedicated Hosts (that is, hypervisor). A Dedicated EC2 instance using the same architecture may share hardware within the AWS account. It gives additional control over host hardware. It helps to meet corporate compliance and regulation requirements. The pricing model for the Dedicated Hosts also can be an On-Demand, reserved (save up to 70%), or spot instance (save up to 90%).

Dedicated EC2 instance has two pricing components:

- Applicable price per hour, based on the selected pricing model
- Additionally, dedicated per region fees. It is $2, applicable per hour for at least one Dedicated EC2 instance of any type running per region

EC2 instance lifecycle

An EC2 instance passes through various statuses throughout its lifecycle. It all starts with launching an EC2 instance using a specific AMI. The following *Figure 5.1* is an illustration of the EC2 instance lifecycle:

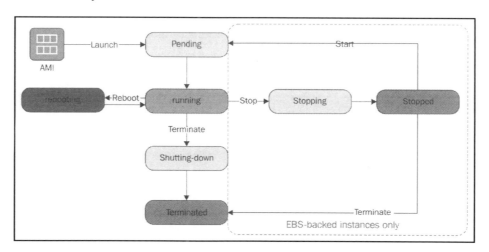

Figure 5.1: EC2 instance life cycle

Instance launch

When an instance is provisioned, it immediately gets into the **pending** state. Depending upon what instance type you have selected, it is launched on a host computer inside AWS virtualized hardware. The instance is launched using the AMI you choose for provisioning. Once the instance is ready for use, it gets into the **running** state. At this moment, you can connect to your instance and start using it. AWS starts billing you for each hour that instance is used once it enters the running state.

Instance stop and start

If you have launched an EC2 instance with an EBS-backed volume, you can stop and start your instance as needed. If your instance fails any status check and is unresponsive, stopping and starting the instance again helps at times.

When you stop an instance, AWS initiates the OS shutdown process and the instance enters into the **stopping** state. As soon as the OS shutdown process completes, the instance enters into the **stopped** state. Once an instance is in the **stopped** state, you are not charged for that instance. However, AWS does charge you for any EBS volume or Elastic IPs associated with that instance. There are certain configuration options that can be used only when the instance is in the **stopped** state. When the instance is in the **stopped** state, you can change the instance type or disassociate/associate root volume of the instance.

When an instance is started back, it enters into the **pending** state. Mostly, AWS moves the instance to another host computer once it is stopped and started again. The instance may remain in the same host computer if there are no hardware related issues on the host computer. AWS adapts this approach for automatically resolving hardware related issues on an instance.

If you are running an instance on EC2-Classic, AWS allocates a new IPv4 address every time an instance is stopped and started again. However, EC2 on a VPC, retains its IP address even if it's stopped and started again.

Every time an instance transitions from the **stopped** to **running** state, AWS charges a full billing hour. That means your billing hour count increases every time you stop and start an instance. It is recommended to exercise the **stop** and **start** options wisely

Instance reboot

An EC2 instance can be rebooted in various ways. You can use AWS console, command-line tools, AWS API, or you can restart the instance from the operating system. AWS recommends rebooting the instance instead of rebooting the operating system. Rebooting the instance is equivalent to rebooting the operating system. When an instance reboots, it remains on the same host computer in the virtualized environment. It retains its IP addresses and public DNS name. It also retains the data on its instance store.

Unlike stopping and starting an instance, rebooting does not initiate a new billing hour.

Instance retirement

In case, there is any irreparable issue in underlying hardware where an instance is hosted, AWS schedules the instance for retirement. The instance is automatically stopped or terminated by AWS when it reaches the scheduled retirement date. If your instance is an EBS backed instance, you can stop and start the instance. Stopping and starting the instance automatically changes the underlying host and you can continue using the instance. If your instance has a root volume with an instance-store-based volume, the instance gets terminated and you cannot use it again.

Instance termination

If an EC2 instance is no longer required, you can terminate the instance. AWS stops charging you as soon as your instance's status changes to **shutting-down** or **terminated**.

AWS provides an option called *termination protection*. If this option is enabled, users cannot terminate an instance without disabling the termination protection. AWS provides this option to prevent accidental termination of an instance.

Once an EC2 instance is terminated, it remains visible with a **terminated** status on the console for a while and automatically disappears from the console after a while. Once an instance is terminated, it cannot be recovered. If a safe backup of the instance is taken, you can launch a new instance from the backup.

Every EC2 instance with EBS-backed volume, supports an attribute that controls its behavior on shutdown. This attribute is called `InstanceInitiatedShutdownBehavior`. While launching the instance, you can select what happens on shutting down the instance. You can select to stop the instance on shutdown or terminate it. Default behavior of an EC2 instance is *stop* on shutdown.

While launching an instance and associating an EBS volume, EC2 provides an option against each EBS volume called `DeleteOnTermination`. If this attribute is selected against an EBS volume, it is automatically deleted when the instance is terminated.

AMI

While launching an instance, you may have a specific requirement such as an operating system, preinstalled software, a number of EBS volumes, and their respective size. To cater to such a requirement, AWS uses a feature called AMI.

An AMI contains a set of information to launch an instance:

- It contains a template that includes information such as operating system, application server, and any other application software
- It contains launch permissions describing which AWS account can use the AMI to spin up new instance
- It also contains block device mapping, describing the volume information to be attached to the instance while launching

You can specify the AMI while launching an instance. An AMI can be used to launch as many instances as required; however, an instance can be based on a single AMI. You can also use multiple AMIs as required to launch different instances. The following *Figure 5.2* helps to understand how multiple EC2 instances from a single AMI can be created:

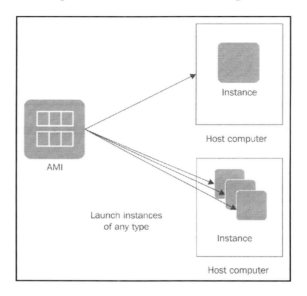

Figure 5.2: Concept of AMI and EC2 instance creation

Reference URL: https://docs.aws.amazon.com/AWSEC2/latest/UserGuide/ec2-instances-and-amis.html

Amazon provides a number of preconfigured AMIs in its marketplace. The AMIs on the marketplaces include AMIs provided by Amazon with base configuration, community AMIs contributed by a large AWS community, and a number of AMIs with third-party software.

All AWS AMIs are internally stored in a S3 bucket. AWS protects these AMIs and these AMIs are not directly visible on S3. You can choose the AMIs only when you launch an instance.

Apart from an underlying operating system and preconfigured software in the AMI, there are two more characteristics of AMI that are critical for choosing an AMI:

- Root device volume type
- Virtualization type

Before launching or planning an EC2 instance OS in the enterprise architecture, it is necessary to understand what these characteristics are.

Root device types

While choosing an AMI, it is essential to understand the root device type associated with the AMI. A bootable block device of the EC2 instance is called *root device*. As EC2 instances are created from an AMI, it is very important to observe the root device type at the AMI. An AMI can have either of two root device types:

- Amazon EBS-backed AMI (uses permanent block storage to store data)
- Instance store-backed AMI (which uses ephemeral block storage to store data)

While creating an EC2 instance using a web console we can see whether an AMI is EBS or instance-backed. The following *Figure 5.3* highlights the root device type while selecting an AMI:

Figure 5.3: Root device type in an AMI

Amazon EBS-backed AMIs launch faster than instance-stored AMIs as you only need to create the volume from the snapshot, for booting the instance. While AMIs with ephemeral storage take longer time to boot, as you need to load all the software on the ephemeral storage before booting the instance.

Ephemeral storage devices are directly attached to the host computer, which makes it faster in accessing the data, however, stored data gets wiped out on restarting or shutting down the EC2 instance.

It is very important to remember that EBS-backed instances can be stopped; If ephemeral-based instances are stopped or terminated, the data stored on the ephemeral storage gets wiped out from the storage.

EC2 instance virtualization types

Similar to root device type, virtualization type is another aspect of an AMI that is critical to understand before choosing an AMI. An AMI can fall into either of the following two virtualization types:

- **Paravirtual (PV):** EC2 instances boots by PV-GRUB
- **Hardware Virtual Machine (HVM):** EC2 instances boots by **Master Boot Record (MBR)**

The main difference between these two virtualization types is in their booting process and their ability to take advantage of special hardware extensions, for a better performance of CPU, network, and storage devices.

For the best EC2 instance performance, it is highly recommended you use the latest instance type with HVM AMIs.

In the case of HVM, the OS can directly run on virtual machines without any modifications. This makes HVM-based instances faster and more efficient. PV-based instances can run on hardware without virtualization support, however, they cannot take advantage of special hardware extensions. Special hardware extensions such as enhanced networking or GPU processing can make a huge difference for running certain application types. Before the enhancement in HVM technologies, PV-based instances used to perform better than HVM, however, with technological enhancements, HVM is leading the race.

While creating an EC2 instance, you can see the type of virtualization against the AMI. The following *Figure 5.4* highlights the virtualization type given against an AMI:

Figure 5.4: AMI - Virtualization type

Creating an EC2 instance

Now, since we have the basic information about EC2, its pricing model, and AMIs, let's understand how to create an EC2 instance using the AWS console.

The following steps describe the process of creating an EC2 instance:

1. Log in to the AWS console using valid credentials and go to the EC2 dashboard.
2. Click on the **Launch Instance** command button.
3. Select the appropriate AMI based on the OS, root device type, and virtualization type. The screen, which displays a number of AMIs to choose from is shown in the following *Figure 5.5*. By default, you can see a number of AMIs in **Quick Start**. If required, you can select **My AMIs**, which contains all the custom AMIs created in a user's account. If you select **AWS Marketplace** from the left menu, it displays a number of third-party AMIs available in **AWS Marketplace**. Marketplace AMIs may not be free. You can also choose **Community AMIs** that contain a number of AMIs contributed by AWS community members. Alternatively, if you just want to create a free tier instance, you can select the checkbox against **Free tier only**:

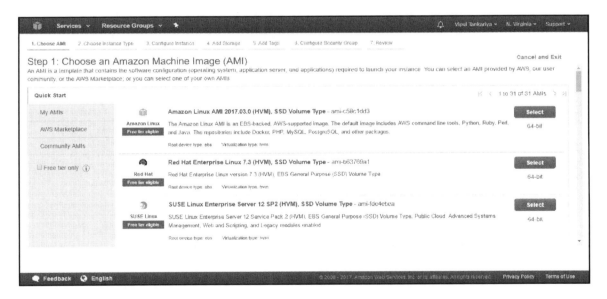

Figure 5.5: Selecting an AMI while launching an instance

4. Once you select an AMI, it displays on the screen as given in the following *Figure 5.6*. Select the appropriate instance type from the screen:

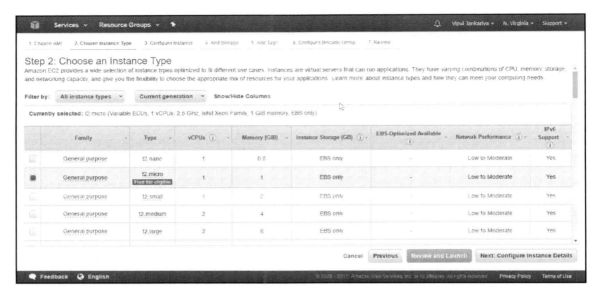

Figure 5.6: Selecting an instance type

5. After selecting the instance type from the screen, click on **Next: Configure Instance Details**. The subsequent screen provides options to **Configure Instance details**, such as number of instances to launch, payment option (spot or on-demand), VPC and Subnet, Public IP, IAM role, Shutdown Behavior, Termination Protection, advanced monitoring, and user data. The following *Figure 5.7* displays the screen with options to configure instance details:

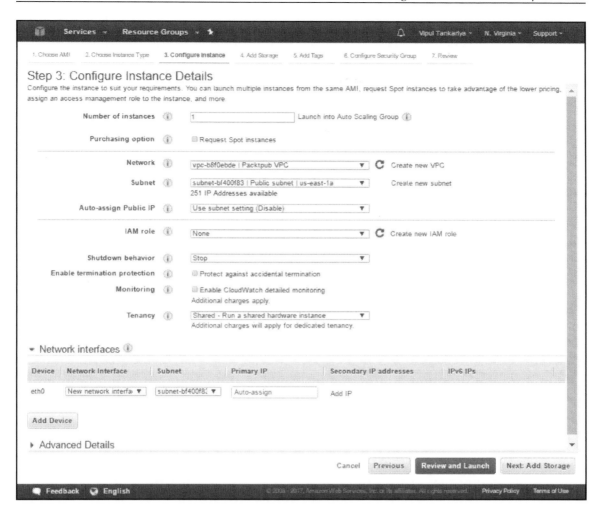

Figure 5.7: EC2 Instance configuration details

6. Add additional EBS volumes as required. Amazon allows up to 30 GB of General Purpose volume in free tier. Also, while creating the EC2 instance, at this stage, it is possible to change the **Delete on Termination** option to true or false for each EBS volume, including root volume. Once an instance is created, you can change the D**elete on Termination** option for EBS only through CLI or API. After selecting the appropriate option, click on the **Next: Add Tags** button as shown in the following *Figure 5.8*:

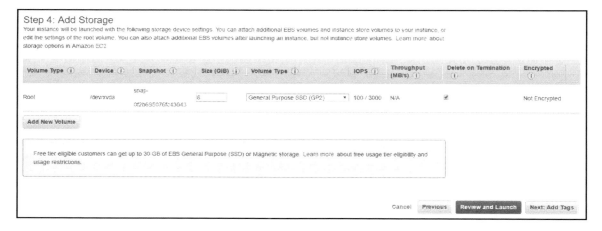

Figure 5.8: Add additional EBS volume

7. In the subsequent screen, as shown, you can add tags to your EC2 instance. Amazon assigns a distinct instance ID to every EC2 instance for uniquely identifying an instance. On top of that you can also add additional tags to the instance for grouping them based on environment, that is, development, testing, pre-production or production, and so on. These tags are key value pairs and are case sensitive:

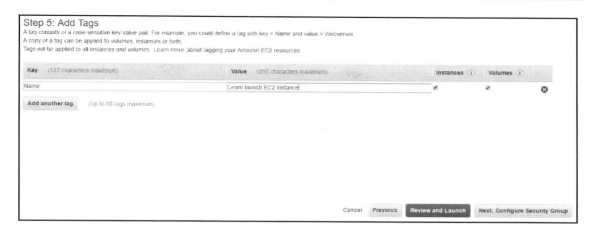

Figure 5.9: Add tags

While creating the tags, by ticking against the **Volumes** column, AWS associates the same tags to each relevant EBS volume associated to the instance. You can see the volume column in the next screenshot. Click on **Next: Configure Security Group** for the next screen.

8. The next screen shows provided options for **Configuring Security Group**. You can open the required port on a specific protocol and source IPs. Generally, inbound rules are defined based on what ports and protocols are used by the application hosted on the server. You can either use an existing security group or you can create a new one based on the requirement. The next *Figure 5.10* shows security group configuration options. After configuring the security group, you can click on **Review and Launch**:

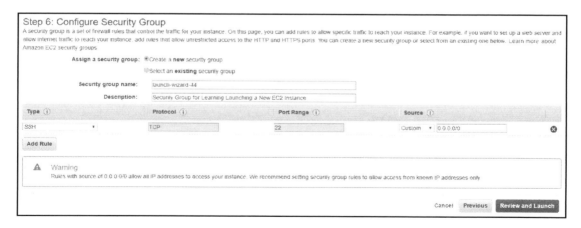

Figure 5.10: Configure security group

9. In the subsequent screen of the wizard, you can finally review the configuration options you have selected during the launch instance wizard. If required, you can click on the **Previous** button and modify the options as needed:

Figure 5.11

10. After verifying all the options, you can click on the **Launch** button. Once you click on the **Launch** button, it asks you to either select an existing key pair or **create a new key pair**. Select an existing key pair or give a suitable key name to create a new key pair. Remember to download the key. The key is available to download during this wizard only. AWS does not provide an option to download the key later on. After providing the key pair detail, you can click on the **Launch Instance** button. It may take a few minutes for the instance to launch. The time for an EC2 instance to come to **running** state, depends on the AMI type and instance type.

You can see all the instances on the EC2 dashboard. You can see all the relevant EC2 properties by selecting a specific instance:

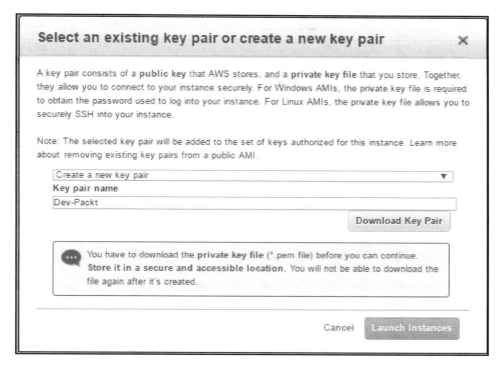

Figure 5.12: Download key pair

Changing EC2 instance type

Once an instance is launched, it may be required to change the instance type based on the need. For example, you may need to change the instance type to accommodate high CPU and memory requirements. Perform the following steps to change the EC2 instance types. An instance can be changed only if the instance is in **Stopped** state. Shut down the instance either from the OS or from the EC2 console and follow these steps:

1. Log in to the AWS dashboard using valid credentials and go to the EC2 dashboard.
2. Go to **Instances** and select desired EC2 instance to change the instance type.

3. Shut down the EC2 instance. Once an EC2 instance is in the **stopped** state, right-click on the EC2 instance and change its type by going to **Instance Settings** | **Change Instance Type** as shown in the following *Figure 5.13*:

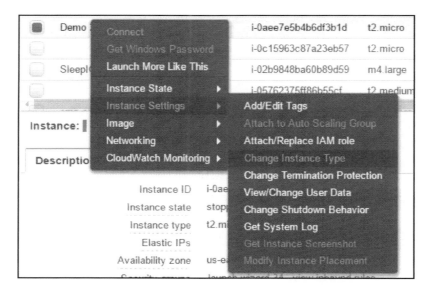

Figure 5.13: Change instance type

4. Once the instance type is changed, you can start the instance again. It may take some time for instance to come back to the **running** state.

Connecting to the EC2 instance

For remotely connecting to an EC2 instance in a public subnet, you need to know its public IP or Elastic IP address. To work with EC2 instances residing in a private subnet, you need to create a bastion host in a public subnet and attach an Elastic IP to access it. For connecting to an instance in a private subnet, first you need to connect to a bastion host and then from bastion host, connect to the EC2 instances in a private subnet. By default, Linux-based EC2 instances can be connected on port 22 using tools such as PuTTY. Microsoft Windows EC2 instances can be connected on port 3389 using the Windows remote desktop utility. To connect to the Linux system, you need to pass a username, port, and private key. The public key is embedded inside EC2 instance.

Default users for various Linux systems are given in the following table:

OS on EC2 instance	AMI (SSH username)
Amazon Linux	ec2-user
BitNami	bitnami
Centos	centos
Debian	admin
Fedora	fedora
FreeBSD	ec2-user
NanoStack	ubuntu
OmniOS	root
RHEL 6.3 and earlier	root
RHEL 6.4 and later	ec2-user
SUSE	root
TurnKey	root
Ubuntu	ubuntu

Connecting to a Linux EC2 instance from a Microsoft Windows system

The prerequisites for connecting to a Linux EC2 instance from a Microsoft Windows system are:

1. Download PuTTY and PuTTYGen on the Microsoft Windows machine. You can get links for downloading PuTTY and PuTTYGen from http://www.putty.org/.
2. Get the public DNS or public/Elastic IP of the desired Linux instance to connect.
3. When IPv6 is assigned to an EC2 instance, connecting to it requires the source machine also to have an IPv6 address.
4. Keep the relevant private key file handy, which is downloaded while creating an instance.
5. Ensure that SSH port 22 is open in inbound rules of the security group assigned to the instance.
6. You need to convert the downloaded key file from .pem to a private key as .ppk.

Converting a PEM file to a private key (PPK)

The following steps describe how to convert a .pem file to a .ppk file:

1. Open PuTTYGen, and click on the **Load** button. Select **All Files** from the dropdown and choose the appropriate .pem file that you need to convert to a .ppk file.

   At the time of loading a file, default filtration is only done on .ppk files. Change it to show **All Files (*.*)** to get a list of desired .pem files to load as follows:

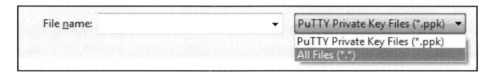

Figure 5.14: Load .pem file

2. In the same PuTTYGen screen, make sure parameters are configured to store a public key as an RSA format and bit size 2048.

Figure 5.15: Parameters to save private key without password phrase

3. Click on the **Save** private key button.

4. When saving the key, a warning dialog box may appear; you can select **Yes** on the warning.

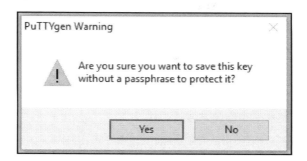

Figure 5.16: Warning dialog box

5. Finally, save the public key with the .ppk extension.

Connecting to an EC2 instance using PuTTY session

Once you have a .ppk file, you are ready for connecting to an AWS EC2 Linux instance. The following steps describe the process to initiate an SSH connection with an EC2 instance using PuTTY:

1. Run an application PuTTY on Microsoft Windows from where you need to connect to the EC2 instance.

2. In the **Category** pane, on the left-hand side select **Session** and provide the following details:

   - Default port is 22 for Linux OS.
   - Connection type should be SSH.
   - Username, default SSH username based on the OS type as shown in the previous table and public DNS or public/ElasticIP. For example:

Syntax:

```
<username>@<PublicIP>
```

Example: to connect to RHEL/CentOS 7 EC2 instance:

```
ec2-user@34.204.99.20
```

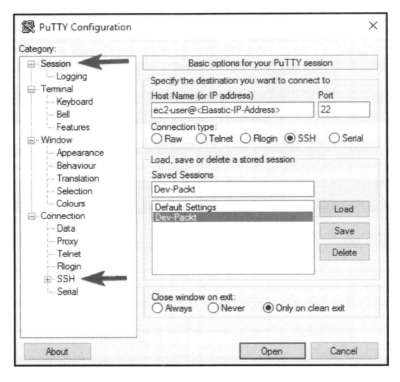

Figure 5.17: Putty session

3. On the left-hand side, in the **Category** pane, select **Connection| SSH| Auth** and click **browse** to provide a private key:

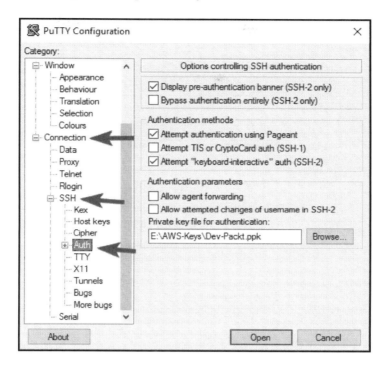

Figure 5.18: Provide private key

4. Once you click **Open**, a security dialog box may appear confirming that you trust the host you are about to connect with. Choose **Yes** and SSH connection takes place.

Troubleshooting SSH connection issues

While establishing an SSH connection with an EC2 instance, if all the required details are properly provided and in spite of that, it fails to establish an SSH connection, check out the following points:

- Ensure that you are giving the correct IP address of the instance.
- Verify the username you have given along with the IP address.

- Make sure an EC2 instance is up and running.
- Ensure that the security group has SSH port 22 open and is accessible.
- Check the OS level firewall and ensure its not blocking the connection.
- If you are behind a network proxy, ensure that your network proxy is not blocking it.
- Ensure that you are using a right .ppk file.
- After verifying all the preceding steps, if you are still not able to log in, you can try stopping and restarting the instance.
- You can also diagnose the issue by stopping the instance, detaching its root drive and attaching and mounting it to another healthy EC2 instance as a secondary drive. Once the drive is attached to another EC2 instance, you can diagnose configuration issues.

EC2 instance metadata and user data

Metadata is data about an EC2 instance. EC2 instance details such as AMI ID, hostname, instance ID, instance Type, private IP address, public IP address, and so on are metadata of the instance. EC2 instance metadata can be retrieved by querying 169.254.269.254 on the same machine. From a Linux system, you can use the following command to retrieve the metadata from the EC2 instance:

```
$ curl http://169.254.169.254/
```

Issuing the curl command gives the following output, categorizing the metadata based on the date it is introduced by AWS:

```
1.0
2007-01-19
2007-03-01
2007-08-29
2007-10-10
2007-12-15
2008-02-01
2008-09-01
2009-04-04
2011-01-01
2011-05-01
2012-01-12
2014-02-25
2014-11-05
2015-10-20
2016-04-19
2016-06-30
```

```
2016-09-02
latest
```

Furthermore, `latest` metadata is divided into three categories, as shown in the following output:

```
$ curl http://169.254.169.254/latest
dynamic
meta-data
user-data
```

An EC2 instance's individual metadata properties can be retrieved by adding the property at the end of the following command:

```
$ curl http://169.254.169.254/latest/meta-data/
```

For example, you can retrieve `ami-id` by querying the following URL:

```
$ curl http://169.254.169.254/latest/meta-data/ami-id
```

Similarly, you can use the following list of properties with the `curl` command to retrieve its value:

```
ami-id
ami-launch-index
ami-manifest-path
block-device-mapping/
hostname
instance-action
instance-id
instance-type
local-hostname
local-ipv4
mac
metrics/
network/
placement/
profile
public-hostname
public-ipv4
public-keys/
reservation-id
security-groups
```

On an Amazon Linux EC2 instance, the `ec2-metadata` command also gives metadata.

Placement group

A Placement group is a logical grouping of EC2 instances within a single AZ. Placement group provides a possible lowest network latency across all the EC2 instances that are part of the same placement group. All EC2 instances do not support high network throughput (that is, placement group). Before launching an instance in a placement group, you need to ensure that the instance type supports a placement group. It is best practice to create all the EC2 instances required in a placement group, and ensure they are created in a single launch request and have the same instance type. In case multiple instance types are mixed in a placement group then the lowest bandwidth among the EC2 instances is considered as the highest network throughput of the placement group. It is recommended you choose an instance type that supports a 10 GBps or 20 GBps network throughput. There is no additional charge for creating an instance group.

Some important points about a placement group:

- A placement group can span across peered VPCs.
- When network traffic is flowing to and from outside the placement group, network throughput is limited to 5 GBps.
- An existing EC2 instance in the same AZ cannot be moved inside a placement group. It requires creating an AMI of the existing instance and then launching a new EC2 instance inside the placement group.
- Even in the same account, placement groups cannot be merged.
- When you stop and start an instance inside a placement group, it remains in the same placement group.
- If you get a capacity error while launching an instance inside a placement group, you can stop and start all instances in the placement group. Stopping and starting instances automatically migrates the instances to another hardware that has capacity to run them.

Introducing EBS

EBS is an AWS block storage service, that provides block level, persistent storage volumes for EC2 instances. EBS volumes are highly available and reliable storage solution. An EBS volume can be attached only to the EC2 instances running in the same AZ. It provides persistent storage and it is independent from the EC2 instance. That means the data on the EBS volume remains intact even if the instance is restarted. AWS charges for the allocated EBS volume sizes, even if the volume is not attached to any instance. Also, charges are based on the allocated volume size and not based on how much data is stored on the volume. EBS volumes can be formatted into the desired block size and filesystem. It is very suitable for the read and write such as database application or throughput of intensive workloads such as big data. Once EBS volumes are attached to EC2 instances, they are used like a normal physical drive. Multiple EBS volumes can be attached to a single EC2 instance; however, one EBS volume can be attached only to a single EC2 instance.

AWS replicates EBS data at least three times within a single AZ. Unlike S3 data, it does not get replicated in multiple AZs within the same region. It is also important to understand that EBS volumes are not directly attached to the hosts (hypervisor), but they are network-attached block storage.

Types of EBS

Currently, AWS provides the following types of EBS volumes. These EBS types have different performance and prices per GB:

- **Solid State Drive (SSD)**:
  - General Purpose SSD (gp2)
  - Provisioned IOPS SSD (io1)
- **Hard Disk Drive (HDD)**:
  - Throughput optimized HDD (st1)
  - Cold HDD (sc1)
- Previous generation volume:
  - Magnetic (Standard)

General Purpose SSD (gp2)

The gp2 volumes are one of the EBS volume types that provides persistent storage. gp2 volume types are ideal for a number of workloads. gp2 volumes are very efficient and provide single-digit millisecond latencies. A gp2 volume is capable of bursting up to 3,000 IOPS for a significant amount of time. You can provision a minimum of 1 GiB size of gp2 volume and a maximum of up to 16 TiB of a gp2 volume. gp2 volume provides 3 IOPS per GiB of volume size. However, if a volume size is 33.33 GiB or less, it provides a minimum of 100 IOPS. As you increase the volume size, the IOPS it provides, also increases. However, a gp2 volume can provide a maximum of 10,000 IOPS. If you use multiple gp2 volumes in an instance, AWS imposes a limit of a maximum of 65000 IOPS per instance.

Where to use gp2 volumes:

- It is recommended for almost all workload types
- Can be used as a root volume for an operating system
- Can be attached to a virtual desktop
- In interactive apps requiring low-latency storage
- Development workloads
- Testing environments

Provisioned IOPS SSD (io1)

Provisioned IOPS SSD (io1) volumes are solid state drive volumes that are intended to address the needs of I/O intensive application workloads. io1 volumes are specifically used for database workloads that require high performance storage and consistent throughput. Unlike gp2 volumes, io1 volume provides a consistent performance. You can specify a consistent IOPS rate while creating the volume. io1 volumes can provide maximum performance out of all other volume types. An io1 volume size can range between 4 GiB to 16 TiB. An io1 volume can have a minimum of 100 IOPS and a maximum of up to 20,000 IOPS. If you use multiple io1 volumes in an instance, AWS imposes a limit of a maximum of 65000 IOPS per instance.

Where to use io1 volumes:

- It can be used in mission critical applications
- Business critical application requiring consistent performance
- It can be used in large databases workloads such as SQL Server, Oracle, and so on

Throughput Optimized HDD (st1)

Throughput Optimized HDD (st1) volumes are designed to provide a financially viable magnetic storage option. st1 volumes are architected to measure the performance in terms of throughput and not on IOPS. st1 volume type is recommended for a large and linear workload such as data warehouse, log processing, Amazon **Elastic MapReduce** (**EMR**), and ETL workloads. It cannot be used as a bootable volume. An st1 volume size can range between 500 GiB to 16 TiB. An st1 volume can have a maximum of 500 IOPS per volumes. If you use multiple st1 volumes in an instance, AWS imposes a limit of a maximum of 65000 IOPS per instance.

Where to use st1 volumes:

- Applications requiring consistent and fast throughput at a low cost
- Big data
- Data warehouse
- Log processing

Cold HDD (sc1)

Cold HDD (sc1) volumes are designed to provide a cost effective magnetic storage option. sc1 volumes are designed to measure the performance in terms of throughput and not on IOPS. sc1 volume type provides a lower throughput limit compared to st1. It is recommended for large, linear cold-data workloads. It's a good low-cost alternative to st1 if you require infrequent access to your data. sc1 volumes cannot be used as bootable root volume. An sc1 volume size can range between 500 GiB to 16 TiB. An sc1 volume can have a maximum of 250 IOPS per volumes. If you use multiple sc1 volumes in an instance, AWS imposes a limit of a maximum of 65000 IOPS per instance.

Where to use sc1 volumes:

- It can be used in throughput-oriented storage
- Use it for large volumes of data when you don't need to access it frequently
- In application needs where there is a need to lower the storage cost

Encrypted EBS

Amazon provides a simple EBS encryption solution that does not require building, maintaining, and securing your own key management infrastructure.

After creating an encrypted EBS volume, when you attach it to a supported instance, it encrypts the following types of data:

- All data at rest, stored inside the volume
- All data that is moving between the volume and the EC2 instance
- All snapshots back up taken from the volume
- AWS encrypts the data on the servers that host EC2 instances and provide encryption of data-in-transit from EC2 instances and on to EBS storage

Amazon EBS encrypts the data using AWS **Key Management Service** (**KMS**) with a customer master key whenever you create an encrypted volume and subsequently any snapshots from them.

When an encryption-enabled EBS volume is attached to the supported EC2 instance type, encryption takes place at EC2 for data-in-transit from EC2 to EBS storage. All future snapshot and disk I/Os are encrypted. An encryption master key from Amazon KMS is used to perform encryption and decryption. Two types of encryption master keys can be used, an Amazon created and custom key or customer provided key. When creating an encrypted EBS volume for the first time in any AWS region, AWS automatically creates a master key in that region. By default, this key can only be used to encrypt the EBS volume. In order to use a custom key to encrypt EBS volumes, you need to create a **Customer Master Key** (**CMK**) in AWS KMS. Creating a CMK gives more control over disabling, defining access control, creating and rotating encryption keys. At present, the root volume attached to the AWS EC2 instance cannot be encrypted. Other than the root, all attached EBS volumes can be encrypted. AWS uses **Advanced Encryption Standard** (**AES-256**) algorithms for encryption.

Monitoring EBS volumes with CloudWatch

Once desired size and type of EBS volumes are created, it is recommended you monitor the performance of the volumes. Monitoring helps in identifying any performance bottleneck, if any, due to any issue. We can use performance logs in the CloudWatch to determine if any volume type needs an upgrade in terms of size, IOPS, or throughput. When an EBS volume is created, AWS automatically creates several CloudWatch metrics for each EBS volumes. Monitoring data is categorized into basic and detailed monitoring. Basic monitoring details are free and include metrics such as read bandwidth (KiB/s), write bandwidth (KiB/s), read throughput (Ops/s), write throughput (Ops/s), and many others.

Only Provisioned IOPS SSD (io1) sends monitoring data to CloudWatch at one-minute intervals. The rest of the EBS volume types such as General Purpose SSD (gp2), Throughput Optimized HDD (st1), Cold HDD (sc1), and Magnetic (standard) sends data to the CloudWatch metrics at five minute intervals.

CloudWatch does not monitor at what rate the disk is being filled or at what percent the disk is utilized or empty. For such requirement, you need to create a custom CloudWatch matrix.

More details about monitoring EC2 instances and EBS volumes are given in `Chapter 7 - Monitoring with CloudWatch`.

Snapshots

EBS snapshot is an AWS service that provides a mechanism to back up EBS volumes. AWS provides a way to back up your EBS data on S3 by taking a point-in-time snapshot. Snapshots are incremental in nature. That means, it only saves data blocks that are changed after the last snapshot backup taken from the volume. This incremental approach of backing up data saves the time and cost of storage. If there are multiple snapshots for an EBS volume and you delete one of the snapshots, AWS deletes only the data relevant to that snapshot. Other snapshots created out of the same volume, refer to the base data and the incremental change relevant to them.

However, AWS stores the snapshot on S3; snapshots are not directly visible to users on S3. AWS stores the snapshot on a separate area in S3, which is inaccessible to end users. Users can see their snapshots on a snapshot dashboard, given within the EC2 dashboard.

Whether EBS volumes are attached to any instance or not, an EBS snapshot can be taken. Snapshot not only provides an option to perform point-in-time backup of EBS volumes, but it also acts as a baseline for new EBS volumes. Snapshot can be used to migrate existing EBS volumes along with its data from one AZ, region, or AWS account to another. Snapshot of an encrypted volume is also encrypted.

The internal mechanism for a snapshot is to write the copy of data from the EBS volume to the S3 where it is stored redundantly across multiple AZs in the same region. When we access S3 using a web console, CLI, or API, we can't see the snapshots in S3.

It is critical for an organization to draft a backup and retention policy that determines how frequently snapshots are taken for EBS volumes. It is advisable that the backup and retention policy also defines a retention period for each snapshot depending on organizational needs. Housekeeping activities should be automated using scripts or tools to take the snapshots as well as delete unwanted snapshots from the account to control unnecessary cost.

Snapshots are the incremental backup. For any EBS volume, when taking the first snapshot all the written blocks are copied to S3 and finally **Table of Contents (TOC)** for the snapshot is written to the S3. TOC points to these blocks. When taking a consequent snapshot for the same EBS volume, it only copies modified blocks from the EBS volume to S3 and creates a relevant table of contents. The table of contents points to the recent blocks copied from EBS to S3 as well as blocks copied during previous snapshots, which are not changed. The following snapshot creation and deletion *Figure 5.19* helps to understand the same. In the same figure, we can see the TOC 2 and TOC 3 is pointing to some of the new and some of the old blocks:

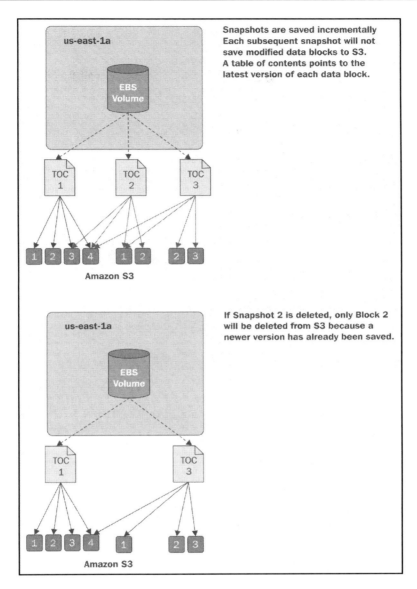

Figure 5.19: Snapshot creation and deletion

It also helps us to understand that when any intermediate snapshot is deleted, only those blocks are deleted that are not referred to by any other snapshot TOCs.

EBS optimized EC2 instances

In a normal EC2 instance, usual network traffic and EBS traffic flows through the same network interface. If network traffic on application processes increases, it adversely affects the EBS performance. Similarly, activities on an EBS volume read and write can adversely affect other network activities on the instance. The following *Figure 5.20* indicates how network traffic from an EC2 instance and EBS volume flows through the same network link:

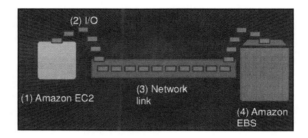

Figure 5.20: Network traffic on EC2 instance and EBS volume

https://cloudnative.io/blog/2015/01/ebs-best-practices-and-performance-tuning/

To handle such performance issues, AWS provides EBS-optimized instance types. EBS optimized instance provides dedicated throughput between EBS volumes and EC2 instance. Such instance types are essential for the application where predictable and consistent disk performance is required. While using Provisioned IOPS SSD volumes, it is recommended you use EBS-optimized instance. It ensures best performance out of Provisioned IOPS SSD volume.

EC2 best practices

The list summarizing EC2 best practices are as follows:

- Ensure that unused EC2 instances are stopped and if not required, terminate them. It reduces unnecessary cost in the monthly AWS billing.
- Closely observe snapshots and AMIs, timely perform housekeeping and discard all the AMIs and snapshots, which are not required. It is recommended you automate and monitor this process.

- Ensure that an instance type is set as per the requirement of the application hosted on the instance. It is recommended you optimize instance type as per application performance.
- To match a seasonal spike in compute requirement, plan for Auto Scaling and load balancing.
- Divide your application load in multiple instances rather than going for one big instance, where possible. Dividing the application workload over multiple instances, in different AZ, can avoid single point of failure.
- Ensure to use On-Demand, Spot, and Reserved Instances in the environment based on the need. Balancing the instance types can significantly reduce cost as reserved and spot instances provide a huge cost benefit.
- Always keep your key pairs safely. Once a key pair is lost, it cannot be recovered from AWS.
- Do not embed access key and secret key into the EC2 instance. Where possible, use EC2 roles for accessing AWS resources from an EC2 instance.
- Attach appropriate IAM roles and policies, at the time of creating an EC2 instance to grant access to other AWS services.
- Periodically update security groups and maintain least permissive rules.
- Periodically update and patch the OS to overcome possible security and other vulnerabilities.
- According to the data storage requirement such as persistent or temporary, select EBS or instance-type backed AMI for provisioning an instance.
- It is recommended you use separate volumes for the operating system and data storage.
- Always tag AWS resources with appropriate and relevant tags. It provides a convenient way to identify the right EC2 instance at the time of performing maintenance.
- Create golden AMIs and update them periodically.
- Periodically perform maintenance to delete obsolete and unwanted AMIs as well as snapshots to minimize monthly AWS billing.
- Monitor EC2 and EBS volumes to identify any performance bottleneck in the environment.

6

Handling Application Traffic with Elastic Load Balancing

Introduction to Elastic Load balancer

Elastic Load Balancer (ELB) is an AWS service that automatically distributes incoming network or application traffic to a number of EC2 instances. It monitors the health of each of the EC2 instances associated with it and forwards traffic only to healthy instances. ELB provides a single point of contact for the EC2 instances behind ELB. Each of the EC2 instances is marked with a status, either *InService* if it is healthy or *OutOfService* if it is unhealthy. Traffic is routed only to *InService* instances. An ELB provides a single point of contact for the application traffic which is hosted on multiple EC2 instances. By routing traffic only to healthy instances, ELB provides fault tolerance to the application and ensures high availability of the application:

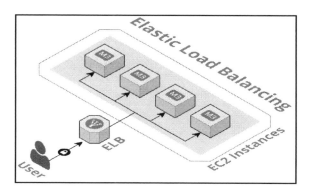

Benefits of using ELB

ELB provides high availability, fault tolerance, elasticity, and security to your environment. We will now look at benefits of ELB in brief:

- **High availability**: An application hosted behind an ELB on a fleet of EC2 instances spread across multiple AZ provides high availability. Consider a scenario where an application is hosted in an EC2 instance without using an ELB. If traffic to the application spikes, EC2 may not be able to handle the traffic and application performance as well as availability is affected. Consider the similar traffic scenario where an application is hosted in multiple E2 instances across AZs behind an ELB. ELB distributes the traffic in a round-robin fashion to all the instances, ensuring that any one EC2 instance is not flooded with traffic.

- **Fault tolerance**: ELB monitors the health of each of the instances associated with it. If an instance is unreachable, it marks the instance as *OutOfService*. Similarly, if an instance is reachable and healthy, it marks the instance as *InService*. The traffic is directed only to the *InService* instances. This way, even if an instance is down, application traffic is not affected and it provides fault tolerance to the application.

- **Elasticity**: In spite of high availability and fault tolerance with a limited number of instances in an ELB, traffic can spike beyond the capacity of the instances in ELB. Other way round, if traffic is very low, the number of instances in an ELB may be underutilized. Over utilization of instances may lead to application performance issues and under utilization results in unnecessary cost. To handle both these scenarios, an ELB can be associated with an Auto Scaling group. It provides elasticity to ELB by automatically increasing the number of instances in an ELB when the traffic is high and automatically reducing the number instances when the traffic is low.

- **Security**: ELB, when used with VPC, provides robust networking and security features. It provides the ability to create an internal-facing ELB, using private IP addresses to route traffic within the VPN. You can also create an internet-facing load balancer to route traffic from the internet to instances in a private subnet. In either case, instances are not directly accessible to the traffic. ELB acts as a frontend to the instances associated with it; and provides a security layer to protect them.

Types of ELB

There are two types of ELB, Classic Load Balancer and Application Load Balancer.

Classic Load Balancer

Classic Load Balancer is one of the initial offerings of AWS. It handles the traffic depending upon application or network level information. It is used for load balancing simple traffic across multiple EC2 instances where the need is to have a highly available, automatic scaling, and secured environment. It is not suitable for the applications that require advanced routing capabilities for handling the application traffic.

Application Load Balancer

Application Load Balancer has been introduced lately in AWS offerings. Unlike Classic Load Balancer, it provides advance application-level routing options. It provides the ability to route the traffic based on application content spread across multiple services, micro services, or container services with multi-tiered application architecture.

Features of ELB

There are several features of an ELB. Each type of load balancer, be it Classic Load Balancer or Application Load Balancer, has its own set of features. The following table illustrates these features and compares the two types of ELBs. This comparison can help in choosing the right load balancer type depending on the requirement:

Features	Classic Load Balancer	Application Load Balancer
Protocols	HTTP, HTTPS, TCP, SSL	HTTP, HTTPS
Platforms	EC2-Classic, EC2-VPC	EC2-VPC
Sticky sessions (cookies)	✓	Load balancer generated
Idle connection timeout	✓	✓
Connection draining	✓	✓
Cross-zone load balancing	✓	Always enabled

Health checks	✓	Improved
CloudWatch metrics	✓	Improved
Access logs	✓	Improved
Host-based routing		✓
Path-based routing		✓
Route to multiple ports on a single instance		✓
HTTP/2 support		✓
WebSockets support		✓
ELB deletion protection		✓

ELB feature comparison

Let's understand each of the features supported by respective load balancer type.

Protocols: As depicted in the table, Classic Load Balancer supports transport layers as well as application layers. Transport layers consist of TCP and SSL protocol, whereas application layers use HTTP and HTTPS protocols. Application Load Balancer takes routing decisions at application layer and supports only HTTP and HTTPS protocols.

Platforms: Classic Load Balancer, being one of the initial offerings, supports EC2-Classic as well as EC2-VPC, whereas Application Load Balancer is introduced later in AWS offerings for advance application-level options, and supports EC2 instances hosted in a VPC only.

Sticky sessions: Sticky session is a way to consistently route traffic requests from a particular user to the same target instance based on HTTP session, IP address, or a cookie. Classic load balancer supports application cookies or if an application does not have a cookie, you can create a session cookie by specifying stickiness duration in ELB configuration. It creates a cookie named AWSELB for mapping the session to an instance.

Application Load Balancer supports sticky sessions using load balancer generated cookies. It's a mechanism to route traffic requests originated from a user to the same target group every time during a session. When a user sends a request to an application for the first time, an ELB routes the request to one of the instances and generates a cookie. This cookie is included in the response back to the user. When the user sends the subsequent requests, the request contains the same cookie. Based on the cookie, this request is sent to the same target instance until the session duration lasts. The name of the cookie generated in Application Load Balancer is AWSALB.

Idle connection timeout: Every time a user makes a request to an ELB, it maintains two connections. One connection is created with the client and another connection is created with the target EC2 instance. For each of these connections, ELB maintains an idle timeout period. If there is no activity during the specified idle time between the client and the target EC2 instance, ELB closes this connection. In short, if there is no traffic flowing from client to EC2 or vice versa, ELB closes the connection. By default, idle time duration is 60 seconds in an ELB.

Connection draining: An ELB stops sending requests to instances that are either unhealthy or are deregistering from the ELB. This can lead to abrupt closure of an ongoing session initiated by a user. Such abrupt closed sessions give unpleasant experience to an application user. To take care of such user experience issues, AWS supports connection draining in an ELB. When connection draining is enabled and an instance becomes unhealthy or deregistering, an ELB stops sending new requests to such instances; however, it completes any in-flight request made to such instances.

The timeout value for connection draining can be specified between 1 second an 3,600 seconds. The default timeout value for connection draining is 300 seconds. The load balancer forces a connection to close and deregisters it if the time limit is reached.

Cross-zone load balancing: When a Classic Load Balancing is created with instances spread across multiple AZs, it distributes the traffic evenly between the associated AZs. If you have an ELB with 10 instances in US-East-1a and two instances in US-East-1b, the traffic is distributed evenly between two AZs. This means—two instances in US-East-1b serve the same amount of traffic as 10 instances in US-East-1a. This is the default behavior of Classic Load Balancing. If you enable cross-zone load balancing, an ELB distributes traffic evenly between all the EC2 instances across multiple AZs.

Cross-zone load balancing is configurable in Classic Load Balancer; however, it is always enabled in Application Load Balancer.

Health checks: To determine whether an instance is capable of handling traffic or not, an ELB periodically sends pings, tries to establish a connection, or sends HTTP/HTTPS requests. These requests are used to determine the health status of an instance and are called health checks. All the healthy instances in an ELB that serve the traffic have a status as *InService* instances. All the unhealthy instances, which cannot serve the traffic, are called *OutOfService* instances. The ELB routes requests only to the healthy instances. It stops routing traffic requests to *OutOfService* instances. It resumes sending traffic to the instances as soon as the instance status becomes healthy and *InService*.

CloudWatch metrics: AWS sends data points to CloudWatch for load balancers and all the instances associated with it. CloudWatch aggregates those data points and creates statistics in an ordered set of time-series data. This time-series data is called CloudWatch metrics for ELB. With CloudWatch metrics, you can verify the number of healthy EC2 instances in a load balancer during a specific time period. It helps to verify whether the system is consistently performing as expected or not. With CloudWatch, you can create an event trigger in case the metric is outside of the acceptable range. Such event triggers can send a mail to stakeholders or take any specific action based on its association with either Lambda function or Auto Scaling group.

Proxy protocol: When an end user request hits ELB, ELB changes source IP and other request header and forwards it to one of the EC2 instance where the application is hosted. This is the default behavior of ELB, which bars an application from obtaining original client connection information. In some enterprise applications, it is required to have original source connection details to perform traffic analysis. It helps the application to understand more about end user's behavior with such information. However, ELB does not provide original connection information to application by default, it supports proxy protocol, which can be used to obtain connection information from ELB. Proxy protocol is nothing but an **Internet Protocol (IP)**, which carries client connection information. You can enable or disable Proxy protocol on ELB with the help of AWS CLI.

For more details on enabling or disabling the proxy protocol, you can refer to the URL: `https://www.linkedin.com/pulse/enable-disable-proxy-protocol-support-aws-elb-using-cli-bhavin-parmar/`.

Access logs: ELB generates access logs for each requests sent to it. With each passing request, it captures information such as time of request, source IP address, latencies, request path, and the server response. The access log can be used to analyze the traffic and for troubleshooting any issue. Enabling a access log is optional and it is disabled by default. Once the access log is enabled for an ELB, it captures the log and stores it in an Amazon S3 bucket. The S3 bucket name can be specified while enabling the access log on an ELB.

AWS does not charge any additional amount for access logs, however, you are charged for the storage you use on S3 bucket for access logs.

Host-based routing: Host-based routing refers to a mechanism of routing traffic to a specific target group based on the hostname specified in the host header of the request. For example, requests to `www.example.com` can be sent to target group A, requests to `mobile.example.com` can be sent to target group B, and requests to `api.example.com` can be sent to target group C.

Host-based routing is only supported in Application Load Balancer.

Path-based routing: Application Load Balancer provides a mechanism to route traffic to a specific target group based on the URL path specified in the host header of the request. For example, requests to `www.example.com/production` can be sent to target group A, requests to `www.example.com/sandbox` can be sent to target group B, and requests to `www.example.com/admin` can be sent to target group C.

Path-based routing is only supported in Application Load Balancer.

Route to multiple ports on a single instance: Application Load Balancer supports routing traffic to multiple ports on an EC2 instance. For example, an EC2 instance can run multiple applications on different ports on a single EC2 instance:

- EC2 can run the main web server on port `80`
- It can run the admin application on port `8080`
- It can run the reporting application on port `5000`

In such a scenario, Application Load Balancer can route all the traffic requests with host header as `www.example.com` to port `80` on the instance, all traffic requests with host header `www.example.com/admin` to port `8080` on the instance, and all the traffic requests with host header `www.example.com/reporting` to port `5000` on the instance.

Routing to multiple ports on a single instance is only supported in Application Load Balancer.

HTTP/2 support: HTTP/2, also called HTTP/2.0 is a major revision of the HTTP network protocol used on the internet. Using HTTP/2 features, web applications can increase its speed. It improves the way data is framed and transported. Websites can increase the efficiency and minimize the number of requests required to load an entire web page.

Application Load Balancer supports HTTP/2, industry standard protocol and provides better visibility on the health of the EC2 instances and micro servers or containers.

WebSockets support: WebSockets are an advanced technological development that enables the application to open an interactive communication session between the browser and an application server. If WebSockets are enabled, it allows you to send a message to an application server and receive event-driven responses from the server without polling the server for its response. It provides a persistent connection between a browser and the application server. The browser establishes the connection with the application server using a process named *WebSocket handshaking*. Once a session is established, the browser or the application can start sending the data unilaterally as and when required. Application Load Balancer supports WebSockets, whereas Classic Load Balancer does not support it.

ELB deletion protection: Application Load Balancer supports a configuration option that ensures that an ELB is not accidentally deleted by anybody. This option is called an ELB deletion protection. It is supported only by Application Load Balancer. If ELB deletion protection is enabled, you cannot delete the ELB unless this option is disabled again.

Step by step – Creating a Classic Load Balancer

Before creating a load balancer, it is necessary to ensure that desired configuration of VPC and EC2 instances are in place. If you create an ELB with EC2 instances spread across multiple AZs, ensure that the required instances are in place in each AZ to perform tests after creating the ELB. Also, verify that the security group attached to the respective EC2 instances allows incoming traffic on required ports and protocols. It is also recommended that the desired application or web server is configured properly on the target EC2 instances. With this background, let's follow the steps to create a Classic Load Balancer:

1. Log in to the AWS web console with sufficient credentials to create an ELB.
2. Go to EC2 dashboard and select **Load Balancers** from the left-hand side pane, as shown in the following *Figure 6.1*:

Figure 6.1: Load Balancer option on EC2 dashboard

3. Click on the **Create Load Balancer** button, as shown in the following *Figure 6.2*:

Figure 6.2: Create a Load Balancer button

4. Select the **Classic Load Balancer** type, as shown in the following *Figure 6.3*:

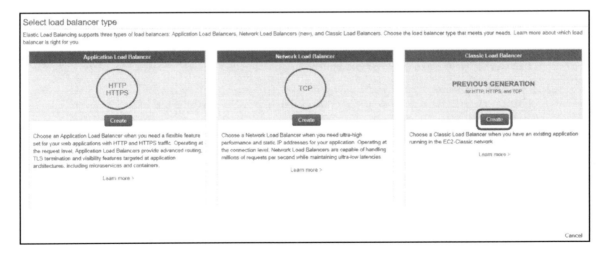

Figure 6.3: Select Classic Load Balancer

5. Next, we define Classic Load Balancer **Basic Configuration**:

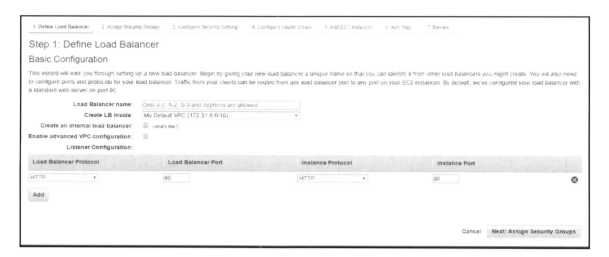

Figure 6.4: Classic Load Balancer -Basic Configuration

In this step, you need to understand the following ELB options:

- **Load Balancer name**: Provide a meaningful and relevant ELB name; it can be alphanumeric (A-Z, a-z, 0-9) and dash (-).
- **Create LB Inside**: Select the desired VPC, where EC2 instances reside. Only one VPC can be selected from the drop-down menu.
- **Create an Internal load balancer**: Select this option when creating a load balancer to manage traffic only from within an AWS environment. An internal load balancer cannot serve internet traffic and can be accessed from within the network or associated VPC.

- **Enable advanced VPC configuration**: Select this option to perform manual selection of available subnets within a selected VPC in the region. When you select this option, other relevant options become visible.
- **Listener Configuration**: Listener defines the ports and protocols which ELB opens for end users to send requests and it defines target ports and protocols on EC2 instances where ELB can forward the incoming traffic. When the listener port on ELB is selected as HTTPS, in consecutive steps, it asks to upload an SSL certificate along with essential cipher configuration.

6. Create a new security group or select an existing security group as shown in the following *Figure 6.5*. It is recommended to create individual security groups for every ELB. Security groups should open only the minimum required ports and protocols:

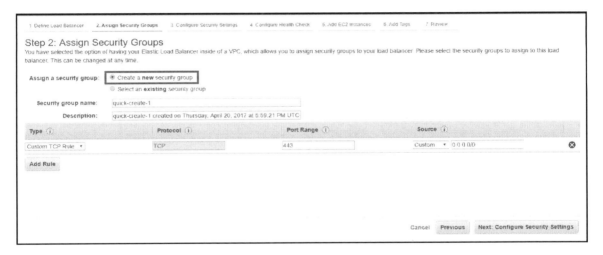

Figure 6.5: Assign Security Groups

7. Configure theSSL certificate. You can either **Choose an existing certificate from AWS Certificate Manager (ACM)**, **Choose an existing certificate from AWS Identity and Access Management (IAM)**, or **Upload a new SSL certificate to AWS Identity and Access Management (IAM)** as shown in the following *Figure 6.6*:

Figure 6.6: Configure Security Settings

When a listener is selected to listen on a HTTPS (443) port, it is essential to provide certificate details to move on to the next step.

8. The next step is to **Configure Health Check.** You can use the health check options table as a reference for configuring the health check options shown as follows:

Figure 6.7: Configure Health Check

The various health check options are listed as follows:

Health check option	Description
Ping Protocol	Ping Protocol can be either HTTP, HTTPS, TCP, or SSL target instance should allow the selected protocol for pinging it.
Ping Port	This is the port on which ELB can send the ping request to instances. This port should be the port on which EC2 hosts the application. The default port is 80, which can be changed based on where the application listens.
Ping Path	Ping Path points to a specific document or page on the EC2 instance. Ideally, this should be the path to the initial page loaded on the application. The ping is considered as a success if it is able to reach the page on a given path. To minimize the time to complete each ping, it is recommended to point it to the document root (/) rather than /index.html.

Healthy threshold	Healthy threshold is the threshold value in the range of 2 to 10. It defines the number of consecutive successful health checks before considering any EC2 instance as healthy instance.
Unhealthy threshold	Unhealthy threshold is the threshold value in the range of 2 to 10. It defines the number of consecutive failed health checks before considering any EC2 instance as unhealthy instance.
Response Timeout	This is an integer value in the range of 2 to 60 seconds. It defines the time interval in seconds. If an instance fails to respond during this time, ELB considers it as a failed health check. The instance is marked as an unhealthy instance if it crosses the Unhealthy threshold. Note: Health check timeout must be smaller than interval.
Interval	Interval can be given as an integer value in the range of 5 to 300 seconds. ELB waits for the number of seconds defined in the interval between two health checks.

9. Add EC2 instances from each of the AZs selected. Select **Enable Cross-Zone Load Balancing** and **Enable Connection Draining** as required. If connection draining is enabled, you can specify the number of seconds against it. ELB waits for the number of seconds defined for in-flight traffic to drain before forcing a session to close on deregistering an EC2 instance:

Figure 6.8: Add EC2 Instances to an ELB

10. Add tags as shown in the following *Figure 6.9*. It is recommended to give meaningful and relevant tags on an ELB as per enterprises naming conventions:

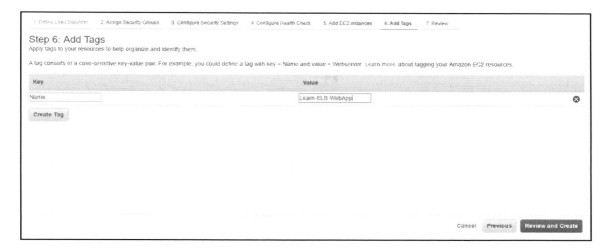

Figure 6.9: Add Tags to the ELB

11. Finally, click on **Review and Create** and verify the configuration. If everything is as per requirement, click on the **Create** button. Once ELB creation is completed, it provides an ELB endpoint. An ELB endpoint can be configured in CNAME record set in DNS to forward end user requests to the ELB.

How ELB works

Since all the ELB terminologies and features are explained, let us understand how exactly ELB works.

The working of a Classic Load Balancer

As per OSI model, Classic Load Balancer runs at Layer 4, which is the transport layer.

A transport layer level load balancer operates at the network protocol level. It does not check the content of actual network packets. A transport layer level load balancer does not check specific details of HTTP and HTTPS requests. In other words, it distributes the load without necessarily knowing much detail about the incoming traffic requests.

A user creates the Classic Load Balancer with instances spread across one or more AZs.

The load balancer configuration includes the following:

- Security group, which defines the security of ELB including the source of traffic that is allowed on the ELB, ports, and protocols open on the ELB for incoming traffic.
- Listener ports and protocols on which ELB listens for incoming traffic and target ports and protocols on EC2 instances where ELB directs the traffic.
- User includes SSL/TLS certification in the configuration.
- User defines health check for the associated instances. Health check enables the ELB to monitor the instances and determines whether an EC2 instance is *InService* or *OutOfService*. ELB routes traffic only to healthy instances with *InService* status.
- User can enable cross-zone load balancing to balance the traffic across all the instances in multiple AZs as required. If cross-zone load balancing is not enabled, traffic is routed on round-robin fashion between AZs.
- User can enable connection draining. If connection draining is enabled, before de-registering an instance from ELB, it allows in-transit sessions to complete for a defined span of seconds.
- Once an ELB is configured and associated with an application, AWS provides an ELB endpoint. ELB endpoint can be used to define a CName in Route53 or any other DNS.
- As described in the following *Figure 6.10*, a user can type in a site URL `www.example.com` in the browser.
- The user's request for the website hits a DNS server, which resolves to an ELB endpoint registered with the DNS and the request is forwarded to the ELB endpoint.
- The ELB endpoint resolves in a public IP address if the ELB is defined as an internet-facing ELB or it resolves in a private IP address if the ELB is defined as an internal-facing ELB:

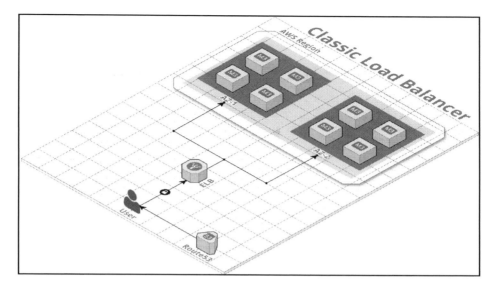

Figure 6.10: Classic Load Balancer

ELB receives the request forwarded by user and checks the source IP, host header, and cookie if sticky session is enabled.

If the source of the request is authorized to access the ELB, it forwards the traffic in a round-robin fashion to the AZs associated with the ELB. If cross-zone load balancing is enabled, the traffic is distributed between all the instances in round-robin fashion instead of distributing it at AZ level. If sticky session is enabled, ELB establishes a persistent session between client browser and EC2 instance. All subsequent requests from this user are forwarded to the same EC2 instance until the user session ends.

The target EC2 instance forwards the response, which is captured by ELB and forwarded back to the user.

The working of a Application Load Balancer

As per OSI model, Application Load Balancer runs at Layer 7, called the application layer.

Application Load Balancer is more powerful than Classic Load Balancer. It checks the traffic packets for more detail. It also has access to HTTP and HTTPS headers of the requests. It fetches more detail from the packets, which empowers it to do a more intelligent job in distributing the load to target instances.

Application Load Balancer supports content-based routing. You can enable host-based and path-based routing on an Application Load Balancer.

It also supports routing to multiple ports on a single instance.

It provides support for HTTP/2, which enables a website to increase efficiency and minimize the number of requests required to load a web page.

With the support of WebSockets, an Application Load Balancer can enable the application to open an interactive communication session between the browser and an application server.

A user creates the Application Load Balancer with instances spread across one or more target group in multiple AZs.

The load balancer configuration includes the following:

- Security Group, which defines the security of ELB including source of traffic that is allowed on the target group, ports, and protocols open on the ELB for incoming traffic.
- Listener ports and protocols on which ELB listens for incoming traffic and target ports and protocols on EC2 instances where ELB directs the traffic.
- Users can also define content-based routing. Content-based routing includes host-based routing or path-based routing. Depending upon the configuration, the traffic requests are forwarded to specific target groups.
- User includes SSL/TLS certification in the configuration.
- User defines health check for the associated instances. Health check enables the ELB to monitor the instances and determines whether an EC2 instance is *InService* or *OutOfService*. ELB routes traffic only to healthy instances with *InService* status.
- Cross-zone load balancing is automatically enabled in Application Load Balancer and the traffic is routed on a round-robin fashion across all the instances.
- User can enable connection draining. If connection draining is enabled, before deregistering an instance from ELB, it allows an in-transit session to complete for a defined span of seconds.
- Once an ELB is configured and associated with an application, AWS provides an ELB endpoint. The ELB endpoint can be used to define a CName in Route 53 or any other DNS.
- A user can type in a site URL www.example.com in the browser.

- User request for the website hits a DNS server, which resolves to an ELB endpoint registered with the DNS and the request is forwarded to the ELB endpoint.
- ELB endpoint resolves in a public IP address if the ELB is defined as an internet-facing ELB or it resolves in a private IP address if the ELB is defined as an internal-facing ELB.

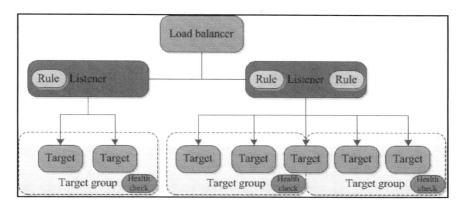

Figure 6.11: Application Load Balancer

ELB receives the request forwarded by the user, and then checks the source IP, host header, and cookie if sticky session is enabled.

If the source of the request is authorized to access the ELB, it forwards the traffic in a round-robin fashion to the target group associated with the ELB. The traffic is distributed between all the instances in round-robin fashion. If sticky session is enabled, ELB establishes a persistent session between client browser and EC2 instance. All subsequent requests from this user are forwarded to the same target until a session lasts.

The target EC2 instance forwards the response, which is captured by ELB and forwarded back to the user.

ELB best practices

ELB best practices are as follows:

- While defining a load balancer, it is recommended to identify target AZs and target group
- Use multiple AZs in ELB as it provides high availability and fault tolerance
- It is highly recommended that a Security group for the ELB opens only required ports and protocols
- Always configure health checks for ELB on appropriate ports and protocols
- If the ELB is created for a web server, use HTTP/HTTPS protocol in health checks instead of TCP protocol
- Do not create internet-facing ELB for internal needs
- Use SSL security certificates to encrypt and decrypt HTTPS connections where possible
- If a heavy traffic spike is expected on a given schedule, contact AWS support and ask them to pre-warm the ELB
- Use ELB deletion protection from accidental deletion
- Use cross-zone load balancing in Classic Load Balancer for evenly distributing the load across all EC2 instances in associated AZs
- Carefully enable connection draining on ELBs associated with critical user applications

7
Monitoring with CloudWatch

CloudWatch is an AWS service, that can be used on the AWS cloud for monitoring various infrastructure and application resources running on your AWS cloud. CloudWatch can be used to collect a number of metrics from the AWS resources. It allows you to track these metrics and also initiate actions based on the threshold you set. CloudWatch can also collect log files, generate metrics out of them, and help to monitor log files. You can set alarms on specific events and trigger an action whenever an event occurs. For example, if CPU utilization for a specific instance crosses a threshold of 80%, you can initiate an action to spin up a new instance.

CloudWatch supports the monitoring of many AWS services such as EC2 instances, DynamoDB, RDS, and so on. You can also generate custom metrics and log files using your own applications and associate them with CloudWatch. Amazon services like Auto Scaling uses CloudWatch alarms to automatically scale an environment up or down, based on the traffic on an environment.

CloudWatch provides a number of graphs and statistics. It gives your system wide insights into how resources are utilized, how to monitor application performances, and track the overall operational health of respective applications in an environment. All these infrastructure and application telemetry data can be used to ensure smooth functioning of your environment.

How Amazon CloudWatch works

CloudWatch acts as a repository of metrics, by collating raw data from various AWS services or applications, converting it into metrics, statistics, graphs, and facilitates certain actions based on specific data points in metrics. The following *Figure 7.1* shows the high-level architecture of CloudWatch:

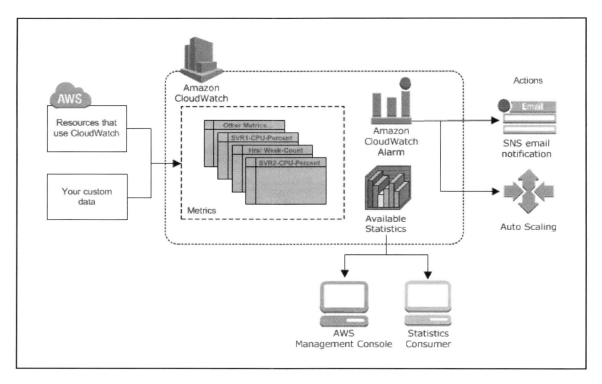

Figure 7.1: High level architecture of CloudWatch

Reference URL: https://docs.aws.amazon.com/AmazonCloudWatch/latest/monitoring/cloudwatch_architecture.html

As shown in the preceding figure, various AWS services and your custom metrics data are stored in CloudWatch. CloudWatch generates various statistical and graphical visualizations out of these metrics which can be consumed directly from the AWS Management Console or by various other means including, but not limited, to AWS CLI, API, custom build applications, and so on. CloudWatch enables the user to set alarms, which can trigger certain actions based on the metrics threshold or events. It can send email notifications or automatically scale an environment up or down using Auto Scaling groups associated with alarms.

Elements of Amazon CloudWatch

To understand and work with AWS-generated and custom metrics, it is important to understand a few basic concepts and terminologies used with Amazon CloudWatch.

Namespaces

CloudWatch namespaces are containers in which metrics for different applications are stored. It is a mechanism to isolate metrics of different applications from each other. Namespaces ensure that an application's metrics, as well as respective statistical data, are not accidentally mixed up with any other application's metrics. All the AWS services that use CloudWatch to register their metrics, use a unique namespace. A namespace name begins with AWS/ and is generally followed by the application name. If you create a custom application and need to store metrics in CloudWatch, you must specify a unique namespace as a container to store custom metrics. Namespace can be defined at the time of creating the metrics. Namespace name can be a string of up to 256 characters including (A-Z, a-z, 0-9), hyphen (-), underscore (_), period (.), slash (/), hash (#), and colon (:).

Some of the namespaces are given in the following table. For more details on namespace, you can refer to URL: http://docs.aws.amazon.com/AmazonCloudWatch/latest/monitoring/aws-namespaces.html.

AWS product	Namespace
Amazon API Gateway	AWS/ApiGateway
Amazon CloudFront	AWS/CloudFront
Amazon CloudSearch	AWS/CloudSearch
Amazon CloudWatch Events	AWS/Events
Amazon CloudWatch Logs	AWS/Logs
Amazon DynamoDB	AWS/DynamoDB
Amazon EC2	AWS/EC2
Amazon EC2 (Spot instances)	AWS/EC2Spot
Amazon EC2 Container Service	AWS/ECS
Amazon EBS	AWS/EBS
Amazon EFS	AWS/EFS

Amazon Elastic Transcoder	`AWS/ElasticTranscoder`
Amazon ElastiCache	`AWS/ElastiCache`
Amazon Elasticsearch Service	`AWS/ES`
Amazon EMR	`AWS/ElasticMapReduce`
Amazon Kinesis Analytics	`AWS/KinesisAnalytics`
Amazon Kinesis Firehose	`AWS/Firehose`
Amazon Kinesis Streams	`AWS/Kinesis`
Amazon RDS	`AWS/RDS`
Amazon Route 53	`AWS/Route53`
Amazon Simple Email Service	`AWS/SES`
Amazon SNS	`AWS/SNS`
Amazon Simple Queue Service	`AWS/SQS`
Amazon S3	`AWS/S3`
Amazon Simple Workflow Service	`AWS/SWF`

Metrics

Metrics are set of data collected over a period of time with a specific time interval for quantitative assessment, measurement, and comparison of performance data generated by a specific application or a service. For example, CPU utilization data for an EC2 instance is stored in a relevant CloudWatch metrics at time interval of 1 minute. Each AWS service stores several metrics in CloudWatch. For an instance, EC2 stores `CPUUtilization`, `NetworkIn`, `NetworkOut`, `DiskReadOps`, `DiskWriteOps`, and so on. CloudWatch by default, stores metrics data at an interval of 5 minutes. If you enable advance monitoring, it can store a metrics data point at an interval of 1 minute.

CloudWatch retains all metrics for 15 months before discarding them, however lower-level granularity of data is deleted to keep the overall volume of data at a reasonable size.

Granularity of data	Data retention period
60 seconds (1 minute)	15 days
300 seconds (5 minutes)	63 days
3600 seconds (1 hour)	455 days (15 months)

CloudWatch also allows you to create custom metrics with a custom name and the required time interval to store data point. Metrics are region based. AWS generated default metrics or custom metrics can be found only in the region where it is created. Metrics cannot be deleted manually. They automatically expire after 15 months from the time of last published data point into the metrics.

Metrics are unique in nature, defined by the combination of a namespace, metric name, and one or more dimensions. Each data point has a timestamp, data point, and optionally, a unit of measurement.

Dimensions

A dimension in a CloudWatch metrics is a mechanism to uniquely identify metrics. It is a name/value pair that is associated with metrics.

For example, CloudWatch stores metrics for EC2 instances in a namespace called AWS/EC2. All EC2 metrics are stored in the specific namespace. If you need to retrieve metrics for a specific InstanceID, you search the metrics with its InstanceID like i-09x7xxx4x0x688x43.

In the preceding example, InstanceID is its name and i-09x7xxx4x0x688x43 is its value which represents a dimension. When you search the metrics with the InstanceID value, you are using a dimension. A dimension is a unique identifier of metrics. When you search with a different value of InstanceId, CloudWatch provides you with a different metrics that is related with another instance. Similarly, you can search metrics with a different dimension name. For example, you can search the EC2 metrics with an ImageID. Metrics can have a maximum of 10 dimensions. Here's the list of dimensions in EC2.

- InstanceId
- ImageId

- `InstanceType`
- `AutoScalingGroupName`

Just like EC2, other services have their own dimensions. You can also create a metrics with it's custom dimensions.

Statistics

Statistics are a collection of aggregated metrics data for a specific period of time. Metrics data is aggregated using namespace, metric name, dimensions, and several data points in a given time period. CloudWatch provides the following statistics on the metrics data.

Statistic	Description
`Minimum`	The least, smallest, or lowest value recorded in the metrics for a specific period of time. For example, lowest CPU utilization recorded during the day on an EC2 instance.
`Maximum`	The largest, biggest, or highest value recorded in the metrics for a specific period of time. For example, highest CPU utilization recorded during the day on an EC2 instance.
`Sum`	Total value resulting from addition of all the matching metrics for a specific period of time. It is useful to study the total volume of activities. For example, total data transferred on an EC2 instance in the past 24 hours.
`Average`	Average value resulting from addition of all the matching metrics for a specific period of time and dividing it by the total number of sample count. For example, average CPU utilization on an EC2 instance for the last one hour.
`SampleCount`	Simply counts the number of data points used for the statistical calculation.
`pNN.NN`	The value represented in percentile. It uses up to two decimal places to specify a number. It helps to study statistics in terms of percentile such as p80.43.

At any given point of time, a data point may contain more than one value as shown in the following table. It describes some statistics with sample data.

Hour	Raw data	Sum	Minimum	Maximum	SampleCount
1	80, 85, 75, 70, 77	387	70	85	5
2	60, 80, 70, 75, 65	350	60	80	5

Percentile

A percentile helps in finding the comparative standing of a value in a set of data. Let us take an example of a data set that contains the CPU utilization of an EC2 instance. The example data is arranged in ascending order for better understanding.

12	17	25	55	58	61	63	70	83	97

Let us consider the percentile for 83 from the preceding data set. In this example, 83 stands at the 90th percentile. That means, 90 percent of data is less than or equal to 83 and the remaining 10 percent is above 83.

Percentile gives a better insight of the data with better understanding on how the data is distributed. The following AWS services support percentiles.

- EC2
- Application Load Balancer
- Classic Load Balancer
- RDS
- Kinesis
- API Gateway

CloudWatch provides options to monitor systems and applications using various statistics such as maximum, minimum, average, sum, or percentile. If you choose percentile, CloudWatch starts displaying the statistics according to percentile value.

Alarms

CloudWatch alarms help in defining a threshold value that is constantly monitored, and an action is triggered when the threshold condition is breached.

For example, you can define a threshold of 80% CPU utilization on an EC2 instance and trigger an action whenever the CPU utilization is >=80 for three consecutive periods.

The action can be one or more SNS notification, Auto Scaling action, or an EC2 action. An SNS notification can be used to send an alert over mail, an SMS over mobile, and it can also trigger a Lambda Function. Auto Scaling action is used for scaling an environment up by adding more instances or scaling an environment down by reducing the number of instances. EC2 action can be used for rebooting, stopping, terminating, or initiating a recovery on the instance.

An alarm can have three possible states:

- Alarm status displays OK when the metric is within the defined threshold
- Alarm status displays ALARM when the metric is outside of the defined threshold
- Alarm status displays INSUFFICIENT_DATA when the alarm is just configured, the metric is not available, or not enough data is available for the metric to determine the alarm state

Creating a CloudWatch alarm

The following steps describe the process of creating a CloudWatch alarm:

1. Open CloudWatch console by navigating to `https://console.aws.amazon.com/cloudwatch/` on your browser. It brings you to the CloudWatch dashboard.
2. Click on **Alarms** as shown in the following *Figure 7.2*:

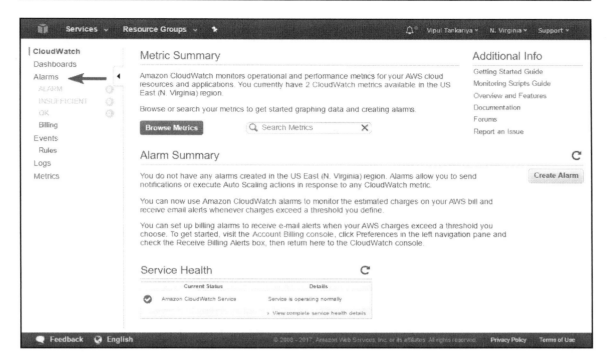

Figure 7.2: CloudWatch dashboard

3. Click on the **Create Alarm** button as shown in the following *Figure 7.3*:

Figure 7.3: Create Alarm

4. Click on **Per-Instance Metrics:** as shown in the next *Figure 7.4*. This window shows multiple categories of metrics depending upon the metrics you have in the account. For example, if you have EC2 instances in the account, it shows **EC2 Metrics:**, if you have ELB resources in the account, it shows **ELB Metrics** and similarly, it shows different categories of metrics for which you have resources in the account. Depending upon the requirement, you can select any of the category metrics as needed:

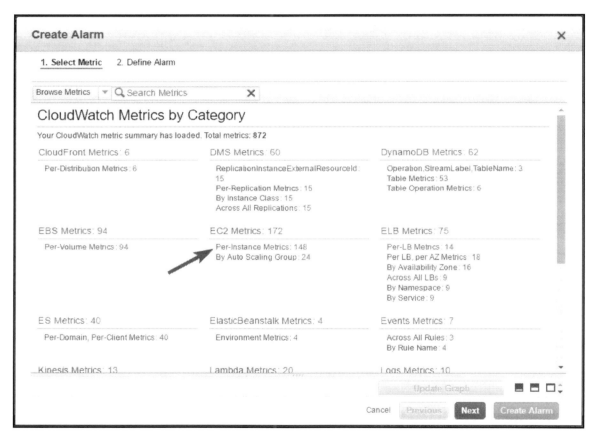

Figure 7.4: CloudWatch Metrics by Category

5. There are a number of metrics such as **CPUUtilization**, **NetworkIn**, **NetworkOut**, and so on. You can select any of these metrics as needed. For this example, select a metrics against an EC2 instance for **StatusCheckFailed_Instance** as shown in the following *Figure 7.5* and click on the **Next** button:

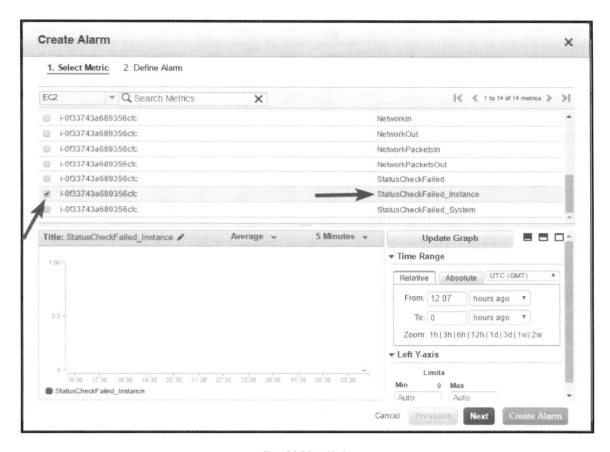

Figure 7.5: Select a Metrics

6. In the subsequent window, provide the alarm **Name**, **Description**, and threshold values:

Figure 7.6: Alarm Threshold

7. In the **Actions** section, action can be one or more from an SNS notification, Auto Scaling action, or an EC2 action. An SNS notification can be used to send an alert over mail or an SMS over mobile. Auto Scaling action is used for scaling an environment up by adding more instances or scaling an environment down by reducing the number of instances. EC2 action can be used for rebooting, stopping, terminating, or initiating a recovery on the instance. For this example, in the same window select the **+ EC2 Action** button which is shown as follows:

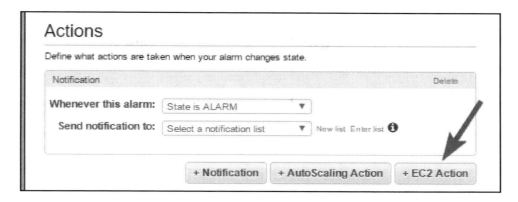

Figure 7.7: Actions

8. When you click **+EC2 Action**, it displays the following *Figure 7.8*. Select **State is ALARM** against **Whenever this alarm** line item and select **Recover this instance** from the action list:

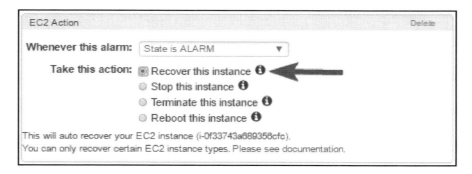

Figure 7.8: EC2 Action

9. If the instance is configured for basic monitoring, you have to select a minimum of 5 minutes or a higher period as shown in the next *Figure 7.9*. An instance can be configured for basic monitoring or it can be configured for advance monitoring. With basic monitoring, instance is monitored at an interval of 5 minutes. With advance monitoring, instance is monitored at an interval of 1 minute. Depending upon the consecutive alarm period selected in the **Alarm Threshold** section and the interval period for checking the alarm, **Alarm Preview** shows the total duration for actions to trigger:

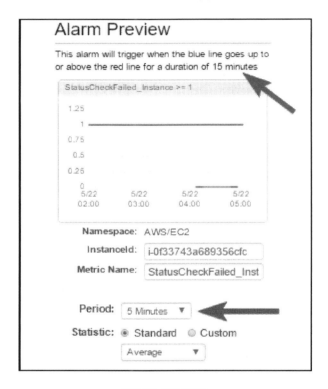

Figure 7.9: Alarm Preview

10. You can click on the **Create Alarm** button after selecting all the required options in the **Create Alarm** window, this creates the alarm. Once the alarm is created, it gets triggered based on the alarm status. In this example, alarm actions are triggered when the instance status is failed for three consecutive periods of 5 minutes each. Instance status failure alarm occurs when there is a hardware issue or any issue with the virtualization host where the EC2 instance is hosted on AWS. If you set this alarm, AWS automatically tries to recover the instance.

You can follow similar steps for creating different types of alarms based on a metric of your choice. For example, if you choose **CPUUtilization** metrics, you can either send an alert to an administrator when the CPU utilization breaches the threshold or you can perform Auto Scaling actions. Auto Scaling actions can add or remove instances in an Auto Scaling group to optimize the resources required for serving the traffic.

Billing alerts

Just as CloudWatch monitors other AWS resources, it can also monitor the monthly billing charges for an AWS account. You can set the threshold for billing. As soon as the billing amount reaches the threshold or shoots above the specified threshold, it notifies the specified administrators. You need to enable billing alerts before you can configure alerts on billing data. You can enable billing alerts from AWS account settings. Remember, only root user can enable the billing alerts, AWS IAM user cannot do that.

The process of enabling billing alerts is discussed as follows:

1. Log in to the AWS account with the root user credentials.
2. Click on the account name and **My Billing Dashboard** as shown in the following *Figure 7.10*:

Figure 7.10: Opening My Billing dashboard

3. From the left hand side pane, click on the **Preferences** and check **Receive Billing Alerts**. Optionally, you can also enable **Receive PDF invoice By Email** and **Receive Billing Reports:**

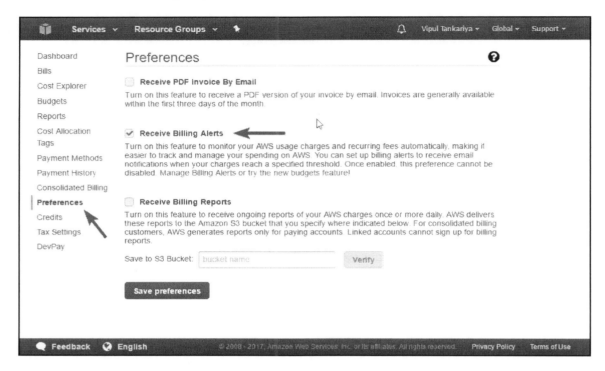

Figure 7.11: Billing dashboard preferences

CloudWatch dashboards

Amazon CloudWatch provides a customizable dashboard inside a web console. It can display a set of critical metrics together. You can create multiple dashboards wherein each dashboard can focus on providing a distinct view of your environment. You can create a custom dashboard to view and monitor the selected AWS resources from the same or different regions. It provides a way to get a single view of critical resource metrics and alarms for observing performance and health of the environment. It gives freedom to add, remove, move, resize, and rename the graphs, as well as change the refresh interval of selected graphs in a dashboard.

Monitoring types – basic and detailed

Amazon CloudWatch monitoring can be broadly categorized into two categories: basic monitoring and detailed monitoring.

- **Basic monitoring:** Basic monitoring is free and it collects data at a 5-minute time interval. By default, when you provision AWS resources, all AWS resources except ELB and RDS start with a basic monitoring mode only. ELB and RDS monitors the resources at a 1-minute interval. For other resources, optionally, you can switch the monitoring mode to detailed monitoring.
- **Detailed monitoring:** Detailed monitoring is chargeable and it makes data available at a 1-minute time interval. Currently, AWS charges $0.015 per hour per instance. Detailed monitoring does not change the monitoring on ELB and RDS which by default collates data at a 1-minute interval. Similarly, detailed monitoring does not change the EBS volumes which are monitored at 5-minute intervals.

You can enable detailed monitoring while launching an instance or after provisioning the instances. While launching an EC2 instance, it provides an option to enable detailed monitoring in the third step as shown in *Figure 7.12*. You can refer to Chapter 5, *Getting Started with Elastic Compute Cloud* which provides more details on how to launch an EC2 instance:

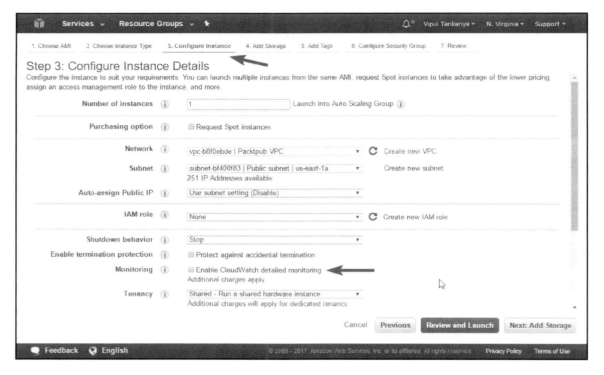

Figure 7.12: Enable detailed monitoring while launching an EC2 instance

For enabling detailed monitoring on an existing EC2 instance, follow these steps:

1. Navigate to https://console.aws.amazon.com/ec2/ for opening an EC2 console from your browser.
2. From the left hand side navigation pane, select **Instances**.
3. Once the instance list is launched, select an instance for which you want to change the monitoring type.
4. Select **Actions | CloudWatch Monitoring | Enable Detailed Monitoring**.
5. In the **Enable Detailed Monitoring** dialog box choose **Yes, Enable**.
6. Click on **Close**.

CloudWatch best practices

Here are the best practices that we can follow in CloudWatch:

- It is best practice to monitor AWS resources and hosted applications using CloudWatch. It helps in identifying performance bottlenecks and also helps in optimizing resource costs.
- It is recommended that you enable billing alerts for an AWS account. It helps to monitor the monthly costs and keep a tab on them.
- For better understanding of CloudWatch visualization, toggle the metrics between UTC and local time.
- By default, CloudWatch provides basic monitoring for resources and records metrics at a 5-minute interval. It is recommended thay you use detailed monitoring for critical resources, which records metrics at a 1-minute interval.
- Enable custom metrics where required. For example, you can enable memory monitoring on EC2 instance, which is not part of the default EC2 metrics.
- Create custom metrics for monitoring application behaviour and link them to CloudWatch. They provide better insight on the application. For example, custom metrics for monitoring JVM can be created for Java-based applications.
- Enable Auto Recovery and Auto Restart Alarms for your critical EC2 instances. It can automatically recover the instances from hardware related or virtualization host related issues on AWS. Also, Auto Restart Alarm can recover the instance from operating system level issues.
- It is recommended that you automate monitoring tasks as much as possible.
- Upload your critical custom logs to CloudWatch for quick statistical analysis.
- While creating custom metrics, verify log files on your EC2 instances with CloudWatch metrics to ensure that the right data synchronizes with CloudWatch.
- Enable SNS notifications for critical metrics threshold breach.
- AWS provides 10 alarms per month per customer for free. If you're intending to operate in a free tier, ensure that you do not exceed this limit.
- AWS supports a maximum of up to 5000 alarms for a customer in a region. If you are a heavy user of alarms, plan your alarms in such a way that all critical alarms are created before reaching the limit.

- CloudWatch does not validate actions while configuring them. Ensure that configured actions exist and are validated properly. For example, ensure SNS group has valid email IDs associated with it. Similarly, ensure that Auto Scaling group has a valid launch configuration associated with it.
- While testing an application associated with an alarm, you can temporarily disable alarms rather than getting flooded with alerts or unwanted actions being triggered.
- Some AWS resources may not send metric data to CloudWatch in certain conditions. For example, an EBS volume does not send data to CloudWatch if it is not attached to an instance. While trouble shooting any metrics availability issue, ensure that the required conditions are met for monitoring the metrics for the resource.

8

Simple Storage Service, Glacier, and CloudFront

Before we understand what Amazon S3 is, let us understand some basic concepts around storage. Storage services are usually categorized based on how they work and how they are used. Specifically, there are three broad types of storage services: block storage, file storage, and object storage:

- **Block storage**: In simple terms, block storage is a type of storage that is not physically attached to a server, but it is accessed as a local storage device just like a hard disk drive. At the backend, the storage service provider creates a cluster of disks, divided into a number of storage blocks. Each block is virtually connected to a server and treated as a local storage. The server operating system manages the block of storage assigned to it. For example, AWS EBS is a block storage type. When you provision a 100 GB EBS volume, a block of 100 GB is assigned from the cluster of disks to that volume. The EBS volume is associated with an EC2 instance. The volume is subsequently formatted and a filesystem is created on it. This volume is managed by the respective operating system installed on the EC2 instance for storing and retrieving data on it.

  As each block of storage is treated as a local disk, block storage works well for creating filesystems, installing operating systems, and databases. Even though the block storage architecture is comparatively complex, it provides high performance.

- **File storage**: File storage is also known as file-based storage. It is a highly available centralized place for storing your files and folders. You can access file level storage using file level protocols such as **Network File System (NFS)**, **Server Message Block (SMB)**, **Common Internet File System (CIFS)**, and so on. You can use file storage for storing and retrieving files and folders. Just like a block storage, you can edit files stored on file storage. Unlike block storage, you do not have access to format file storage, create a filesystem, and install an operating system on it. It is centrally managed by the service provider.
- **Object storage**: Object storage is a type of storage architecture wherein the data is stored as objects. Each object consists of the data, metadata, and a globally unique identifier. Metadata is data about data, and provides basic information about the data stored in an object. Unlike block storage and file storage, you cannot edit the data stored on object storage. If you need to edit a file, you have to create a new file and delete the old file (or keep multiple versions of the same file).

The following table provides a comparison between block storage, file storage, and object storage:

	Block storage	File storage	Object storage
Unit of transaction	Blocks	Files	Objects, files with metadata
How you can update	You can directly update the file	You can directly update the file	You cannot update the object directly. You create a new version of the object and replace the existing one or keep multiple versions of the same object
Protocols	SCSI, Fiber Channel, SATA	SMB, CIFS, NFS	REST/SOAP over HTTP/HTTPS
Support for metadata	No metadata support; it stores only filesystem attributes	No metadata support; it stores only filesystem attributes	Supports custom metadata

Usage	For creating filesystems, installing operating systems, and storing transactional data	Used as centralized and shared file storage	Used as a cloud storage for storing static files and data
Strength	High performance	Simple to access, highly available, and easy for sharing files	Scalable, available over the internet and distributed access
Weakness	Restricted to data center capacity	Restricted to data center capacity	Not suitable for in-place editing of data
Can you format it?	Yes, you get complete access to format it and manage filesystems on it	No, you cannot format it. It's a shared service wherein you have access just to manage data on it	No, you cannot format it. It's a shared service wherein you have access just to manage objects on it.
Can you install OS on it?	Yes, block storage can be used as a root volume and you can have an OS on it.	No, you cannot install an OS on it	No, you cannot install an OS on it
Pricing	You are charged based on allocated volume size irrespective of how much data you store on it	You are charged based on the amount of data you store on it	You are charged based on the amount of data you store on it
Example of specific storage service	EBS	Amazon **Elastic File System** (EFS)	S3

Amazon S3

S3 is a cloud-based object storage service from Amazon. It is highly scalable and makes it easy to access storage over the internet. You can use S3 for storing and retrieving virtually unlimited amounts of data at any time from anywhere. It provides you with access to a highly scalable, reliable, efficient, and low-cost storage infrastructure that is used by Amazon to run its own global network of websites.

S3 is ideally suggested for storing static content such as graphics files, documents, log files, audio, video, compressed files, and so on. Virtually any type of data in any file format can be stored on S3. Currently, the permissible object size in S3 is 0 bytes to 5 TB. Objects in S3 are stored in a bucket. A bucket is a logical unit in S3 that is just like a folder. Buckets are created at root level in S3 with a globally unique name. You can store objects and also folders inside a bucket. Any number of objects can be stored in each bucket. There is a soft limit of 100 buckets per account in S3.

S3 can be used for content storage and distribution, static website hosting, big data object store, backup and archival, storing application data, as well as for disaster recovery. Using Java Script SDK and DynamoDB, you can also host dynamic applications on S3.

The following section describes the concepts and terminologies used in S3:

- **Buckets**: A bucket is a logical unit in S3, just like a folder. It is a container wherein you can store objects and also folders. Buckets are created at root level in S3 with a globally unique name. Any number of objects can be stored in each bucket. For example, if you store an object named `books/acda.pdf` inside the `packtpub` bucket, then it is accessible using the URL `https://packtpub.s3.amazonaws.com/books/acda.pdf`.
- Buckets are generally used for organizing objects in S3. It is associated with an AWS account that is responsible for storing and retrieving data on the bucket. The account, which owns the bucket, is charged for data transfer. Buckets play a vital role in access control and paves the way for creating usage reports on S3.
- Buckets can be created in a specific region. You can enable version control on a bucket. If version control is enabled on a bucket, it maintains a unique version ID against each object stored in it.
- **Objects**: Objects are the basic entities stored in S3. Each object consists of the data, metadata, and a globally unique identifier. Metadata is data about data, and provides basic information about the data stored in an object. Metadata is stored in a set of name-value pairs, which describes the information associated with the object. For example, `Date Last Modified`, `Content Type`, `Content-Length`, and so on. There can be two types of metadata associated with an object: system-defined metadata and user-defined metadata.
- An object is identified with a unique key (name) within the bucket and a version ID if versioning is enabled on the bucket.

- **Keys**: A key is the name that is assigned to an object. It is a unique identifier or name for an object within a bucket. Every object in a bucket has only one key associated with it. The combination of a bucket, key, and its respective version ID uniquely identifies an object within a bucket. Every object within a bucket has a unique address for accessing it through a web service endpoint. The address URL consists of the bucket name, key, and a version number if versioning is enabled on the bucket.

Example: `https://packtpub.s3.amazonaws.com/books/acda.pdf`. In this example, `packtpub` is the name of the bucket and `books/acda.pdf` is the key as follows:

Figure 8.1: Object URL in S3

- **Region**: A region is a geographical region where Amazon S3 stores a bucket based on user preferences. Users can choose a region while creating a bucket based on the requirement. Ideally, a bucket should be created in the closest geographical region where the bucket is needed to be accessed. Choosing a closest region while creating a bucket optimizes latency while accessing the bucket, reduces costs, and complies with any regulatory requirements an organization may have.

Currently, Amazon has the following regions:

Region	Location of S3 servers
US East (N. Virginia)	Northern Virginia
US East (Ohio)	Columbus Ohio
US West (N. California)	Northern California
US West (Oregon)	Oregon
Canada (Central)	Canada
Asia Pacific (Mumbai)	Mumbai
Asia Pacific (Seoul)	Seoul
Asia Pacific (Singapore)	Singapore

Asia Pacific (Sydney)	Sydney
Asia Pacific (Tokyo)	Tokyo
EU (Frankfurt)	Frankfurt
EU (Ireland)	Ireland
EU (London)	London
South America (Sao Paulo)	Sao Paulo

S3 supported regions

When you create an object in a region, it is stored in the same region unless you explicitly copy it over to any other region:

- **S3 data consistency model**: Amazon provides two types of consistency model for S3 data when you perform various input/output operations with it: read-after-write consistency and eventual consistency.

The following table describes both of these data consistency models in S3:

Input/output operation	Data consistency model	Exception, if any
PUTS of new object	read-after-write consistency	S3 gives eventual consistency for HEAD or GET requests while retrieving the key name before creating an object
Overwrite PUTS and DELETES	Eventual consistency	No exception

Data consistency model

Amazon provides read-after-write consistency for PUTS of a new object. That means, if you create a new object in S3, you can immediately read it.

Amazon provides eventual consistency for overwrite PUTS and DELETES operations. That means, it takes a few seconds before the changes are reflected in S3 when you overwrite an existing object in S3 or delete an existing object.

Amazon replicates data across the region in multiple servers located inside Amazon data centers. This replication process provides high availability for data. When you create a new object in S3, the data is saved in S3, however, this change must replicate across the Amazon S3 regions. Replication may take some time and you may observe the following behavior:

- After you create a new object in S3, Amazon immediately lists the object keys within the bucket and the new object keys may not appear in the list
- When you replace an existing object and immediately try to read the object, Amazon may return old data until the data is fully replicated
- When you delete an object and immediately try to ready it, Amazon may read the data for the deleted object until the deletion is fully replicated
- When you delete an object in a bucket and immediately list the contents of the bucket, you may still see the deleted object in the content of the bucket until the deletion is fully replicated

Creating a bucket

The following steps describe the process of creating a bucket using the AWS Management Console:

1. Sign-in to your AWS account and go to the S3 console or visit `https://console. aws.amazon.com/s3/`. If you already have any buckets in the account, it displays a list of the buckets or the following *Figure 8.2* stating that you do not have any buckets in the account:

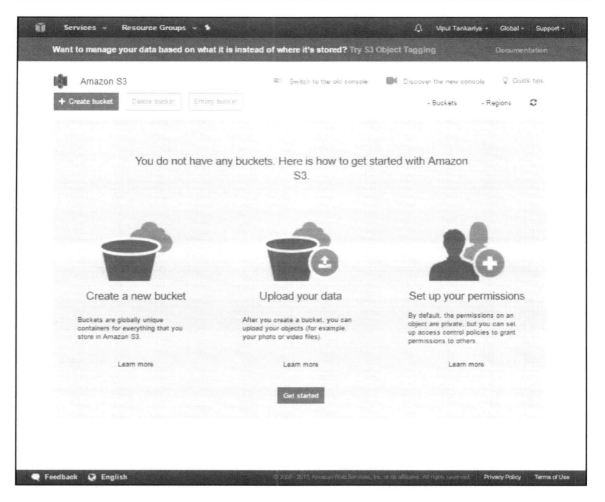

Figure 8.2: S3 console

2. Click on the **Create bucket** icon, as displayed in the following *Figure 8.3*:

Figure 8.3: Create bucket

3. Clicking on the **Create bucket** button, display a pop-up as shown in the *Figure 8.4*. Enter a DNS compliant bucket name. **Bucket name** must be unique across all existing bucket names in S3. Since S3 is a shared service, it is likely that you may not always get the bucket name you want as it might have been already taken by some one.

Select the appropriate region where you want to create the bucket from the drop-down menu as indicated in the following *Figure 8.4*. If you already have some buckets, you can **Copy setting from an existing bucket**. You can also click on the **Create** button if you do not want to follow the remaining steps. You need to set bucket properties and permissions later on, if you directly click on the **Create** button. To understand these steps, you can click on the **Next** button:

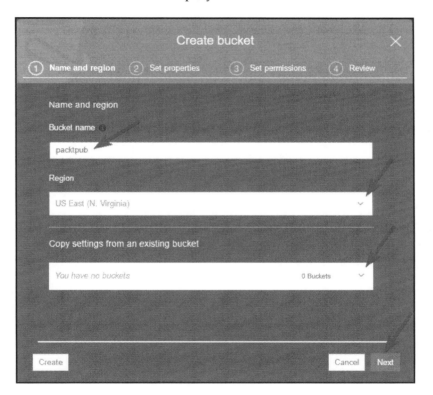

Figure 8.4: Create bucket screen

4. In the subsequent screen, as shown in the following *Figure 8.5*, you can set the required properties. You can see in the screen that by default **Versioning** is **Disabled**, **Logging** is **Disabled**, and there are no **Tags**. You can click on **Versioning** and **Logging** as required or add tags as needed. When you click on these items, it displays respective pop-ups as shown in the following *Figure 8.5*. You can set the required properties as needed:

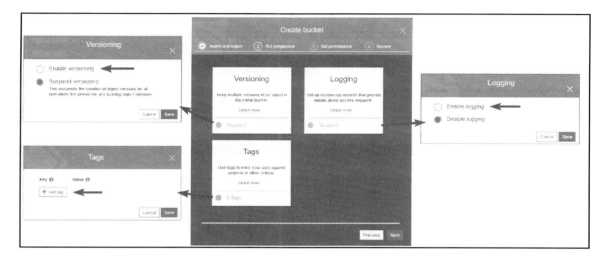

Figure 8.5: Bucket properties in Create bucket wizard

5. In the subsequent screen, as shown in the following *Figure 8.6*, you can set folder permissions. You can set individual user permissions, manage public permissions, and manage system permissions:

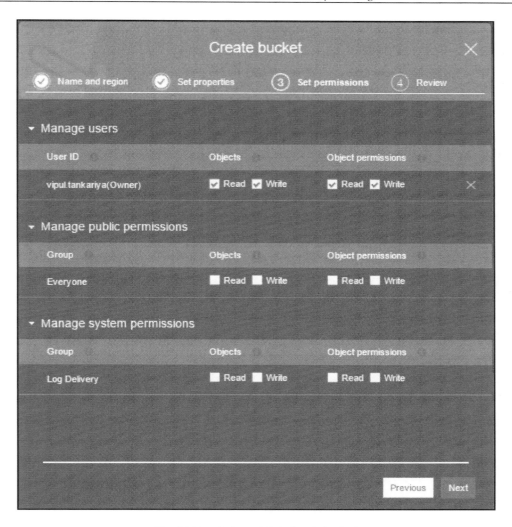

Figure 8.6: Manage bucket permission in Create bucket wizard

6. In the subsequent screen, as shown in the following *Figure 8.7*, review your selection. If required, you can edit your selection under individual categories. After reviewing everything, click on the **Create bucket** button. It creates a bucket as per the input given by you:

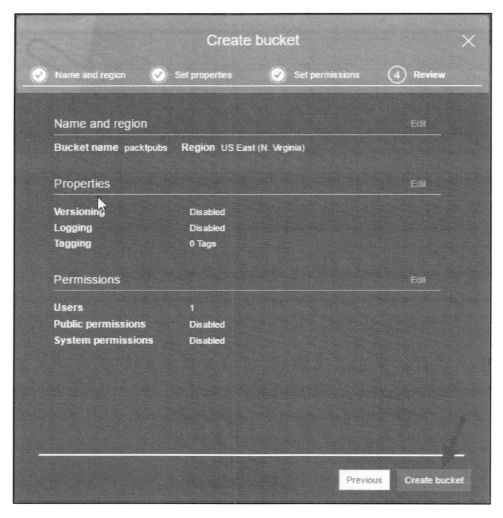

Figure 8.7: Review your steps in the Create bucket wizard

Bucket restriction and limitations

Bucket restrictions and limitations are listed as follows:

- You can create a bucket using the S3 console, APIs, or the CLI.
- Amazon imposes a soft limit of 100 buckets on an AWS account. You can increase this soft limit by raising a support request with Amazon.
- When you create a bucket, it is associated with the AWS account and the user you have used to create it. Bucket ownership cannot be transferred to another AWS account or another user within the same AWS account.
- There is no limit on the number of objects that can be created in a bucket.
- A bucket is created at the root level in S3; you cannot create a bucket inside a bucket.
- If you use an application that automatically creates a bucket, ensure that the application chooses a different bucket name in case the bucket name generated by the application already exists.

Bucket names should comply with DNS naming conventions as follows:

- Bucket names can range between 3 to 63 characters
- Bucket names must be in lowercase letters. They can contain number and hyphens
- Bucket names must start with a lowercase letter or a number and similarly, must end with a lowercase letter or a number
- Bucket names must not be given as an IP address, that is, `192.168.1.10`
- It is recommended to avoid using periods `(.)` in bucket names

Bucket access control

Each bucket in S3 is associated with an access control policy, which governs how objects are created, deleted, and enumerated within the bucket.

When you create an S3 resource, all S3 resources, including buckets, objects, lifecycle policy, or static website configuration, are by default private. Only the resource owner who creates the resource, can access that resource. After creating the resource, the resource owner can optionally grant permissions to other users using an access control policy.

There are two types of access control policy:

- Resource-based policies
- User policies

Access policies that you associate with buckets and objects are called resource-based policies. Bucket policies and **Access Control Lists (ACL)** are examples of resource-based policies. Access policies that you associate with users are called user policies. You can use a resource-based policy or user policy and at times a combination of both, to control access to your S3 resources.

Bucket policy

A bucket policy, generally, comprises of the following elements:

- **Resource**: This indicates Amazon S3 resources such as buckets and objects. While creating a policy, you can specify ARN to allow or deny permissions on that resource.
- **Action**: This indicates one or more actions that are either allowed or denied. For example, s3:GetObject specifies the permission to read the object data. Similarly, s3:ListBucket specifies the permission to list objects in the bucket.
- **Effect**: This specifies action type, either Allow or Deny access. If permission is not explicitly granted on a resource, by default, access is denied. When you explicitly Deny access, it ensures that the user cannot access the resource even if another policy grants access.
- **Principal**: This indicates the account or a user who is allowed or denied access to the resources mentioned in the policy statement. In a user policy, you may not need to specify a principal. A user policy implicitly applies to the associated user.
- **Sid**: This is an optional identifier known as **statement ID**, which is specified for the policy statement. Sid values must be unique within the policy statement.
- Here is an example of a bucket policy. The example policy allows the user Heramb following three permissions on the bucket named packtpubs:
  - s3:GetBucketLocation
  - s3:ListBucket
  - s3:GetObject

In the policy statement, `Account-ID` should be replaced with the AWS account number:

```
{
    "Version": "2012-10-17",
    "Statement": [
        {
            "Sid": "Statement1",
            "Effect": "Allow",
            "Principal": {
                "AWS": "arn:aws:iam::Account-ID:user/Heramb"
            },
            "Action": [
                "s3:GetBucketLocation",
                "s3:ListBucket",
                "s3:GetObject"
            ],
            "Resource": [
                "arn:aws:s3:::packtpubs"
            ]
        }
    ]
}
```

In the same policy, if you change the effect from `Allow` to `Deny`, it explicitly denies access to the user `Heramb` on the `packtpubs` bucket to perform the specific set of actions mentioned in the policy statement.

User policies

Access policies are associated with users or groups. Unlike a bucket policy, you don't need to specify `Principal` in a user policy. A policy is implicitly applied to the user with whom it is associated.

Example of user policy is as follows:

```
{
    "Version":"2012-10-17",
    "Statement":[
        {
            "Effect":"Allow",
            "Action":[
                "s3:ListAllMyBuckets"
            ],
            "Resource":"arn:aws:s3:::*"
        },
        {
```

```
            "Effect":"Allow",
            "Action":[
               "s3:ListBucket",
               "s3:GetBucketLocation"
            ],
            "Resource":"arn:aws:s3:::packtpubs"
      },
      {
            "Effect":"Allow",
            "Action":[
               "s3:PutObject",
               "s3:GetObject",
               "s3:DeleteObject"
            ],
            "Resource":"arn:aws:s3:::packtpubs/*"
      }
   ]
}
```

There are three parts to the preceding user policy example:

- The first part describes permission to list all the buckets using a
  ListAllMyBuckets action against arn:aws:s3:::*, which signifies all
  resources in S3 for the account
- The second part describes ListBucket and GetBucketLocation permissions
  on the packtpubs bucket
- The third part describes permissions to create, read, and delete objects in the
  packtpubs bucket

Once a user policy is created, it can be attached to a user or a group to grant them respective access specified in the policy.

Transfer Acceleration

When you need to transfer a very big amount of data between your on-premises environment and S3, time, efficiency, and the security of the data plays a very vital role. In such requirements, S3 Transfer Acceleration can be very handy. It provides a fast, easy, and secure way to transfer files between S3 and any other source or target of such data transfers. For Transfer Acceleration, Amazon uses CloudFront edge locations. CloudFront edge locations are spread across the Globe, which facilitates the Transfer acceleration process.

The scenarios in which you should use Transfer Acceleration are:

- You have a centralized bucket, which your end customers use from across the Globe for uploading data
- You regularly transfer GBs and TBs of data across continents
- If available bandwidth is underutilized while you transfer data to S3

Enabling Transfer Acceleration

The steps for enabling Transfer Acceleration are as follows:

1. Log in to the AWS Management Console and go to the S3 Console or browse to `https://console.aws.amazon.com/s3`.
2. Open the bucket on which you need to enable Transfer Acceleration.
3. Click on the **Properties** tab as shown in the following *Figure 8.8*:

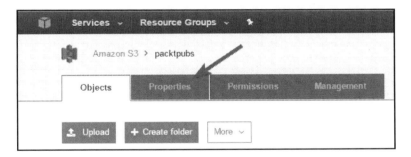

Figure 8.8:Selecting Bucket Properties

4. In the **Properties** tab, click on **Transfer acceleration**. It brings a pop-up to enable or suspend Transfer acceleration as shown in the following *Figure 8.9*. You can select **Enabled** in this pop-up to enable the Transfer Acceleration on the selected bucket. Click on the `Save` button after the selection is done:

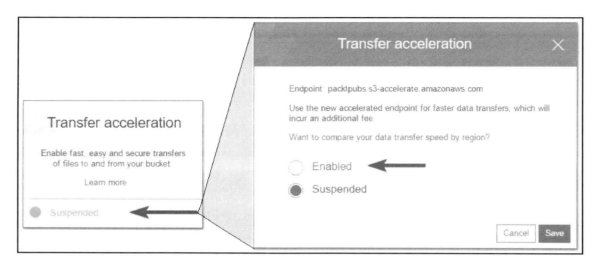

Figure 8.9: Enable Transfer acceleration on a bucket

Requester Pay model

Generally, when you create a bucket in S3, you pay for data storage and data transfer. Based on your usage, charges are added to the AWS account associated with the bucket. Amazon provides an option wherein you can configure your bucket as **Requester Pays** bucket. When you configure a bucket as a Requester Pays bucket, the requester pays for the requests they initiate to download or upload data in the bucket. You just pay for the cost of the data you store in S3:

- You can enable Requester Pays on a bucket when you want to share the data, but do not want to get charged for the requests received, data downloads, or upload operations
- When you enable Requester Pays, AWS does not allow you to enable anonymous access on the bucket
- All requests to Requester Pays buckets must be authenticated. When you enable authentication, S3 can identify requesters and charge them for their respective usage of the bucket

- If a system or application makes requests by assuming an IAM role, AWS charges the account where the assumed role belongs
- If you make calls to the bucket using an application, the request must include x-amz-request-payer in the header section if you make POST, GET, and HEAD requests
- If you make a REST request, you need to include x-amz-request-payer as a parameter in the request
- Requester Pays buckets do not support anonymous request, BitTorrent, and SOAP requests
- Amazon does not allow you to enable end user logging on a Requester Pays bucket and similarly, you cannot enable Requester Pays on a bucket where end user logging is enabled

Enabling Requestor Pays on a bucket

You can enable Requestor Pays a bucket in steps that are very similiar to those you followed in Transfer Acceleration:

1. Log in to the AWS Management Console and go to the S3 console or browse to https://console.aws.amazon.com/s3.
2. Open the bucket on which you need to enable Transfer Acceleration.
3. Click on the **Properties** tab as shown in the *Figure 8.8*.
4. Click on **Requester Pays** to enable it.

Understanding objects

Objects are the basic entities stored in S3. Amazon has designed S3 as a simple key, value store. You can store a virtually unlimited number of objects in S3. You can segregate objects by storing them in one or more buckets.

Objects consist of a number of elements, that is, key, version ID, value, metadata, subresources, and access control information. Let us understand these object elements:

- **Key**: Key is the name that is assigned to an object. It's just like a filename and can be used to access or retrieve the object.

- **Version ID**: If you enable versioning on a bucket, S3 associates a version ID with each object. The bucket may have one or more objects with the same key, but a different version ID. The version ID helps in uniquely identifying an object when there are multiple objects with the same key.
- **Value**: Value refers to the content or data that is stored on the object. It is generally a sequence of bytes. the minimum size of an object can be zero and the maximum 5 TB.
- **Metadata**: S3 stores reference information related to an object in its metadata in the form of name-value pairs. There are two types of metadata, that is, system-metadata and user-defined metadata. System-metadata is used for managing objects and user-defined metadata is used for managing information related to objects.
- **Subresources**: An object can have subresources associated with it. Subresources are defined and associated with objects by S3. There can be two types of subresources associated with an object, that is, ACL and torrent:
    - ACL contains a list of users and respective permissions granted to them. When you create an object, the ACL entry contains just an owner. Optionally, you can add more users with required permissions for each user.
    - Torrent is another subresource of an object. AWS supports the BitTorrent protocol. It is very simple to access S3 objects using a BitTorrent client. If you assign anonymous permission on an object, that object can be accessed by a BitTorrent client by referring to the object URL with `?torrent` at the end. Once an object URL is accessed with `?torrent` at the end of it, AWS automatically creates a `.torrent` file for that object. Subsequently, you can distribute the `.torrent` file to end users to access the object using BitTorrent client.
- **Access control information**: Amazon S3 enables you to control access on the objects you create using ACL, bucket policies, and user policies. Access control information is nothing but the information containing permissions in the form of ACL, a bucket policy, or user access policies.

Object keys

When you create an object in S3, you need to give a unique key name to the object in the bucket. A key name uniquely identifies an object in the bucket. When you browse a bucket in the S3 console, it displays a list of objects within the bucket. The list of names within the bucket are object keys.

An object key is a sequence of Unicode characters in UTF-8 encoding. A key name can be a maximum of 1024 bytes long.

Object key naming guide

Each application applies its own mechanism to parse special characters. It is recommended to follow best practices while naming an object key. These best practices provide maximum compliance with DNS, web safe characters, XML parsers, and various other APIs:

- An object key name consists of alphanumeric characters [0-9a-zA-Z] and special characters such as !, -, _ ., *, ', (,).
- S3 can store buckets and objects. It does not have any hierarchical structure; however, prefixes and delimiters used in an object key name allows S3 to use folders.
- Key name examples of how S3 supports folders:
  - `projects/acda-guide.xlsx`
  - `books/aws-networking.pdf`
  - `outlines/vpc.xlsx`
  - `help.txt`
- In the previously mentioned examples, S3 uses key name prefixes such as `projects/`, `books/`, `outlines/`. These key name prefixes with / as delimiter, enable S3 to represent a folder structure. The following *Figure 8.10* shows the folder structure in S3:

Figure 8.10: Folder structure in S3

When you open a folder, it displays objects inside the folder. The S3 console displays the bucket and folder in the breadcrumb as shown in the following *Figure 8.11*:

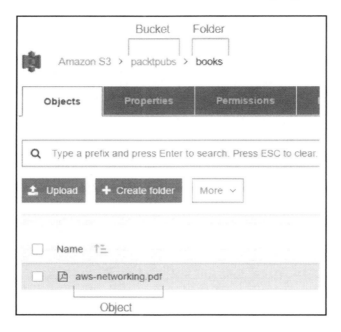

Figure 8.11: Objects inside a folder

Special characters in an object key name

The following is a list of special characters that require special handling if you use them in an object key name. Some characters may not be properly rendered by a browser or application. If you plan to include these characters in S3 object key names, it is recommended to build appropriate logic to handle them in your application.

Ampersand (&)	Dollar ($)	ASCII character ranges 00-1F hex (0-31 decimal) and 7F (127 decimal)
At (@)	Equals (=)	Semicolon (;)
Colon (:)	Plus (+)	Space - significant sequences of spaces may be lost in some uses (especially multiple spaces)
Comma (,)	Question mark (?)	

AWS recommends avoiding following characters in object key names.

Backslash (\)	Left curly brace ({)	Non-printable ASCII characters (128-255 decimal characters)
Caret (^)	Right curly brace (})	Percent character (%)
Grave accent / back tick (`)	Right square bracket (])	Quotation marks
Greater than symbol (>)	Left square bracket ([)	Tilde (~)
Less than symbol (<)	Pound character (#)	Vertical bar / pipe (|)

Object metadata

S3 stores reference information related to an object in its metadata in the form of name-value pairs. There are two types of metadata: system-metadata and user-defined metadata.

System-metadata

Amazon stores a set of system-defined metadata with every object in S3. For example, S3 stores the object creation date as well as size of the object in object metadata. There are two types of system-metadata, one wherein only S3 can change the value of metadata such as object creation date and size. There are other types of system-metadata such as storage class and server-side encryption that can be controlled by users based on selection.

The following table displays a list of system-defined metadata:

Name	Description	Can user modify the value?
Content-Length	Indicates object size in bytes	No
Content-MD5	Indicates a base64-encoded 128-bit MD5 digest of the object	No
Date	Indicates current date and time	No
Last-Modified	Indicates date of last modification on object. It can be the creation date if object is not modified after initial creation	No

`x-amz-delete-marker`	It is displayed against objects in a bucket where versioning is enabled. It indicates if an object is marked for deletion	No
`x-amz-server-side-encryption`	This metadata indicates if server-side encryption is enabled on an object or not.	Yes
`x-amz-server-side-encryption-aws-kms-key-id`	When `x-amz-server-side-encryption` is enabled on an object and it includes `aws:kms`, it indicates the ID of the KMS master encryption key that is used for the object	Yes
`x-amz-server-side-encryption-customer-algorithm`	It indicates if server-side encryption is enabled with customer-provided encryption keys (SSE-C)	Yes
`x-amz-storage-class`	It indicates what storage class is used for storing the object	Yes
`x-amz-version-id`	When versioning is enabled on a bucket, this metadata indicates version of the object	No
`x-amz-website-redirect-location`	When website hosting is enabled on an S3 bucket, this metadata indicates the redirection URL if request redirection is configured	Yes

User-defined metadata

Amazon S3 allows users to assign user-defined metadata to an object. When you create an object in S3, you can provide optional metadata as name-value pair.

User-defined metadata is generally used for associating additional information with an object. Such metadata can help in identifying objects. It can also be used for automating data management tasks using scripts. For example, a script may traverse through all the objects in a bucket and check for specific metadata on an object. If a desired key value pair of a metadata is assigned to an object, the script may further process the data in the object. User-defined metadata must begin with `x-amz-meta-`.

Here is how you can assign metadata to an object using the S3 console:

1. Log in to the AWS console and go to the S3 console.
2. Open the required bucket.
3. Click on the object on which you want to define metadata.
4. Click on the **Properties** tab.
5. Click on **Metadata**.
6. Click on **Add Metadata**.
7. Select **x-amz-meta-book-type** from the drop-down and type the remaining value in the **Key** as well as the **Value** box as shown in the following *Figure 8.12*.
8. Click on **Save:**

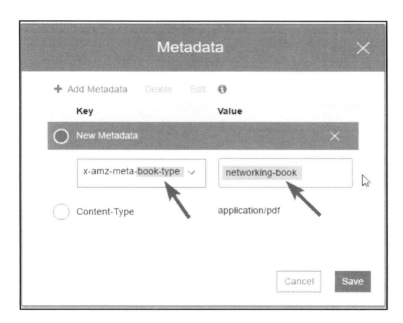

Figure 8.12: Add metadata to an S3 Object

Versioning

S3 allows you to keep multiple versions of an object in a bucket. Versioning can be enabled at bucket level. Once versioning is enabled, it protects you from accidental updates and deletes on an object. When you overwrite or delete an object, it keeps multiple copies with version numbers.

For example, when you enable versioning on a bucket called `packtpub`, for each action on an existing object in the bucket, S3 creates a new version and associates a version ID with it, as shown in the following table:

Object	Last activity	Version ID
developer-guide.pdf	Jun 12, 2017 9:42:02 AM	VAgAtLChtLoMkKF4ZVoq.NAGRRBA1hSp
developer-guide.pdf	Jun 11, 2017 8:41:23 AM	3mWAzx.l25VRt3.V.1ExutyOAEG1npX3
developer-guide.pdf	Jun 10, 2017 5:39:58 PM	hV_2iz3GgRvOTt1NoiL8KXg3FpLJkFI7

When you delete an object in a version-enabled bucket, S3 does not actually delete the object but instead adds a delete marker to it.

Enabling versioning on a bucket

The steps for enabling versioning on a bucket are as follows:

1. Sign in to your AWS Management Console and go to the S3 console on `https://console.aws.amazon.com/s3/`.

2. Click on the bucket on which you want to enable versioning, as shown in the following *Figure 8.13*:

Figure 8.13: Select bucket to enable versioning

3. Click on the **Properties** tab:

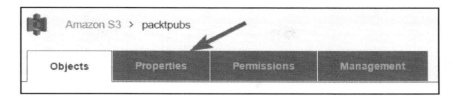

Figure 8.14: Select bucket properties

4. Click on **Versioning, Enable versioning,** and save the changes:

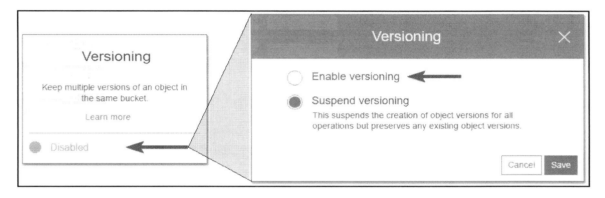

Figure 8.15: Enabling Versioning

Object tagging

S3 allows you to add tags to your objects. Tagging an object helps in categorizing the objects. Each tag is a key and value pair.

Example of tags on an object: Let's consider a scenario wherein an application processes data stored in an S3 bucket. While traversing through the objects in a bucket, it checks for a tag before processing the data in the object. In such scenarios, you may add the following tag to the objects:

```
Processed=True
```

Or:

```
Processed=False
```

The application may check for the tag in an object before processing the data in it. If the tag indicates `Processed=False` then the application should process the data stored in the object and change the tag to `Processed=True`.

You can add tags to an object from object properties in the S3 console. You can also add tags to an object using the AWS CLI as follows:

AWS CLI syntax for adding tags to an object:

```
aws s3api put-bucket-tagging --bucket <Bucket> --tagging
'TagSet=[{Key=<key>,Value=<value>}]'
```

Example:

```
aws s3api put-bucket-tagging --bucket packtpubs --tagging
'TagSet=[{Key=Processed,Value=True}]'
```

S3 storage classes

Amazon S3 provides a number of storage classes for different storage needs. Storage classes are divided into four main types, based on how they are used.

Storage classes include:

- S3 Standard storage
- S3-**Infrequently Accessed (IA)** storage
- S3 **Reduced Redundancy Storage (RRS)**
- Glacier

S3 Standard storage

S3 Standard storage is used as general-purpose storage for frequently accessed data. It provides high availability, durability, and high-performance storage for frequently accessed data. S3 Standard storage can be used in content distribution, cloud applications, big data analytics, mobile or gaming applications, and dynamic websites. The key features of S3 Standard storage are listed as follows:

- Provides low-latency and high-throughput performance
- Ensures 99.999999999% durability for objects

- Provides 99.99% availability in a year backed by Amazon S3 **Service Level Agreement (SLA)**
- Enables SSL encryption of data in transit using SSL
- Supports AES-256 encryption of data at rest
- Supports data lifecycle management for automatically migrating data from one class of storage to another

S3-IA storage

S3-IA storage is meant for data that is less frequently used, but needs to be available immediately when needed. It provides low-latency, high throughput, and durable data storage. It incurs relatively low per GB storage and retrieval costs. Being a low-cost and high performance storage, S3-IA is best suited for backups, disaster recovery, and any long-term storage needs. You can keep S3-IA class objects within the same bucket with other class objects. It also supports object lifecycle policies for automatically transitioning objects to other storage classes without requiring any modification of applications using objects. The key features of S3-IA are as follows:

- Suitable for long-term data storage, backups, and disaster recovery
- Provides low-latency and high-throughput performance same as S3 Standard
- Ensures 99.999999999% durability for objects
- Provides 99.99% availability in a year backed by Amazon S3 SLA
- Enables SSL encryption of data in transit using SSL
- Supports AES-256 encryption of data at rest
- Supports data lifecycle management for automatically migrating data from one class of storage to another

S3 RRS

As the name suggests, S3 RRS provides reduced levels of redundancy as opposed to standard S3 storage. It is suitable for storing noncritical and reproducible data. It is a highly available storage solution for content distribution as a secondary storage for data that is available elsewhere as well. It is ideal for storing thumbnails, transcoded media, or any other processed data that can be reproduced.

S3 stores RRS objects across multiple facilities and provides 400 times durability than a local disk drive; however, RRS objects are replicated relatively infrequently compared to S3 Standard objects:

- Provides reduced level of redundancy
- Comparatively cheaper than S3 Standard storage
- It is backed by Amazon S3 SLA
- Provides 99.99% durability in a given year
- Provides 99.99% availability in a given year
- Architected for absorbing data loss in a single facility
- Enables SSL encryption of data in transit using SSL
- Supports AES-256 encryption of data at rest

Glacier

Glacier is very low-cost, secure, and durable data archival storage. You can virtually store unlimited amounts of long-term data on Glacier for much cheaper rate. Glacier is ideal for storing long term data, backups, archives, and data for disaster recovery. Unlike S3, data stored on Glacier is not immediately available for access. You need to initiate a data retrieval request for accessing data on Glacier. For keeping the costs low and still making it suitable for different retrieval requirements, Glacier provides the following three options for data retrieval:

Data retrieval option	Minimum time for retrieval	Comparative costs
Expedited retrieval	1 to 5 minutes	$$$
Standard retrieval	3 to 5 hours	$$
Bulk retrieval	5 to 12 hours	$

Comparison of S3 storage classes and Glacier

The following table compares the three storage classes of S3 with glacier:

Description	Standard	Standard-IA	Reduced Redundancy	Glacier
Availability SLA	99.9%	99%	N/A	N/A
Concurrent facility fault tolerance	2	2	1	N/A
Availability	99.99%	99.9%	99.99%	N/A
Durability	99.999999999%	99.999999999%	99.99%	99.999999999%
First byte latency	milliseconds	milliseconds	milliseconds	Select minutes or hours
Lifecycle transitions	yes	yes	yes	yes
Minimum object size	N/A	128KB	N/A	N/A
Maximum object size	5TB	5TB	5TB	40TB
Minimum storage duration	N/A	30 days	N/A	90 days
Retrieval fee	N/A	per GB retrieved	N/A	per GB retrieved
SSL support	yes	yes	yes	yes
Storage class	object level	object level	object level	object level
Supported encryption at rest	AES-256	AES-256	AES-256	AES-256
Data retrieval time	immediately	immediately	immediately	minimum 3 to 5 hours
Recommended multipart upload size	100 mb	100 mb	100 mb	100 mb

Lifecycle management

Lifecycle management is a mechanism in S3 that enables you to either automatically transition an object from one storage class to another storage class or automatically delete an object, based on configuration. Lifecycle rules can be applied to a group of objects based on filter criteria set in the rule.

S3 allows you to configure one or more lifecycle rules, wherein each rule defines a specific action. There are two types of action you can define in Lifecycle rules:

- **Transition actions**: This defines when an object storage class changes from an existing storage class to target storage class. For example, you can define a rule for all object keys starting with `data/` in a bucket to transition from Standard storage to STANDARD_IA after 15 days. Similarly, you can define a rule to transition for all objects keys starting with `data/` from STANDARD_IA to Glacier storage. Let's say, you have a bucket named `packtpubs` and inside the bucket you have a folder named `data`. Within the data folder you have `.csv` files. In such scenarios, this transition rule applies to all the files present in the data folder.
- **Expiration actions**: This defines when objects expire. When objects expire, Amazon S3 automatically deletes them for you. For example, you can set a rule for object keys starting with `backup/` in a bucket to expire after 30 days. In such scenarios, all the files from the backup folder in a specific bucket expire after 30 days and are automatically deleted from S3.

Lifecycle configuration use cases

It is advisable to configure lifecycle rules on objects wherein there is absolute clarity on the lifecycle of the objects. The following are example scenarios wherein you can consider defining lifecycle rules:

- You have an application that generates and upload logs to an S3 bucket. The application does not need these logs after a week or a month. In such scenarios, you may want to delete these logs.
- You have a bucket wherein users and applications are uploading objects. These objects are frequently accessed for a few days. After a few days of uploading, these objects are accessed less frequently.

- You are archiving data to S3 and you need to keep this data only for regulatory compliance purposes. You need this data in an archive for a specific period of time to cater for regulatory needs and subsequently this data can be deleted.
- You are taking a back up of your databases on S3 and your organization has a predefined retention policy for this data. Based on the retention policy, you may want to keep the backup for a specific period and then delete it.

Defining lifecycle policy for a bucket

Object lifecycle rules can be configured using the Amazon S3 console, using the AWS SDK, or using the REST API. The following list describes the steps for configuring lifecycle rules using the Amazon S3 console:

1. Sign in to your AWS account and go to the S3 console on `https://console.aws.amazon.com/s3`.
2. Click on the bucket for which you want to create the lifecycle policy.
3. Click on the **Management** tab and then click on **+ Add lifecycle rule** as in following *Figure 8.16*:

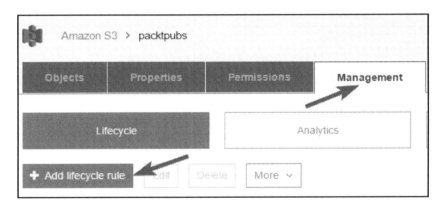

Figure 8.16: Adding lifecycle rule

4. In the subsequent window enter the name for your rule as shown in the following *Figure 8.17*. The rule name must be unique in the bucket. You cannot create more than one rule with the same name in a bucket.

5. Specify filter criteria for filtering the objects in a bucket. The filter criteria can be a string expression, for example `backup/`. You can also specify one or more object tags and limit the scope of the rule accordingly, for example, `backup/ | processed`. You can select a prefix and tags while entering the filter value as shown in the following *Figure 8.17*. You can initially enter prefix value `backup/` and then click on tag as shown in *Figure 8.17* for entering tag value. S3 user pipe (|) delimiter for separating prefix and tag in the rule:

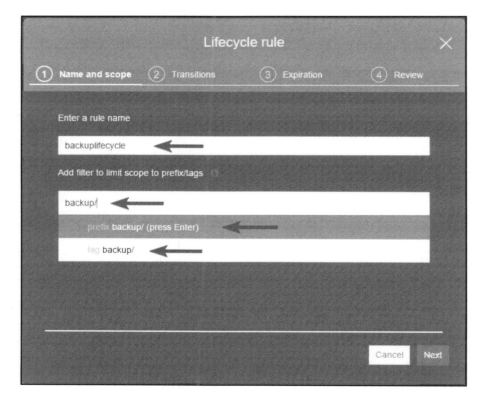

Figure 8.17: Enter lifecycle rule filter

6. In the next screen you can define whether the rule you create applies to the current and latest version of the object or the previous version. If versioning is enabled on the bucket, there may be more than one version of an object. Based on your preference you can select **Current version** or **Previous versions** or both as required:

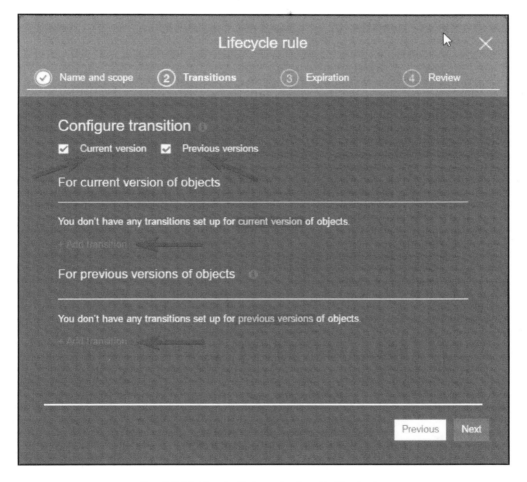

Figure 8.18: Select Current or Previous versions for applying lifecycle policy

7. Click on **+Add transition** as shown in the preceding *Figure 8.18*. It expands the options for selecting transition options as shown in the following *Figure 8.19*. Select the transition action from the combo box, either **Transition to Standard-IA after** or **Transition to Amazon Glacier after**. Also enter the number of days after object creation when an object should transition, as shown in the following *Figure 8.19*. You can also specify similar transition criteria for **Previous versions** of objects:

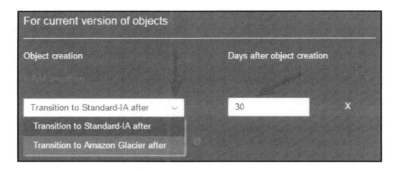

Figure 8.19: Object transition options for lifecycle policy

8. In the subsequent screen, configure expiration options. Similar to the previous steps, you can select either **Current version** or **Previous versions** or both of them as required. You can additionally select to clean up expired object delete markers and clean up incomplete multipart uploads:

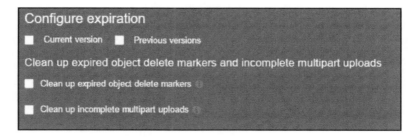

Figure 8.20: Configure expiration options

Based on the version selected, you get options for further selection. As shown in the following *Figure 8.21*, you can choose to expire the current version after a specific number of days. You can also choose to **Clean up expired object delete markers**. Delete markers are not created for expired objects. If you choose to expire objects, you cannot select the option to clean up delete markers. Optionally, you can opt to **Clean up incomplete multipart uploads** after a specific number of days. This is useful in a situation wherein you upload a large object to S3 and the upload process is abruptly closed. S3 can automatically clean up such incomplete multipart uploads based on the selection here:

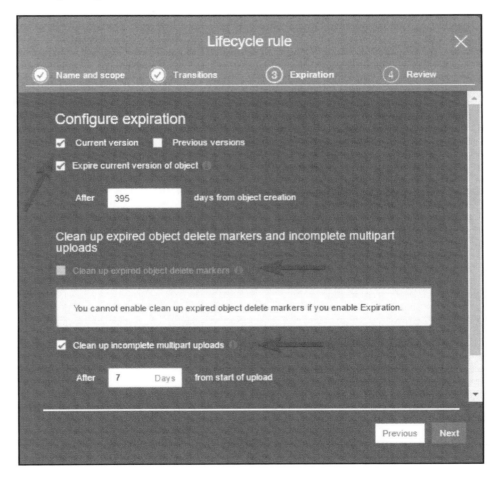

Figure 8.21: Provide additional data for expiration options

9. In the subsequent screen, review the **Lifecycle rule** and click on the **Save** button:

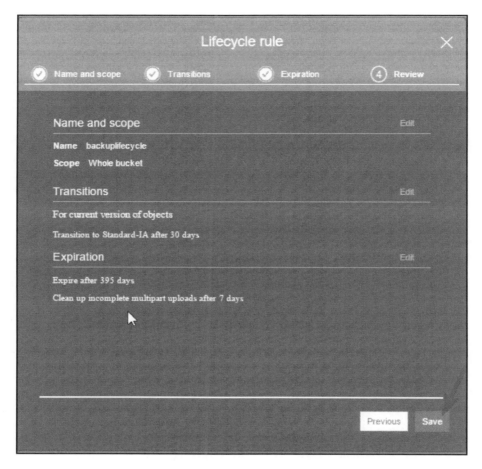

Figure 8.22: Review lifecycle rule and save

Hosting static website on S3

Amazon S3 allows you to host a static website. A static website can contain web pages with static content as well as client-side scripts. S3 does not support service side scripting and due to that, you cannot host a site with any server side scripting such as PHP, JSP, ASP.Net.

You can host HTML pages, CSS, client-side scripts like JavaScripts, and so on. Here's step-by-step process to enable static website hosting on an S3 bucket:

1. Sign in to your AWS console and go to S3 console at `https://console.aws.amazon.com/s3`.
2. Click on the bucket on which you want to enable static website hosting.
3. Click on **Properties** tab as shown in following *Figure 8.23*:

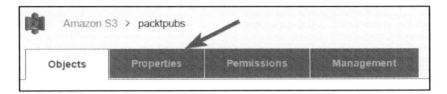

Figure 8.23: Bucket properties tab

4. Click on **Static website hosting** as shown in the following *Figure 8.24*:

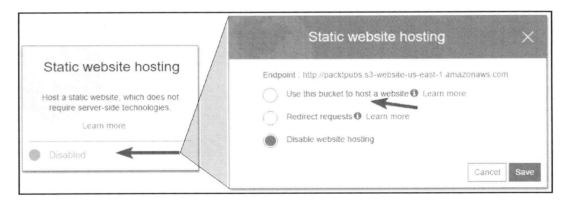

Figure 8.24: Enable static website hosting

5. Specify index and error document for your website as shown in following *Figure 8.25* and click on **Save**. You can also configure **Redirect requests** as needed and optionally specify **Redirection rules**. After configuring the options, you can browse your site from the endpoint URL of the bucket shown as follows:

Figure 8.25: Specify index and error documents for static website

Cross-Origin Resource Sharing (CORS)

Before understanding CORS, let us understand the significance of same origin policy. The cross-origin policy is a critical aspect of web application security model. In web application security model, by default, a web browser does not allow a script file associated with a web page to access data associated on a page in different hostname, domain, or port number. The purpose of cross-origin policy is to prevent any malicious script embedded on one page to access sensitive data on another web page.

For example, a script hosted in a page `books.html` on `www.packtpub.com`, can access **Document Object Model (DOM)** of any page within the same domain that is, `www.packtpubs.com`. If it tries to access DOM of a page hosted on another domain, the access is denied. Even if a page is hosted on a subdomain like `books.packtpubs.com`, tries to access DOM of another page on `projects.packtpubs.com`, it is denied the access. This is a way to maintain the security of the page based on cross-origin web application security model.

The CORS as the name suggests, is an exact opposite of cross-origin policy.

CORS is a mechanism for client web applications hosted on one domain to use resources hosted on another domain. You can host rich client-side web applications using CORS support on S3. You can selectively enable CORS support on S3 using S3 console, S3 REST API, and AWS SDKs.

Using CORS in different scenarios

- **Use case 1**: Suppose you host a website on an S3 bucket named `packtpubs`. End users can access this site using the URL: `https://packtpubs.s3-website-us-east-1.amazonaws.com`. Amazon's S3 API endpoint for the bucket is assigned as `packtpubs.s3.amazonaws.com`. If you try to make authenticated GET and PUT javascript requests on the pages hosted in the bucket using S3 API endpoint, these requests are blocked by a browser. You can allow such requests using CORS by explicitly allowing requests from `packtpubs.s3-website-use-east-1.amazonaws.com`.

- **Use case 2**: Consider a scenario wherein you host a web site on a bucket and need to load fonts from a different bucket. In such scenario, browser denies access to fonts bucket as it refers to a different origin. CORS can help in such scenario. You can explicitly allow cross-origin request from font bucket.

Configuring CORS on a bucket

For configuring CORS on a bucket, you need to create an XML document which defines the rule to allow cross-origin access on your bucket. You can either open full access to all domains or open access for specific origin domains or URL. For maintaining the security of your site, it is recommended to open access for specific domain. To further strengthen the security of the site, you can allow a specific HTTP methods like GET, POST, PUT, DELETE, and so on.

CORS configuration example XML

```
<!-- Sample policy -->
<CORSConfiguration>
  <CORSRule>
    <AllowedOrigin>*</AllowedOrigin>
    <AllowedMethod>GET</AllowedMethod>
    <MaxAgeSeconds>3000</MaxAgeSeconds>
    <AllowedHeader>Authorization</AllowedHeader>
  </CORSRule>
</CORSConfiguration>
```

The preceding policy, is the default policy that you see when you enable CORS on a bucket. It allows GET requests from all origin. `MaxAgeSeconds` is number of seconds browser can cache response from S3. `AllowedHeader`, by default, allows authorization requests. If you want to allow all headers, you can specify * in `AllowedHeader`. It is recommended to exercise caution while configuring CORS and create one or more rules to allow specific domain and HTTP actions. The following example is more specific:

```
<!-- Sample policy -->
<CORSConfiguration>
<CORSRule>
    <AllowedOrigin>http://www.packtpub.com</AllowedOrigin>
<AllowedMethod>PUT</AllowedMethod>
<AllowedMethod>POST</AllowedMethod>
<AllowedMethod>DELETE</AllowedMethod>
<AllowedHeader>*</AllowedHeader>
</CORSRule>
</CORSRule>
<CORSRule>
  <AllowedOrigin>*</AllowedOrigin>
  <AllowedMethod>GET</AllowedMethod>
</CORSRule>
</CORSConfiguration>
```

There are two rules in the preceding example, first rule allows PUT, POST, and DELETE actions from `http://www.packtpub.com`. The second rule allows GET requests from all origins with `AllowedOrigin` as *.

Enabling CORS on a bucket

1. Sign in to your AWS console and go to S3 console at `https://console.aws.amazon.com/s3`
2. Click on the bucket on which you want to enable CORS.
3. Click on **Permissions** tab as shown in following *Figure 8.26*:

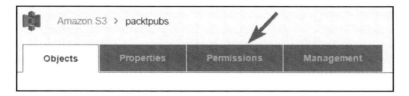

Figure 8.26: Bucket permission tab

4. Click on **CORS configuration** button as shown in the following *Figure 8.27*:

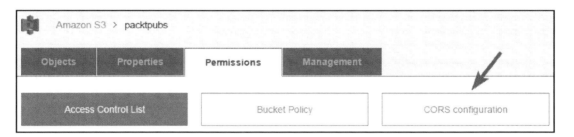

Figure 8.27: Click on CORS configuration

5. Edit the configuration XML as required and click on **Save** as shown in the following *Figure 8.28:*

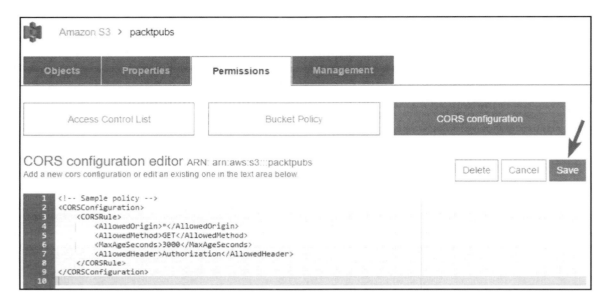

Figure 8.28: Edit CORS configuration and save

Cross-region replication

Amazon S3 enables you to automatically and asynchronously copy objects from a bucket in one AWS region to another AWS region. This is a bucket level feature, which can be configured on source bucket. In the replication configuration, you can specify destination bucket where you want your source bucket objects to be replicated. In the configuration, you can specify a key-name prefixes. S3 replicates all the objects starting with the specific key prefixes to destination bucket. Cross-region replication is generally used for compliance requirements, for minimizing latency in accessing objects, and for any operational reasons wherein compute resources in multiple regions need to access data from region specific bucket.

There are some requirements for enabling cross-region replication:

- Both, source as well as destination bucket must have versioning enabled on them
- Source and destination buckets must be in different regions
- S3 allows you to replicate objects from a source bucket to only one destination
- You must provide permission to Amazon S3 for replicating objects from source to destination bucket
- If source and destination bucket owners are different, source bucket owner must have permission for `s3:GetObjectVersion` and `s3:GetObjectVersionACL` actions
- If source and destination bucket are in different AWS accounts, source bucket owner must have access to replicate objects in the destination bucket

Enabling cross-region replication

1. Sign in to your AWS console and go to S3 console at `https://console.aws.amazon.com/s3`.
2. Click on the bucket on which you want to enable cross-region replication.
3. Click on **Properties** tab as shown in the following *Figure 8.29*:

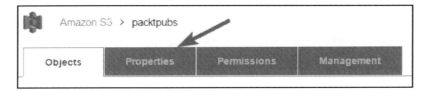

Figure 8.29: Bucket properties tab

4. Click on **Cross-region replication** and **Enable cross-region replication** as shown in following *Figure 8.30*:

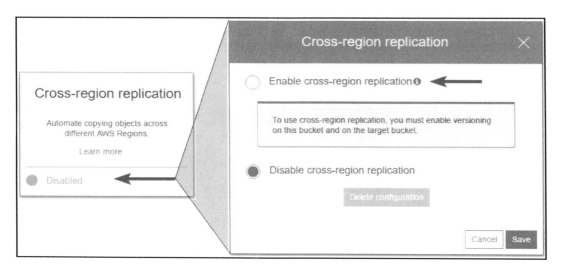

Figure 8.30: Enable cross-region replication

5. As shown in the following *Figure 8.31*, you can select **Whole bucket** or a specific key-name prefix in the bucket for source objects. You need to select a destination region from the drop-down menu. Depending upon available bucket in the destination region, which have versioning enabled, it displays a list of buckets for selection in destination buckets. In addition, you can also select an existing role or create a new role for the cross-region replication on the bucket:

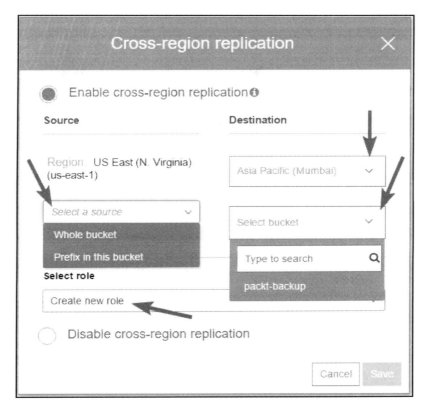

Figure 8.31: Configure cross-region replication</span>

9
Other AWS Storage Options

AWS offers a variety of highly available, scalable, reliable, and secure storage services to address various organizational needs. It provides a rich web console for all of the services, which is easy to access and navigate. It's easy to use UI complements efficient services for quickly performing day-to-day administrative. AWS also provides a set of API and CLI interfaces. You can use API and CLI to perform advanced operations or to automate various tasks using customized applications and scripts. The following table describes a number of storage and backup services provided by AWS.

AWS service	Description
Amazon S3	S3 is a cloud-based object storage over the internet. It is ideally suggested for storing static content such as graphics files, documents, log files, audio, video, compressed files, and so on. Virtually, any type of data in any file format can be stored on S3. Currently, permissible object size in S3 is 0 bytes to 5 TB. Objects in S3 are stored in a bucket. A bucket is a logical unit in S3 which is just like a folder. Buckets are created at root level in S3 with a globally unique name. You can store objects and also folders inside a bucket. Any number of objects can be stored in each bucket. There is a soft limit of 100 buckets per account in S3. **Common usage:**S3 can be used for content storage and distribution, static website hosting, big data object store, backup and archival, storing application data as well as for DR. Using Java Script SDK and DynamoDB, you can also host dynamic applications in S3.

Amazon Glacier	Glacier is a highly secure, durable, and a very low-cost cloud storage service for archiving data and taking long-term backups. Each file or an object stored in Amazon Glacier is called an archive. These stored archives are immutable, which means that contents of the archive cannot be modified. If required, another version of the archive can be stored and the existing version can be deleted. Size of each archive can range from 1 byte to 40 TB. With the help of the S3 lifecycle rules, objects from S3 can be automatically transferred to Glacier. These archives can be logically isolated in containers called vaults. A maximum of 1,000 vaults per account per region can be created. A few important characteristics: • Very economical for storing long term archival data, which is rarely accessed • Retrieval incurs charges and may take a minimum of 3 to 4 hours or more depending on the size of the data • Amazon charges early deletion fees if data is deleted within three months from the date of storing **Common usage**: Glacier can be mainly used for data archival. It is widely used for media asset archiving, healthcare information archiving, regulatory and compliance archiving, scientific data storage, digital preservation, magnetic tape replacement, and so on. It is rarely retrieved for audit or other business purposes.
Amazon EFS	AWS EFS is a simple to use and scalable file storage, which can be used with EC2 instances. It is a fully managed storage service from AWS which can be used for storing GBs to TBs of data. EFS volumes can be mounted and accessed by multiple EC2 instances at the same time. It uses the **Network File System versions 4.1 (NFSv4.1)** protocol. When using any EFS volume for the first time, you simply need to mount and format it to the desired filesystem. Subsequently, you can mount this volume on other EC2 instances directly and start using it. EFS volumes can also be accessed from on-premise environments using Direct Connect. You cannot access it from an on-premise environment over VPN connectivity. EFS is available in two modes, General Purpose mode and Max I/O mode. **Common usage**: EFS is designed to provide very high disk throughput. It can be used for big data and analytics, media, content management, web serving, and home directories.

Amazon EBS	EBS is a persistent, block-level storage service from Amazon. Persistent storage is a type of storage which retains the data stored on it even after power to the device is turned off. Block level storage is a type of storage which can be formatted to support a specific filesystem like NFS, NTFS, SMB, or VMFS. EBS volumes can be attached to an EC2 instance. Because of its persistent nature, data on EBS volume remains intact even after restarting or stopping an EC2 instance. There are five variants of EBS: 1) General Purpose SSD (gp2) 2) Provisioned IOPS SSD (io1) 3) Throughput optimized HDD (st1) 4) Cold HDD (sc1) 5) Magnetic (Standard) Each of these variants, differs in terms of price and performance. EBS volumes are connected as a network storage to an EC2 instance. It can be sized from 1 GB to 16 TB. You can take a snapshot of an EBS volume. A Snapshot is a point-in-time backup of an EBS volume. Snapshots can be used to restore the volume as and when required. **Common usage**: EBS volumes can be used as a root partition and for installing operating systems. It is also used for storing enterprise applications, application data, and databases.
Amazon EC2 instance store	Instance store is a temporary block-level storage service from Amazon. Unlike EBS, instance store is temporary in nature. Data stored in instance store volume is deleted when EC2 instance is either restarted, stopped, or terminated. Instance store volumes are directly attached to the underlying hosts where an EC2 instance is provisioned. Instance store volumes are faster in comparison to EBS, however, it is a temporary data store. Performance of the instance store volume attached to an EC2 instance, size of each of the volumes, and the number of such volumes that can be attached to an EC2 instance, depending on the EC2 instance type. **Common usage**: It is widely used to store swap files, temporary files, or in applications where good disk throughput is required but data persistence is not required.

AWS Storage Gateway	AWS Storage Gateway is a hybrid storage service which connects on-premise environments with cloud storage using a software appliance. It seamlessly connects on-premise environments with Amazon's block-level and object-level storage services such as EBS, S3, and Glacier. Storage Gateway uses standard storage protocols such as NFS and iSCSI. It provides low-latency for exchanging data from on-premise to S3, Glacier, or EBS volumes and vice versa. Storage Gateway can provide high performance for frequently accessed data by caching them at source in on-premise environment. **Common usage**: Storage Gateway can be configured for use as a file server in conjunction with S3. It can also be used as a virtual tape library for backup on S3 and virtual tape shelf for archival on Glacier. It can also be configured to be used as a local iSCSI volume. Storage Gateway can also be handy for transferring data from on-premise environments to AWS or transferring the data from AWS to on-premise environments.
AWS Snowball	AWS Snowball is a petabyte-scale level data transport solution that uses physical appliances to transfer large-scale of data from on-premise environments to the AWS cloud and vice versa. A single Snowball appliance can transport up to 80 TB of data. Snowball comes in two sizes, 50 TB and 80 TB. Data can be copied over to multiple physical appliances and transported to and from an AWS. Transferring large scale data over the internet can take a significant amount of time depending upon the size of data. The purpose of the Snowball service is to minimize the data transfer time by transferring the data using a physical medium rather than transferring data over the internet. Snowball can efficiently compress, encrypt, and transfer data from the on-premise host to the intended Snowball device. Once the data is copied over to one or more snowball devices, these devices are transported back to the nearest AWS data center. Subsequently, AWS transfers data from Snowball devices to S3. **Common usage**: Snowball is used for rapidly and securely transferring bulk data between on-premise data centers and the AWS cloud at a very economical rate.

AWS Snowmobile	AWS Snowmobile is an exabyte-scale data transport solution that uses physical containers to transfer extremely large-scale of data from on-premise environment to the AWS cloud and vice versa. A Snowmobile container literally comes in a truck which can transfer up to 100 PB of data per snowmobile. The truck carries a high cube shipping container which is 45 foot long, 8 foot wide, and 9.6 foot tall. If your data is more than 100 PB, you can ask Amazon for more than one Snowmobile. At a time, more than one Snowmobile can be connected to the on-premise network for transferring data. When connected to an on-premise network, Snowmobile appears as a standard NFS mounting point on the network. It may require up to 350 KW of power supply. Once the data is transferred from the on-premise network to the Snowmobile, it returns to the nearest AWS data center in the region and subsequently, the data is transferred to the S3 of the respective customer account. **Common usage**: Snowmobile is used for rapidly and securely transferring extremely large scale data between the on-premise data center and the AWS cloud at a very economical rate.
Amazon CloudFront	Amazon CloudFront is a **Content Delivery Network (CDN)** offered by AWS. It is a system of distributed servers spread across edge locations. It is mainly used for caching static content such as web page, stylesheets, client-side scripts, images, and so on. It can also speed up dynamic content distribution. When a user hits a URL which is served through CloudFront, it routes the user request to the nearest edge location. The nearest edge location gives minimum latency in serving the request and provides the best possible performance to the user. **Common usage**: CloudFront is used for providing seamless performance on delivery of a website or web application for a user base spread across multiple geographic locations. It can be used for distributing software or other large files, streaming media files, offering large downloads, and delivering live events.

S3, Glacier, EBS, EC2 instance store, and CloudFront are elaborated in other relevant chapters. Subsequent section of this chapter touches up on EFS, AWS Storage Gateway, AWS Snowball, and AWS Snowmobile.

Amazon EFS

AWS EFS is a simple to use and scalable file storage which can be used with EC2 instances. It is a fully managed storage service from AWS which can be used for storing GBs to TBs of data. EFS volume can be mounted and accessed by multiple EC2 instances at the same time. It uses the NFSv4.1 protocol. When using any EFS volume for the first time, you simply need to mount and format it to the desired file system. Subsequently, you can mount this volume on other EC2 instances directly and start using it. EFS volumes can also be accessed from an on-premise environment using Direct Connect. You cannot access it from on-premise environment over VPN connectivity. EFS is available in two modes, General Purpose mode and Max I/O mode.

In the industry, it is a common requirement to share file systems across the network, which be used as a common data source. EFS is a simple, secure, fully managed, scalable, and reliable block storage, to fulfill common file storage requirements. For using EFS with Linux EC2 instance, you may require installing the latest NFS packages. AWS recommends using the NFSv4.1 client on EC2 instances. Unlike EBS, EFS does not require provisioning a fixed volume size in advance. Being a managed service, you can store as much data as you need and pay only for what you use.

 Currently, EFS does not support Windows-based EC2 instances.

An EFS volume is created at the VPC level. At the time of creating an EFS volume, you can specify the AZ from where it can be accessed. EC2 instances from all selected AZ within the same VPC can access the EFS volume. Optionally, you can add tags to your EFS volume. It is recommended to provide a relevant and meaningful name to your EFS volume along with tags for better identification and reference. While creating an EFS volume, it is essential to select the type of EFS volume. Types of EFS volume are General Purpose and Max I/O. The default EFS volume type is General Purpose. Once an EFS volume is successfully created, it returns a DNS endpoints. You can mount the EFS volumes on an EC2 instance or on-premises environment using the endpoint. Remember, you can mount EFS volume on an on-premise network only if you use Direct Connect.

Successful creation of an EFS volume also creates mount points in each AZ. EFS carries properties such as mount target ID, the file system ID, private IPv4 address, the subnet ID in which it is created and the mount target status. It is possible to mount EFS volume using a DNS name. The following *Figure 9.1* elaborates an EFS:

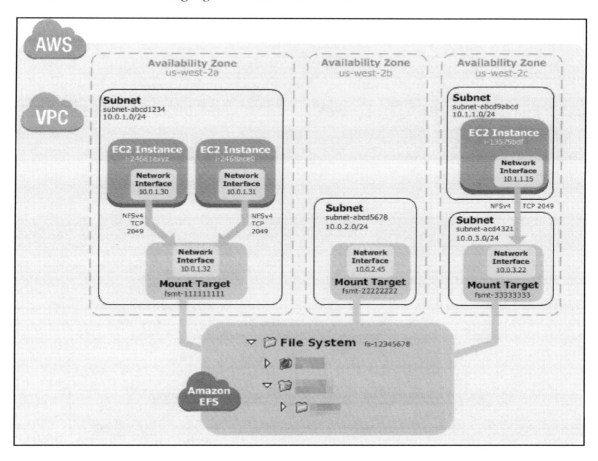

Figure 9.1: EFS

Reference URL: https://docs.aws.amazon.com/efs/latest/ug/how-it-works.html

An EC2 instance does not require a public or elastic IP to mount an EFS volume. You can enable or disable any existing EFS volume as required. You can perform all such changes from the **Manage file system access** option. Once you delete any EFS volume, it cannot be recovered.

Snapshots can be created for EFS volumes. It is also possible to design a backup solution using AWS Data Pipeline for copying data from one EFS volume to another EFS volume. You can also configure a copy operation schedule.

AWS Storage Gateway

AWS Storage Gateway is a hybrid storage service provided by Amazon. With Storage Gateway services, your on-premises applications can seamlessly use AWS cloud storage. The following are some of the important points of AWS Storage Gateway:

- AWS Storage Gateway connects on-premise software appliances with the AWS cloud storage to provide a seamless integration experience and data security between the on-premises data center and the AWS storage services
- It is a scalable and cost-effective storage solution which also maintains data security
- It provides an iSCSI interface, which can be used to mount a volume as a local drive for easily integrating it with the existing backup applications
- AWS Storage Gateway uses incremental EBS snapshots for backing up data to AWS
- AWS provides a VM image for running Storage Gateway on an on-premise data center and you can also run it as an EC2 instance on AWS and in case of any issue, such as if the on-premise data center goes offline, you can deploy the gateway on an EC2 instance
- You can use a Storage Gateway hosted on an EC2 instance for DR, data mirroring, and as an application storage
- By default, Storage Gateway uploads data using SSL and provides data encryption at rest using AES-256 when the data is stored on S3 or Glacier
- Storage Gateway compresses data in-transit and at-rest for minimizing the data size

AWS Storage Gateway provides three types of solutions: file gateways, volume gateways, and tape-based gateways. A file gateway creates a file interface into Amazon S3. It allows you to access S3 using the **Network File System (NFS)** protocol. When using volume gateways, you can mount a volume as a drive in your environment. Tape-based gateways can be used similarly to a tape drive for backup.

File gateways

A file gateway creates a file interface into Amazon S3. It allows you to access S3 using the NFS protocol. When you opt for a file gateway, a software appliance is hosted in the on-premise environment on a virtual machine running on VMware ESXi. Once the file gateway is created, it enables you to directly access S3 objects as files using an NFS volume mounted on a server.

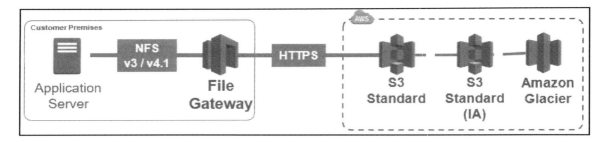

Figure 9.2: File gateway

Here is what file gateways can do for you:

- It allows you to directly store files on S3 using the NFS 3 or NFS 4.1 protocol
- You can directly retrieve files from S3 using the same NFS mount point
- It also allows you to manage S3 data with lifecycle polices, manage cross-region replication, and enable versioning on your data

Volume gateways

When you create a volume gateway, it creates a cloud-backed storage volume, which you can mount as iSCSI devices on your on-premises servers where iSCSI stands for **Internet Small Computer System Interface**. Volume gateways stores all data securely on AWS. There are two types of volume gateway, which determine how much data is stored on-premises and how much data is stored on AWS storage and are discussed as follows:

Gateway–cached volumes

Cached volumes enable you to store complete data on S3 and cache a copy of only frequently used data on on-premise. By reducing the amount of data stored on on-premise environment, you can reduce the overall storage cost. It also boosts performance by providing low-latency access to frequently accessed data using a cache.

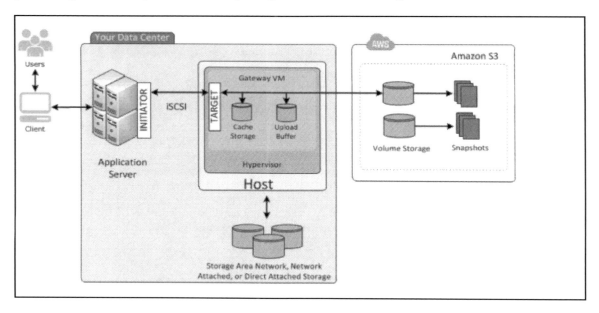

Figure 9.3: Gateway-cached volumes

The key features of gateway-cached volumes are as follows:

- A cached volume stores data in S3 and serves as a primary data storage
- It creates a local copy of frequently accessed data, which provides low-latency access for subsequent data access requests from applications
- By reducing the amount of data stored on an on-premise environment, you can reduce the overall storage cost
- You can create up to 32 gateway-cached volumes in a single storage gateway
- You can store from 1 GiB to 32 TiB in each volume with a maximum storage volume limit of 1,024 TiB (1 PiB)
- You can attach gateway-cached volumes as iSCSI devices on on-premise application servers
- You can take incremental snapshots of gateway-cached volumes
- Gateway-cached volume snapshots are stored on S3 as EBS snapshots
- Gateway-cached volume snapshots can be restored as gateway storage volume or you can create an EBS volume out of them and use it on an EC2 instance
- A maximum size of an EBS volume created out of a snapshot is 16 TiB and you cannot create an EBS volume out of the snapshot if it is more than 16 TiB in size
- AWS stores gateway-cached volume data and snapshots in Amazon S3 and the data is encrypted at rest with **server-side encryption** (**SSE**); you cannot access the data with S3 API or any other tools
- Gateway VM allocates storage in two parts:
  - Cache storage
    - It serves as on-premise durable storage
    - It caches the data locally before uploading it to S3
    - It provides low-latency access to frequently accessed data
  - Upload buffer
    - Upload buffer serves as a staging location prior to uploading the data to s3
    - It uploads data on an encrypted SSL connection to AWS and stores it in an encrypted format on S3

Gateway–stored volumes

You can use gateway-stored volumes when you need low-latency access to your entire data set. It stores all your data locally first and then asynchronously takes a point-in-time backup of this data as a snapshot to S3. It is generally used as an inexpensive off-site backup option for DR.

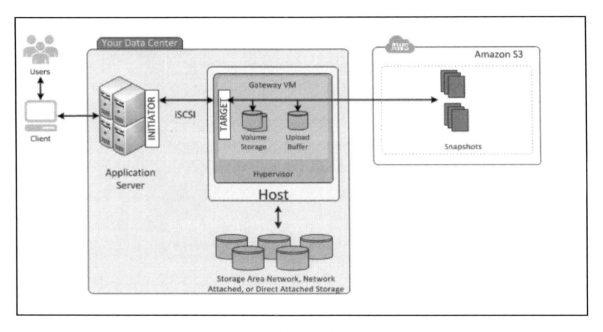

Figure 9.4: Gateway stored volume

The key features of a gateway-stored volume are as follows:

- It maintains the entire data set locally, providing low-latency access to the data
- It stores all your data locally first and then asynchronously takes a point-in-time backup of this data as a snapshot to S3
- You can attach gateway-stored volumes as iSCSI devices on on-premise application servers
- It supports up to 12 gateway-stored volumes per storage gateway applications
- Each gateway stored volume can be from 1 GiB to 16 TiB in size with a total volume storage limit of 192 TiB

- Gateway-stored volumes can be restored as an EBS volume on EC2 instance
- Gateway-stored volume snapshots can be restored as gateway storage volume or you can create an EBS volume out of it and use it on an EC2 instance
- A maximum size of an EBS volume created out of a snapshot is 16 TiB and you cannot create an EBS volume out of the snapshot if it is more than 16 TiB in size
- AWS stores gateway-stored volume data and snapshots in Amazon S3 and the data is encrypted at rest with SSE; you cannot access the data with S3 API or any other tools
- Gateway VM allocates storage in two parts:
    - Volume storage
        - It is used for storing actual data
        - You can map it to an on-premise **DAS (Direct-Attached Storage)** or **SAN (Storage Area Network)**
    - Upload buffer
        - Upload buffer serves as a staging location, before uploading the data to S3
        - It uploads data on an encrypted SSL connection to AWS and stores it in an encrypted format on S3

Tape-based storage solutions

A tape gateway serves as a replacement for an on-premise tape drive for backup purposes. It stores data on Amazon Glacier for long-term archival. It provides a virtual tape, which can scale based on requirement. It also reduces the burden of managing the physical tape infrastructure.

There are two types of tape-based storage solutions: **Virtual Tape Library (VTL)** and **Virtual Tape Shelf (VTS)**.

VTL

VTL is a scalable and cost effective virtual tape infrastructure, which seamlessly integrates with your existing backup software.

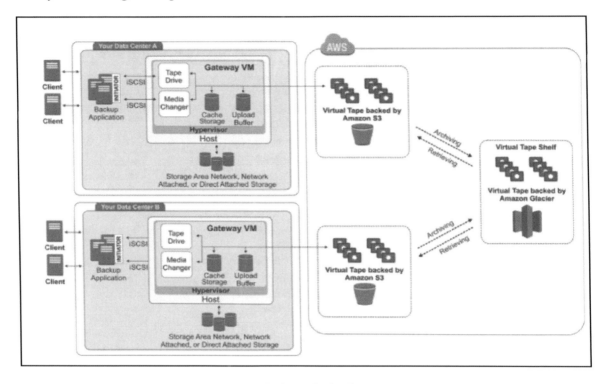

Figure 9.5: Gateway-Virtual tape library

- It provides a low-cost and long-duration archival option in Glacier.
- It provides a virtual tape infrastructure, which can scale based on requirements. It also reduces the burden of managing the physical tape infrastructure.
- It allows you to continue using your existing tape-based backup software for storing data on virtual tape cartridges, which can be created on a gateway-VTL.
- Each gateway-VTL is equipped with preconfigured media changer and tape drives. These are made available to existing backup applications as iSCSI devices. You can add tape cartridges as needed for archiving the data.

- A Gateway VTL contains the following components :
    - Virtual tape
        - Virtual tape emulates a physical tape cartridge wherein the data is stored in AWS storage solutions
        - You can have up to, 1500 tapes in each gateway or up to 150 TiB of total tape data
        - Each tape can store from 100 GiB to a maximum of 2.5 TiB of data
    - VTL
        - VTL emulates a physical tape library wherein the data is stored in S3
        - When a backup software writes data to the gateway, at first the data is stored locally and, subsequently, asynchronously uploaded to virtual tapes in S3
    - VTS
        - VTS works just like an offsite tape holding facility
        - In VTL, data is stored on S3 whereas VTS stores data in Glacier
        - As it uses Glacier for data archival, it becomes an extremely low-cost data archival option
        - VTS resides in the same region where the Storage Gateway is created and there is always only one VTS irrespective of the number of gateways created in an AWS account
        - The gateway moves a virtual tape to VTS when the backup software ejects a tape
        - You can retrieve tapes from VTS only after retrieving the tapes from VTL and it takes around 24 hours for the tapes to be available in the VTL

- Gateway allocates storage in two parts:
  - Cache storage
    - It serves as an on-premise durable storage
    - It caches the data locally before uploading it to S3
    - It provides low-latency access to frequently accessed data
  - Upload buffer
    - Upload buffer serves as a staging location, prior to uploading the data to S3
    - It uploads data on an encrypted SSL connection to AWS and stores it in an encrypted format on S3

AWS Snowball

AWS Snowball comes in a hardware form and can be used with the AWS dashboard or API. It is available in two different sizes, 50 TB and 80 TB. It can be used to transfer **petabytes** (**PB**) of data into and from AWS S3. Dedicated Snowball software is made available by AWS to perform data transfer in a compressed, encrypted, and secure manner. You can attach multiple AWS Snowball devices at the same time to on-premises network backbone. Perfom the following steps to obtain AWS Snowball:

- Sign in to your AWS account and create a job inside the AWS Snowball management console. While creating a job, you need to provide information such as shipping details to receive Snowball device(s), job details mentioning the region, the AWS S3 bucket name, and so on. You also need to provide security details such as ARN of the AWS IAM role and master key from AWS KMS.

- Once the job is created, the Snowball device is shipped to the given shipping address. The following *Figure 9.6* illustrates a Snowball device:

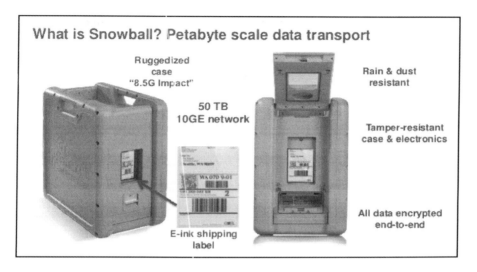

Figure 9.6: Snowball device and its features

- Once the device is received, connect it to the network. It has two panels, one in the front and another in the back. Flipping the front panel on the top gives access to the E Ink-based touch screen to operate. Network and power cables can be connected on the back side.
- When a Snowball is connected to an on-premise network, it becomes ready to transfer data. Snowball requires credentials to start a data transfer job. These credentials can be retrieved from the AWS dashboard or API. These credentials are encrypted with a manifest file and unlock code. Without the manifest file and unlock code, it is not possible to communicate with the Snowball. AWS provides a Snowball client, to transfer data from on-premise to the Snowball device.
- It is highly recommended that you do not delete the on-premise copy of the data until the data is successfully migrated to the AWS S3 bucket.

- Once the job is complete, disconnect the device from the network and return the device to the shipping address displayed on the display panel. When you create a job, at that time only regional shipping carriers are assigned. For India, Amazon logistics and for rest of the world, UPS are the shipping carrier partners.
- Once the device is shipped back to AWS, the job progress status indicating the movement of data from Snowball to AWS S3 bucket can be tracked on the AWS dashboard or through APIs.

AWS Snowmobile

AWS Snowmobile is an exabyte data transfer service. This hardware come in a high cube shipping container of dimensions, 45 feet long, 8 foot wide, and 9.6 foot tall. Each Snowmobile truck can store up to 100 PB of data and at the same time multiple Snowmobile trucks can be connected to an on-premise infrastructure. It uses 256-bit encryption and a master key for encryption can be managed with AWS KMS. It comes with GPS tracking, alarm monitoring, 24/7 video surveillance, and an optional escort security vehicle while in transit.

When you request for a Snowmobile, AWS performs an assessment and subsequently transports the snowmobile to your designated location. An AWS resource configures it so that you can access it as network storage. During the entire period when the Snowmobile stays at your location, AWS personnel work with your team for assistance. The AWS personnel connect a network switch from your Snowmobile to your local network. Once the setup is ready, you can start the data transfer process from multiple sources in your network to the Snowmobile.

10
AWS Relation Database Services

AWS **Relational Database Service (RDS)** is a fully managed relational database service from Amazon. RDS makes it easier for enterprises and developers who want to use a relational database in the cloud without investing much time and resources in managing the environment. AWS RDS supports six database engines: Amazon **Aurora**, **PostgreSQL**, **MySQL**, **MariaDB**, **Oracle**, and **Microsoft SQL Server**. It provides easy to use, cost-effective, and scalable relational databases in the cloud.

The advantages of Amazon RDS as follows:

- It's a fully managed service, which automatically manages backups, software and OS patching, automatic failover, and recovery.
- It also allows taking a manual backup of the database as a snapshot. Snapshots of a database can be used to restore a database as and when required.
- RDS provides fine-grained access control with the help of AWS IAM.

AWS RDS does not provide root access to the RDS instance. In short, RDS not allow the user to access the underlined host operating system. That means, you cannot login to server operating system. It also restricts access to certain system procedure and tables, which may require advance privileges.

After launching RDS in their service offerings, AWS was not providing option to stop an RDS instance for a very long time. Recently, an option to stop the RDS instance is introduced by Amazon. However, unlike EC2 instances, there are some limitations in stopping an RDS instance:

- Only a single AZ RDS instance can be stopped.

- An RDS instance can be stopped for maximum 7 consecutive days. After 7 days, the instance is automatically restarted

This way, by stopping an RDS instance, you can cut the cost for limited period of time. However, there is no limitation on restarting the instance or terminating all unused RDS DB instances to stop incurring the cost.

If a manual snapshot is not taken before terminating the RDS DB instance, it prompts you to take a final snapshot. Once an RDS DB instance is deleted, it cannot be recovered.

Amazon RDS components

Amazon RDS components are as follows:

DB instances

Each Amazon RDS engine can create an instance with at least one database in it. Each instance can have multiple user-created databases. Databases names must be unique to an AWS account and are called DB instance identifier. Each DB instance is a building block and an isolated environment in the cloud. These databases can be accessed using the same tools that are used to access standalone databases hosted in a data center. On top of standard tools AWS RDS instance can also accessed by the AWS Management Console, the API, and the CLI.

Each DB engine has its own version. With the help of a DB parameter group, DB engine parameters can be configured. These parameters help to configure DB instance performance. One DB parameter group can be shared among the same instances types of the same DB engine and version. These sets of allowed parameters vary according to the DB engine and its version. It is recommended to create individual DB parameter groups for each database to have legacy to fine tune as per business need each of them individually. When you choose an RDS instance type, it determines how many CPUs and memory is allocated to it. The most suitable instance type can be selected based on the performance need. Each DB instance can store a minimum of 5 GB and a maximum of 6 TB.

However, there some exceptions like Microsoft SQL Server RDS DB instances supports up to 4 TB of storage. Also, AWS periodically keeps revising this limit for different RDS engines. The minimum and maximum supported storage capacity may vary for each instance type. RDS supports magnetic, general purpose (SSD), and provisioned IOPS (SSD) storage types. RDS instances can be deployed within VPC. Based on the architectural needs, it can be deployed in a public subnet for accessing over the internet or in a private subnet for accessing it within the network.

Region and AZs

AWS hosts its computing resources in data centers, spread across the Globe. Each geographical location where the data centers are located is called a region. Each region comprises multiple distinct locations that are called AZs. Amazon creates AZs in isolated locations such that a failure in one AZ does not impact other AZs in the region. AZs are interconnected with low-latency network connectivity within a region. When you launch an application in multiple AZs, it provides you with high availability and protects you from the failure of an AZ.

An RDS DB instance can be provisioned in several AZs by selecting the Multi-AZ deployment option. It can also be used for DR sites. It is advisable to create RDS in multiple AZs for avoiding single points of failure. It automatically maintains synchronous replicas across multiple AZs. RDS synchronizes DBs between primary and secondary instances. In case a primary instance fails, the load is automatically shifted to a secondary instance.

Security groups

Security groups acts like a firewall. They controls access to a RDS DB instance, by specifying the allowed source port, protocol and IPs. Three types of security group can be attached with Amazon RDS DB instances – DB security groups, VPC security groups, and EC2 security groups.

In general, a DB security group is used when the RDS instance is not in the VPC. The VPC security group is used when RDS instance is within the VPC. The EC2 security group can be used with EC2 instances as well as RDS instances.

DB parameter groups

Over a period when a RDS instance is used in enterprise applications, it may be required to tune certain allowed and common parameters to optimize the performance based on the data insertion and retrieval pattern. The same DB parameter group can be attached to one or more DB instances of the same engine and version type. If not specified then the default DB parameter group with default parameters will be attached. Before creating an RDS instance it is recommended to create DB parameter groups.

DB option groups

DB options groups are used to configure RDS DB engines. With the help of the DB option groups, some of the DB engines can provide additional features for data management, database management, and can also provide additional security features. RDS supports DB options group for MariaDB, Microsoft SQL Server, MySQL, and Oracle. Before creating an RDS instance, it is recommended to create DB option groups.

 Amazon RDS charges are based on instance type, running time, storage size, type and I/O requests, total backup storage size, and data in and out transfers.

RDS engine types

Amazon RDS supports six DB engine types: **Amazon Aurora**, **MySQL**, **MariaDB**, **Microsoft SQL Server**, **Oracle**, and **PostgreSQL**. The following table helps us understand the connecting port and protocol for each of these DB instances:

Amazon RDS engine types	Default port	Protocol
Aurora DB	3306	TCP
MariaDB	3306	TCP
Microsoft SQL	1433	TCP
MySQL	3306	TCP
Oracle	1521	TCP
PostgreSQL	5432	TCP

Default port and protocol to connect with each of Amazon RDS engine types

The Amazon RDS engine for Microsoft SQL server and Oracle supports two licensing models: license included and **Bring Your Own License (BYOL)**. In case you are already invested in purchasing licenses for such databases, it can also be used as a BYOL with Amazon RDS to minimize monthly billing.

 Supported instance types may vary for each Amazon RDS engine.

Amazon Aurora DB

Amazon Aurora is a MySQL and PostgreSQL-compatible fully managed **Relational Database Management System (RDBMS)**. It provides a rare combination of performance and reliability like commercial databases and the cost effectiveness of open source databases. Amazon RDS also provides push-button migration tools to convert your existing Amazon RDS for MySQL applications to Amazon Aurora. It is also possible to use the code, tools, and applications you use today with your existing PostgreSQL databases with Aurora (PostgreSQL).

Creating an Amazon Aurora DB instance will create a DB cluster. It may consist of one or more instances along with a cluster volume to manage the data. These clusters consist of two types of instance: Primary instance and Aurora Replica. Actually the Aurora cluster volume is a virtual database storage volume of type SSD and it spans across multiple AZs in the same region. Each AZ will have a copy of the cluster data. Each Aurora cluster grows automatically as the amount of data in the database grows. It can grow up to 64 TB. Table size is limited to the cluster volume size hence the table can grow up to 64 TB in size:

- **Primary instance**: Performs read, writes, and modifies data to the cluster volume. Each Aurora DB cluster has one primary instance.

- **Aurora Replica**: Performs only read operations. Each Aurora DB cluster supports up to 15 Aurora Replicas plus one primary instance. Amazon RDS Aurora instance availability can be increased by spreading Aurora Replicas across multiple AZs. The following *Figure 10.1* helps to understand this:

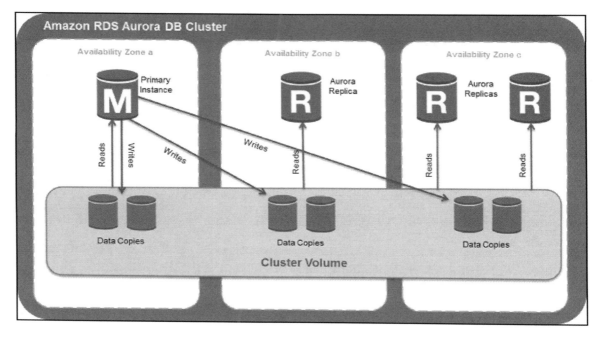

Figure 10.1: Amazon RDS Aurora primary and replica

Reference URL: https://docs.aws.amazon.com/AmazonRDS/latest/UserGuide/Aurora.Overview.html

With the help of various endpoints such as the cluster endpoint, reader endpoint, and instance endpoint it is possible to connect to the Aurora DB cluster. Each endpoint consists of a domain name and port separated by a colon and both are discussed as follows:

 An endpoint is a URL to access an AWS resource. It can be used to access the DB instance from an application, script, or as a CNAME in a DNS.

- **Cluster endpoint**: To connect with primary instances to perform data read, write, and modification operations. The primary instance also has its own endpoint. An advantage of the cluster endpoint is, it always points to the current primary instance.

- **Reader endpoint**: To connect with one of the Aurora Replicas to perform read operations. This endpoint automatically loads a balanced connection across available Aurora Replicas. In case a primary instance fails, then one of the Aurora Replicas will be promoted as a primary instance and in that situation all the read requests will be dropped.
- **Instance endpoint**: To directly connect with the Primary or Aurora replica instance.

It is designed to be a highly durable, fault tolerant, and reliable and provides the following features:

- **Storage Auto-repair**: It maintains multiple copies of data in three AZs to minimize the risk of disk failure. It automatically detects the failure of a volume or a segment and fixes it to avoid data loss and point-in time recovery.
- **Survivable cache warming**: It *warms* the buffer pool page cache for known common queries, every time a database starts or is restarted after failure to provide performance. It is managed in a separate process to make it survive independently of the database crash.
- **Crash recovery**: Instantly recovers from a crash asynchronously on parallel threads to make a database open and available immediately after crash.

Amazon RDS upgrades the newer major version of Aurora to the cluster only during the system maintenance windows. Timing may vary from region to region and cluster settings. Once a cluster is updated, the database restarts and may experience a downtime for 20 to 30 minutes. It is highly recommended to configure maintenance windows setting to match an enterprise's business requirement to avoid unplanned downtime. But in the case of a minor version upgrade, Amazon RDS schedules an automatic upgrade for all Aurora DB database engines for all Aurora DB clusters. It is optional to allow that update at that scheduled time. It can be manually selected and updated at the desired schedule. Otherwise, it gets applied at the next automatic upgrade for a minor version release.

Amazon Aurora offers *lab mode*. By default it is disabled. It can be enabled for testing current instance and available features in the currently offered version. New features can be tested before applying to production instance.

Comparison of Amazon RDS Aurora with Amazon RDS MySQL

The following table helps in understanding difference between Aurora and MySQL DB engines:

Feature	Amazon RDS Aurora	Amazon RDS MySQL
Read scaling	Supports up to 15 Aurora Replicas with minimal impact on the write performance.	Supports up to only five Read Replicas with some impact on the write operation.
Failover target	Aurora Replicas are automatic failover targets with no data loss.	Manually Read Replicas are promoted as a master DB instance with potential data loss.
MySQL version	Supports only MySQL version 5.6.	Supports MySQL version 5.5, 5.6, and 5.7.
AWS region	Not available in some regions.	Available in all regions.
MySQL storage engine	It supports only InnoDB storage engine type. Tables from other types of storage engine are automatically converted to InnoDB.	Supports both MyISAM and InnoDB.
Read replicas with a different storage engine than the master instance	MySQL (non-RDS) Read Replicas that replicate with an Aurora DB cluster can only use InnoDB.	Read Replicas can use both MyISAM and InnoDB.
Database engine parameters	Some parameters apply to the entire Aurora DB cluster and are managed by DB cluster parameter groups. Other parameters apply to each individual DB instance in a DB cluster and are managed by DB parameter groups.	Parameters apply to each individual DB instance or Read Replica and are managed by DB parameter groups.

Detailed comparison between Amazon RDS Aurora and Amazon RDS MySQL

Reference URL: https://docs.aws.amazon.com/AmazonRDS/latest/UserGuide/Aurora.Overview.html

MariaDB

MariaDB is a community version of MySQL RDBMS under GNU GPL license. It maintains a high level of compatibility with MySQL.

Amazon RDS MariaDB manages versions as X.Y.Z where X.Y denotes a major version and Z is the minor version. For example, a version change from 10.0 to 10.1 is considered a major version change, while a version change from 10.0.17 to 10.0.24 is a minor version change. In general, within three to five months it will be introduced in Amazon RDS MariaDB. Amazon RDS Management Console, CLIs, or APIs can be used to perform common tasks such as creating an instance, resizing the DB instance, creating and restoring a backup, and so on.

 Minor version support may not be available in all AWS regions.

Amazon RDS MariaDB supports multiple storage engines, but all of them are not optimized for recovery and durability. At present, it fully supports the **XtraDB** storage engine. It supports point in time restore and snapshot restore. It also supports the **Aria** storage type engine, but it may have a negative impact on recovery in the case of instance failure. However, to manage spatial geographical data, it is suggested to use the Aria storage type as the XtraDB storage type doesn't support.

 Amazon RDS MariaDB is available in all regions except AWS GovCloud (US) (us-gov-west-1).

Amazon RDS supports two kinds of upgrade for running instances: major version upgrades and minor version upgrades. Minor version upgrades can take place automatically when auto minor version upgrade is enabled from the instance configuration options. In all other cases, upgrading minor versions or major versions requires manual upgrades.

Microsoft SQL Server

It is possible to run Microsoft SQL Server as an RDS instance. It supports various versions of MS SQL such as from SQL Server 2008 R2 to SQL Server 2016. There are a few limitations for Microsoft SQL Server DB instances:

- Each Amazon RDS Microsoft SQL instance can have a maximum of 30 databases. Master and model databases are not counted as a database in this count.
- Some ports are reserved for internal purposes, and cannot be used for general purposes.
- It is not possible to rename a database when an RDS instance with Microsoft SQL Server is deployed in Multi-AZ mirroring.
- The minimum storage required is 20 GB with maximum 400 GB for the Web and Express edition. For the Enterprise and Standard edition a minimum of 200 GB and a maximum of 4 TB of storage is required. In case of larger storage is required, with the help of sharding across multiple DB instances this can be achieved.
- It is recommended to allocate storage based on future considerations. Once storage volume is allocated it cannot be increased due to the extensibility limitations of striped storage attached to Windows Server.
- It doesn't support some of the features of SQL Server such as SQL Server Analysis Services, SQL Server Integration Services, SQL Server Reporting Services, Data Quality Services, and Master Data Services. To use these features it is required to configure Microsoft SQL Server on an Amazon EC2 instance.
- Due to the limitations of Microsoft SQL Server, point in time restore may not work properly until the database has been dropped successfully.

Amazon RDS Microsoft SQL instances support two licensing options: License Included and BYOL. License Included mode is good for the enterprise if you have not already purchased a license. In case you have already purchased a license and are using it in an existing infrastructure, when migration to AWS cloud has been done, once the instance is running with the help of management console or CLI, BYOL can be implemented. When it is deployed in a Multi-AZ mode, the secondary instance is passive and only provides read operations until failover takes place. BYOL is supported for the following Microsoft SQL Server database editions:

- Microsoft SQL Server Standard Edition (2016, 2014, 2012, 2008 R2)
- Microsoft SQL Server Enterprise Edition (2016, 2014, 2012, 2008 R2)

It may be required to upgrade the Amazon RDS Microsoft SQL Server instance, Amazon RDS supports major version and minor version upgrades. In either type, it is essential to perform such upgrades manually. It requires downtime and the total time depends on the engine version and the size of the DB instance.

MySQL

Amazon RDS supports various versions of MySQL. It is also compliant with many leading industry leading standards such as HIPAA, PHI, BAA, and many others. MySQL versions are organized as X.Y.Z where X.Y indicates a major version and Z indicates a minor version. Most of the major versions are supported in most of the regions, but it is recommended to check the availability of desired major and minor version in region, where you are planning to create primary and DR sites. A new version of MySQL is available with the Amazon RDS MySQL instance usually within three to five months. While upgrading MySQL to a newer version, it is possible to maintain compatibility with specific MySQL versions. Major versions can be upgraded from MySQL 5.5 to MySQL 5.6 and then MySQL 5.6 to MySQL 5.7. Usually major version upgrades complete within 10 minutes, but it may vary based on the DB instance type. Minor versions automatically get updated when AutoMinorVersionUpgrade is enabled. Amazon RDS policy on deprecation of MySQL is as follows:

- The major version is supported for three years from the release such as 5.5, 5.6, 5.7, and upcoming
- The minor version is supported for a year from release such as MySQL 5.546
- Three months of grace are provided from the date of version deprecation date

 It is essential to perform an OS update (if any are available) before upgrading Amazon RDS MySQL 5.5 DB instance to MySQL 5.6 or later.

Amazon RDS MySQL 5.6 and later supports memcached in an option group. Amazon RDS MySQL also supports various storage engines, but point in time recovery is only supported by InnoDB. Amazon RDS currently does not support the following MySQL features:

- Global Transaction IDs
- Transportable table space
- Authentication plugin

- Password strength plugin
- Replication filters
- Semi-synchronous replication

It is possible to create a snapshot for an Amazon RDS MySQL instance storage volume. Each snapshot is based on the MySQL instance engine version. As it is possible to upgrade the version of an Amazon RDS MySQL instance, it is also possible to upgrade the engine version for DB snapshots. It supports DB snapshot upgrades from MySQL 5.1 to MySQL 5.5.

Oracle

At the time of writing, the following Oracle RDBMS versions are supported by Amazon RDS Oracle engine:

- Oracle 12c, Version 12.1.0.2
- Oracle 11g, Version 11.2.0.4

Amazon RDS Oracle engine also supports the following Oracle RDBMS versions, but soon they will be deprecated:

- Oracle 12c, Version 12.1.0.1
- Oracle 11g, Version 11.2.0.3 and Version 11.2.0.2

Oracle RDS can be deployed within VPC and can perform point-in-time recovery and scheduled or manual snapshots. Optionally, it can be deployed in Multi-AZ to get high-availability and failover. At the time of creating a DB instance master user gets DBA privileges with some limitations, for example SYS user, SYSTEM user, and other DB administrative user accounts cannot be used.

Amazon RDS Oracle instances support two licensing options: License Included and BYOL. Once an instance is running with the help of management console or CLI, BYOL can be implemented. In the case of License Included, it supports the following Oracle database versions:

- Oracle Database Standard Edition One (SE1)
- Oracle Database Standard Edition Two (SE2)

BYOL supports the following license models:

- Oracle Database Enterprise Edition (EE)
- Oracle Database Standard Edition (SE)
- Oracle Database Standard Edition One (SE1)
- Oracle Database Standard Edition Two (SE2)

Amazon allows you to change Oracle RDS instance types, however, if your DB instance uses a deprecated version of Oracle, you cannot change the instance type. Such RDS instances are autocratically updated to new version based on a cut-off date provided by Amazon. For more details on supported versions, deprecated version, and cut-off date for upgrading the deprecated versions, you can check following URL: `http://docs.aws.amazon.com/AmazonRDS/latest/UserGuide/CHAP_Oracle.html`.

It supports both major and minor version upgrades. While upgrading an Amazon RDS Oracle instance from 11g to 12c is a major version upgrade, it has to be done manually and it requires downtime. This downtime may vary based on the current engine version and size of the DB instance. While upgrading engine version it takes two snapshots. The first snapshot is taken just before upgrading, in the case of failure due to any reason it can be used to restore the database. The second snapshot is taken just after engine upgrade is completed. Once DB engine is successfully upgraded, it cannot be undone. If there is any requirement to rollback to previous version, you can create a new instance with the snapshot taken before upgrading the version. Oracle engine upgrade path may vary depending up on the current version running on the instance.

PostgreSQL

The Amazon RDS PostgreSQL engine supports various versions of PostgreSQL. It also supports point-in-time recovery using periodically or manually taken snapshots, Multi-AZ deployment, provisioned IOPS, Read Replicas, SSL connection to DB and VPC. Applications such as *pgAdmin* or any other tool can be used to connect to PostgreSQL and run SQL queries. It is also compliant with many industry leading standards such as HIPAA, PHI, BAA, and many others.

At the time of creating an Amazon RDS PostgreSQL instance master user (super user) a system account is assigned to `rds_superuser` role with some limitations. More details about various supported PostgreSQL supported versions and their features, can be obtained from the URL: `http://docs.aws.amazon.com/AmazonRDS/latest/UserGuide/CHAP_PostgreSQL.html`.

Amazon RDS supported and unsupported database engines can be installed and configured on Amazon EC2 instances as well. Compared to Amazon RDS, installing DB on Amazon EC2 gives more power to fine-tune database engines as gets root level access. Usually, when enterprise is looking for a managed service solution, Amazon RDS is preferred and when they are looking for more detailed fine-tuning hosting on Amazon EC2 is preferred.

Creating an Amazon RDS MySQL DB instance

Amazon RDS MySQL DB instances can be created using Amazon Management Console, CLIs, or APIs and the steps are as follows:

1. Log in to the AWS Management Console with the appropriate user privileges and go to the Amazon RDS dashboard.
2. Select **Launch a DB Instance** as shown in the following *Figure 10.2*:

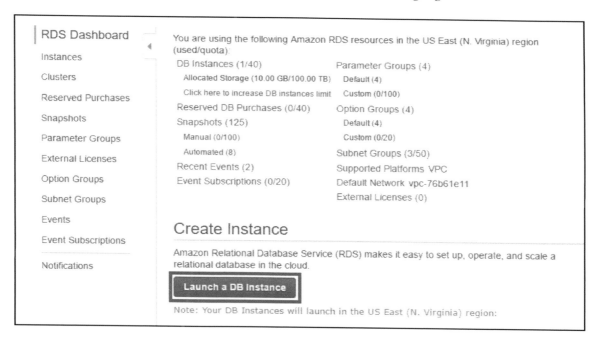

Figure 10.2: Select a DB instance

3. Select the engine type as MySQL, as shown in the following *Figure 10.3*:

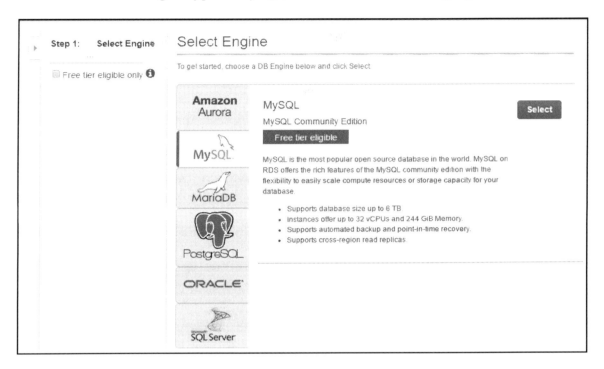

Figure 10.3: Select Amazon RDS engine type as MySQL

 Free tier allows us to create a t2.micro single-AZ instance for the first year.

4. Select the **Production** type: **Dev/Test** or **MySQL** Multi-AZ, as shown in the following *Figure 10.4*. It is also suggested to switch to Amazon Aurora as it is seamlessly compatible with MySQL:

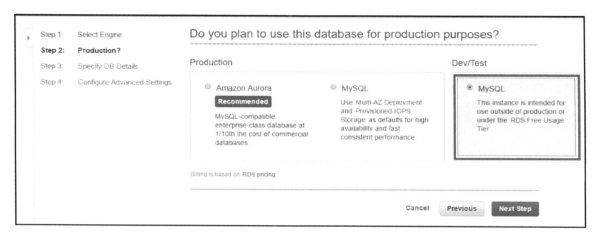

Figure 10.4: Select Amazon RDS MySQL instance to deploy in a single or Multi-AZ

5. Specify Amazon RDS MySQL DB details as follows:

- **Licence Model**: At present it has only one license model: **general-public-licence**.
- **DB Engine Version**: Amazon RDS MySQL engine supports various versions. Based on the enterprise IT requirement, the optimum and latest can be selected.
- **DB Instance Class**: Select the RDS instance type. It decides the size of RAM, CPU, network performance, and EBS performance.
- **Multi-AZ Deployment**: Select **Yes** to enable a standby replica of DB instance in another AZ for failover support.
- **Storage Type**: Supports three types: **Magnetic, General Purpose (SSD)**, and **Provisioned IOPS (SSD)**. Storage type can be selected based on the required number of read/write operations.
- **Allocated Storage**: Size of the storage volume to attach to the Amazon RDS DB instance.
- **DB Instance Identifier**: It is a unique DB name for each DB within the AWS account.

- **Master Username** and **Master Password**: Master user is the user with the highest level of privileges within each Amazon RDS instance. It is used to create enterprise level users and grant them privileges to perform day-to-day activities and applications. It also defines passwords.

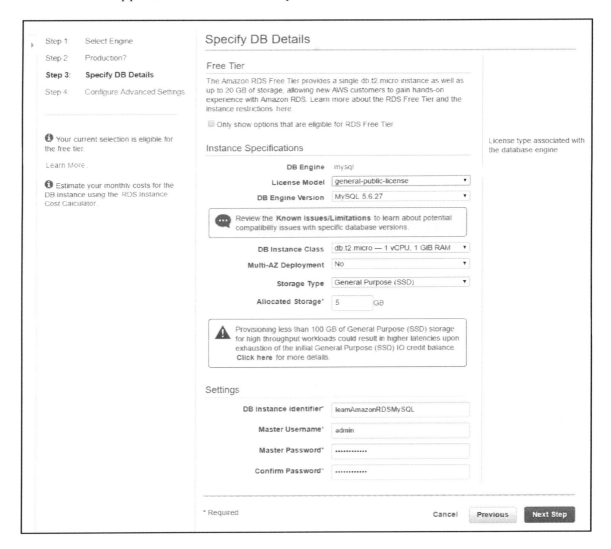

Figure 10.5: Amazon RDS MySQL DB instance details

6. **Configure Advanced Settings** as shown in *Figure 10.6*:

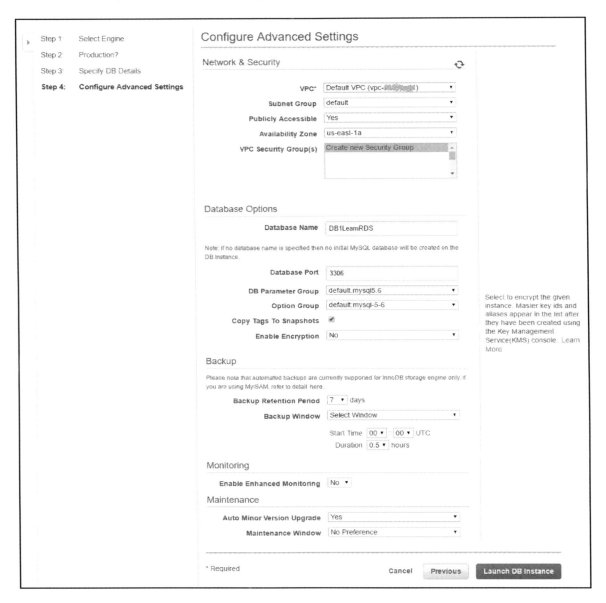

Figure 10.6: Amazon RDS MySQL DB instance advanced configuration

- **VPC**: Select a suitable network VPC.
- **Subnet Group**: Subnet selection depends on architectural design. It can be public or private based on requirements.
- **Publicly Accessible**: It should be selected as **Yes**, if you want to allow the access to the DB from the Internet. It creates a public DNS endpoint, which is Globally resolvable. Select No if you want this DB instance to be accessible only from within the network or VPC.
- **Availability Zone**: If you have any preference on which AZ you want to launch your instance, you choose the specific AZ as required. If you do not have any preference AZ, you can select **No Preference**. In this case, Amazon automatically launches the instance in appropriate AZ to balance the resource availability.
- **VPC Security Group(s)**: Security groups act as a software firewall. One or more security groups can be attached to each Amazon RDS instance.
- **Database Name**: It can be a maximum of 64 alpha-numeric characters. For a given name, it will create a database within the DB instance. It can be blank also.
- **Database Port**: For Amazon RDS MySQL DB instances the default port is 3306. A default port list for all supported DB engines is given in a table.
- **DB Parameter Group**: It helps to configure DB engine parameters. It is recommended to create the DB parameter group before creating a DB instance. Once it is created it will appear in available drop-down list to use at the time of creating a DB instance. If it is not created before creating a DB instance then the default DB parameter group will be created. This group of parameters can be applied to one or more DB instances of the same engine type. When any dynamic parameter value is changed in the DB parameter group it gets applied immediately whether **Apply Immediately** has been enabled or not. In the case of static parameter value change to get effect, it is required to manually reboot the DB instance.
- **Option Group**: It is supported by the MariaDB, Microsoft SQL Server, MySQL, and Oracle Amazon RDS engines. With the help of option groups it is possible to fine-tune databases and manage data. Option groups can consist of two types of parameter: permanent and persistent.
- To change the persistent options value, it is required to detach the DB instance from the DB option group. When the option group is associated with any DB snapshot, then to perform point-in-time recovery using that DB snapshot it is required to create a new DB instance with the same DB options group. On the other hand, it is not possible to remove permanent options from option group. Also, an option group with permanent options cannot be detached from a DB instance.

- **Copy Tags To Snapshots**: In a backup window, it creates an instance level backup (that is, a snapshot) for the entire volume. By enabling this parameter, each snapshot will copy tags from the DB instance. These metadata can be very helpful to manage access policies.
- **Enable Encryption**: Enabling this option will encrypt data at rest in the DB instance's storage volume and subsequent snapshots. The industry standard AES-256 encryption algorithm is used. Amazon RDS automatically takes care of authentication and encrypts/decrypts data with a minimal impact on performance.
- **Backup Retention Period**: You specify snapshot retention period here in number of days. Snapshots which are older than specified number of days are automatically deleted after specified number of days. Any snapshot can be retained for maximum of 35 days.
- **Backup Window**: An automated backup time window can be specified in a UTC. During this scheduled time, everyday a snapshot will be taken. When any snapshot is aged for a backup retention period it will be automatically obsolete. It will help to achieve an organizational backup retention policy and minimize AWS billing by obsolete old snapshots.
- **Enable Enhanced Monitoring**: Amazon RDS maintains various performance metrics in an Amazon CloudWatch. The main difference between normal and enhanced monitoring is the source of the data. In the case of normal monitoring, CPU utilization of data is derived from the hypervisor. But for enhanced monitoring it is derived from the agent installed on a hypervisor. Data collection from these two sources may vary. In the case of small instance types, this difference can be bigger.
- **Auto Minor Version Upgrade**: Amazon RDS Instances can have two types of upgrade: major and minor. Major version upgrades may require down-time hence they are not performed automatically. Also it may not be possible to revert a major version upgrade. Minor version upgrades are compatible with previous versions and may not require down-time; hence it is performed automatically during scheduled maintenance.

- **Maintenance Window**: Amazon allows you to specify maintenance window. During the maintenance window, Amazon may upgrade DB instance's minor version or DB cluster's OS. Upgrade of the underlined OS or DB version may bring performance implications. Considering this, you should carefully define the maintenance window. Maintenance window definition allows you to define the starting day of the week, hour of the day, minute of the hour, and the total allocated time to perform maintenance activity. Once the maintenance activity begins and if it requires more time to complete the maintenance, it doesn't terminate in between. It stops only after completing the maintenance tasks.

Monitoring RDS instances

Once an Amazon RDS instance is created as per the present need, it is very important to observe its performance with constantly changing business requirements and application loads. It is possible to monitor the instance's CPU utilization, DB connections, free storage space, free memory, and many other parameters. It helps to identify bottlenecks and also will give the opportunity to minimize monthly billing by reducing the resource size if it is underutilized.

An alarm can be configured to take action on a specified threshold. For example, if CPU usage is above 70% for a specified consecutive time period, then send SNS notifications to the DBA. Such an alarm can be created either from the CloudWatch dashboard or from the Amazon RDS dashboard.

To create a CloudWatch alarm from the Amazon RDS dashboard perform the following steps:

1. Go to the Amazon RDS dashboard and select the desired DB instance from the list of running DB instances.
2. Click **Show Monitoring** to get the list of supported metrics. For example, here we have selected the CPU utilization metric and selected **Create Alarm**.

3. Create an alarm by specifying the threshold and other relevant details such as the SNS topic to use to send notifications, CPU utilization threshold, consecutive time period, and alarm name as shown in the following *Figure 10.7*:

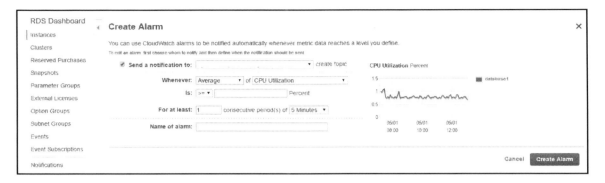

Figure 10.7: Create CloudWatch alert and action from Amazon RDS dashboard.

Creating a snapshot

A snapshot is a frozen image of the DB instance's storage volume. It helps to restore a database to a particular point-in-time. Usually, point-in-time recovery is performed when a database is corrupted or by mistake some data has been dropped (that is, deleted) to bring a database back to the last healthy state. At the time of creating an Amazon RDS instance, a daily snapshot schedule has been already configured. But sometimes it may be required to take a manual snapshot of the DB instance before performing any maintenance task on the database. Snapshot will back up an entire DB instance. It will include all databases and tables and other resources existing on it.

Creating a snapshot for a Multi-AZ DB instance doesn't bring many performance implications. But taking a snapshot for a single-AZ DB instance may suspend DB I/O for a few seconds to minutes. Manual snapshots can be taken using Amazon Management Console, CLI, or APIs. To take a manual snapshot using the management console perform the following steps:

1. Select the desired DB instance.
2. Select **Take Snapshot** from the drop-down menu **Instance Actions,** available above the list of the running RDS instances:

Figure 10.8: Take manual Amazon RDS DB instance snapshot

3. Provide the relevant **Snapshot Name** as shown in the following *Figure 10.9*:

Figure 10.9: Provide Snapshot Name, while taking manual snapshot

Restoring a DB from a snapshot

A snapshot can only be restored by creating a new instance. You cannot restore a snapshot to an existing instance. While restoring the snapshot to a new RDS instance, you can have a different storage volume type from the one used in the snapshot.

Creating an RDS DB instance from a snapshot, automatically attaches a default parameter group and security group to it. Once a DB instance is created, it is possible to change the attached parameter group and security group for that instance.

By restoring a snapshot, the same option group associated with the snapshot will get associated to the newly created RDS DB instance. Options groups are platform-specific: VPC or EC2-Classic.

Creating a RDS DB instance inside a particular VPC will link a used option group with that particular VPC. It means when the snapshot is created for that DB instance it cannot be restored in a different VPC. To do that it requires us to either attach a default options group or create a new options group and attach it to the newly created DB instance from the snapshot.

Creating a DB instance from a snapshot also requires us to provide parameters such as **DB Engine, Licence Model, DB Instance Class, Multi-AZ Deployment, Storage Type, DB Instance Identifier, VPC, Subnet Group, Publicly Accessible, Availability Zone, Database Name, Database Port, Option Groups**, and other parameters that we define at the time of creating a new Amazon RDS DB instance.

> It is also possible to copy and share an Amazon RDS snapshot from one region to another and share it among multiple AWS accounts respectively. It may require us to create a DB instance from a snapshot in a different region or AWS account.

Changing a RDS instance type

An RDS instance type is generally changed to accommodate additional resource requirement or for downgrading an existing instance type which is underutilized. For changing the instance type, perform the following steps:

1. From the list of RDS DB instances select the desired instance to modify the instance type and select **Modify** from the **Instance Actions** drop-down menu. The drop-down menu is shown in the following *Figure 10.10*:

Figure 10.10: Instance Actions drop down menu to select Modify

2. Modifying a DB instance does not only allow us to change the DB instance type, it also allows us to change many other parameters that are provided at the time of creating a DB instance such as subnet group, security group, and many more options. At the end of the parameters that can be changed, an option is available to apply changes now or wait until a next maintenance window, as shown in the following *Figure 10.11*:

Figure 10.11: DB instance change parameters to Apply Immediately or wait till next maintenance window

3. If DB performance is throttling, you can change the DB instance parameters and apply them immediately. If you do not apply them immediately, the changes are automatically applied during the next maintenance window. Some modifications such as parameter group changes may require us to reboot DB instances. It is advisable to test any changes in a test environment first, before making the changes into productions environment directly.

It is best practice to test such changes in a test environment first, before making changes into productions directly.

Amazon RDS and VPC

Before 2013, AWS used to support EC2-Classic. All AWS account created after 2013-1-04, it only supports EC2-VPC. If an AWS account only supports EC2-VPC, then a default VPC is created in each region and a default subnet in each AZs. Default subnets are public in nature. To meet enterprise requirements, it is possible to create a custom VPC and subnets. This custom VPC and subnet can have a custom CIDR range and can also decide which subnet can be public and which one can be private. When an AWS account only supports EC2-VPC, it has no custom VPC is created, then Amazon RDS DB instances are created inside a default VPC. Amazon RDS DB instances can also be launched into a custom VPC just like EC2 instances. Amazon RDS DB instances have the same functionality in terms of performance, maintenance, upgrading, recovery, and failover detection capability, irrespective of whether they are launched in a VPC or not.

Amazon RDS and high availability

ELB and Auto Scaling can be used with Amazon EC2 to perform load balancing and launching or terminating an EC2 instance to match the load requirement. Auto Scaling cannot be used with Amazon RDS. Amazon RDS supports Multi-AZ deployment to provide high availability and failover. By enabling Multi-AZ deployment, Amazon RDS creates two instances of the same instance type and configuration with individual endpoints in two separate AZs. The sole purpose of another DB instance is to maintain a synchronous standby replica. The standby replica receives traffic only when failover takes place. It can not be used for load balancing or serving read-only traffic. For serving read-only traffic, read replicas can be created, which is different from creating Multi-AZ instances. At present while writing this book, Amazon RDS supports six DB engines. Four out of the six DB engines that is, Oracle, PostgreSQL, MySQL, and MariaDB can perform failover from primary DB instance to secondary DB instance using Amazon's failover mechanism. Microsoft SQL Server RDS engine uses SQL Server mirroring for high availability. Amazon Aurora cluster creates at least three copies of data across Multi-AZs within the same region, which can fulfill high availability requirement. In Amazon Aurora, in case of primary DB instance fails, one of the Aurora Replicas is promoted as a primary.

The following *Figure 10.12* helps to understand the Amazon RDS DB primary and secondary instance in a VPC where the primary instance is denoted as **M** and secondary instance is denoted as **S**:

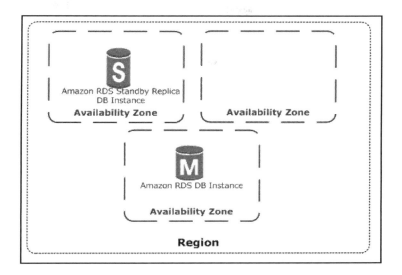

Figure 10.12: Amazon RDS DB instance in a Multi-AZ

Reference URL : https://docs.aws.amazon.com/AmazonRDS/latest/UserGuide/Concepts.MultiAZ.html

 When using the BYOL licensing model, you must have a license for both the primary instance and the standby replica.

Connecting to an Amazon RDS DB instance

Once the Amazon RDS DB instance is created, you can connect to it for performing read/write operation as well as for performing day-to-day maintenance activities. Before connecting to the DB instance, ensure that the port to connect with DB instance is allowed in the firewall or security group. Also ensure that the source IP from where you need to connect to DB instance is allowed in the security group.

Connecting to an Amazon Aurora DB cluster

Aurora DB clusters consist of a primary instance and Aurora Replica. A separate endpoint is available for the primary instance, Aurora Read instance, or a group of Aurora Read Instances. In line with the task you want to carry out, it is possible to use any of these endpoints in scripting, application, or manually connecting them. Tools used to connect with MySQL databases can be used to connect to Amazon Aurora cluster DB instances.

You can refer to following syntax for connecting to an Aurora DB:

```
mysql -h <aurora-cluster-endpoint> --ssl-ca=[full path]rds-combined-ca-
bundle.pem --ssl-verify-server-cert
```

Connecting to a MariaDB Instance

Amazon RDS MariaDB instance up and running has a valid endpoint. It can be used with an application, client, or tool to connect with the DB instance. By default it uses port 3306 and the TCP protocol.

Amazon RDS MariaDB instances can be accessed from the mysql command line utility. HeidiSQL is a GUI-based utility and it can be used to connect MariaDB instances.

The following mysql command helps to understand syntax:

```
mysql -h <endpoit> -p 3306 -u <masteruser> -p
```

It is possible to provide a password immediately after the -p parameter. Best practice is not to provide it with the command, but to provide it at runtime when prompted for it. Based on the memory (instance type) the number of connection limit is derived. DB instances with higher memory have a higher connection limit. MariaDB maximum possible connection number is defined in the max_connections parameter.

Connecting to a MySQL instance

By providing an Amazon RDS endpoint, MySQL DB instances can be connected using a standard MySQL client application or utility. Connecting to MySQL DB instances is similar to connecting MariaDB using a MySQL command-line tool:

```
mysql -h <endpoit> -p 3306 -u <masteruser> -p
```

 Amazon RDS DB instance endpoints can be obtained from the RDS console or using CLI `describe-db-` instances.

Optionally it is also possible to use SSL encryption to connect Amazon RDS MySQL DB instance. The `--ssl-ca` parameter is used to provide a public key (`.pem`) for SSL encrypted communication.

Following two tips are repeating, same as MariaDB.

 It is possible to pass a password immediately after `-p` parameter. Best practice is not to provide it with the command but to provide at runtime when prompted. The number of connection limit for a MySQL instance is dependent instance type. DB instances with higher memory have a higher connection limit. MySQL's maximum possible connection number is defined in the `max_connections` parameter.

Connecting to an Oracle instance

SQL*Plus is an Oracle command-line utility. It can be downloaded from the Oracle website. Before connecting to the Amazon RDS Oracle DB instance, it is essential to find out Amazon RDS endpoint, port, and protocol. When connecting for the first time, we must connect using master user credentials. Once Amazon RDS relevant application and real entity users are created, it can be used for day-to-day maintenance activity. The following `sqlplus` command line example helps us to understand this:

```
sqlplus 'mydbusr@(DESCRIPTION=(ADDRESS=(PROTOCOL=TCP)(HOST=<dns name of
db instance>)(PORT=<listener port>))(CONNECT_DATA=(SID=<database name>)))'
```

Where:

- User: `mydbuser` could be the master user or any other valid user
- `PROTOCOL`: TCP is a protocol and it remains TCP only
- `PORT`: By default, Oracle DB can be connected on `1521`
- `SID`: Database name, intended to connect where one instance may have more than one database

RDS best practices

RDS best practices are as follows:

- Create an individual AWS IAM user to perform DBA tasks. Grant the minimum privileges required to perform day-to-day tasks. Remove unused access key and secret key. Have a strong password policy and rotate the password periodically.
- Before creating an RDS instance identify Amazon RDS essential characteristics to be specified such as VPC, security group, failover or Read Replica requirement, the region and AZs to use, and storage and backup requirements.
- Before creating an RDS instance it is recommended to create a DB options group and DB parameter group.
- Monitor Amazon RDS instance resources such as CPU, memory, and astorage to avoid performance bottlenecks.
- It is recommended to keep some extra buffer in memory and a storage volume while choosing RDS instance types.
- It is recommended to test your environment for failover as it may take different time depending on the use case, instance type, and underlined data size.
- Amazon RDS provides an endpoint to connect to the RDS instance. The IP address beneath that endpoint may change after failover takes place. So if an application caches DNS IP address, set the TTL to under 30 seconds in your application environment.

11
AWS DynamoDB - A NoSQL Database Service

DynamoDB is an easy to use and fully managed NoSQL database service provided by Amazon. It provides fast and consistent performance, highly scalable architecture, flexible data structure, event driven programmability, and fine-grained access control.

Before we get into much details about DynamoDB, let us understand some fundamental characteristics of RDBMS/SQL and NoSQL databases. For a long time, the developer community has been working with **Relational Database Management Service (RDBMS)** and **Structured Query Language (SQL)**. If you have used RDBMS and SQL, you will naturally want to compare and understand the fundamental differences as well as similarities between SQL and NoSQL database.

Let us first understand what an RDBMS is

RDBMS enables you to create databases that can store related data. A database is a collection of information that stores data in database objects, called tables. A table is a collection of related data entries, which consists of columns and rows.

RDBMS enables you to create a link between these tables by establishing a relationship between them. Such a relational model helps in obtaining related information from multiple tables using SQL. You can see in the following *Figure 11.1* that there are three tables, `Employee_Master`, `Department_Master`, and `Emp_Dept`, respectively. All these tables are related with a key field which is called as the primary key. In the following example, you can see how the `Emp_Dept` table, which provides department detail for employees, is linked with the `Employee_Master` and `Department_Master` tables:

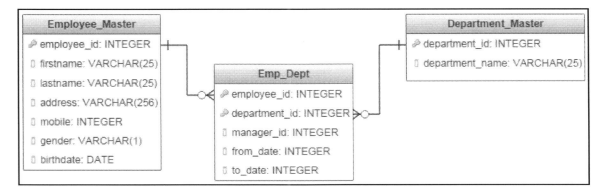

Figure 11.1: Relation between tables in an RDBMS

This is how in a nutshell, RDBMS co-relates with data stored in tables.

What is SQL?

SQL is a standardized language to interact with relational databases. It can execute queries against a database and retrieve data from one or more tables. It can insert, update, and delete records from database tables and perform many other database-related activities. In short, SQL can help you manage your databases.

Here's a simple example of an SQL statement.

```
Select * from Employee_Master
```

The preceding example simply retrieves all the records from `Employee_Master` database. Let's understand one more simple example of an SQL statement, which retrieves related information from multiple tables.

```
Select a.employee_id, b.firstname, b.lastname, c.department_name from
Emp_Dept a, Employee_Master b, Department_Master c where a.employee_id =
b.employee_id and a.department_id = c.department_id
```

The preceding example retrieves related employee information from three different tables. The key to retrieving the information is in the relationship between them. The relationship is established based on key fields in the respective tables.

This is how, in a nutshell RDBMS and SQL work.

What is NoSQL?

A NoSQL database provides a way to store and retrieve data that is in a non-tabular format. It is also referred to as **Non SQL**, **Non Relational** or **Not only SQL** database. NoSQL databases are used for managing large sets of data that are frequently updated in a distributed system. It eliminates the need for a rigid schema associated with an RDBMS.

There are basically four types of NoSQL databases:

- Key-value pair databases
- Document databases
- Graph databases
- Wide column stores

Key-value pair databases

It uses a very simple data model that stores data in a pair of unique keys and the associated value. Commonly, it is used for storing time series data, click stream data, and application logs.

Examples of key-value pair databases are: DynamoDB, Riak, Redis, Aerospike.

Key	Value
Name	Abhishek
Mobile	0987654321
Address	Mumbai

DynamoDB is a key-value pair database. In subsequent sections of the chapter, we will get into more details of a key-value pair databases.

Document databases

It stores data elements in a structure that represents a document-like format such as JSON, XML, YAML and so on. Document databases are commonly used for content management and monitoring applications.

Examples of document databases: MongoDB, CouchDB, MarkLogic, and so on.

Unlike RDBMS, the document database schema design is flexible and can combine multiple entities in a single schema. The following example shows how employee information can be stored in a MongoDB document:

```
db.employee.insert(
{
    {
      employee_id:'10001', firstname: 'Tony', lastname: 'Stark', birthdate:
'1965-04-04'
    },
    {
      employee_id:'10002', firstname: 'Thor', lastname: 'Odinson',
birthdate: '1983-08-11'
    },
    {
      employee_id:'10003', firstname: 'Natalia', lastname: 'Romanoff',
birthdate: '1984-11-22'
    }
})
```

Graph databases

A graph database is a NoSQL database type that uses graph structures and stores related data in nodes. It emphasizes on the connection between the data elements to accelerate query performance. It is mainly used for storing geographical data and recommendation engines.

Examples of graph databases: Allegrograph, IBM graph, Neo4J, and so on.

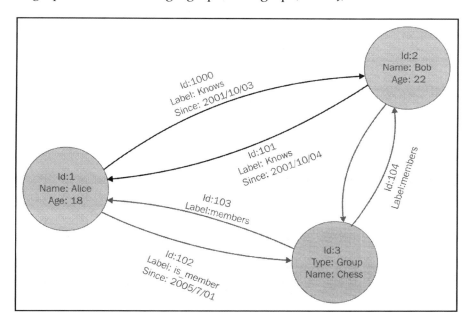

Figure 11.2: Graph database

Image Source: https://upload.wikimedia.org/wikipedia/commons/3/3a/GraphDatabase_PropertyGraph.png

Wide column databases

The wide column database is a type of NoSQL database that stores data using a column-oriented model. It is also called a table-style database or column store database. It stores data in a table-like structure and it can store large number of columns.

Wide column databases are generally used for storing data related to internet search and other similar large-scale web applications.

Examples of wide column databases: Cassandra, HBase, SimpleDB, Accumulo, Hypertable, and so on.

Employee_id	Firstname	Lastname	Birthdate
10001	Tony	Stark	1965-04-04
10002	Thor	Odinson	1983-08-11
10003	Natalia	Romanoff	1984-11-22

In a wide column database, each column is stored in a separate file as depicted in the preceding example.

When to use NoSQL databases?

A relational database stores data in one or more related tables. The relational model and tabular format minimizes data duplication. However, scaling relational databases can become very resource-intensive. In contrast, NoSQL databases stores related data in a single document, which can improve accessibility and scalability. A NoSQL database trades some of the query and transaction capabilities of RDBMS in favor of better performance and high scalability.

NoSQL is generally used for big data, advertisement technologies, gaming, mobile applications, time series data, logs, IoT, and many other applications where heavy write performance, reduced latency, and a dynamic schema are required.

SQL versus NoSQL

Following are some of the key differences between SQL and NoSQL databases:

SQL	NoSQL
Database systems are termed RDBMS.	Database systems are termed non-relational or distributed systems.
It follows a rigid and pre-defined schema model.	It uses a dynamic schema.
It stores data in tabular form and is also known as a tabular database.	It stores data in a collection of key-value pair, graph database, documents, and wide column stores.
Databases can be scaled vertically.	Databases can be scaled horizontally.

It uses SQL for defining and managing data.	It uses an unstructured query language, which varies from database to database.
It is best suited for complex queries.	It is not suitable for complex queries as it does not use the relational data model.
It is not suitable for hierarchical data stores.	It is best suited for hierarchical data stores.
Oracle, SQL Server, MySQL, PostgreSQL, and so on are SQL databases.	DynamoDB, MongoDB, Bigtable, Cassandra, Hbase, CouchDB, and so on are NoSQL databases.

Introducing DynamoDB

Amazon DynamoDB is a fully managed NoSQL database service from Amazon that provides fast and flexible NoSQL database service for applications that need consistent and low-latency access at any scale. It supports key-value and document data models. It provides a dynamic schema model and predictable performance. DynamoDb is best suited for big data, advertisement technologies, gaming, mobile applications, time series data, logs, IoT, and many other applications where heavy write performance, reduced latency, and a dynamic schema are required.

DynamoDB allows you to store any amount of data and handle any level of user traffic. It allows you to scale up or down a table's read/write capacity without affecting the up time and performance of the table. You can use the management console for monitoring DynamoDB resource utilization and it's effective performance metrics.

It helps you reduce storage usage by automatically deleting the expired items from a table. Since it can help you automatically delete expired data, the cost for storing data can be significantly optimized.

DynamoDB tables are spread across a cluster of servers that are sufficient for handling the desired throughput and the required storage for consistent and reliable performance. It stores data in **Solid State Drive** (**SSD**) and the data is replicated across multiple AZs for obtaining high availability and data durability.

DynamoDB components

There are basically three core components of a DynamoDB table: tables, items, and attributes.

Let us understand these core components in detail:

- **Tables**: DynamoDB stores data in an entity called a table. A table consists of a set of data; for example, the following employee table shows how you can store employee information in a DynamoDB table.
- **Item**: A table consists of multiple items. An item consists of a group of attributes. An item is like a record or row in an RDBMS table. In the following employee table example, you can see the data of two employees. Each employee data represents an item in DynamoDB.
- **Attributes**: An item in a table consists of multiple attributes. An attribute is a basic data element of an item. It is similar to a field or a column in an RDBMS. However unlike RDBMS, attributes in a table item can have sub attributes. You can see that in the following employee data example, the address attribute is further broken down into multiple attributes for representing specific data:

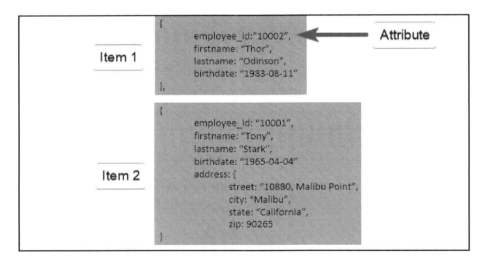

Figure 11.3: DynamoDB table items and attributes

As you can see in the preceding example, the first record in a table does not contain an address whereas, the next record has an address and its subset attributes in the record. This shows the flexibility in the schema of a DynamoDB table. You can have different attributes in subsequent records based on need.

Primary key

While creating a DynamoDB table, you need to specify the table name and the primary key of the table. It is mandatory to define a primary key in the DynamoDB table. A primary key is a mechanism to uniquely identify each item in a table. A primary key does not allow two items with the same key value in a table. There are two types of primary keys:

- **Partition key**: It is a simple primary key that is composed of a single attribute named partition key. DynamoDB partitions the data in sections based on the partition key value. The partition key value is used as an input to an internal hash functions, which determines in which partition the data is stored. This is the reason partition key is also called the *hash* key. No two items in a table can have the same partition key. Since the data is divided into partitions based on its partition key value, data retrieval becomes faster. You can observe in the preceding *Figure 11.3*, employee_id is an example of a simple primary key. You can rapidly access employee information from a table by providing the employee_id.

- **Partition key and sort key**: Partition key and sort key are composed of two attributes and that's why it is also called as a composite primary key. As the name suggest, the first attribute of the key is the partition key and the second attribute is the sort key. Just like the partition key, the composite key also uses the partition key as an input to an internal hash function. This hash function determines the place of an item in a partition. The partition is a physical storage, which is internal to DynamoDB, for arranging the item to get the best possible performance from the table.

DynamoDB stores all items with the same partition key together. In a partition, items are ordered based on a sort key value. Thus, the partition key determines the first level of sort order in a table whereas the sort key determines the secondary sort order of the data stored in a partition. A sort key is also called a *range key*.

A table with both partition key and sort key can have more than one item with the same partition key value; however, it must have a different sort key. In the following example, you can see that `department_id` is a partition key and `employee_id` is a sort key. A department can have multiple employee records, which leads to repeating the `department_id`; however, `employee_id` cannot repeat with the same department name:

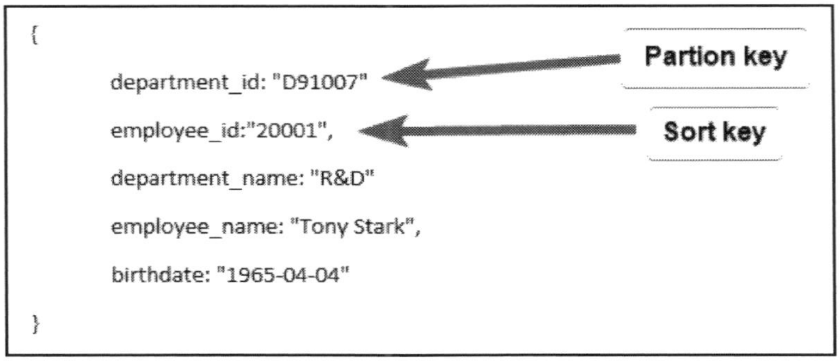

Figure 11.4: Partition key and sort key

In a nutshell, there can be two types of primary keys:

- Single attribute *partition key*
- Two attributes: *partition key and sort key*

Secondary indexes

DynamoDB allows you to create secondary indexes on a table. It is an alternate way to query table data in addition to querying it using the primary key. It is not necessary to use indexes, but using secondary indexes provides some flexibility in querying the data.

There are two types of secondary indexes:

- **Global Secondary Index (GSI)**: It consists of a partition key and a sort key, which has to be different from the primary keys defined on the table
- **Local Secondary Index (LSI)**: It uses the same partition key as of the table but uses a different sort key

DynamoDB allows you to create 5 GSI and 5 LSI on a table.

- Every index is associated with a table, called the base table for the index.
- DynamoDB automatically maintains the indexes. Whenever data is added, updated, or deleted from the base table, DynamoDB adds, updates, or deletes the corresponding item in the related indexes.
- While defining the index, you can choose what all attributes are copied to the index. At minimum, DynamoDB projects at least the key attributes from the table.

DynamoDB Streams

DynamoDB Streams provides an optional feature that can capture data modification events whenever a DynamoDB table is changed. The event data is captured in the steam in near real time in chronological order as the event occurs. Each of the events are recorded by a stream record.

When you enable a stream on a DynamoDB table, it writes a stream record as and when one of the following events occurs:

- When a new item is added to a table, the stream captures an image of the entire item including all of the item attributes
- When an item is updated, the stream captures the *before* and *after* values of all the attributes modified during the process
- When an item is deleted from the table, the stream captures an image of the entire item before it is deleted

A stream record consists of the name of the table, the timestamp when the event occurs, and other metadata. A stream record can last for 24 hours; after that it is automatically deleted from the stream.

You can also use AWS Lambda to create a trigger along with DynamoDb streams. A Lambda function can execute whenever a defined event occurs in a stream. Let us consider the Employee table used in the previous examples. When a new employee record is created, you want to send an email to all the employees in the department to welcome the new joinee. In such cases, you can enable a stream on the Employee table and then associate the stream with a pre-defined Lambda function, which sends an email to all the employees in a department where a new employee joins.

The Lambda function executes whenever there is a new record available in the stream; however, it processes only new items added to the employee table. The Lambda function invokes the Amazon **Simple Email Service (SES)** for sending emails to the users in the department. The following *Figure 11.5* illustrates this scenario:

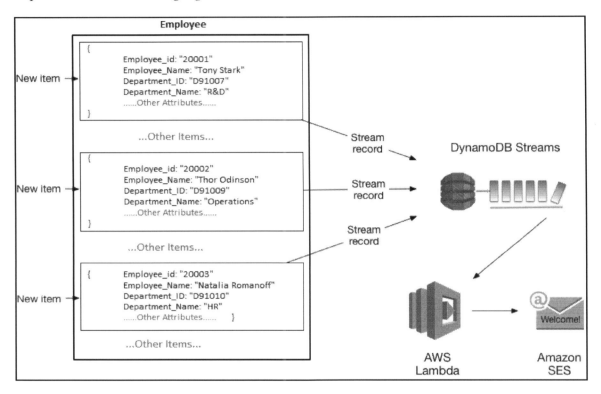

Figure 11.5: DynamoDB Streams with Lambda Function

Apart from triggers, DynamoDB streams can be used for data replication within a specific region or across multiple regions. They can also be used for materialized views of DynamoDB tables. A materialized view is a database object that contains the result of a query just like *views* in RDBMS terminology. DynamoDB stream can also be used for data analysis with Kinesis materialized views.

Read consistency model

Amazon provides DynamoDB in multiple AWS regions across the globe. All of these regions are independent and physically isolated from each other. If you create a DynamoDB table `Employee` in us-east-1 region and similarly create another table `Employee` in the us-west-2 region, these tables are two separate and isolated tables. An AWS region consists of multiple AZs. Each of the AZs are isolated from failures in any of the AZs in a region. Amazon provides an economical and low-latency network connection between all the AZs in a region.

Whenever you write data to a DynamoDB table, AWS replicates this data across multiple AZs to provide high availability. After writing data to a DynamoDB table, you get an HTTP 200 response. HTTP 200 (OK) indicates that the data is safely updated to all the replicated copies stored in different AZs. AWS provides two types of read consistency models: eventually consistent read and strong consistent read. These models are based on the mechanism of how soon the data is replicated across the AZs.

Eventually consistent reads

While reading data from a DynamoDB table using with eventually consistent reads, the result you may get might not reflect any recently completed write operations. Since the data is stored in multiple AZs, it takes few seconds to synchronize the data in multiple location. Eventually, the consistency of data is achieved. In such cases, if you repeat your read operation after a short while, it returns the latest copy of the data.

Strong consistent reads

If you opt for a strongly consistent read on a DynamoDB table, it provides the response with the most up-to-date data. It reflects changes from all prior write operations which were successful. While working with strongly consistent reads, if there is any outage or delay in the network, the data may not be available immediately.

By default, DynamoDB uses eventually consistent reads. If you need to use strongly consistent reads, you need to specify as much while creating the table.

Read operations such as GetItem, Query and Scan provide a `ConsistentRead` parameter. When you set this parameter to True, DynamoDB uses strongly consistent reads.

Naming rules and data types

DynamoDB supports a number of data types. This section describes these data types as well as DynamoDB naming rules.

Let's start by understanding naming rules first.

Naming rules

Each table, attributes, and any other object in DynamoDB should have a names. All the names that you use in DynamoDB should be concise and meaningful. For example, a table can be named `Employee`, `Department`, `Books`, and so on. Just like these names, whatever name you use should be self-explanatory.

Here are some of the naming rules for DynamoDB:

- Names are case-sensitive and must be encoded in UTF-8
- A table name and an index name may range between 3 to 255 characters
- Names may contain only the following characters:
    - a-z
    - A-Z
    - 0-9
    - _ (underscore)
    - - (dash)
    - . (dot)
    - Attributes can have a number of characters between 1 to 255.

 There are a number of special characters and reserved words in DynamoDB. These reserved words are given in the link `http://docs.aws.amazon.com/amazondynamodb/latest/developerguide/ReservedWords.html`.

Apart from these reserved words, the following characters have special meaning in DynamoDB:

- # (hash)
- : (colon)

Although, DynamoDB allows you to use this list of reserved names and special characters, it is recommended you not use them for naming purposes in DynamoDB.

Data types

DynamoDB supports a number of data types for attributes in a table. These data types can be categorized in three parts

- **Scalar types**: Scalar data type represents one value. It includes data types such as number, string, binary, boolean, and null.
- **Document types**: A document data type contains of a complex structure with nested attributes. Examples of such structures are JSON and XML. DynamoDB supports list and map document data types.
- **Set types**: A set data type contains a group of scalar values. The set types supported by DynamoDb are string set, number set, and binary set.

You need to specify names and respective data types for each of the primary key attributes while creating a DynamoDB table. In addition to that, each primary key, be it a partition key or sort key, must be defined as one of the following scalar data types:

- string
- number
- binary

DynamoDB is a schemaless NoSQL database. While creating a table, you need to define the primary key and its respective data types. Apart from that you do not need to define other attributes and their data types while creating a table. In contrast, while creating a table in RDBMS, you need to specifically define a schema with field names and its data types. DynamoDB has a flexible schema that allows you to directly store the data without defining the schema. You just need to define the primary key;the rest of the attributes can be taken care dynamically as you store the data in the table.

The following section describes each of these data types along with an example format.

Scalar data types

The scalar data type includes number, string, binary, boolean and null.

- **String**

Encoding	Unicode with UTF-8 binary encoding
Length	Greater than 0 and less than 400 KB
Partition key length	Maximum 2048 bytes

Sort key length	Maximum 1024 bytes
Usage	To represent string, alternatively date, and timestamp in string format

- **Number**

Can store	Positive, negative or zero
Precision	Maximum up to 38 digits
Positive range	1E-130 to 9.9999999999999999999999999999999999999E+125
Negative range	-9.9999999999999999999999999999999999999E+125 to -1E-130

- **Binary**

Can Store	Binary data such as images, compressed text, encrypted data
Length	Great than 0 and less than 400 KB
Binary attribute as partition key	Maximum length 2048 bytes
Binary attribute as sort key	Maximum length 1024 bytes
Supported encoding	Application must send the data in base64-encoded format

- **Boolean:** Boolean is also a scalar data type and it can store either *true* or *false* values
- **Null:** Null data type indicates an undefined or unknown state of the data

Document types

DynamoDB supports two document data types: **List** and **Map**. You can create a complex data structure by nesting these data types up to 32 levels deep.

DynamoDB does not limit on the number of values it can store in a list of a map data types; however, a table item must not exceed a total item size of 400 KB..

DynamoDB does not support empty scalar data types or set data types; however, it does support empty list and maps data types.

- **List:** A list data type can store a collection of values in square brackets [...]. You can compare the list data types with a JSON array. You can store any data types within the list and all elements in the list may or may not be of the same data type.
- Simple list example:
    - TechGiants: ["Amazon", "Apple", "Google", "Facebook"]
- Multiple data type list example:
    - DeckOfCards: ["Ace", 2, 3, 4, 5, 6, 7, 8, 9, 10, "Jack", "Queen", "King"]

- **Map:** A map data type attribute can consist of a collection of name-value pairs. This collection of values can be in any order. Map values are stored in curly braces { ... }. You can compare map with a JSON format. DynamoDB does not restrict you from storing any data type in a map element. You can also store multiple data types in an element. They do not need to be of the same size.
- Generally, maps are used for storing JSON documents in DynamoDB.

Example of map with a nested list:

```
{
employee_id: "D10007",
employee_name: "Tony Stark",
address: [
        home:
        {
                street: "10880, Malibu Point",
                city: "Malibu",
                state: "California",
                zip: 90265
        },
        office:
        {
                street: "890, Fifth Avenue, Manhattan",
                city: "New York",
                state: "New York",
                zip: 10019
        }

    ]
}
```

Set types

DynamoDB supports set data types that contains a group of scalar values. The set types supported by DynamoDB are string set, number set, and binary set.

When you use a set type, all the values within a set must be of the same data type. If you declare a set of type string, the set can contain only string values. If you declare an attribute of type number, the set can contain only number values within the set.

DynamoDB does not restrict you on the number of values within a set; however, the item containing the set data cannot exceed the DynamoDB item size limit of 400 KB.

The set must contain unique values. DynamoDB does not preserve the order of set values. Considering that, your application should not rely on any static element order in a set; also, it is important to note that DynamoDB does not support an empty set.

Examples of string, number and binary sets are as follows:

```
["Amazon", "Google", "Microsoft", "Facebook", "Apple"]
[-3.14159, 0, 1, 1.4142, 2, 4, 8, 16, 32]
["eNrLz0sFAAKRAUM=", "eNorKc8HAAK8AVs=", "eNoryShKTQUABm4CGQ=="]
```

Creating a DynamoDB table – basic steps

After going through the core components of a DynamoDB table, it's time to create a table. This section describes the process of creating a DynamoDB table:

1. Log in to your AWS account and open the DynamoDB console at `https://console.aws.amazon.com/dynamodb/`.
2. Click on the **Create Table** button.
3. In the **Create DynamoDB table** dialog, you can choose various options as given in the following *Figure 11.6*:

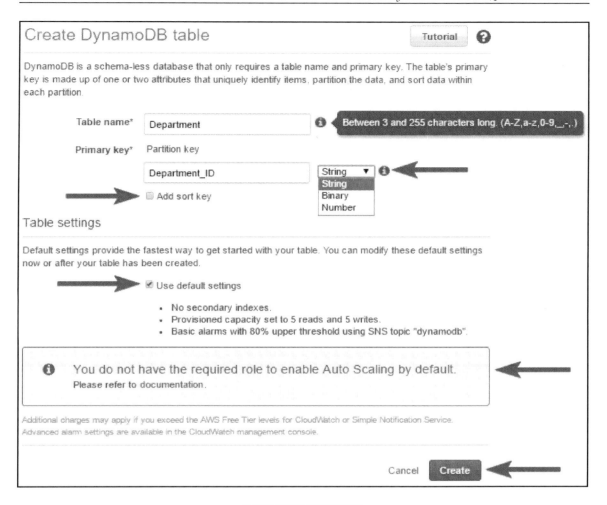

Figure 11.6: Create DynamoDB table

1. Enter the desired table name as shown in the preceding screen. **Table name** can be between 3 to 255 characters long.

2. Enter the partition key name and select the key type from the drop-down menu. Any primary key can be only a scalar data type that is **String, Binary** or **Number**.

3. Check **Add sort key** if required and enter the sort key name and data type. This is required only if you want to create a composite primary key with a combination of a *partition key* and a *sort key*.

4. With the default settings, Amazon creates a table without any secondary indexes and provisions a 5 read with 5 write capacity. It also creates a **Basic alarms with 80% upper threshold using SNS topic "dynamodb"**. You can customize these settings by unchecking the **Use default settings** checkbox.

5. As you can see in the preceding *Figure 11.6*, there is a warning saying that **You do not have the required role to enable Auto Scaling by default**. This warning comes only if you do not have any such role in your IAM roles. You can safely ignore this, as DynamoDB creates a new role when you create a table with default settings. In the advanced settings, there is an option to create a new Auto Scaling role for DynamoDB or to use an existing one. This is explained in the subsequent points.

4. Click on **Create**, after choosing the appropriate options.

Now, let us understand some of the advanced settings in the table creation process.

Adding a sort key while creating a DynamoDB table

You can add a sort key while creating a table by selecting the **Add sort key** checkbox as follow:

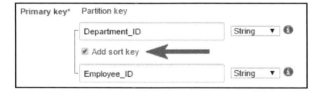

Figure 11.7: Adding a sort key

Using advanced settings while creating a DynamoDB table

With the default setting, Amazon creates a table without any secondary indexes and provisions a 5 read with 5 write capacity. It also creates a **Basic alarm with 80% upper threshold using the SNS topic "dynamodb"**. You can customize these settings by unchecking the **Use default settings** checkbox. Let us understand the options in advanced settings.

On the create table screen uncheck **Use default settings**. It displays the screen shown as follow:

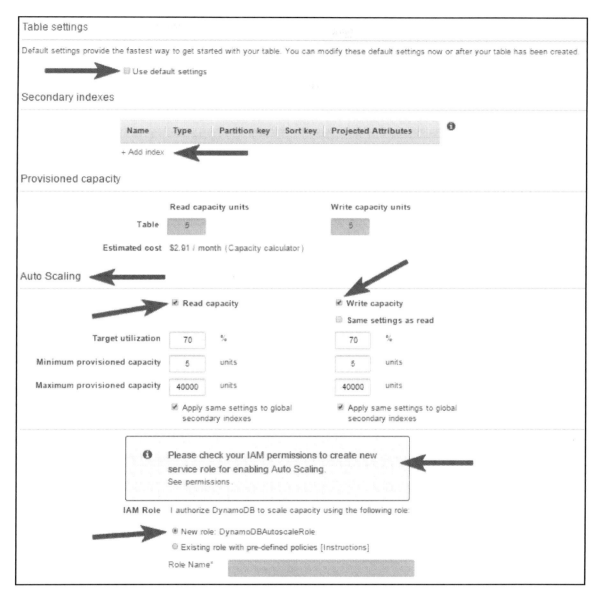

Figure 11.8: Create table screen - advanced settings

As you can see in the advanced settings, there is a provision to create secondary indexes and set up Auto Scaling and also an option to create a **New role: DynamoDBAutoScaleRole** or to choose an existing role for Auto Scaling permissions. Let us understand each of these options one by one.

Creating secondary indexes – table settings

The create table screen allows you to create secondary indexes while creating a table. For creating secondary indexes, click on **Add index** in the **Table settings** screen, as shown in the previous *Figure 11.8*.

Clicking on **Add index** brings up the following *Figure 11.9* with further options:

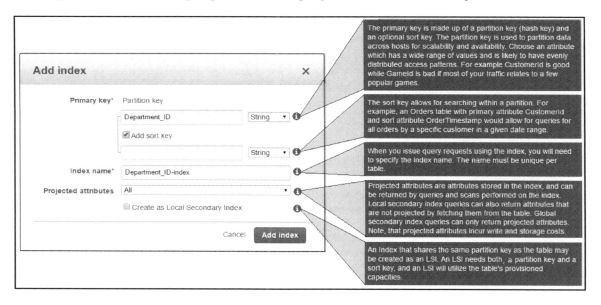

Figure 11.9: Create secondary index

As shown in the preceding *Figure 11.9*, you can enter the **Partition key** name and optionally a sort key name based on the requirement. Index name is automatically populated with the **Partition key** name and the -index suffix. You can change the index name, if required. The index name must be unique per table.

Projected attributes are attributes which are stored in the index. While creating an index, you can specify what all attributes you want to add to the index. You can select these projected attributes from the drop-down box. There are three options in the drop-down box. You can either choose **All** attributes or you can choose **Keys only** or you can select **Include** and add specific attributes that you want to add to the index. Whatever attributes you choose here, are returned by query and scan performed on the index.

Provisioned capacity – table settings

If you choose to customize the default settings, you can configure the **Provisioned capacity** for the table. Provisioned capacity settings are disabled if Auto Scaling is enabled. For a custom read or write capacity, you need to disable the **Read capacity** and **Write capacity** checkbox. After disabling the Auto scaling, you can choose the specific **Read capacity** units and **Write capacity** units. You can refer to *Using advanced settings while creating a DynamoDB Table* section. Table read and write capacity is automatically taken care if you enable Auto Scaling on the table.

Auto Scaling – table settings

You can configure the Auto Scaling options from **Table settings**. You can selectively choose Auto Scaling for Read Capacity and/or Write Capacity as per your needs. There are three options you need to configure in order to use Auto Scaling shown as follow:

- **Target utilization**: Default value for **Target utilization** is 70%. You can change this value based on the need. DynamoDB automatically scales up the read/write capacity of the table , in case the utilization goes beyond the target utilization percentage configured here. The table capacity scales up to **Maximum provisioned capacity** configured. You can individually specify **Target utilization** thresholds for read as well as write operations.
- **Minimum provisioned capacity:** While creating the table, you can specify the **Minimum provisioned capacity** for a table. Irrespective of utilization, DynamoDB provisions the minimum read and/or write capacity as configured here. DynamoDB does not scale itself down beyond **Minimum provisioned capacity**. You can separately specify the **Minimum provisioned capacity** for read as well as write operations.

- **Maximum provisioned capacity:** While using Auto Scaling on a table, you can configure the maximum scaling capacity of a table. DynamoDB does not scale beyond this capacity during Auto Scaling events. You can separately specify the **Maximum provisioned capacity** for read as well as write operations:

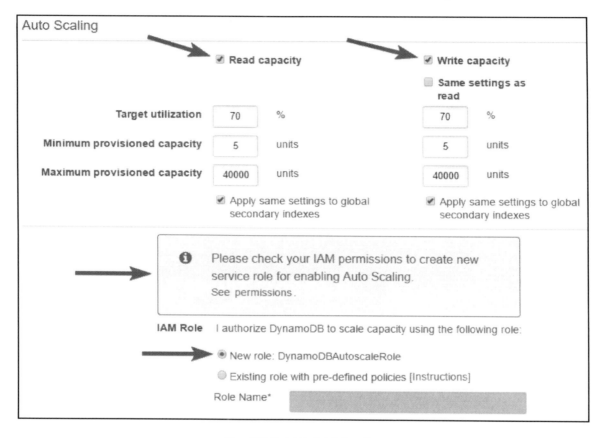

Figure 11.10: Create table -Auto Scaling settings

You can enable or disable Auto Scaling for **Read capacity** and **Write capacity** separately as displayed in the preceding *Figure 11.10*. Unchecking **Read Capacity** disables Auto Scaling for read capacity. Similarly, unchecking the **Write Capacity** disables Auto Scaling for write capacity.

For Auto Scaling the table capacity, DynamoDB requires permission. As shown in the previous snapshot, you need to either select **New role: DynamoDBAutoscaleRole** or choose **Existing role with pre-defined policies**. If you select **Existing role with pre-defined policies**, you need to specify an existing role name, which carries sufficient permissions for Auto Scaling the DynamoDB table.

> For more details on creating a role for DynamoDB Auto Scaling, you can refer to the URL: http://docs.aws.amazon.com/amazondynamodb/latest/developerguide/AutoScaling.CLI.html#AutoScaling.CLI.CreateServiceRole.

Methods of accessing DynamoDB

Amazon provides a DynamoDB console, CLI and API interface to access DynamoDB resources.

Let's understand each of these interfaces.

DynamoDB console

Amazon provides a DynamoDB AWS Management Console. You can access the console on the URL: https://console.aws.amazon.com/dynamodb/home.

Here's what you can do with the DynamoDB AWS Management Console:

- You can access the DynamoDB dashboard for monitoring recent alerts, the total provisioned capacity of tables, health of the service, and latest news on DynamoDB.
- The console allows you to create, update, and delete tables. It also provides a capacity calculator that can help you estimate the capacity units you may need based on the information you provide.
- You can manage DynamoDB Streams.
- The console also helps you to see items stored in a table, add new items, update existing items, and delete items.
- You can also manage **Time To Live (TTL)** for items stored in a table. TTL is defined for automatically deleting an item from the table when it expires.
- Console also helps you to query items in a table and perform a scan on a table.

- The interface also helps you to create and view alarms for monitoring a table's capacity usage.
- You can view in real time a table's top monitoring metrics graph, directly from CloudWatch onto the DynamicDB console.
- Console provides you an interface to change the provisioned capacity of a table.
- There is a provision in the console to create and delete GSIs.
- It enables you to create triggers that can connect DynamoDB streams to a Lambda function.
- You can also add tags to your DynamoDB resources for better identification and categorization of resources.
- Using Console, you can also purchase reserved capacity.

The console also provides a number of navigation tabs. The following list provides a quick reference to each of the tabs available on the console:

Navigation tab	Description
Overview	Displays table details and manage Streams and TTL
Items	Manages table items and executes queries and scans against table and indexes
Metrics	Views and monitors CloudWatch metrics related to DynamoDB
Alarms	Views and manages CloudWatch alarms
Capacity	Views and updates provisioned capacity of a table
Indexes	Views and manages GSIs
Triggers	Manages triggers that can connect DynamoDB streams to a Lambda function
Access control	Manages fine-grained access control and configures web identity federation
Tags	Adds tags to resources for better identification and categorization of resources

DynamoDB CLI

AWS provides CLI to manage AWS services using the command line. You can use CLI for a number of purposes such as creating a script to automate a task or creating a table and performing many other DynamoDB tasks using utility scripts.

If you have not already setup AWS CLI, you can follow the instructions for downloading and configuring it at the URL: `http://aws.amazon.com/cli`.

Working with DynamoDB CLI is very simple if you understand the basics right. Here's the syntax for working with DynamoDB CLI:

```
aws dynamodb <operation-name> <--parameters-name> <parameter-value> ... <--
parameters-name> <parameter-value>
```

The following command creates a DynamoDB table named `employee` with the attributes `Employee_ID` and `Employee_Name`. It also creates a partition key on the attribute `Employee_ID`:

```
aws dynamodb create-table \
    --table-name employee \
    --attribute-definitions \
        AttributeName=Employee_ID,AttributeType=S \
        AttributeName=Employee_Name,AttributeType=S \
    --key-schema AttributeName=Employee_ID, KeyType=HASH
    --provisioned-throughput ReadCapacityUnits=1,WriteCapacityUnits=1
```

Similarly, the following commands add new items to the `employee` table:

```
aws dynamodb put-item \
--table-name employee \
--item \
    '{"Employee_ID": {"S": "10001"}, "Employee_Name": {"S": "Vipul
Tankariya"}, "Country": {"S": "India"}}' \
--return-consumed-capacity TOTAL

aws dynamodb put-item \
--table-name employee \
--item \
    '{"Employee_ID": {"S": "10002"}, "Employee_Name": {"S": "Bhavin
Parmar"}, "Country": {"S": "India"}}' \
--return-consumed-capacity TOTAL
aws dynamodb put-item \
    --table-name employee \
    --item '{ \
        "Employee_ID": {"S": "10003"}, \
        "Employee_Name": {"S": "Gajanan Changadkar"}, \
        "Country": {"S": "India"} }' \
    --return-consumed-capacity TOTAL
```

Sometimes the complex JSON format may create problems on the command line. AWS provides a way to handle this format using a file as an argument on the command line. The following example shows how you can run CLI with JSON file arguments.

Let us assume that all the command line arguments are stored in a JSON file called `condition-file.json` for creating items in the employee table:

```
aws dynamodb query --table-name employee --key-conditions file://condition-
file.json
```

AWS provides a number of commands to work with DynamoDB.

 You can refer to the URL `http://docs.aws.amazon.com/cli/latest/reference/dynamodb/index.html` for more of such commands.

Working with API

Apart from the AWS Management Console and CLI, AWS also provides APIs to work with DynamoDB. These APIs can be used to develop applications that can manage various DynamoDB operations. For using APIs, you need to install AWS SDKs. AWS provides SDKs for a number of programming languages such as Java, JavaScript in the browser, .Net, Node.js, PHP, Python, Ruby, C++, Go, Android, and iOS.

The following table describes where you can start working with these SDKs:

Language	Reference URL
Java	`https://aws.amazon.com/sdk-for-java`
JavaScript in the browser	`https://aws.amazon.com/sdk-for-browser`
+.Net	`https://aws.amazon.com/sdk-for-net`
Node.js	`https://aws.amazon.com/sdk-for-node-js`
PHP	`https://aws.amazon.com/sdk-for-php`
Python	`https://aws.amazon.com/sdk-for-python`
Ruby	`https://aws.amazon.com/sdk-for-ruby`
C++	`https://aws.amazon.com/sdk-for-cpp`
Go	`https://aws.amazon.com/sdk-for-go`
Android	`https://aws.amazon.com/mobile/sdk/`
iOS	`https://aws.amazon.com/mobile/sdk/`

DynamoDB provisioned throughput

DynamoDB provides the Auto Scaling feature for automatically scaling the read and write capacity of a table; however, if you do not use it, you need to manually handle the throughput requirement of your table. DynamoDB measures the throughput capacity using read and write capacity units.

Read capacity units

DynamoDB processes the read operations based on the type of read consistency used. Using one read capcity unit, DynamoDb can process one strongly consistent read per second. In the same line, DynamoDB can process two eventual consistent reads per second using one read capacity unit. Using one read capacity unit, DynamoDB can process an item of up to 4 KB in size. If the item size is more than 4 KB, it requires an additional read capacity unit to process it. In short, item size and consistency model determines the total number of read capacity units required to process it.

- 1 read capacity unit = 1 strongly consistent read
- 1 read capacity unit = 2 eventual consistent reads
- 1 read operation can process an item of up to 4 KB in size
- If an item is more than 4 KB in size, it requires additional read operations
- If an item is less than 4 KB in size, it still requires 1 read capacity units

Write capacity units

Using one write capcity unit, DynamoDb can process one write per second and write an item of maximum 1 KB in size. If the size of the item is larger than 1 KB, it requires additional write capacity units. In short, the number of write capacity units required to process an item depends up on the size of the item.

- 1 write capacity unit = 1 write operation of up to 1 KB in size
- If an item is larger than 1 KB, it requires additional write capacity units
- If an item is less than 1 KB in size, it still requires 1 write capacity unit

Calculating table throughput

If you create a table with a throughput of 5 read capacity units and 5 write capacity units:

- It can perform a strongly consistent read of up to 20 KB per second
  - 5 read capacity units x 4 KB

- It can perform an eventual consistent read of up to 40 KB
  - 5 read capacity units x 4 KB x 2
- It can write 5 KB per second
  - 5 write capacity units x 1 KB
- When you manually configure the throughput of a table, it determines the highest amount of capacity an application can utilize from a table or associated index. If your application consumes more throughput than configured in the provisioned throughput settings, application requests start throttling. This can either crash the application or give a lackluster performance.
- Let's consider a couple of examples to understand the throughput calculation:

Example 1: You have an application that requires reading 15 items per second. Each item is of 3 KB in size. If the application requires strongly consistent reads, what read capacity is required to address this need?

Explanation:

One read capacity unit can process one strongly consistent read of up to 4 KB item in size. If the item size is less than 4 KB, it still requires one read capacity to process the read operation.

Let us formulate this understanding:

Read throughput = (Item size rounded-up in multiples of 4KB) / 4 KB x number of items

Read throughput = 4 / 4 x 15 (Item size is 3 KB, which is rounded-up to 4 KB)

Read throughput = 1 x 15

Read throughput = 15

The answer is 15 read capacity units.

In the same example if the requirement changes to an eventual consistent read, then you just need to divide the result by 2 as one read capacity unit can process two eventual consistent reads.

Example 2: You have an application that requires reading 80 items per second. Each item is 5 KB in size. If the application requires using strongly consistent read, what read capacity is required to address this need?

In this example, the item size is 5 KB, which is greater than 4 KB. We need to round it up to a multiple of 4 KB, which is 8 KB in this case. Remember, if an item is more than 4 KB in size, it requires additional read capacity. This is the reason why we need to always use multiples of 4 while calculating the read throughput.

Let's add the values in the formula for this example:

Read throughput = (Item size rounded-up in multiples of 4KB) / 4 KB x number of items

Read throughput = 8 / 4 x 80

= 2 x 80

= 160

The answer is 160 read capacity units.

Similarly, if the requirement changes from strong consistent read to eventual consistent read, you need to divide the answer by 2.

Example 3: You have an application that requires reading 60 items per second. Each item is 3 KB in size and the application requires using eventual consistent read. What read capacity is required to address this need?

Here's the formula for calculating read capacity for eventual consistency:

Read throughput = ((Item size rounded-up in multiples of 4 KB) / 4 KB x number of items) / 2

= (4 / 4 x 60) / 2

= (1 x 60) / 2

= 60/2

= 30

The answer is 30 read capacity units.

Example 4: You have an application that writes 10 items per second with each item being 8 KB in size. How many write capacity units are required to address this need?

Remember, 1 write capacity unit = 1 write operation of up to 1 KB in size. Here's the formula that can help us in calculating the required write throughput

Write Throughput = (Item size rounded-up in multiples of 1KB) / 1KB x number of items

= Item size rounded-up in multiple of 1KB x number of items

= 8 x 10

= 80

The answer is 80 write capacity units.

DynamoDB partitions and data distribution

Table partitioning is a mechanism to segregate a large table into smaller, more manageable parts without creating a separate table for each part. A partitioned table physically stores data in groups of rows. These groups of rows are called partitions. You can separately access and maintain each partition.

DynamoDB also manages data in partitions. DynamoDB uses SSDs for storing data and automatically replicates data across multiple AZs in an AWS region. DynamoDB automatically manages partitions; you as a consumer do not need to manage the partitions.

While creating a table, DynamoDB allocates a sufficient number of partitions to the new table such that it can handle any provisioned throughput needs. However, DynamoDB can allocate additional partitions to a table in certain situations. The following are the scenarios when DynamoDB allocates additional partitions:

- In case a table's provisioned throughput goes beyond what the existing partitions can handle
- In case an existing partition consumes allocated storage space and more storage space is required

Partition management tasks are performed automatically in the background without affecting the provisioned throughput of a table. It is also important to note that GSIs are also segregated in partitions. The data in an index is stored separately from the base data of a table. Index partitions and table partitions act in a similar manner in DynamoDB.

Data distribution – partition key

As we have seen earlier in this chapter, DynamoDB allows you to create a primary key either with a single attribute partition key or with a composite key comprising of a combination of a partition key and sort key. If we create a table with only the partition key, each item in the table is retrieved based on the partition key value.

DynamoDB uses an internal hash function for writing an item to the table. The partition key value acts an input to the hash function. Based on the partition key value, the hash function determines the target partition for storing the item.

It is required to provide the partition key value for reading an item from the table. This value is used in the hash function to locate the partition where the item can be found.

Let us consider an example to understand how the items are stored in a partition. The following *Figure 11.11* describes the details of a `Cars` table. The table spans in multiple partitions. The primary key for the table is `CarType`. For simplifying the concept, only the primary key attribute is included in the *Figure 11.11*. While storing data in a table, DynamoDB uses an internal hash function to determine the target partition for storing a new item. In this example, the hash function determines the target partition based on the hash value of `CarType`, which is `Sedan`. Here, it is important to understand that the items are not stored in a sorted order. The location of each item is determined based on the value of the partition key:

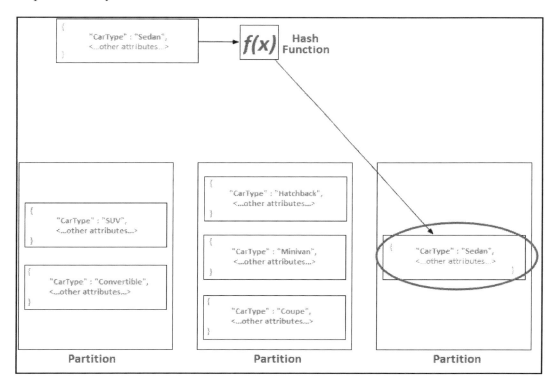

Figure 11.11: Partitioning and hash function

The preceding example with `CarType` is given for simplifying the data distribution concept in DynamoDB partition. While designing a DynamoDB table, you should choose a partition key that has a large number of distinct values. If the partition key values are similar, data may end up getting stored in some specific partitions and may not give optimum performance.

Let's understand this scenario with an example:

If you're creating a Vendor table, `Vendor_ID` is a good candidate for the partition key, however, you need to ensure that the values in the `Vendor_ID` are distinct.

If you choose values in Vendor_ID as `V0001`, `V0002`, `V0003`, and so on, it works and items are distributed in multiple partitions depending up on the table size. However, the best way to optimize partitioning is to use more distinct values such as `FMG001`, `ITV001`, `SRV001`. In this example, `Vendor_ID` includes the vendor type like **FMG** for **Fast-moving consumer goods** vendor, **ITV** for **IT vendor**, **SRV** for **service vendor,** and so on. Such approaches create more distinct values in the table and distributes data optimally in more partitions.

Data Distribution – partition key and sort key

When you use the composite key in a DynamoDB table, which includes the partition key and the sort key, the approach for calculating the hash value remains the same. In addition to keeping partition key values physically close to each other, DynamoDB orders the data by the sort key value.

As described in the previous section, while storing an item in a table, DynamoDB uses the partition key value. The partition key value is supplied to the hash function, which determines the target partition for storing the item. The target partition may already have a number of items. In such scenarios, DynamoDB stores the item in the ascending order of sort key values in the table.

For reading an item from the table, you need to supply the partition key value as well as sort key value. DynamoDB uses the partition key value to determine the source partition where the item can be found. DynamoDB even allows you to read multiple items from a table using a single query. However for reading multiple items in a single query requires that the items must have the same partition key value. While querying the table you can optionally apply a condition to the sort key such that the times within a specific range value is returned.

DynamoDB global and LSI

DynamoDB provides primary keys for quickly accessing items in a table by supplying primary key values in a query. The primary key is useful and it can certainly speed up data retrieval from the table; however, in certain scenarios, applications can take advantage of secondary indexes. Secondary indexes can speed up item retrieval from a table based on any other attributes than the primary key. For fulfilling such requirements, you need to create secondary indexes on the DynamoDB table. Once a secondary index is created on an attribute, you can use a `Query` or `Scan` request on specific indexes to retrieve items.

Secondary index refers to a data structure which is made up of a subset of attributes in a table. The main purpose of a secondary index is to provide an alternate key for query operations. You can use secondary indexes to read data using a query, in the same manner as you query a DynamoDB table. DynamoDB allows you to create multiple secondary indexes, which can help you to access the data using different query patterns.

A secondary index is linked with a table, which becomes the source of data for it. The source table from which an index takes data, is also called as the base table for the index. While defining an index, you need to define an alternate key, which can be a partition key and sort key. You can also choose what all attributes you want to associate with the index. You can choose, all attributes, primary keys or you can choose a specific set of attributes from the table. DynamoDB copies all the attributes you choose, into the index along with primary key attributes. Once the index is created, you can query or scan the index in the same way as you query a table.

DynamoDB automatically maintains secondary indexes. When you change anything on the base table, the change automatically reflects into indexes. If you add, modify, or delete any item in the table, DynamoDB automatically updates this change in the index.

There are two types of secondary indexes:

- **GSI**: It is an index, which can have a different partition key and sort key as compared to the base table. With GSI, you can query data spanned across all the partitions in a base table. In short, when any query is executed against a GSI, its scope spans across all the partitions in a table. This is the reason it is called **Global Secondary Index (GSI)** .

- **LSI**: It is an index which has the same partition key as its base table, however, it has a different sort key. Every partition in a LSI is mapped with a base table partition, which carries the same partition key value. In short, LSIs scope is associated with its base table partition and this is the reason it is called **Local Secondary Index (LSI)**.

Difference between GSI and LSI

Characteristic	Global secondary index	Local secondary index
Key schema	Primary key of a GSI can be a single attribute key which is called a partition key or, it can be a composite key with two attributes, the partition key and the sort key.	Primary key of a LSI has to be a composite key, a combination of the partition key and sort key.
Key attributes	Partition key and sort key of the index, can be any attributes from the base table.	Partition key of the index must be the same as the base table partition key. Sort key can be any attribute from the base table.
Size restrictions per partition key value	There is no restriction on the size of the index.	Total size of all items for a specific partition key value must be less than or equal to 10 GB in size.
Online index operations	GSI can be created while creating a table. DynamoDB also allows you to add additional GSIs to an existing table or delete an existing index as and when required.	LSIs can be created while creating a table, however, DynamoDB does not allow you to add additional LSIs to an existing table. It does not even allow you to delete any existing LSI.
Queries and partitions	You can query the entire table stored across all the partitions in a GSI.	You can query only a single partition with a partition key value specified in the query.
Read consistency	GSI supports only eventual consistency reads.	LSI supports eventual consistency or strong consistency reads based on your requirement.

Provisioned throughput consumption	You need to configure a separate provisioned throughput for GSI. You need to explicitly specify the read and write capacity units while creating a GSI. When you query a GSI, it uses read and write capacity units on top of base table consumption.	LSI does not have their own provisioned throughput. It utilizes read and write capacity units from the base table when you query or scan a table or write data to base table.
Projected attributes	While executing a query or scan or a write request against a GSI, you can specify only the attributes, which are projected while creating the index. It cannot handle any request for attributes which are not defined as part of the index.	While executing a query or scan or a write request against a LSI, you can specify any attributes from the table, even if these attributes are not projected while creating the index. When you query any additional attributes, which are not part of the index, DynamoDB automatically gets these attributes from the base table.

DynamoDB query

DynamoDB query is a mechanism to request items from a table. Using queries, you can request data from a table or any secondary index that has a composite primary key. While querying a table or index, you have to provide the name of the partition key attribute and a value for the same. The query returns all the items with that partition key value. You can also select a sort key attribute and filter the search result using any of the comparison operators.

For working with Query in GUI, you need to go to the DynamoDB dashboard in the URL: `https://console.aws.amazon.com/dynamodb`. From the dashboard, you can select **Tables** -> **Movies** -> **Items** tab. In this example, we are working with the **Movies** table. You need to select the specific table name that you want to work with on your dashboard.

In the following *Figure 11.12* , you can see the Query window for the **Movies** table, which has **year** as the partition key and **title** as the sort key:

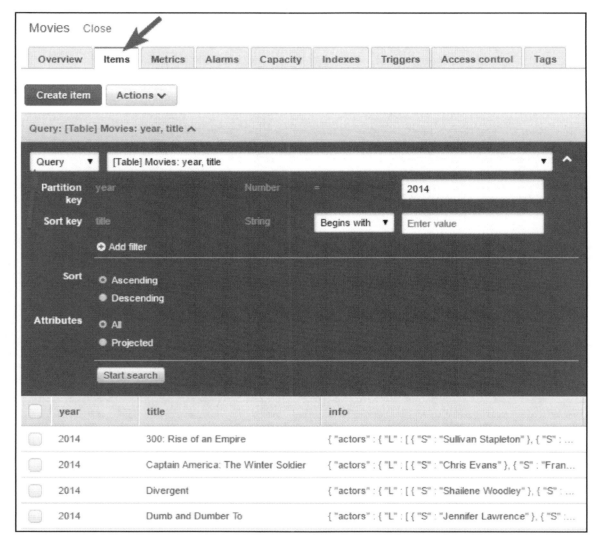

Figure 11.12: DynamoDB query

Do remember to select **Query** from the dropdown box as shown in the preceding figure. By default, the item window is loaded with the **Scan** option as selected instead of **Query**.

For querying the table, you need to provide the partition key value and optionally provide the sort key value. In this example, the partition key is the **year** and **2014** is given as the value. You can click on the **Start search** button after entering the required values. As you can see in the preceding *Figure 11.12*, the table displays all items with the partition key value as **2014**.

For sort keys and filters, you can use a number of key condition expressions. These expressions are described in the following table:

Key condition exptressions

Operator	Example	Description
=	a = b	true if the attribute a is equal to the value b
<	a < b	true if a is less than b
<=	a <= b	true if a is less than or equal to b
>	a > b	true if a is greater than b
>=	a >= b	true if a is greater than or equal to b
Between	a BETWEEN b AND c	true if a is greater than or equal to b, and less than or equal to c
Begins with	begins_with (a, substr)	true if a begins with a specified substring

While working with Query, you can sort the output in ascending or descending order. You can opt to display all the attributes of the table or you can choose to project specific attributes from the table.

Query with AWS CLI

Here are some examples of using DynamoDB Query with AWS CLI:

```
aws dynamodb query \
    --table-name Items \
    --key-condition-expression "Item_ID = :id" \
    --expression-attribute-values  '{":id":{"S":"i10001"}}'
```

The query retrieves all records for Item_ID i10001 from the table Items. As you can see in the preceding example, for initiating a query request to DynamoDB, you need to use the aws dynamodb query command on AWS CLI. aws dynamodb query requires some parameters. Let's understand the query with the following table:

Command/Expression	Description
aws dynamodb query	AWS CLI command to initiate a query request to DynamoDB.
\	Backward slash \ is used for indicating continuation of code in next line.
--table-name	Indicates the name of the DynamoDB table.
--key-condition-expression	Describes the key condition. In this example it indicates the attribute Item_ID with id as the expression attribute. Expression attributes can be any string to describe the expression. It is different from table attributes. It is a custom name given to an expression. The value of the custom expression is declared in --expression-attribute-values as described in the example.
--expression-attribute-values	Describes the value for the key-condition-expression attribute defined in --key-condition-expression. In this example, a custom expression attribute id is declared. Here you need to declare the value type and the value for the expression attribute. In this example id is of type S (String) with the value i10001. For the numeric expression attribute, you need to specify N instead of S.

If you need to deep dive into Queries, you can take a look at the URL.
http://docs.aws.amazon.com/amazondynamodb/latest/developerguide/
Query.html.

DynamoDB Scan

When you use Query on DynamoDB, it uses only primary key attribute values to perform a search on the table. You can further refine the result by using filters on attributes other than primary keys. Unlike a Query, the Scan operation can perform a search on any attribute of the table. It also allows you to refine the search by applying filters to the scan result.

When you perform a Scan operation on a table, it reads all the items in the table or indexes and by default returns all the items and attributes. If you do not want to retrieve all the attributes, you can use the `ProjectionExpression` parameter to retrieve only specific attributes.

Irrespective of whether the items are found with the matching criteria or not, Scan always returns a result set. If items with the specified criteria are found, it returns the result set with the items else it returns an empty result set.

Every Scan operation can retrieve a maximum of 1 MB data. You can apply a filter to the scan for further narrowing down the result based on the filter conditions.

Example: The following AWS CLI example scans the `Movies` table and returns only the items with `ReleaseYear` as `2017`:

```
aws dynamodb scan \
    --table-name Movies \
    --filter-expression "ReleaseYear = :name" \
    --expression-attribute-values '{":name":{"N":"2017"}}
```

Reading an item from a DynamoDB table

You can use the GetItem operation for reading an item from a DynamoDB table. While performing a GetItem operation, you need to provide a table name and the primary key of the table item.

Example: Following example shows how to read an item from the employee table using AWS CLI. In this example, `employee_id` is the primary key of the table:

```
aws dynamodb get-item \
   --table-name employee \
   --key '{"employee_id":{"S":"E10001"}}'
```

For reading an item from the table, it is necessary to specify the entire primary key. If a table has a composite key, you need to specify the partition key as well as the sort key in `get-item`. It performs an eventual consistent read by default; however, you can use a strongly consistent read by using the `ConsistentRead` parameter. Also by default, `get-item` returns all the attributes of a table. If you want to return specific attributes of the table, you can use the project expression parameter. You can also set the `ReturnConsumedCapacity` parameter to `TOTAL` for returning the number of read capacity used by the `get-item` operation.

Example:

```
aws dynamodb get-item \
    --table-name employee \
    --key '{"employee_id":{"S":"E10001"}}' \
    --consistent-read \
    --projection-expression "FirstName, LastName, JoiningDate, Gender,
DateOfBirth" \
    --return-consumed-capacity TOTAL
```

Writing an item to a DynamoDB table

DynamoDB provides the following operations for creating, updating, and deleting an item from a table:

- PutItem
- UpdateItem
- DeleteItem

For performing either of these operations, you need to specify the complete primary key. If the table has just a partition key, you can provide the partition key. If the table has a composite key, you need to provide both, the partition key as well as the sort key. Providing just the partition key or the sort key alone does not work for these operations. You need to specify both the keys for composite key table.

If you want the operation to return write capacity consumed by the operation, you can set `ReturnConsumedCapacity` parameter with one of the following values:

- `TOTAL`: Indicates total number of write capacity units consumed by the operation
- `INDEXES`: Indicates total number of write capacity units consumed by the table along with the secondary indexes affected by the operation

- NONE: Does not return any details for write capacity consumed by the operation. If you do not explicitly specify the ReturnConsumedCapacity parameter, by default it considers NONE.

PutItem

It is used for writing a new item in the table. If the table already has an item with the same key, it is replaced with the new item.

Example:

```
aws dynamodb put-item \
    --table-name employee \
    --item file://employee-item.json
```

Details of the --item argument are stored in the file employee-item.json:

```
{
    "FirstName": {"S": "Gini"},
    "LastName": {"S": "Davidson"},
    "JoiningDate": {"S": "20120817"},
    "Gender": {"S": "Female"},
    "DateOfBirth": {"S": "19850719"}
}
```

UpdateItem

UpdateItem is used for updating an item in a table. If you use an existing primary key with UpdateItem, it updates the existing item. If the specified key does not exist, it creates a new item in the table.

While, you can specify the attributes that you want to modify with the update expression. Along with the udpate expression, you can use expression attribute values that act as placeholders for the real values.

Example:

```
aws dynamodb update-item \
    --table-name employee \
    --key file://employee-key.json \
    --update-expression "SET FirstName = :fname, LastName = :lname,
JoiningDate = :jdate" \
    --expression-attribute-values file://expression-attribute-values.json \
    --return-values ALL_NEW
```

The values for the arguments against `--key` parameter are stored in the file `employee-key.json`:

```
{
    "employee_id": {"S": "E10001"},
    "DateOfBirth": {"S": "19850719"}
}
```

The values for arguments against `--expression-attribute-values` are stored in the file `expression-attribute-values.json`:

```
{
    ":fname": {"S":"Johnson"},
    ":lname": {"S":"David"},
    ":jdate": {"S":"19850720"}
}
```

DeleteItem

The deleteItem operation is used for deleting an item from a DynamoDB table. You need to supply a specific key value as a parameter with the DeleteItem operation.

```
aws dynamodb delete-item \
    --table-name employee \
    --key file://key.json
```

It is important to note that if the table has a composite key, you need to specify both the partition key and the sort key.

Contents of the `key.json` file:

```
{
    "employee_id": {"S": "E10001"},
    "DateOfBirth": {"S": "19850719"}
}
```

Conditional writes

You can perform write operations in a DynamoDB table using PutItem, UpdateItem, and DeleteItem. By default, these operations are unconditional in nature; this means that when you perform write operations using these statements, they overwrites an existing item with the same primary key value specified in the operation.

If you do not want to overwrite an existing item, or write an item only based on a specific condition, you can use conditional write with these operations. Conditional write succeeds only in case it meets an expected condition; else, it returns an error. Conditional writes can be used in multiple scenarios.

Example scenarios when conditional writes can be used:

- You want to write an item using the PutItem operation, only if the item with the specific key does not exist
- You want to update an item using the UpdateItem operation, only if the item attribute contains a specific value
- You want to update an item using the UpdateItem operation, only if it is not already been modified by another user

Conditional writes can be handy in situations where multiple users try to update the same item. Let's consider the following *Figure 11.13* to understand this scenario in which Vipul and Bhavin are trying to update the same item in a DynamoDB table:

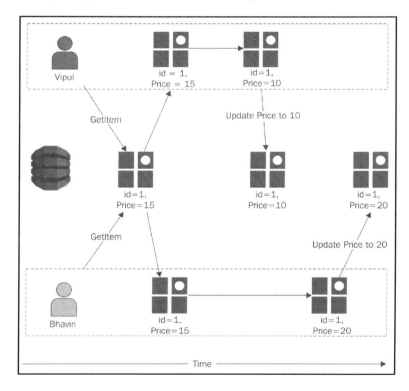

Figure 11.13: No Condition write

Let's assume that Vipul tries to update the `Price` attribute to `10` in the `ProductMaster` table:

```
aws dynamodb update-item \
    --table-name ProductMaster \
    --key '{"Id":{"N":"1"}}' \
    --update-expression "SET Price = :newprice" \
    --expression-attribute-values file://expression-attribute-values.json
```

As we explained earlier, the arguments for `--expression-attribute-values` should be stored in a separate JSON file. In this case, arguments are stored in the file named expression-`attribute-values.json` with the following content:

```
{
    ":newprice":{"N":"10"}
}
```

Now let's consider that Bhavin updates the same item using the UpdateItem request and changes the price to `20`. For Bhavin, the `--expression-attribute-values` parameter file can contain the following values:

```
{
    ":newprice":{"N":"20"}
}
```

The UpdateItem operation initiated by Bhavin succeeds but it overwrites the change made by Vipul.

For performing a conditional write, you need to specify the condition expression along with PutItem, DeleteItem, or UpdateItem. A condition expression contains a string with attribute names, conditional operators, and built-in functions. The operation executes only if the entire expression evaluates to true else; if not, the operation fails.

Let us understand the conditional write using the following figure, which shows how the conditional write prevents Bhavin from overwriting Vipul's changes on the same item. You can compare the previous *Figure 11.13* and the following *Figure 11.14* and observe how the condition is highlighted shown as follow:

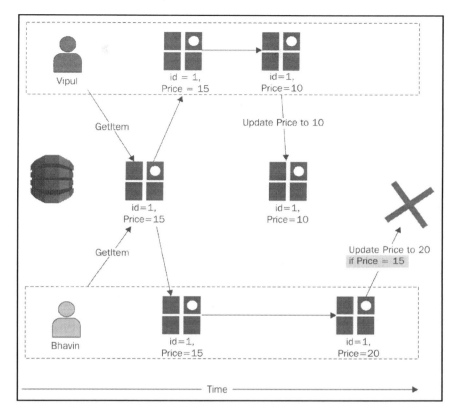

Figure 11.14: Conditional write

Let us understand how you can achieve this using AWS CLI.

While updating the `Price`, Vipul gives a condition to update the Price to 10 only if the Price is 15:

```
aws dynamodb update-item \
    --table-name ProductMaster \
    --key '{"Id":{"N":"1"}}' \
    --update-expression "SET Price = :newprice" \
    --condition-expression "Price = :currprice" \
    --expression-attribute-values file://expression-attribute-values.json
```

The arguments for `--expression-attribute-values` should be stored in a separate JSON file. In this case, arguments are stored in the file named `expression-attribute-values.json` with the following content:

```
{
    ":newprice":{"N":"10"},
    ":currprice":{"N":"15"}
}
```

Vipul's update succeeds as the condition evaluates to be true.

Similarly, Bhavin tries to update the `Price` to 20 with a conditional expression that checks for the current price as 15 before updating it.

For Bhavin, the `--expression-attribute-values` parameter file can contain the following values:

```
{
    ":newprice":{"N":"20"},
    ":currprice":{"N":"15"}
}
```

Since Vipul has already changed the `Price` to 10, the condition expression in Bhavin's request evaluates to false and his update fails.

User authentication and access control

For accessing DynamoDB you need credentials. The credentials should have the permission to access the DynamoDB table. This section provides details on how you can use IAM to secure DynamoDB resources.

There are a number of ways in which you can access DynamoDB resources:

- AWS root user account
- IAM user
- IAM role
  - Identity federation
  - Cross-account access
  - AWS service access
  - Application running on EC2

If you have valid credentials that can authenticate against DynamoDB you can initiate the request to access but, unless you have permissions associated with your credentials, you cannot perform any operation against DynamoDB. For example, for creating a new DynamoDB table, you need to have the table creation permission.

Before understanding these permissions, let us understand the resources in DynamoDB.

Tables are the primary resources in DynamoDB. Apart from tables, there are indexes and streams, which are part of DynamoDB. Indexes and streams are associated with a table and they are sub-resources of a table. DynamoDB maintains unique ARNs with each of the resources and sub-resources as shown in the following table:

Resource type	ARN format
Table	arn:aws:dynamodb:*region*:*account-id*:table/*table-name*
Index	arn:aws:dynamodb:*region*:*account-id*:table/*table-name*/index/*index-name*
Stream	arn:aws:dynamodb:*region*:*account-id*:table/*table-name*/stream/*stream-label*

Managing policies

Access to any resource is determined by a permission policy. In Chapter 3, *Getting Familiar with Identity and Access Management*, managing policy is discussed in detail. This chapter emphasizes on IAM with respect to DynamoDB. There are two types of policy: identity-based policies and resource-based policies. Identity-based policies are attached to an IAM identity and resource-based policies are attached to a resource. This section discusses about identity-based policies only, as DynamoDB does not support resource-based policies.

There are three identities in IAM

- User
- Group
- Role

You can attach a policy to a user or a group and grant them access to DynamoDB resources such as table, indexes, and streams.

You can attach a policy to a role for granting cross-account permissions.

Here's an example of a permission policy. This example policy allows
`dynamoDB:ListTables` permission for all resources:

```
{
    "Version": "2012-10-17",
    "Statement": [
        {
            "Sid": "ListTables",
            "Effect": "Allow",
            "Action": [
                "dynamodb:ListTables"
            ],
            "Resource": "*"
        }
    ]
}
```

Here's one more example of a permission policy. In this example policy, access is granted on three actions, namely DescribeTable, Query, and Scan. As you can observe in the previous policy, access is granted to all resources with * and, unlike the previous policy, in this policy, access is granted to a specific table using an ARN for the table:

```
{
    "Version": "2012-10-17",
    "Statement": [
        {
            "Sid": "DescribeQueryScanEmployeeTable",
            "Effect": "Allow",
            "Action": [
                "dynamodb:DescribeTable",
                "dynamodb:Query",
                "dynamodb:Scan"
            ],
            "Resource": "arn:aws:dynamodb:us-east-1:account-
id:table/employee"
        }
    ]
}
```

DynamoDB API permissions

While setting up a permission policy, you can refer to the following table which lists DynamoDB API operations, associated actions, and the ARN format for the resource. For more information, refer to `http://docs.aws.amazon.com/amazondynamodb/latest/developerguide/api-permissions-reference.html`.

API Actions	Resources

dynamodb:BatchGetItem	`arn:aws:dynamodb:region:account-id:table/table-name`
	or
	`arn:aws:dynamodb:region:account-id:table/*`

dynamodb:BatchWriteItem	`arn:aws:dynamodb:region:account-id:table/table-name`
	or
	`arn:aws:dynamodb:region:account-id:table/*`

dynamodb:CreateTable	`arn:aws:dynamodb:region:account-id:table/table-name`
	or
	`arn:aws:dynamodb:region:account-id:table/*`

dynamodb:DeleteItem	`arn:aws:dynamodb:region:account-id:table/table-name`
	or
	`arn:aws:dynamodb:region:account-id:table/*`

dynamodb:DeleteTable	`arn:aws:dynamodb:region:account-id:table/table-name`
	or
	`arn:aws:dynamodb:region:account-id:table/*`

dynamodb:DescribeLimits	`arn:aws:dynamodb:region:account-id:*`
dynamodb:DescribeReservedCapacity	`arn:aws:dynamodb:region:account-id:*`

dynamodb:DescribeStream	`arn:aws:dynamodb:region:account-id:table/table-name/stream/stream-label`
	or
	`arn:aws:dynamodb:region:account-id:table/table-name/stream/*`

dynamodb:DescribeTable	`arn:aws:dynamodb:region:account-id:table/table-name`
	or
	`arn:aws:dynamodb:region:account-id:table/*`

dynamodb:DescribeTimeToLive	`arn:aws:dynamodb:region:account-id:table/table-name`
	or
	`arn:aws:dynamodb:region:account-id:table/*`

dynamodb:GetItem	`arn:aws:dynamodb:region:account-id:table/table-name`
	or
	`arn:aws:dynamodb:region:account-id:table/*`

dynamodb:GetRecords	`arn:aws:dynamodb:region:account-id:table/table-name/stream/stream-label`
	or
	`arn:aws:dynamodb:region:account-id:table/table-name/stream/*`

dynamodb:GetShardIterator	`arn:aws:dynamodb:region:account-id:table/table-name/stream/stream-label`
	or
	`arn:aws:dynamodb:region:account-id:table/table-name/stream/*`

dynamodb:ListStreams	`arn:aws:dynamodb:region:account-id:table/table-name/stream/*`
	or
	`arn:aws:dynamodb:region:account-id:table/*/stream/*`

dynamodb:ListTables	`*`

dynamodb:ListTagsOfResource	`arn:aws:dynamodb:region:account-id:table/table-name`
	or
	`arn:aws:dynamodb:region:account-id:table/*`

dynamodb:PutItem	`arn:aws:dynamodb:region:account-id:table/table-name`
	or
	`arn:aws:dynamodb:region:account-id:table/*`

dynamodb:Query	To query a table:
	`arn:aws:dynamodb:region:account-id:table/table-name`
	or:
	`arn:aws:dynamodb:region:account-id:table/*`
	To query an index:
	`arn:aws:dynamodb:region:account-id:table/table-name/index/index-name`
	or:
	`arn:aws:dynamodb:region:account-id:table/table-name/index/*`

dynamodb:Scan	To scan a table:
	`arn:aws:dynamodb:region:account-id:table/table-name`
	or:
	`arn:aws:dynamodb:region:account-id:table/*`
	To scan an index:
	`arn:aws:dynamodb:region:account-id:table/table-name/index/index-name`
	or:
	`arn:aws:dynamodb:region:account-id:table/table-name/index/*`

dynamodb:TagResource	`arn:aws:dynamodb:region:account-id:table/table-name`
	or
	`arn:aws:dynamodb:region:account-id:table/*`

dynamodb:UpdateItem	`arn:aws:dynamodb:region:account-id:table/table-name`
	or
	`arn:aws:dynamodb:region:account-id:table/*`

dynamodb:UpdateTable	`arn:aws:dynamodb:region:account-id:table/table-name`
	or
	`arn:aws:dynamodb:region:account-id:table/*`

dynamodb:UpdateTimeToLive	`arn:aws:dynamodb:region:account-id:table/table-name`
	or
	`arn:aws:dynamodb:region:account-id:table/*`

dynamodb:UntagResource	`arn:aws:dynamodb:region:account-id:table/table-name`
	or
	`arn:aws:dynamodb:region:account-id:table/*`

DynamoDB best practices

DynamoDB best practices are as follows:

- Create a primary key that spans across multiple partitions. Choose the primary key that has more distinct values. If the number of distinct values is less in a primary key attribute, items may be distributed in a limited number of partitions instead of all available partitions.

- In DynamoDB each item can have a maximum size of 400 K; however, there is no limit on the number of items in a table. To efficiently store large items in a table, use one of the mechanism such as one to many table, multiple tables to support varied access patterns, compress large attribute values, store large attribute values in Amazon S3, or break up large attributes across multiple items.

- By default, Scan reads the entire table with all items and consumes more throughput. Use Query instead of Scan, as it is more economical.

- Create LSIs for frequently queried attributes on the table apart from primary key attributes. It improves the query performance.

- If it is required to use the Scan operation, design an application to use the Scan operation in a way that minimizes the impact on read requests on the table.

- One or more secondary indexes can be created to perform efficient search and query on the attributes other than primary and sort key.

- Rather than Scan, use parallel scan to retrieve a large data set from the table as it uses multiple work threads in the background at low priority without affecting the production traffic. These background processes are called as sweepers.

- It is suggested to plan LSIs very carefully as they can only be defined at the time of creating a table and later they cannot be deleted throughout the table lifecycle. On top of that they share primary read and write throughput from the base table.

- GSI allows creating a secondary index with a different primary key and sort key from the base table. This secondary index can be created and deleted separately at any given time on the base tables. These indexes are maintained automatically with the base table but have their own read/write throughput. Hence create them wisely.

12

Amazon Simple Queue Service

Before understanding **Simple Queue Service (SQS)**, let us understand what a message queue is. A message queue is a queue of messages exchanged between applications. Messages are data objects that are inserted in the queue by sender applications and received by the receiving applications. Receiving applications get the data objects from the queue and process the data received from the queue based on the application requirement. The following *Figure 12.1* describes the message queue in a simple way:

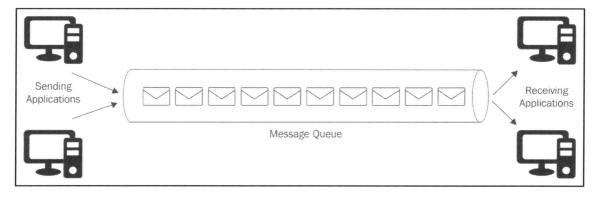

Figure 12.1: Message queue

SQS is a highly reliable, scalable, and distributed message queuing service provided by Amazon. It's a hosted solution provided by Amazon so that you do not need to manage the service infrastructure. SQS stores the messages in transit as they travel between various applications and micro services. Amazon provides a host of web services APIs, which can be accessed using any programming language supported by AWS SDK.

The purpose of this chapter is to introduce readers to basic concepts of SQS with respect to the scope of the AWS Certified Developer - Associate exam. From a development perspective, SQS is a wide topic and a full book can be written on SQS. Considering the scope of the exam, this chapter does not intend to teach the reader how to code SQS applications but focuses more on fundamental aspects of SQS.

Why to use SQS?

There are many reasons to use SQS. Let us start by understanding a simple use case followed by a brief insight on a few more use cases.

Consider a scenario wherein you have a collaborative news site or application that accepts images from the users, optimizes these images to display in multiple devices, and stores them for future retrieval. If the application users are spread across the globe, the application may get a huge number of traffic that uploads images. If these images are directly offloaded to the processing server, the server may not be able to handle the traffic. If you use a scaled up environment to process the images, you end up incurring more costs. Also, a scaled up environment may miss processing some of the images if the process gets interrupted or crashes.

In such scenarios, a message queue comes in handy. The application can send all the image processing requests to a message queue. At the other end, the image processing component of the application can read the message queue and process the requests one by one. This way, the application is not flooded with requests and all the images are processed irrespective of the amount of traffic.

Here are a few more use cases for SQS:

- **Decoupling application processes**: When you start a project, you may not be able to predict what the future needs of the project would be. By segregating the data generation process, the data consumption process and implementing a message queue in between the processes, you can create a data-based interface. All the processes involved in the application can implement this data-based interface. In such a scenario, any process involved in the overall application workflow, can be changed without disturbing other processes.
- **Application scalability**: Since the application processes are decoupled with a message queue, you can easily scale up the data generation and data consuming processes to control the rate at which the data is processed. Without changing the underlying code and by simply adding more processing resources, you can scale up the whole process.

- **Guaranteed message delivery**: Use of a message queue ensures that a message is delivered at least once and eventually processed by the processing application as long as the process continues reading the queue. Depending on the configuration of the queue, you can also ensure that a message is processed only once. Such a guarantee is possible by SQS, as when a process retrieves the message from the queue, it temporarily removes the message from the queue. When the client informs the queue that it has finished processing the message, SQS deletes the message from the queue. If the client does not respond back to the queue in a specific duration, SQS places the message back in the queue. This way, if the message is not processed by a client, it would be available for another client to process.

- **Message order guarantee**: In many scenarios, the order in which the data is processed is very important. SQS provides a mechanism to process the data in a predefined order.

- **Asynchronous data processing**: There are certain requirements wherein you do not need to process the data immediately. SQS allows you to process the messages asynchronously. That means, you can add a message on the queue but do not need to process it immediately. You can add as many messages as required and process them later.

- **Building resilience in the system**: If some processes in your application environment go down, your entire environment does not go down with it. Since SQS decouples the processes, if a client processing a message goes down, the message is re-added to the queue after a specific duration. This message is either processed by another client or the same client after it recovers. This way, SQS builds resilience in the system.

- **Bringing elasticity to application with SQS**: When your application hits an unusual amount of high traffic, it should be able to sustain the load with additional resources. When the traffic subsides, it is wasteful to keep resources on standby for future needs. In such a scenario, using SQS you can build elasticity into your application. Since SQS helps you decouple the processes, you can host data publisher as well as data consumer processes in separate resources. Data publisher and data consumer resources can be scaled up when there is a high amount of traffic and the resources can be scaled down when the traffic is low.

- **Analyzing data flow and performance of the processes**: When you build a distributed system, it is very critical to understand how each of the components performs and if there is any delay, what is the reason for that delay. SQS can easily help in identifying underperforming resources with the insight on rate at which each of the resources perform.

- **Building redundancy with SQS**: Sometimes processes do fail while processing the data. In such scenarios, if the data is not persisted, it is lost forever. SQS takes care of such a data risk by persisting the data till it's completely processed. There is something called the put-get-delete paradigm used by SQS. It requires a queue to explicitly state that the data it has, has finished processing the message it pulled from the queue. The message data is kept safe with the queue and gets deleted from the queue only after confirmation that it is processed.

How queues work?

As shown in the following *Figure 12.2*, SQS works on put-get-delete paradigm:

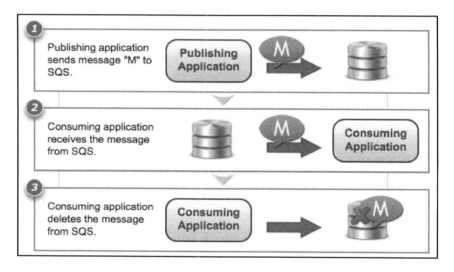

Figure 12.2: Working of SQS

1. The publishing application pushes message *M* into the queue.
2. The consuming application pulls the message *M* from the queue and processes it.
3. The consuming application confirms to the SQS queue that processing on the message is completed and deletes the message from the SQS queue.

Main features of SQS

SQS provides a scalable and reliable messaging platform. It enables you to build operational efficiency in your application without any operational overhead. Some of the benefits of using SQS are explained as follows:

- **Redundant infrastructure**: Amazon SQS provides redundant infrastructure. With its redundant infrastructure, it ensures that a message is delivered at least once in a standard queue and it ensures that a message is delivered exactly once in a **First In First Out (FIFO)** queue. It provides concurrent access mechanism and a highly available environment for queue producer and consumer applications.

- **Multiple producers and consumers**: Multiple components of a distributed application can concurrently send and receive messages at the same time. When a client picks up a message from the queue, SQS locks up that message until the client confirms that it has completed processing the message. If the queue does not receive a response from the client for a specific duration of time, the queue unlocks the message and makes it available for other clients to pick it up from the queue.

- **Queue wise configurable settings**: SQS provides options to configure each queue independently. You do not need to have the same configuration for all the queues. For example, queue *A* may take longer time than queue *B* for processing a request. Such a requirement requires you to configure your queues differently and SQS allows you to configure each queue independent of each other.

- **Variable message size**: SQS supports a message size of maximum 256 KB. If you need a larger size, which is more than 256 KB, you can store it in S3 or DynamoDB. SQS holds the pointer to the S3 object in the queue.

- **Queue access control**: SQS allows you to control producers and consumers that can send and receive messages to or from the queue.

- **Delay queue:** SQS enables you to set a delay time in a queue. Delay time ensures that a message inserted in the queue is postponed for the time configured as *delay time* in the queue. This delay time can be set while creating a queue. You can also change the delay time later on, however, any change in the delay time is effective only with the new messages added to the queue.

- **Payment Card Industry (PCI) compliance**: PCI standard mandates that any service that handles payment data, must adhere to PCI standards in order to be PCI compliant. SQS supports handling of credit card payments with storage and transmission of credit card data. Considering this need, Amazon has built a PCI compliant service.
- **Health Insurance Portability and Accountability Act (HIPAA) compliance**: SQS supports HIPAA compliance. If you have a **Business Associate Agreement (BAA)** with AWS, it enables you to use SQS for building a HIPAA-compliant application that can store **Protected Health Information (PHI)**.

Types of queue

SQS supports mainly two types of queues:

- Standard queues
- FIFO queues

A standard queue generally sends the data in the same order as it receives it, however, in certain occasions, the order may change. Unlike a standard queue, the order in which the data is sent is fixed in FIFO queues.

Let us understand the difference between these queue types with the help of the following table:

Description	Standard queue	FIFO queue
Availability	It's available in all AWS regions.	It's available only in the US East (N. Virginia), US East (Ohio), US West (Oregon), and EU (Ireland) regions.
Throughput	It supports almost all unlimited number of **Transaction Per Second (TPS)** with each API action.	It supports limited throughput. It can support up to 300 messages per second without any batching. With a batch size of 10 messages, it can support up to 3,000 messages per second.
Order	It generally sends the data in the same order as it receives, however, in certain occasions the order may change.	It ensures that the data is sent in FIFO order.

Delivery guarantee	Standard queue guarantees that a message will be delivered at least once, however, occasionally a message may be delivered more than once.	FIFO queue guarantees that a message will be delivered exactly once. The message remains in the queue until the consumer confirms that the message is processed.
Usage	It is used when the throughput is more important than the order in which the data is processed.	It is used when the order in which the data is processed is more important than the throughput.

Dead Letter Queue (DLQ)

A DLQ is used by other queues for storing failed messages that are not successfully consumed by consumer processes. You can use a DLQ to isolate unconsumed or failed messages and subsequently troubleshoot these messages to determine the reason for their failures.

SQS uses redrive policy to indicate the source queue, and the scenario in which SQS transfers messages from the source queue to the DLQ. If a queue fails to process a message for a predefined number of times, that message is moved to the DLQ.

While creating a queue you can enable redrive policy and set the DLQ name as well as maximum receive count after which if the messages is still unprocessed, it can be moved to DLQ.

Queue attributes

SQS uses certain queue attributes that defines the behavior of a queue. While creating a queue, you can either create a queue with default attributes or customize these attributes as per your needs. The following table describes these queue attributes with their acceptable ranges:

Queue attribute	Description	Minimum acceptable range	Maximum acceptable range
`Default visibility Timeout`	The length of time that a message is received from a queue will be invisible to other receiving components.	0 seconds	12 hours

Message Retention Period	The amount of time that SQS retains a message if it does not get deleted.	1 minute	14 days
Maximum Message Size	Maximum message size accepted by SQS.	1 KB	256 KB
Delivery Delay	The amount of time to delay the first delivery of all messages added to the queue.	0 seconds	15 minutes
Receive Message Wait Time	The maximum amount of time that a long polling receive call waits for a message to become available before returning an empty response.	0 seconds	20 seconds
Content-Based Deduplication	FIFO queue uses more than one strategy to prevent duplicate messages in a queue. If you select this checkbox, SQS generates SHA-256 hash of the body of the message to generate the content-based message deduplication ID. When an application sends a message using SendMessage for FIFO queue with message dedupication ID, it is used for ensuring deduplication of the message.	N/A	N/A

Creating a queue

Since you have developed a basic understanding of what SQS is, let us go through the following steps and create and configure our first SQS queue:

1. Log in to the AWS Management Console and navigate to `https://console.aws.amazon.com/sqs/`.

2. Click on a **Create New Queue** button as shown in the following *Figure 12.3*:

Figure 12.3: Create New Queue

3. In the subsequent page, type the name of the queue as shown in the following *Figure 12.4*, ensuring that you are in the intended region. If required, you can change the region from the top-right corner of the screen. Also note that **Queue Name** is case sensitive and can have a maximum of up to 80 characters. When you're creating a FIFO queue, **Queue Name** must end with `.fifo` suffix:

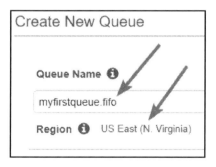

Figure 12.4: Provide queue name

4. By default, the SQS wizard has a **Standard** queue select. Depending on your requirement, you can choose **Standard** or **FIFO** as shown in the following *Figure 12.5*:

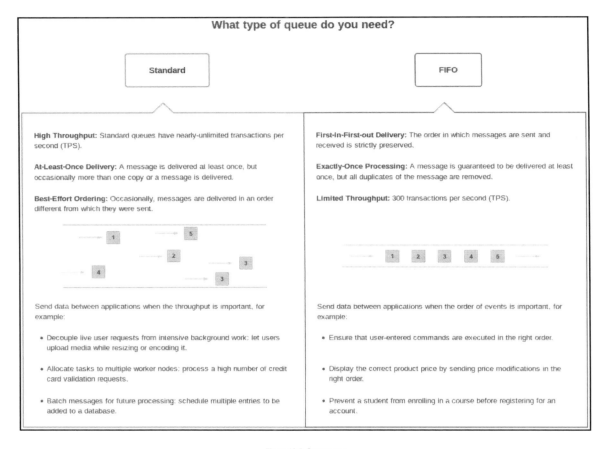

Figure 12.5: Queue types

5. If you want to create a queue with the default parameters, you can click on the **Quick-Create Queue** button. Alternatively, you can click on the **Configure Queue** button for configuring the queue parameters. You can enter appropriate values in the queue attributes as shown in the following *Figure 12.6*. These queue attributes are described in the previous table:

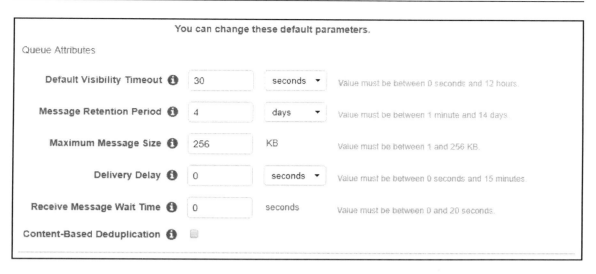

Figure 12.6: Queue Attributes

6. On the same screen, optionally you can enable redrive policy as shown in the following *Figure 12.7*. This is an optional step and is required only if you want to divert unprocessed messages to a DLQ. If you enable the redrive policy, you need to specify the name of an existing queue that can act as a DLQ. You also need to specify the maximum receive count. If a message is received back for the specified number of time, it is moved to the DLQ:

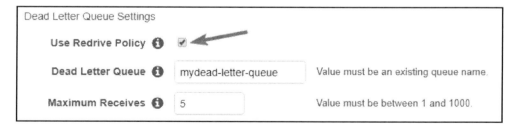

Figure 12.7: Dead Letter Queue Settings

7. In this step, you can optionally enable **Server Side Encryption (SSE)** as shown in the following *Figure 12.8*. If you choose to enable SSE, you can either use the default **Customer Master Key (CMK)** from the AWS **Key Management Service (KMS)** or you can specify any other existing CMK you have in KMS. If you select any other key than the default CMK, you need to manually specify the key ARN. You also need to specify a **Data Key Reuse Period** which can range between 1 minute and 24 hours. For encrypting or decrypting data, SQS needs a data key which is provided by KMS. Once a key is obtained from KMS, it can be used by SQS for the time specified in a **Data Key Reuse Period** before again going to KMS for a new data key:

Figure 12.8: Server-Side Encryption (SSE) Settings

8. After giving all the required input on the screen, you can click on the **Create Queue** button. Once the queue is created, you can see the queue in the SQS dashboard as shown in the following *Figure 12.9*:

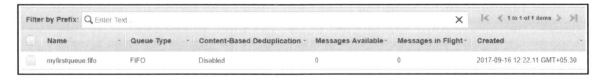

Figure 12.9: SQS dashboard with newly created queue

You can select the queue and see more description on the dashboard. You can also perform other actions on the queue such as configure queue, send a message, delete a queue, and so on.

Sending a message in a queue

For sending a message in a queue, you can follow the following steps:

1. Go to the SQS dashboard and select the queue you want to send the message to as shown in the following *Figure 12.10*:

Figure 12.10: Queue list

2. Click on the **Queue Actions** button and select **Send a Message** as shown in the following *Figure 12.11*:

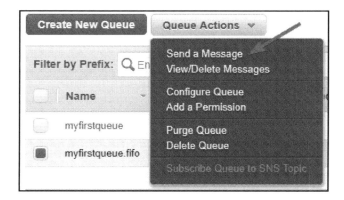

Figure 12.11: Queue Actions-Send a Message

3. In the subsequent screen, enter the message that you want to send to the queue. Enter the **Message Group ID** and also specify the **Message Deduplication ID,** as shown in the following *Figure 12.12.* **Message Group ID** is mandatory. It is used for grouping the message. When you specify a **Message Group ID,** messages sent to a specific group ID in a FIFO queue are guaranteed to be delivered in the First In First Out order. If you have enabled **Content-Based Deduplication** checkbox while creating the queue, **Message Deduplication ID** given in the following *Figure 12.12* is optional:

Figure 12.12: Send a Message-options

Optionally, you can also specify **Message Attributes** as shown in the following *Figure 12.13*:

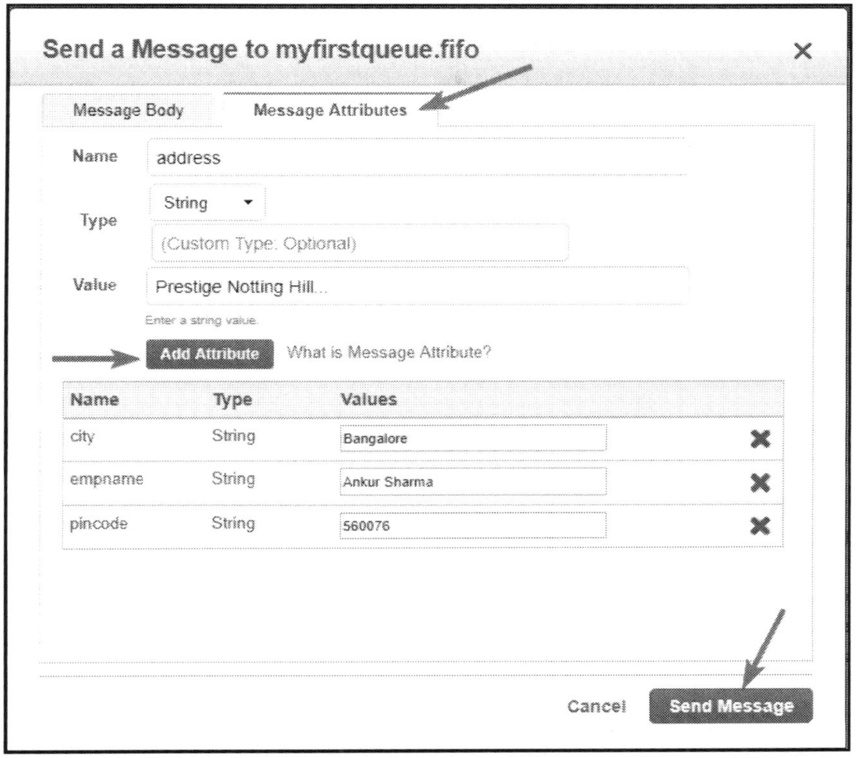
Send a Message to myfirstqueue.fifo
Message Body
Message Attributes
Name
address
Type
String
(Custom Type: Optional)
Value
Prestige Notting Hill...
Enter a string value.
Add Attribute
What is Message Attribute?
Name
Type
Values
city
String
Bangalore
empname
String
Ankur Sharma
pincode
String
560076
Cancel
Send Message

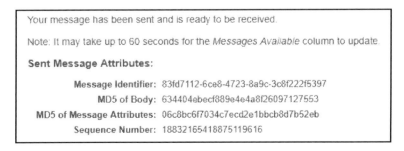

Figure 12.13: Message Attributes

4. Finally, click on the **Send Message** button. It displays a confirmation message as shown in following *Figure 12.14*:

Your message has been sent and is ready to be received.
Note: It may take up to 60 seconds for the Messages Available column to update.
Sent Message Attributes:
Message Identifier: 83fd7112-6ce8-4723-8a9c-3c8f222f5397
MD5 of Body: 634404ebecf889e4e4a8f26097127553
MD5 of Message Attributes: 06c8bc6f7034c7ecd2e1bbcb8d7b52eb
Sequence Number: 18832165418875119616

Figure 12.14: Message sent confirmation

You can either send another message or close the window after reading the confirmation.

Viewing/deleting a message from a queue

After the message is sent to the queue you can retrieve it from the queue. While retrieving a message from the queue, you cannot specify which message you want to retrieve from the queue, however, you can specify how many messages you want to retrieve. Here are the steps for viewing a message from the queue:

1. Select a queue from the queue list as shown in the following *Figure 12.15*:

Figure 12.15: Queue list

2. Click on **Queue Actions** and then **View/Delete Messages** shown as follows:

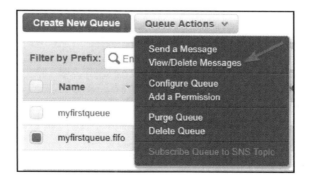

Figure 12.16: Queue Actions-View/Delete Messages

3. From the subsequent screen, you can click on **Start Polling for Messages** as shown in the following *Figure 12.17*:

Figure 12.17: Polling for messages

4. In the subsequent screen you can see up to 10 messages available in the queue as specified in the previous step. The screen resembles the following *Figure 12.18*:

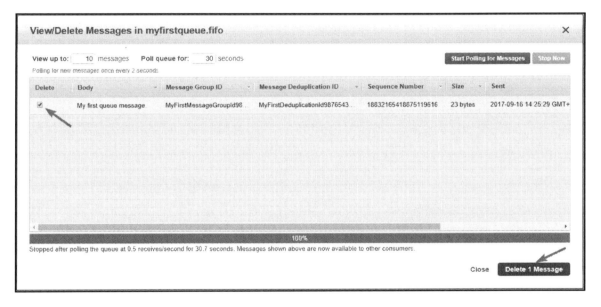

Figure 12.18: Messages in a queue

5. You can select one or more messages from the list that you want to delete and click on **Delete 1 Message**. It displays **Delete Messages** dialog box as shown in following *Figure 12.19*. You can click on **Yes, Delete Checked Messages**. This action deletes the selected message.

Figure 12.19: Delete message confirmation

Purging a queue

Purging a queue means deleting all the messages from a queue. For purging a queue, you can follow these steps:

1. Select a queue from the queue list as shown in the following *Figure 12.20*:

Figure 12.20: Queue list

2. Click on **Queue Actions** and then **Purge Queue** shown as follows:

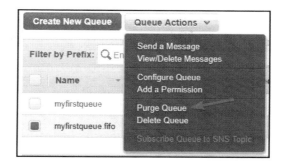

Figure 12.21: Queue Actions - Purge Queue

3. The subsequent screen displays a confirmation message with a number of messages that it would purge from the queue as shown in the following *Figure 12.22*. Clicking on **Yes, Purge Queue** button purges the queue:

Figure 12.22: Purge Queues-confirmation

Deleting a queue

You can perform the following steps to delete a queue:

1. Select a queue from the queue list shown as follows:

Figure 12.23: Queue list

2. Click on **Queue Actions** and then **Purge Queue** as shown in the following *Figure 12.24*:

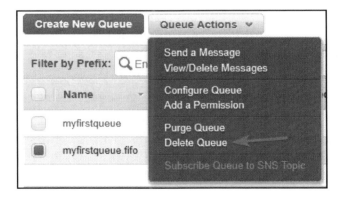

Figure 12.24: Queue Actions - Delete Queue

3. The subsequent screen displays a confirmation message with the number of message the queue contains as shown in the following *Figure 12.25*. Clicking on **Yes, Delete Queue** button deletes the queue:

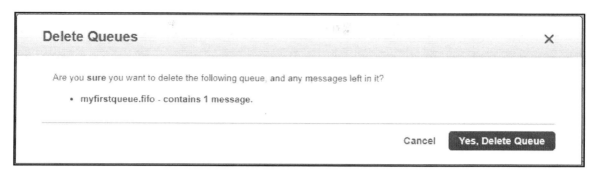

Figure 12.25: Delete Queues-confirmation

Subscribing a queue to a topic

SQS enables you to subscribe your queues to SNS topics. You can choose from a list of already-available SNS topics and subscribe the queue to that topic. Subscription permission is automatically managed by SQS. When a message is published to a topic in SNS, that message automatically goes to all the queues subscribed to that topic. For more details on SNS, you can refer to `Chapter 13`, *Simple Notification Service.*

At present, only standard queues can subscribe to an SNS topic. FIFO queues are presently not supported for topic subscription.

Here are the steps to subscribe a queue to an SNS topic:

1. Select a queue from the queue list as shown in the following *Figure 12.26*:

Figure 12.26: Queue list

2. Click on **Queue Actions** and then on **Subscribe Queue to SNS Topic** as shown as follows:

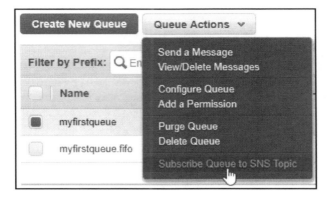

Figure 12.27: Queue Actions-Subscribe Queue to SNS Topic

3. From the subsequent screen, select the appropriate region where your SNS topic is available, choose a topic from the list available. A topic's ARN is automatically populated depending on the topic you select. Alternatively, you can manually type the ARN as required. Finally, you can click on the **Subscribe** button as shown in the following *Figure 12.28*:

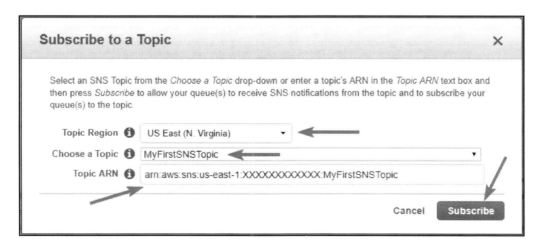

Figure 12.28: Subscribe to a Topic

It displays a confirmation dialog box as shown in the following *Figure 12.29*. You can click on **OK**, the queue is now subscribed to the topic:

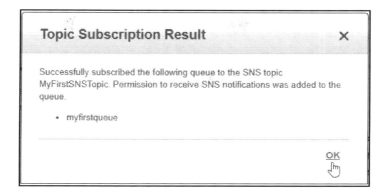

Figure 12.29: Topic Subscription Result

Adding user permissions to a queue

SQS allows you to define permission for your queue. This permission determines the ability of your queue to interact. You can allow or explicitly deny some permissions. The following steps can guide you to set permissions for a queue:

1. Select a queue from the Queue list as shown in the the following *Figure 12.30*:

Figure 12.30: Queue list

2. Click on **Queue Actions** and then **Add a Permission** as shown in the following *Figure 12.31*:

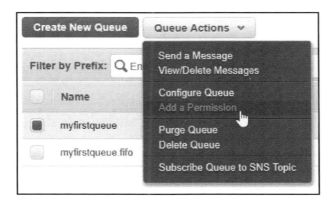

Figure 12.31: Queue Actions - Add a Permission

3. In the subsequent screen, select **Allow** or **Deny** effect as required. You can specify a specific account in the **Principal**, whom you want to assign the permission or choose the **Everybody** checkbox to assign the permission to everybody. From the **Actions** tab, you can choose specific actions that you want to assign or alternatively **All SQS Actions** checkbox to assign permissions for all actions as shown in the following *Figure 12.32*:

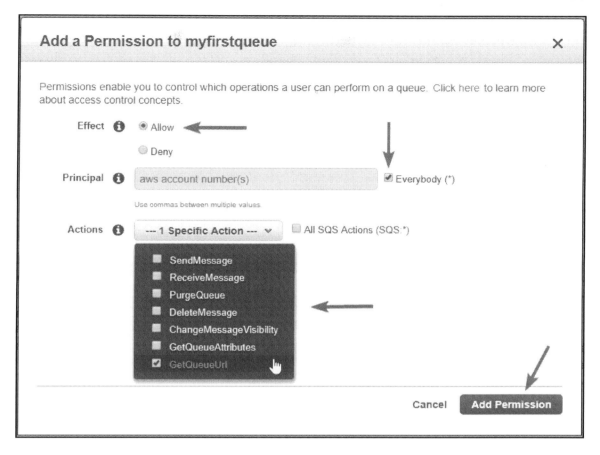

Figure 12.32: Add permission to a queue

SQS limits

It is important to understand SQS limits with respect to queues, messages and policies. This topic describes various limits

- Limits related to queues
- Limits related to messages
- Limits related to policies

The following table describes these limits:

Limit	Applies to	Description
In flight messages per queue	Queues	Standard queue: Maximum 120,000 inflight messages. FIFO queue: Maximum 20,000 inflight messages. SQS returns `overLimit` error if this limit is exceeded.
Queue name	Queues	Queue name can have a maximum of 80 characters. FIFO queue name must end with `.fifo`. Queue name can have alphanumeric characters, hyphen, and underscore.
Message attributes	Message	A message can have a maximum of 10 metadata attributes.
Message batch	Message	A message batch can have a maximum of 10 messages per batch.
Message content	Message	A message content can include only XML, JSON, and any unformatted text.
Message retention	Message	A queue can retain a message for a minimum of 60 seconds, maximum of 14 days and by default, the message is retained for 4 days.
Message throughput	Message	Standard queue: Nearly unlimited TPS, FIFO queue maximum 300 messages per second without batch, and 3,000 message per second with a maximum batch size of 10 messages per operation.
Message size	Message	Minimum size: 1 byte, maximum size: 256 KB.
Message visibility timeout	Message	Maximum 12 hours visibility timeout for a message.
Policy information	Policies	A policy can have a maximum of 8192 bytes, 20 statements, 50 principals, or 10 conditions.

Queue monitoring and logging

Monitoring SQS queues plays a vital role in an application lifecycle. There are many functions that are dependent on monitoring using CloudWatch and relevant triggers. For example, you monitor the size of a queue and define a trigger to automatically scale up EC2 instances with an Auto Scaling group. Similarly, you can scale the number of instances serving the consumer process in case the size of a queue is smaller. Considering the criticality of monitoring with SQS, CloudWatch and SQS are integrated such that you can easily view and analyze various CloudWatch metrics for SQS queues. Queues metrics can be viewed and analyzed using an SQS console, CloudWatch console, programmatically using APIs or using the CLI.

Amazon automatically gathers CloudWatch metrics for an SQS queue and pushes it to CloudWatch with an interval of five minutes. Amazon gathers metrics for all active SQS queues. A queue is said to be active for up to six hours in case it has messages or in case any API action is performed on the queue.

Amazon does not charge you for the SQS metrics collated in CloudWatch. It's provided as part of the SQS queue service without any additional charges. SQS does not support detail, one minute interval monitoring. CloudWatch supports metrics for both the types of queues, that is, standard queues as well as FIFO queues.

CloudWatch metrics available for SQS

CloudWatch supports a list of metrics for SQS. Each of these metrics are explained in following table:

Metrics	Description	Units	Statistics
ApproximateAgeOfOldestMessage	It indicates the approximate age of the oldest message in the queue that is not deleted.	Seconds	Average, Minimum, Maximum, Sum, Data Samples

ApproximateNumberOfMessagesDelayed	It indicates the number of delayed messages in the queue that are not available for reading immediately.	Count	Average, Minimum, Maximum, Sum, Data Samples
ApproximateNumberOfMessagesNotVisible	It displays the number of messages that are inflight.	Count	Average, Minimum, Maximum, Sum, Data Samples
ApproximateNumberOfMessagesVisible	It indicates the number of messages that are available in the queue for retrieval.	Count	Average, Minimum, Maximum, Sum, Data Samples
NumberOfEmptyReceives	It denotes the number of empty responses received by ReceiveMessage API calls.	Count	Average, Minimum, Maximum, Sum, Data Samples
NumberOfMessagesDeleted	It provides the number of messages that are deleted from the queue.	Count	Average, Minimum, Maximum, Sum, Data Samples
NumberOfMessagesReceived	It describes the number of messages that are returned by the ReceiveMessage API calls.	Count	Average, Minimum, Maximum, Sum, Data Samples

NumberOfMessagesSent	It captures the number of messages that are pushed to a queue.	Count	Average, Minimum, Maximum, Sum, Data Samples
SentMessageSize	It calculates the size of messages that are added to a queue.	Bytes	Average, Minimum, Maximum, Sum, Data Samples

Logging SQS API actions

While using SQS, producer, and consumer applications perform a number of actions using API calls. It is very critical to log all these API calls made by various components of a distributed application. Apart from that, there are many operations performed on SQS queues using SQS consoles, their activity should also be logged. In short, any change or operation performed on any SQS queue using APIs, should be logged for auditing and troubleshooting. To cater to this requirement, Amazon has integrated SQS with CloudTrail. CloudTrail is a service that captures any API call initiated to perform SQS operations on a queue. Irrespective of the type of SQS queue, CloudTrail records all the activities performed on a queue.

CloudTrail supports the following actions and records detailed log for these actions:

- AddPermission
- CreateQueue
- DeleteQueue
- PurgeQueue
- RemovePermission
- SetQueueAttributes

Every time, any of the above actions are performed on a queue, CloudTrail generates a detailed log entry along with requestor information which initiated the action. With this information, you can verify if the actions were performed by a root account or an IAM user. It also includes the details if the requested operation was performed with any temporary credentials, a federated user, or any other AWS service. Log files can be stored in an S3 bucket for as long as required. Alternatively, you can define any S3 lifecycle rule to archive it to Glacier or delete it.

You can also integrate it with SNS for generating notification when a new log file is created. It can help you to quickly analyze the log and take any quick actions as needed. AWS also allows you to aggregate SQS log files from more than one AWS regions into a single S3 bucket. This makes it easy to keep track of logs and perform an aggregated analysis on the environment.

SQS security

Amazon's SQS service is built securely. It requires credentials to initiate any request to SQS queues. Even if you supply credentials while initiating a request to a queue, you may not be able to access it unless you have sufficient permission to access the queues and messages. In this section, let us understand authentication and access control related to SQS queues.

Authentication

AWS allows you to access SQS with any of the following identities:

- Root user
- IAM user
- IAM role
    - Federated access
    - Cross-account access
    - AWS service access
    - EC2 applications

SSE

Sometimes it becomes necessary to protect your data using the SSE due to some compliance requirement or due to criticality of the data used in the SQS queue. Amazon provides SSE to protect sensitive data in SQS. SSE helps you to transmit sensitive data in encrypted queues. Amazon uses KMS to manage encryption keys. These keys are used for encrypting the queue.

Messages are encrypted by SSE as soon as the messages are added to the queue. The queue stores these messages in an encrypted format. These messages are decrypted when they are sent to a consumer who is authorized to use it. When using SSE in SQS, requests initiated with the queues must be on HTTPS protocol.

13

Simple Notification Service

AWS **Simple Notification Service (SNS)** works on a push technology. It is also called a server push. In this mechanism, the message or transaction is initiated by the publisher or a central server and AWS SNS delivers the same to the subscribers. It is opposite to the pull mechanism. Pull mechanism is also called a client pull, where the client raises a request to fetch or pull data from the server. Just for a note here, unlike SNS, AWS SQS works on a pull mechanism.

In enterprise architecture, it is often required to send notifications to the subscribers. Some of the following real-time notification use cases help us to understand how and where they are used:

- When an EC2 instance is under or over-utilized for a specific time frame it should send a notification to system administrators and stack holders. For example, at any given time when average CPU usage is above 70% or below 30% for a specific time frame, it sends notification to the system administrator or Auto Scale to scale-out or scale-in number of EC2 instances as per the configuration.
- Usually, installed mobile applications on a smart phone occasionally send push notifications on various offers and discounts based on the user's interaction with the mobile app.
- To send a mobile application push notification the end-user may need to install an application on the smart phone. On the other hand, SMS notifications can be sent on any mobile device. It is irrelevant if the end user has installed your mobile application or not.

- When any new message is published to an SNS topic it can invoke a subscribed Lambda function. Some of the example use cases are:
  - Serverless architecture
  - Automated backups and other daily administrative tasks
  - Processing uploaded objects in S3 buckets

In this chapter, we will cover the following topics:

- Introduction to Amazon SNS
- Creating an Amazon SNS topic
- Subscribing to SNS topic
- Publising a message to an SNS topic
- Deleting an SNS topic
- Managing access to an SNS topic

Introduction to Amazon SNS

Amazon SNS is a managed notification service. It works on a push mechanism, the publisher raises a request to send a message to the subscribers. The following *Figure 13.1* helps to understand the same:

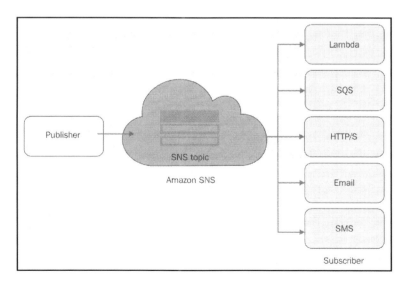

Figure 13.1: Introduction to SNS
Reference URL: http://docs.aws.amazon.com/sns/latest/dg/images/sns-how-works.png

Firstly you need to create an Amazon SNS topic. An SNS topic acts as an access point in between the publisher and subscriber applications. The publisher communicates asynchronously with the subscribers using SNS. Subscribers can be an entity such as a Lambda function, SQS, HTTP or HTTPS endpoint, email, or a mobile device that subscribes to SNS topic for receiving notifications. To receive notifications, subscribers must specify the protocol (that is, **HTTP, HTTPS, Email, Email-JSON, Amazon SQS, Application, AWS Lambda, SMS**). When a publisher has new information to notify to the subscribers, it publishes a message to the topic. Finally, SNS delivers the message/notification to all subscribers.

Topic policy controls who can publish message and subscribe to a topic.

Amazon SNS fanout

Amazon SNS and Amazon SQS are key services to create loosely coupled, scalable, cloud based, and serverless applications in the cloud. One of the common architecture concepts is fanout. In this concept, several Amazon SQSs act as a subscriber. A publisher sends a message to an SNS topic and it distributes it to many SQS queues in parallel. The following image helps us to understand the same concept. For example, a virtual multinational ecommerce company daily introduces hundreds of products for sale in many countries. Now when a new product is saved in a web application, it will send a message to SNS topic. Immediately, the SNS topic sends notifications in parallel to all subscriber SQS queues.

Let's consider a scenario to understand this point.

Consider a scenario wherein there is a web application hosted in multiple regions for a number of countries. Each web application is hosted on a specific web endpoint with URLs ending with a country specific **Top Level Domain (TLD)** such as .in for India, .uk for UK, .nz for New Zealand, and so on. Global site is hosted on .com domain. When a new product is introduced at the .com portal, it sends a push notification to all the subscriber SQS queues. Application hosted in different countries reads the queue on periodic basis and update the product details. The message fans out from SNS to multipe SQS and finally to a number of country specific web applications.

In certain scenario, web applications can directly subscribe to SNS topic with HTTP or HTTPS endpoint URL, however, that is not a fan out mechanism. It's a direct communication between SNS and web application endpoint.

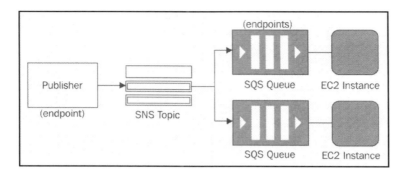

Figure 13.2: Amazon SNS Fanout

Reference URL: http://docs.aws.amazon.com/sns/latest/dg/images/sns-fanout.png

Application and system alerts

It is important to monitor AWS resources over various parameters (that is, **CPUUtilization**, **MemoryUtilization**, **NetworkIn**, **NetworkOut**, and so on) to avoid bottlenecks and to deliver consistent web application performance to the end user. As resource consumption crosses the defined threshold, the administrator should get an alert. This alert can be in the form of an SMS and/or email to the system, network, or a DB administrator, based on the resource type. Other AWS services also use SNS to send notifications on certain events. For example, an Auto Scaling group can also optionally inform the administrator upon scale-out and scale-in.

Mobile push notifications

Mobile push notifications directly send a notification to mobile apps. User interaction with the mobile app helps applications to understand the subscribers interests and accordingly, time-to-time related notifications are only sent to their mobile to update them about offers on products, services, or company news.

Push email and text messaging

Email and text messages (SMS) are two common notification means to convey important messages to an individual or group(s) of people. Usually with this method, subscribers get notification in the form of email or SMS on their subscribed email address or mobile number respectively. This notification contains important messages and URLs to find out more about the same.

Creating Amazon SNS topic

First it is essential you create an SNS topic, then it is possible for a publisher to publish a message and for subscribers to subscribe to get a notification. New SNS topics can be created by the following steps:

1. Sign in to the AWS account with the IAM user who has sufficient privileges to work with Amazon SNS. On successful login to the AWS account, make sure that the appropriate AWS region is selected from the right-hand side top toolbar as shown in the following *Figure 13.3*:

Figure 13.3: AWS web console, select desired region

2. From the AWS dashboard, select **Simple Notification Service** from the **Messaging** services group as shown in the following *Figure 13.4*:

Figure 13.4: AWS web console, select SNS

3. Select **Create topic** from the **SNS dashboard** as shown:

Figure 13.5: SNS dashboard, select Create topic

4. In the **Create new topic** pop-up box provide appropriate input and click on the **Create topic** as shown in the following *Figure 13.6*:

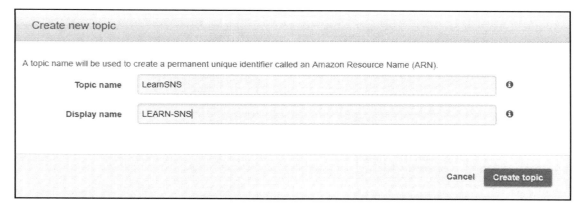

Figure 13.6: Provide appropriate Topic name and Display name

- **Topic name**: This can be up to 256 characters in size. Alphanumeric, underscore (_) and hyphens (-) are allowed, For example, LearnSNS.
- **Display name**: This is mandatory for the SMS protocol only. A maximum of 10 characters are allowed. For example, LEARN-SNS.

On successful creation of the SNS topic, the **Topic** counter becomes **1** from **0** on the AWS SNS dashboard, as shown in the following *Figure 13.7*:

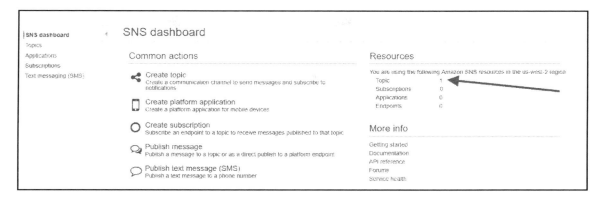

Figure 13.7: SNS dashboard

To see a complete list of SNS topics in a specific AWS region, select **Topics** from the left-hand side pane on the SNS dashboard, as shown in the following *Figure 13.8*:

Figure 13.8: SNS dashboard, select Topics

 Copy the SNS Topic ARN as shown in the preceding screen. This ARN is used in the subsequent step for subscribing to the topic.

Subscribing to a SNS topic

Each SNS topic can have multiple subscribers. Each subscriber may use the same or different protocol. Copy the ARN of the recently created SNS topic. It is required to subscribe to a topic in this step-by-step guide. Subscribers can receive a notification over a desired protocol as and when the publisher sends any message to the same topic. The steps for subscribing to an SNS topic are as follows:

1. Go to the **SNS dashboard** and select **Subscriptions** as shown in the following *Figure 13.9*:

Figure 13.9: SNS dashboard, select Subscriptions

2. Click **Create subscription** as shown in the following *Figure 13.10*:

Figure 13.10: Create subscription

3. A pop-up will appear as shown in the following *Figure 13.11*. Provide a valid **Topic ARN**, **Protocol**, and **Endpoint**. Finally, click on **Create subscription**.

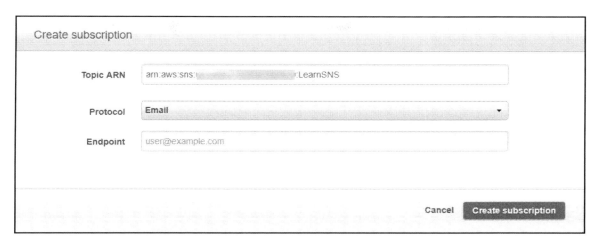

Figure 13.11: Create subscription

- **Topic ARN**: Paste the copied ARN of the recently created SNS topic.
- **Protocol**: Select the appropriate protocol (**HTTP, HTTPS, Email, Email-JSON, Amazon SQS, Application, AWS Lambda,** or **SMS**).
- **Endpoint**: According to the protocol, provide an appropriate endpoint (that is, domain name, email address, SQS ARN, application ARN, Lambda function ARN or mobile number respectively).

4. Amazon SNS will send an email on a specified endpoint, to confirm the subscription. Click on the link in an email. It will lead to a web browser displaying a confirmation of a subscription response from Amazon SNS.

Publishing a message to a SNS topic

As soon as the publisher sends a message to a topic, Amazon SNS will try to deliver a notification/message to all the subscribers. The subscriber may have different protocols and individual endpoints. With the help of the following steps, a message can be published over a SNS topic:

1. Go to the **SNS dashboard**, and select **Topics** from the left-hand side pane, it will display a list of topics as shown in the following *Figure 13.12*:

Figure 13.12: SNS Topics dashboard

2. Click on the topic ARN as shown in the following *Figure 13.13*:

Figure 13.13: Select Topic, to get ARN

3. Click on **Publish to topic** as shown in the following *Figure 13.14*:

Figure 13.14: SNS Topic details

4. To publish a message, provide the details as follows:

Figure 13.15: Publish a message on a Topic

- **Subject**: This is optional and can be up to 100 printable ASCII characters. In the case of an email notification, it will appear as an email subject line.
- **Message format**: This can be either **Raw** or **JSON**.
    - **Raw**: This is the actual plain text message to send to all the subscribers
    - **JSON**: This is the formatted message to customize the message for each of the protocol
- **Message**: Based on the message format type, the actual message will either be plain text or JSON. SMS message can have up to 160 ASCII or 70 unicode characters, while email messages can be up to 256 KB in size.
- **JSON message generator**: This helps to format a plain text message into a JSON format to support the subscriber's desired protocol. On using it the message format becomes JSON type. It shows the pop-up as shown in the following *Figure 13.16*. Select the required protocols to meet the subscriber's configuration. The target platform can be customized as per the actual requirement:

Figure 13.16: JSON message generator

- **Time to live (TTL)**: This is in seconds and will be the same for all mobile platforms push notifications. It is an additional capacity to configure TTL apart from the existing capacity of setting TTL within the SNS message body. It specifies the time to expire metadata about a message. Within a specified time, **Apple Push Notification Service (APNS)** or **Google Cloud Messaging (GCM)** must deliver messages to the endpoint. If the message is not delivered within the specified time, then the message will be dropped and no further attempts will take place to deliver the message.

5. Finally, after following the previous steps, the message that you want to publish looks like the following *Figure 13.17*. To publish a notification that sends an email and SMS to the subscribers, click on the **Publish message** button as shown in the following *Figure 13.17*:

Figure 13.17: Publish a message

Deleting SNS topic

To delete an SNS topic, you first need to unsubscribe the subscribers, and then delete an SNS topic. The following steps can be followed to unsubscribe subscribers and to delete an SNS topic:

1. Go to Amazon **SNS dashboard** and click **Subscriptions** as shown in the following *Figure 13.18*:

Figure 13.18: SNS dashboard

2. Before you can delete a topic, you need to unsubscribe all the subscribers from that topic. Select all the relevant subscribers for the topic and click on **Delete subscriptions** from the **Actions** drop-down menu as shown in the following *Figure 13.19*:

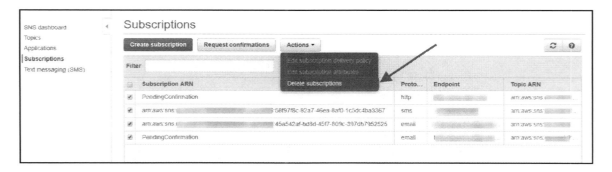

Figure 13.19: Delete subscriptions

3. Before unsubscribing the selected subscribers, click on **Delete** in the confirmation dialog box that appears as shown in the following *Figure 13.20*:

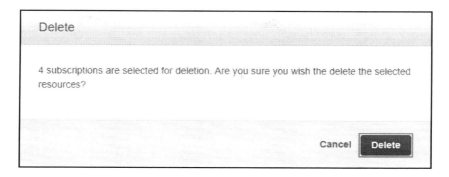

Figure 13.20: Popup, delete subscriptions confirmation

 All the subscriptions that are pending for confirmation, cannot be deleted manually. They are automatically deleted after three days if the confirmation is not received for those subscriptions.

Now, it is safe to delete the SNS topic.

4. Select **Topics** from the left-hand side pane as shown in the following *Figure 13.21*:

Figure 13.21: SNS Subscriptions dashboard, select Topics

5. Select a desired SNS topic to delete and click on **Delete topics** from the **Actions** drop-down menu as shown in the following *Figure 13.22*:

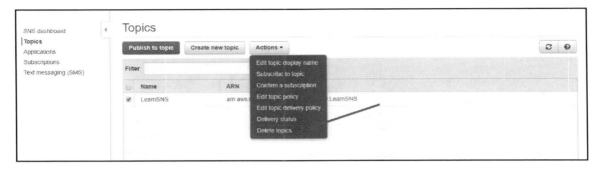

Figure 13.22: SNS Topics dashboard, select desired topic to delete

Managing access to Amazon SNS topics

Amazon SNS supports multiple protocols such as **HTTP, HTTPS, Email, Email-JSON, Amazon SQ**S, **Application, AWS Lambda,** and **SMS**. SNS subscribers can receive the message or notification over one of the supported protocols. Apart from the protocols, SNS also provides topic policy, which can be used to control who can subscribe or publish to a topic. The subsequent point describes when to use the topic policy for access control over an SNS topic.

When to use access control

Access control policy helps to define the way to control access to an SNS topic. There can be a number of scenario wherein you may need to use access control policy for an SNS topic. Some of the examples are given as following:

- You can use access control policy when you want to allow an IAM user to publish a message to one or more SNS topic. This IAM user can be in the same or different AWS account.
- SNS topic allows subscribers to use multiple supported protocols. With the help of access control policy subscriber can be restricted to use one or more specific protocols. For example, on an SNS topic, you can allow the subscribe to use only email and HTTPS.

- You can also define access control policy to restrict an SNS topic to publish a message only to an SQS queue.

Key concepts

Understanding the following key concepts is essential to effectively write the access policy:

- **Permission**: Permission is used for allowing or disallowing access to a specific resource. Permission can be either allow or disallow.
- **Statement**: A statement describes a single permission written in an access policy language such as JSON. One or more statements are part of a policy.
- **Policy**: A policy is a JSON document, this includes one or more statements. The following *Figure 13.23* helps to understand the concept of single and multiple statements in a policy:

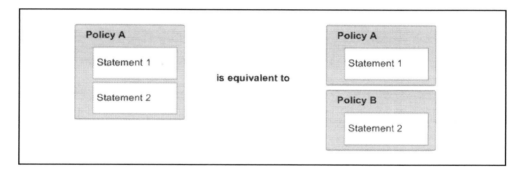

Figure 13.23: Policy and statements

Reference URL: https://docs.aws.amazon.com/sns/latest/dg/images/AccessPolicyLanguage_Statement_and_Policy.gif

One statement allows Jack to subscribe to a `TestTopic` using email protocol only. Another statement restricts Adam to publish messages to a `TestTopic`. As shown in the preceding figure, these two statements can be placed in a single policy or they can also be placed separately in each policy.

- **Issuer**: In general, an issuer is a resource owner. A person who writes access policy on a resource is called the issuer. For example, Bob has created an SNS topic named `TestTopic`. He has full privileges to the `TestTopic`. AWS doesn't allow other IAM users to write access policy on the same. Bob can write access policy to specify who can publish or subscribe with which protocols to a `TestTopic`.

- **Principal**: When an issuer writes an access policy, the person to whom the privilege is granted/restricted in the policy is called a principal. It can be an actual identity such as a username or an IP address such as CIDR range. A principal can be anyone just by mentioning `*`. For example, in the statement, Jack to subscribe to a `TestTopic` using email protocol only; Jack is a principal.
- **Action**: Action specifies the activity that a principal can perform on a resource. One or more actions can be specified in a policy.
- **Resource**: This is an object (that is, SNS topic) that a principal is requesting to access. For example, in the statement, Jack to subscribe to a `TestTopic` using email protocol only; `TestTopic` is a resource.
- **Conditions and keys**: Using conditions you can apply specific restrictions on the permission. For example, we can write a statement in a policy which allow jack to subscribe to a topic, however, it adds a condition which allows jack to subscribe to the topic only using Email protocol.
A key is a specific characteristic such as date and time. It acts as a base for an access restriction. Keys and conditions are used in a pair to define restriction. For example, when the issuer wants the principal to deny access to a resource before 1st Jan 2018, then the condition to be used is **DateLessThan** and the key should be **aws:CurrentTime** and the set value to the `2018-01-01T00:00:00Z`.

- **Requester**: The person or entity sends the access request to the resource called requester. For example, requester asks AWS service: *Will you allow me to do B to C where D applies?*
- **Evaluation**: Evaluation is a process to conclude whether to allow or deny a requester based on the applicable policies. In detail, we will see it in an evolution logic.
- **Effect**: Possible values for an effect can be deny or allow. At the time of policy evaluation, it helps to decide whether the requester can perform action against configured conditions or not.
- **Default deny**: When a policy statement is evaluated, by default, if a permission is not explicitly allowed to perform an action, the statement considers it as deny. In short, if any permission is not explicitly allowed in the policy statement, the user is denied the permission for such actions which are not defined in the policy.
- **Allow**: Policy evaluation is allow when a policy statement has `effect=allow` and defined conditions are met, a requester can perform an action on the resource.
- **Explicit deny**: Policy evaluation is deny, when a policy statement has `effect=deny` and defined conditions are met, a requester cannot perform an action on the resource.

Architectural overview

The following *Figure 13.24* helps us to understand the architectural overview at high-level. It helps us to understand from the beginning, from when the resource is created till access allow or deny is evaluated:

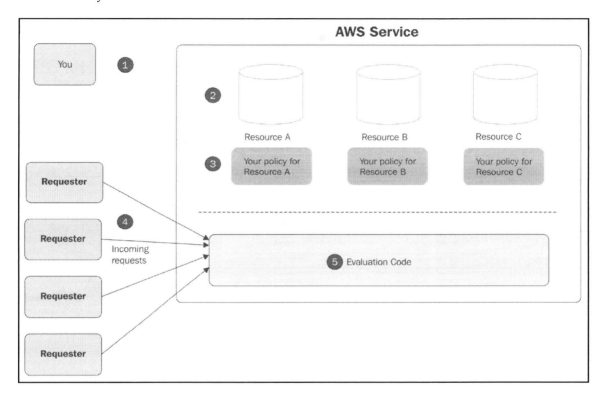

Figure 13.24: Architectural overview (Policy evaluation)

Reference URL: https://docs.aws.amazon.com/sns/latest/dg/images/AccessPolicyLanguage_Arch_Overview.gif

Each of the points given in the preceding *Figure 13.24*, are explained as follows. Readers are requested to refer to the preceding figure and co-relate the point numbers given in the figure:

1. A user creates an AWS resource. For example, Bob creates SNS topics. Bob is the owner for SNS topics.
2. Topics are created within AWS SNS.
3. An owner, also called an issuer, creates an access policy. Usually, one policy with one or more statements is created rather than multiple policies, as it is easy to manage.
4. Requests are incoming from the requesters to AWS SNS. Requesters can be subscribers or publishers.
5. All incoming requests to access AWS resources (that is, in this case SNS topics) are evaluated against applicable policies and it is determined whether the requester can access the resource or not. Evaluation is carried out by the access policy language evaluation code.

Access request evaluation logic

Whenever any request to access an AWS resource is initiated, policy evaluation logic evaluates the related policies to determine whether to allow an incoming request or deny. Basic policy evaluation rules are given as following:

- First and foremost, policy evaluation logic applies default deny rule. That means, except the resource owner all other requests are denied if there is no explicit allow permission is specified in the policy.
- Explicit allow statement or a policy overrides the default deny. As a result, request gets an access.
- Explicit deny statement or a policy overrides the explicit allow statement.

The following flowchart helps to understand in detail how the request to allow or deny decision is made:

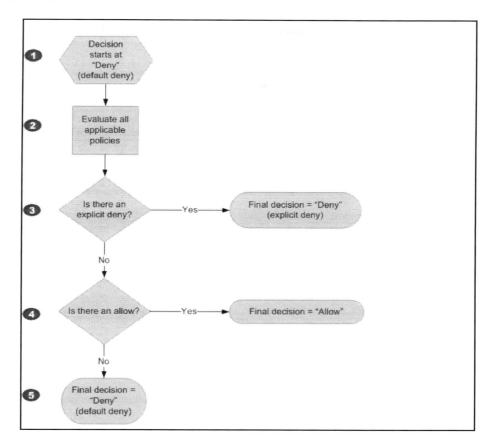

Figure 13.25: Policy evaluation flowchart

Reference URL: https://docs.aws.amazon.com/sns/latest/dg/images/AccessPolicyLanguage_Evaluation_Flow.gif

1. By default, the default deny rule applies. Any request apart from the owner is denied.
2. AWS evaluates a policy based on evaluation logic, relevant resource, principal, and conditions specified in the policies. If there are more than one policies associated with a resource, order of the policy evaluation is not important. Any policy can be evaluated first irrespective of on what order they are associated with the resource

3. During evaluation of policies, if any policy has an explicit deny, the final decision is to *deny* the request.
4. If there is no explicit deny specified in the policy and there is an explicit allow available in the policy, the final decision is to allow the request.
5. If there is no explicit *allow* or *deny* policy, default deny rule is applied.

Invoking Lambda function using SNS notification

An AWS Lambda function can be invoked with Amazon SNS notifications. When a publisher publishes a message to an SNS topic and a Lambda function is subscribed to the same SNS topic, that Lambda function is invoked with the payload of a published message. When a publisher publishes a message to an SNS topic, SNS provides the message delivery status to the publisher stating that the message is sent to the Lambda function. The payload message acts as an input parameter for the Lambda function. The function can process the message (payload) as needed.

As SNS topic can be configured to execute a Lambda function with the help of the following steps:

A prerequisite is to have an SNS topic and a Lambda function.

1. Go to the **SNS dashboard**, and select **Topics** from the left-hand side pane, it will display a list of topics as shown in the following *Figure 13.26*:

Figure 13.26: SNS Topics dashboard

2. Click on the topic ARN for a topic to subscribe a Lambda function shown as follows:

Figure 13.27: SNS Topics dashboard

3. Click on **Create subscription** as shown in the following *Figure 13.28*:

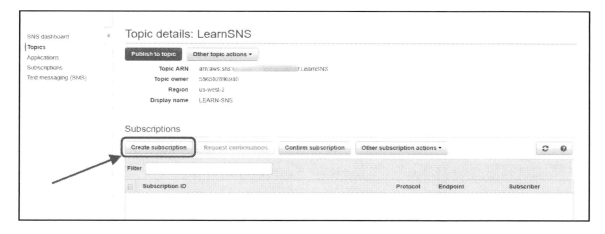

Figure 13.28: SNS Topics dashboard

4. It will come up with a pop-up as shown in the following *Figure 13.29*. Select **Protocol** as **AWS Lambda** and provide a Lambda function **Endpoint**. It also allows you to customize whether to trigger specific alias or a version of alias. Finally, click on the **Create subscription**.

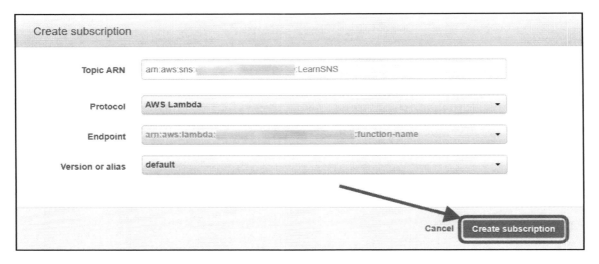

Figure 13.29: Create subscription

Sending Amazon SNS message to Amazon SQS queues

Amazon SNS topic's publisher can send a notification to an Amazon SQS queue. It is essential that the SQS queue is subscribed to a topic.

 A prerequisite is to have an SNS topic and an SQS queue.

1. Go to the SQS dashboard as shown in the following *Figure 13.30*:

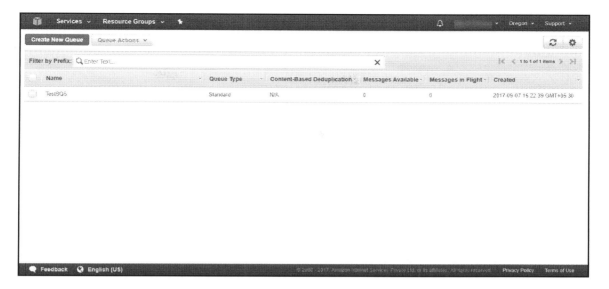

Figure 13.30: Amazon SQS dashboard

2. Select the queue and click on the **Queue Actions** drop-down menu. Select **Subscribe Queue to SNS Topic** as shown in the following *Figure 13.31*:

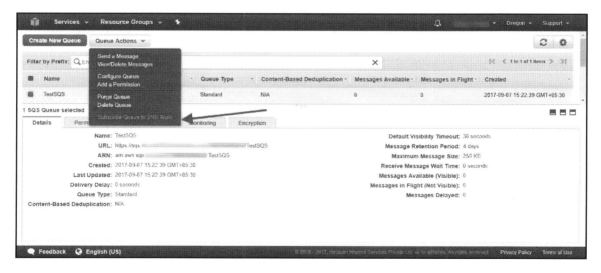

Figure 13.31: Subscribe Queue to SNS Topic

3. In the pop-up, select the appropriate AWS region where the SNS topic is created, choose the appropriate SNS topic to subscribe to the selected SQS queue and click on **Subscribe** as shown in the following *Figure 13.32*:

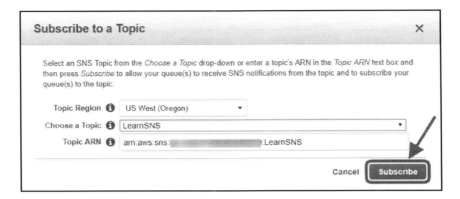

Figure 13.32: Subscribe to a Topic

 In the preceding pop-up, typing an ARN helps an SNS topic in another AWS account.

4. On successful subscription of a SQS queue to an SNS topic a pop-up will appear, as shown in the following *Figure 13.33*:

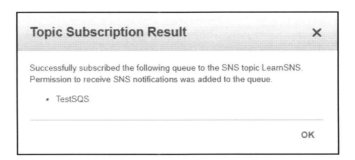

Figure 13.33: Subscription result

5. To verify whether the SQS queue has been successfully subscribed to a desired SNS topic, select the SNS topic from the **SNS dashboard | Topics** and click on ARN to see details. It is visible that the SQS topic has been subscribed as shown in the following *Figure 13.34*:

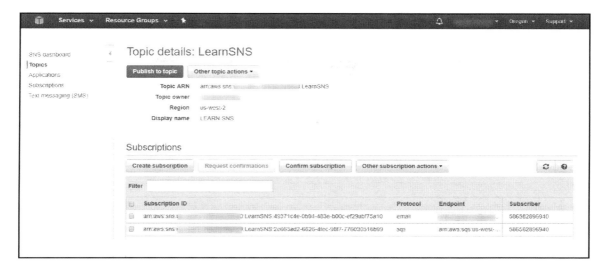

Figure 13.34: SNS Topic dashboard

6. Now when the publisher publishes a message, the SQS queue will get a notification. Visible messages at the SQS queue will be increased. To see a visible message, go to the SQS dashboard, select the queue, and in the lower-pane, **Messages Available** can be seen as shown in the following *Figure 13.35*:

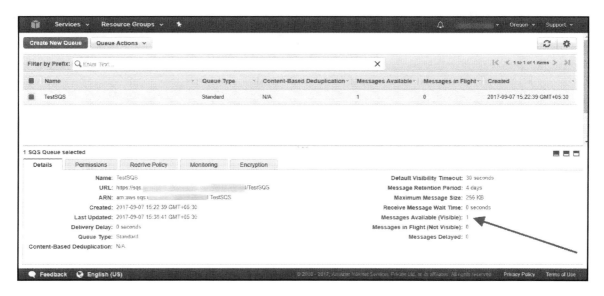

Figure 13.35: SQS dashboard

The Amazon SQS queue will receive messages in a JSON format. A sample message is as follows:

```
{
  "Type" : "Notification",
  "MessageId" : "153697k2i-5672-9k8g-6fp8-159hn86d4h97",
  "TopicArn" : "arn:aws:sns:us-west-2:123456789012:TestTopic",
  "Subject" : "Testing message published to a subscribed queue",
  "Message" : "Hello world!",
  "Timestamp" : "2017-09-02T05:08:40.901Z",
  "SignatureVersion" : "1",
  "Signature" :
"EXAMPLEd4f5h7a3f5VO0FFbh75fkl97JLRfySEoWz4uZHSj6ycK4ph71Zmdv0NtJ4dC/El9FOG
p3VuvchpaTraNHWhhq/OsN1HVz20zxmF9b88R878hqjfKB5woZZmz87HiM6CYDTo3l7LMwFT4VU
7ELtyaBBafhPTg9O5GhsKkg=",
  "SigningCertURL" :
"https://sns.us-west-2.amazonaws.com/SimpleNotificationService-f3ecfb7224c7
233fe7bb5f59f96de52f.pem",
  "UnsubscribeURL" :
"https://sns.us-west-2.amazonaws.com/?Action=Unsubscribe&SubscriptionArn=ar
n:aws:sns:us-west-2:123456789012:MyTopic:c7fe3a54-ab0e-4ec2-88e0-
db410a0f2bee"
}
```

Monitoring SNS with CloudWatch

Amazon SNS and Amazon CloudWatch both are integrated. Every SNS topic publishes standard metrics and dimensions in a CloudWatch. CloudWatch metrics for each SNS topic can be viewed by using the following steps:

1. Go to the CloudWatch dashboard with the IAM user who has sufficient privileges. Click on **Metrics** as shown in the following *Figure 13.36*:

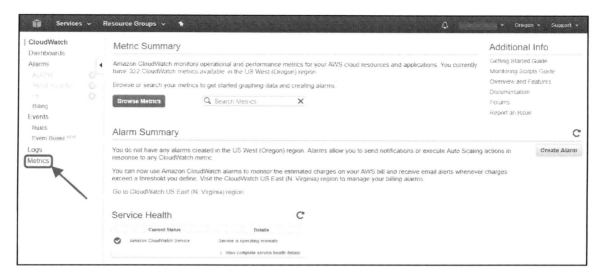

Figure 13.36: CloudWatch Metrics dashboard

2. Select **SNS** to explore all metrics as shown in the following *Figure 13.37*:

Figure 13.37: CloudWatch Metrics dashboard

3. Click on **Topic Metrics** to explore an SNS topic metrics as shown in the following *Figure 13.38*:

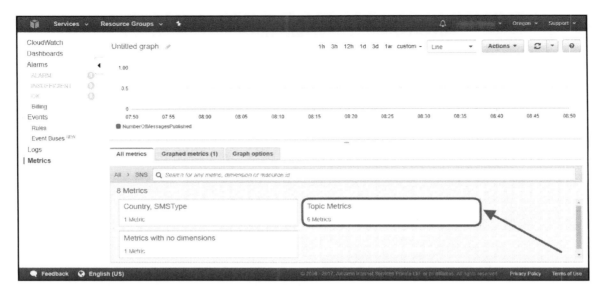

Figure 13.38: CloudWatch Metrics dashboard

4. Select the appropriate metric from the lower-pane to see the activity graph on the upper-pane as shown in the following *Figure 13.39*:

Figure 13.39: CloudWatch Metrics dashboard

 It is a best practice to configure alarms on critical metrics such as NumberOfNotificationsFailed.

SNS best practices

SNS best practices are as follows:

- It is recommended to configure alerts on various SNS standard metrics to observe performance parameters such as success rates, failure rates, deliveries to SQS, and so on.
- Configure access policy to control who can publish a message to and receive a notification from a SNS topic.
- In order to delete an SNS topic, ensure that all the subscriptions for that topic are deleted first.
- Use Amazon SNS and SQS services to build loosely coupled applications or a server less architecture.

14

Simple Workflow Service

Amazon **Simple Workflow Service (SWF)** is a workflow management service which helps in building applications that can handle work through distributed components. Using SWF, you can define a number of tasks that can be executed in a predefined sequence. You can build scalable, resilient, and truly distributed applications using Amazon SWF. You can schedule tasks, define dependencies, and concurrency depending upon the logical workflow of the application. This chapter introduces you to workflows, workflow history, actors, tasks, domains, object identifiers, task lists, workflow execution closure, lifecycle, polling for tasks, execution, access key and secret key, SWF endpoints, and managing access with IAM.

The purpose of this chapter is to introduce to the readers basic concepts of SWF with respect to the scope of the AWS Certified Developer – Associate exam. From a development perspective, SWF is a wide topic and a full book can be written on SWF. Considering the scope of the exam, this chapter does not intent to teach the reader how to code SWF applications but, focuses more on the fundamental aspects of SWF.

When to use Amazon SWF

Here are some scenarios when SWF can be used:

- When you have multiple tasks that need to be coordinated and executed in a specific sequence based on some dependency or in parallel
- When you have multiple application components and need to dispatch tasks to these application components

- When you have a distributed application and you need to coordinate and process tasks in a distributed application environment
- When you need to execute ordered application steps
- When you need to manage the application state during distributed execution
- When you need to reliably execute periodic tasks and audit the execution
- When you need to asynchronously execute event-driven tasks

Some of the SWF use cases are:

- Media processing
- Customer order processing workflow
- Web application backend
- Business process workflow
- Analytics pipelines

Now since we know what SWF is and what it can do, let us understand some basic concepts of SWF such as workflows, workflow history, actors, tasks, domains, object identifiers, task lists, workflow execution closure, execution lifecycle, and polling for tasks.

Workflow

A workflow is a mechanism to execute a number of distributed application tasks in an asynchronous way. With workflow, you can manage multiple activities asynchronously using more than one computing resources. The execution of the workflow tasks can be sequential and parallel as needed. While creating a workflow you need to determine the tasks to be executed in the workflow. SWF recognizes these tasks as activities. You can define the coordination logic in the workflow that determines the order in which the activities are executed.

Example workflow

As shown in the following *Figure 14.1*, customer order processing workflow can be implemented using SWF:

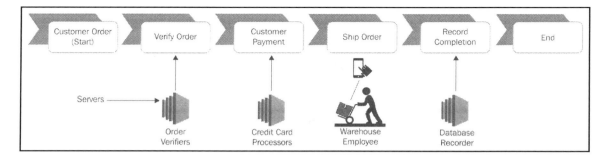

Figure 14.1: SWF customer order processing workflow

1. The workflow starts with the customer placing an order.
2. The order is verified by the order verifiers component of the application, which is hosted on a separate environment.
3. Once the order is verified, the customer is charged by the **Credit Card Processors** component of the application.
4. After a successful payment, the warehouse employee processes the order and ships it.
5. The order detail is updated in the database by the **Database Recorder**.
6. The workflow ends.

Workflow history

SWF keeps the history or execution progress of any workflow in the workflow history. Once the execution of a workflow starts, SWF keeps a detailed history of each and every step of the workflow. Whenever the workflow execution state changes, such as a new activity is scheduled in the workflow or an activity is completed, it is represented as an event in the workflow history. It records events that change the state of the workflow, such as when an activity is scheduled or completed, a task execution timeouts, and so on. It does not record any event that does not change the state of the workflow.

How workflow history helps

Workflow history can be helpful in a number of ways. The following list describes some of the ways, workflow history can be helpful:

- It stores all details about the workflow execution and thus eliminates the need for the application to maintain the state.
- It provides the current status of each of the activities scheduled along with its results. SWF executes the next steps based on this information.
- It provides an audit trail, which can be used to monitor and verify the workflow execution.

```
Order0001

Start Workflow Execution

Schedule Verify Order
Start Verify Order Activity
Complete Verify Order Activity

Schedule Customer Payment
Start Charge Customer Payment Activity
Complete Customer Payment Activity

Schedule Ship Order
Start Ship Order Activity
```

Actors

In simple terms, an actor is a program or an entity that performs different types of activities in a workflow. An actor can be any of the following:

- Workflow starter
- Decider
- Activity worker

Actors can interact with SWF using APIs. Actors can be developed in any programming language. The following *Figure 14.2* shows SWF architecture along with its actors:

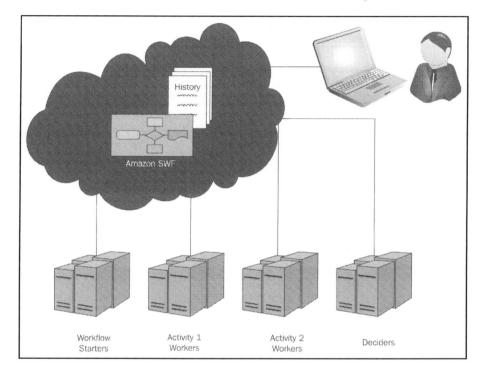

Figure 14.2: Amazon SWF architecture

Reference URL: https://docs.aws.amazon.com/amazonswf/latest/developerguide/swf-dev-actors.html

Workflow starter

A workflow starter is a program or an application that starts the execution of a workflow. In the customer order-processing example, the workflow starter can be a shopping site where the customer orders an item. It can also be a mobile application from where the customer places an order.

Decider

A decider is a program or an application that decides the coordination logic of a workflow. It decides on the order of execution, concurrency, and scheduling of the tasks as per the application logic. Whenever there is any change in the workflow execution such as an activity is completing, the underlined client polls for the tasks for making decisions and it passes them to the programmatic entity called a decider. The decider receives the decision tasks along with the workflow history. The job of the decider is to analyse the execution history and decide which step should be executed next. Once the decider takes the decision, it communicates this decision back to SWF. Interactions between workers and the decider is facilitated by Amazon SWF. It provides consistent views into the progress of tasks and allows initiating new tasks in an ongoing manner. The tasks are stored by SWF and assigned to workers as and when they are ready. SWF monitors the tasks and ensures that a task is assigned only once and is never duplicated.

Remember, a decision is a data type in SWF, which represents next actions.

Activity worker

An activity worker is a program or an application that receives tasks from SWF, executes the tasks and returns the result back to SWF. Activity tasks are tasks, which are identified by you in your application.

For using an activity task, you need to register the activity task in a SWF console or programmatically by using the **RegisterActivityType** action.

All the activity workers are registered in SWF polls for new activity tasks. SWF assigns activity tasks to a worker. There may be some tasks that can be performed by specific activity workers only. Once the activity worker receives a task from SWF, it starts the execution of the task and reports it to SWF on completion along with the results. Subsequently, it polls the SWF for next tasks. This entire process of polling for a task and executing it, goes on until the entire workflow execution is completed.

Tasks

The work assignments that SWF provides to activity workers and deciders are called tasks. There are basically three types of tasks in SWF, namely, activity task, Lambda task, and decision task. Let us understand these task types in the following points:

- **Activity task**: An activity task describes the actions to be performed by an activity worker. The action depends upon the function of the activity worker. For example, an activity worker may be asked to check the inventory for a specific product or it may be asked to initiate a credit card transaction. The task contains all the detail that an activity worker requires to perform the actions.
- **Lambda task**: A Lambda task and activity task are similar. As the name suggests, it executes a Lambda function instead of any SWF activity.
- **Decision task**: A decider determines the next activity in a workflow based on the decision task. It tells the decider that the workflow execution status has changed. The current workflow history is carried along with the decision task.

SWF can schedule a decision task as and when the workflow starts and when the status of the workflow changes, that is, activity task scheduled, activity task completed, and so on.

SWF domains

Domains in SWF are a mechanism to scope SWF resources such as workflows, activity types, workflow execution, and so on. All the resources are scoped to a domain. Domains isolate one set of types, executions, and task lists from other ones within an AWS account. When you work with SWF, you need to first define a domain. All the other resources are defined within a domain. You can define multiple domains in SWF. Similarly, one domain can have multiple workflows, however, workflows defined in different domains cannot interact with each other.

While registering a domain in SWF, you need to define the workflow history retention period. SWF maintains the history of a workflow for the time specified in the workflow history retention period even after the execution of the workflow is completed.

Object identifiers

Object identifiers are a way of uniquely identifying SWF objects. The following list describes how different types of objects are identified in SWF:

- **Workflow type**: A registered workflow type is distinguished by its domain, workflow name and workflow version. You can specify the workflow type in call to the **RegisterWorkflowType**.
- **Activity type**: A registered activity type is distinguished by its domain, activity name, and activity version. You can specify the activity types in the call to **RegisterActivityType**.
- **Decision tasks and activity tasks**: SWF uses a unique task token to identify decision tasks and activity tasks. It generates a task token and returns it with other task information when `PollForDecisionTask` or `PollForActivityTask` is called. Mostly, the token is used by the process that is assigned to the task but the token can also be passed on to other processes. Subsequently, the process with the token can report completion or failure of the task.

Task lists

Task lists are a mechanism to organize different tasks related to a workflow. Task lists can be considered like dynamic queues. While scheduling a task in SWF, you can specify a task list. The task list works in a similar way as a queue. While polling SWF for tasks, you can specify the task list from where the task can be fetched.

Task list offers a way to route tasks to worker processes based on the requirement of your application workflow. You don't need to explicitly create a task list, it is automatically created when a task is scheduled, if the task list is not already there. SWF maintains a separate task list for activity tasks and decision tasks. A task belongs to only one task list, it is not shared between multiple task lists. Just like activities and workflows, task list also has a restricted scope. The scope of a task list is restricted to a specific AWS region and a specific SWF domain.

Workflow execution closure

When a workflow execution is started, it gets into an open state. An open workflow execution can be closed as one of the following:

- completed
- cancelled
- failed
- timed out

Open workflow execution can be closed by a decider process, an administrator, or by SWF. As and when the activities of the workflow finishes, the decider process identifies and marks the workflow execution as completed. The decider uses RespondDecisionTaskCompleted action and forwards the CompleteWorkflowExecution decision to SWF.

Similarly, a decider process can also close the workflow execution as cancelled or failed. The decider process uses RespondDecisionTaskCompleted action and forwards the CancelWorkflowExecution decision to SWF.

Whenever a task enters a state which is outside the purview of normal completion, a decider should fail that workflow execution. For failing the workflow execution, the decider uses RespondDecisionTaskCompleted action and forwards FailWorkflowExecution decision to SWF.

Workflow executions are continuously monitored by SWF to confirm that the workflow execution does not exceed the timeout limit specified by the user in workflow settings. As and when a workflow exceeds timeout, SWF closes the workflow.

At times, certain workflows run for too long and the history grows too large over a period of time. The decider may close the execution of such a workflow and continues running it as a new workflow execution. For such a scenario, a decider uses RespondDecisionTaskCompleted action and forwards ContinueAsNewWorkflowExecution decision to SWF.

Last but not the least; a user can terminate a workflow execution directly from the SWF console. You can also terminate the execution programmatically with TerminateWorkflowExecution API.

When you initiate termination of a workflow through console or API, it automatically forces closure of the running workflow execution based on the selected workflow from the console or given domain, runId, and workflowId in an API call.

SWF can also terminate a workflow in case it exceeds any service defined limits. It can also terminate a child workflow if the parent workflow is terminated and the child policy associated with the workflow is defined to terminate the child workflows.

Lifecycle of workflow execution

SWF starts communicating with actors from the start to the completion of a workflow and allocates respective activities and decision tasks to these actors. The following *Figure 14.3* describes the life cycle of a customer order processing workflow execution:

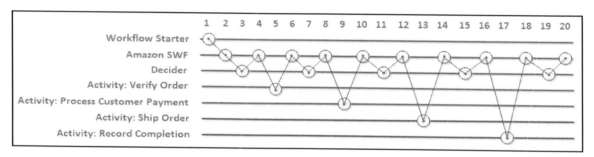

Figure 14.3: Workflow execution lifecycle

Here are the steps shown in the preceding *Figure 14.3*:

1. The workflow starter starts the workflow execution by calling `StartWorkflowExecution` action with order information.

2. SWF gets the request to start the workflow execution, sends it back with a `WorkflowExectuionStarted` event and schedules a decision task raising a `DecisionTaskScheduled` event.

3. A process configured as a decider in the workflow, polls for a decision task using `PollForDecisionTask` action, receives the decision task from SWF along with the task history. The decider then uses coordination logic to ensure that the execution is not already run. After verification, it schedules the verify order activity using `ScheduleActivityTask` decision and returns the decision detail to SWF with `RespondDecisionTaskCompleted` action.

4. SWF gets the decision from the decider, schedules the verify order activity task and raises `ActivityTaskScheduled` event. After scheduling the task, SWF waits for the task until it gets completed or times out.

5. An activity worker polls for the tasks using `PollForActivityTask` action and receives the verify order activity task. After receiving the task, an activity worker performs his task and responds back to SWF along with the result using `RespondActivityTaskCompleted` action.

6. SWF receives the result of verify order activity shared by the activity worker and raises `ActivityTaskCompleted` event. It adds the result to the workflow history. At the end of the step, it schedules a decision task and raises the `DecisionTaskScheduled` event.

7. The decider polls for the decision task using `PollForDecisionTask` action and receives the decision task from SWF along with the task history. The decider then uses coordination logic to ensure that the execution is not already run. After verification, it schedules a process customer payment activity using the `ScheduleActivityTask` decision and returns the decision detail to SWF with `RespondDecisionTaskCompleted` action.

8. SWF gets the decision from the decider through `DecisionTaskCompleted` event, schedules the process customer payment activity task and raises `ActivityTaskScheduled` event. After scheduling the task, SWF waits for the task until it gets completed or times out.

9. An activity worker that can perform process customer payment, polls for the task using `PollForActivityTask` action and receives the process customer payment activity task. After receiving the task, the activity worker performs the task and responds back to SWF along with the result using `RespondActivityTaskCompleted` action.

10. SWF receives the result of process customer payment activity shared by the activity worker and raises the `ActivityTaskCompleted` event. It adds the result to the workflow history. At the end of the step, it schedules a decision task and raises the `DecisionTaskScheduled` event.

11. The decider polls for the decision task using `PollForDecisionTask` action and receives the decision task from SWF along with the task history. The decider then uses the coordination logic to ensure that the execution is not already run. After verification, it schedules to ship the order activity using `ScheduleActivityTask` decision and returns the decision detail to SWF with `RespondDecisionTaskCompleted` action.

12. SWF gets the decision from the decider through the `DecisionTaskCompleted` event, schedules the ship order activity task and raises the `ActivityTaskScheduled` event. After scheduling the task, SWF waits for the task until it gets complete or times out and raises.

13. An activity worker that can perform the ship order, polls for the task using the `PollForActivityTask` action and receives the activity task. After receiving the task, the activity worker performs the task and responds back to SWF along with the result using the `RespondActivityTaskCompleted` action.

14. SWF receives the result of the ship order activity shared by the activity worker through `ActivityTaskCompleted` event. It adds the result to the workflow history. At the end of the step, it schedules a decision task and raises a `DecisionTaskScheduled` event.

15. The decider polls for the decision task using the `PollForDecisionTask` action and receives the decision task from SWF along with the task history. The decider then uses coordination logic to ensure that the execution is not already run. After verification, it schedules a record completion activity using the `ScheduleActivityTask` decision and returns the decision detail to SWF using the `RespondDecisionTaskCompleted` action.

16. SWF gets the decision from the decider through `DecisionTaskCompleted` event, schedules the record completion activity task and raises the `ActivityTaskScheduled` event. After scheduling the task, SWF waits for the task until it is completed or it times out and raises.

17. An activity worker that can perform record completion task, polls for the task using the `PollForActivityTask` action and receives the activity task. After receiving the task, the activity worker performs the task and responds back to SWF along with the result using the `RespondActivityTaskCompleted` action.

18. SWF receives the result of record completion activity shared by the activity worker through `ActivityTaskCompleted` event. It adds the result to the workflow history. At the end of the step, it schedules a decision task and raises the `DecisionTaskScheduled` event.

19. The decider polls for the decision task using `PollForDecisionTask` action and receives the decision task from SWF along with the task history. The decider then uses coordination logic and decides to close the workflow execution. It returns the `CompleteWorkflowExecution` decision to SWF with `RespondDecisionTaskCompleted` action along with any result.

20. At the end, SWF closes the workflow execution, archiving the history for any future reference and raises the `WorkflowExecutionCompleted` event.

Polling for tasks

Deciders and activity workers interact with SWF using long polling. They regularly send messages to SWF indicating that they are ready to receive a task from a predefined task list. In case there is any task already available to assign, SWF responds with the task immediately. If the task is not available, SWF keeps the TCP connection alive for up to 60 seconds. If the task is available in these 60 seconds, it responds back with the task. If there is no task available within these 60 seconds, SWF responds back with an empty response and the connection is closed. In cases wherein the decider or activity worker receives an empty response, they should poll for the task again.

Long polling is suitable where there is a high-volume of tasks available for processing. It is recommended you keep deciders and activity workers behind a firewall.

SWF endpoints

Amazon provides SWF endpoints in multiple regions. These endpoints are provided to reduce latency while accessing the service and storing or retrieving the data from AWS. SWF endpoints are independent from each other. Your SWF domains, workflows, and activities registered in a region are isolated from the other regions and they do not share data or attributes with each other. For example, you can register a domain named `SWF-Mydomain-1` in multiple regions. Even though the domain name remains the same, they are distinct domains specific to respective regions. A domain registered in **us-east-1** cannot share any data or attributes with a domain registered in **us-west-1**.

SWF endpoints available in different AWS regions are shown in the following table. For more details refer http://docs.aws.amazon.com/general/latest/gr/rande.html#swf_region.

Region Name	Region	Endpoint	Protocol
Asia Pacific (Mumbai)	ap-south-1	swf.ap-south-1.amazonaws.com	HTTPS
Asia Pacific (Seoul)	ap-northeast-2	swf.ap-northeast-2.amazonaws.com	HTTPS
Asia Pacific (Singapore)	ap-southeast-1	swf.ap-southeast-1.amazonaws.com	HTTPS
Asia Pacific (Sydney)	ap-southeast-2	swf.ap-southeast-2.amazonaws.com	HTTPS
Asia Pacific (Tokyo)	ap-northeast-1	swf.ap-northeast-1.amazonaws.com	HTTPS
Canada (Central)	ca-central-1	swf.ca-central-1.amazonaws.com	HTTPS
EU (Frankfurt)	eu-central-1	swf.eu-central-1.amazonaws.com	HTTPS
EU (Ireland)	eu-west-1	swf.eu-west-1.amazonaws.com	HTTPS
EU (London)	eu-west-2	swf.eu-west-2.amazonaws.com	HTTPS
South America (São Paulo)	sa-east-1	swf.sa-east-1.amazonaws.com	HTTPS
US East (N. Virginia)	us-east-1	swf.us-east-1.amazonaws.com	HTTPS
US East (Ohio)	us-east-2	swf.us-east-2.amazonaws.com	HTTPS
US West (N. California)	us-west-1	swf.us-west-1.amazonaws.com	HTTPS
US West (Oregon)	us-west-2	swf.us-west-2.amazonaws.com	HTTPS

Managing access with IAM

You can manage controlled access to SWF resources using IAM. Using IAM, you can create users in your AWS account and provide them respective permissions. Each IAM user has a separate set of IAM keys. These IAM keys provide the users with access to respective resources on AWS. An IAM policy can be attached to a user which controls what resources a user can access. Using IAM policies you can control the access at the granular level, such as allow or deny access to specific set of SWF domains.

SWF uses the following principles for access control:

- Access to various SWF resources is controlled only on the basis of IAM policies
- IAM uses denying by default policy. That means, if you do not explicitly allow any access, by default, access is denied.
- You need to attach IAM policies to the actors of the workflow for controlling access to the SWF resources.
- You can specify resource permissions only for domains.
- You can use conditions in the permission to further restrict the permission in a policy.

SWF – IAM policy examples

The following is a simple policy that allows all SWF actions on all the domains in the account:

```
{
    "Version": "2012-10-17",
    "Statement" : [ {
        "Effect" : "Allow",
        "Action" : "swf:*",
        "Resource" : "arn:aws:swf:*:123456789012:/domain/*"
    } ]
}
```

The following policy allows all SWF actions but restricts access to a specific domain in the account:

```
{
    "Version": "2012-10-17",
    "Statement": [ {
        "Effect" : "Allow",
        "Action" : "swf:*",
        "Resource" : "arn:aws:swf:*:123456789012:/domain/mydomain1"
    } ]
}
```

The following policy allows all SWF actions on two specific domains `mydomain1` and `mydomain2`:

```
{
    "Version": "2012-10-17",
    "Statement": [
        {
            "Effect" : "Allow",
            "Action" : "swf:*",
            "Resource" : "arn:aws:swf:*:123456789012:/domain/mydomain1"
        }, {
            "Effect" : "Allow",
            "Action" : "swf:*",
            "Resource" : "arn:aws:swf:*:123456789012:/domain/mydomain2"
        }
    ]
}
```

The following policy allows access to `StartWorkflowExecution` action on the domain `mydomain1` and specifically to `version1` of `myworkflow1`:

```
{
    "Version": "2012-10-17",
    "Statement": [
        {
            "Effect" : "Allow",
            "Action" : "swf:StartWorkflowExecution",
            "Resource" : "arn:aws:swf:*:123456789012:/domain/mydomain1",
            "Condition" : {
                "StringEquals" : {
                    "swf:workflowType.name" : "myworkflow1",
                    "swf:workflowType.version" : "version1"
                }
            }
        }
    ]
}
```

15
AWS CloudFormation

AWS infrastructure can be created and customized using the AWS dashboard (GUI), CLI, or APIs. These methods may be quick to build an infrastructure for once but, over a long period of time, to create a whole or partial infrastructure repeatedly in a different region to build DR, or in a subsidiary AWS account, those methods would be costly not only in terms of time and cost but also in terms of management, modification, and maintenance. It is a case of re-inventing the wheel every time and it is also error prone. For resolving this issue, Amazon provides CloudFormation service. AWS CloudFormation allows you to create and customize the AWS infrastructure using code. It enables you to create your infrastructure as a code. The program or code is called a template in AWS CloudFormation. These templates are also referred to as **CloudFormation templates (CFTs)**. For fulfilling various tasks, you may write one or more CFTs. Each CFT can be written in one of the supported scripting languages (JSON/YAML). You can use these CFTs to re-create same infrastructure in a different region or in a different AWS account. With little or no changes in the template using runtime parameters, the infrastructure gets ready in different region or different AWS account.

AWS does not charge you for using CloudFormation service. You pay only for the chargeable resources that you create using it. For example, you can create a web application infrastructure using CFT that includes a VPC, few EC2 instances, and RDS instances. In this case, AWS account incurs charges only for the EC2 instances and RDS instances based on its configuration such as instance size, attached EBS volumes, and so on as these are chargeable services. However, for a custom VPC and CloudFormation services, there are no charges applied, as both of these services are free.

 In case the AWS account is eligible for the free tier, the same advantage will be leveraged in the monthly AWS billing, whether AWS resources are created using templates or any other possible methods.

What is a template?

AWS CFTs describes all AWS resources and their properties in JSON or YAML format. Templates can be written using any text editor. It is recommended to give relevant and meaningful filenames to each templates. Template extensions can be .json, .yaml, or .txt. When these templates are executed, the defined AWS resources are created in the respective AWS account. You can either upload the template to an S3 bucket and specify the template URL or you can upload the template file using browse button in template creation wizard. Even if you upload the template file using the browse button on the template creation wizard, it is internally stored in S3.

The following *Figure 15.1* helps us to understand this:

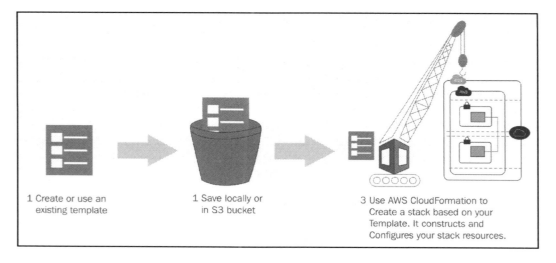

1 Create or use an existing template

1 Save locally or in S3 bucket

3 Use AWS CloudFormation to Create a stack based on your Template. It constructs and Configures your stack resources.

Figure 15.1: AWS CloudFormation flow

Reference URL: http://docs.amazonaws.cn/en_us/AWSCloudFormation/latest/UserGuide/images/create-stack-diagram.png

While creating a stack, if the template path is pointing to the local machine, then automatically it will upload the CloudFormation template to the AWS S3 bucket in the relevant region. In each region, AWS CloudFormation will create its own bucket for that.

While writing a template, it is not required to identify AWS resource dependencies. It automatically identifies the resource dependencies and creates them sequentially. For example, when a template is written to create a custom VPC and an EC2 instance, it first creates a custom VPC and an EC2 instance is created in the same VPC only after the VPC is available. Templates can be used to create simple or complex AWS infrastructures.

Generally, it is recommended to write a template for each layer of architecture. For example, separate templates for networking components, database servers, web servers, and so on. As a result, the required down-time during the maintenance and its impact on the business can be minimized. In a single template, multiple AWS resources can be specified. As the enterprise requirement changes with time, these templates can be modified accordingly. These modified templates can be stored in a version control repository such as Git to maintain the history of the CFTs.

AWS CFT creation is not just restricted to be written in a text editor using JSON or YAML code, but it can also be created using the GUI tool, AWS CloudFormation Designer. For designing your own templates with AWS CloudFormation Designer, you can refer to `https://console.aws.amazon.com/cloudformation/designer`. For more details on CloudFormaton Designer, you can refer to following URL: `http://docs.aws.amazon.com/AWSCloudFormation/latest/UserGuide/working-with-templates-cfn-designer.html`.

 To use AWS CloudFormation Designer, you may require to log in to your AWS account.

What is a stack?

A stack is created on a successful execution of a template in CloudFormation. Executing a template creates a defined set of AWS resources. A group of these AWS resources defined in CloudFormation is called a stack. During template execution, if CloudFormation is unable to create any resource, the whole stack creation fails. When a CloudFormation execution fails, it rolls back all execution steps and deletes any resources created during the process. CloudFormation execution may fail due to several reasons including insufficient privileges. Due to limited IAM privileges, if rollback process unable to delete the created resources, the incomplete stack remains in the AWS account until it is deleted by any IAM user having sufficient privileges to delete the stack.

At the time of creating a stack from the template, AWS CloudFormation only checks for the syntax error in JSON/YAML notation. It does not check whether the IAM user executing the template has sufficient privileges to complete the template execution or not. Also it does not check if any resource creation may violate AWS soft limits for the resources in the account.

Stack helps to efficiently manage several AWS resources as a single unit. The property of each resource created inside a stack can also be modified manually, but it is a best practice to modify stack resource properties by modifying the CFTs only. With the help of the update stack option, modifications can be carried out in an existing stack.

An existing CloudFormation stack can be updated by submitting a modified version of the original stack template, or by giving different input parameter values during the execution. During the re-execution of the template, AWS CloudFormation compares the updated template with the original template and creates a change set. The change set includes changes required to update the stack. You can review the proposed changes and execute it for updating the stack or you can opt for creating a new change set. The following *Figure 15.2* summarizes the workflow for updating a stack:

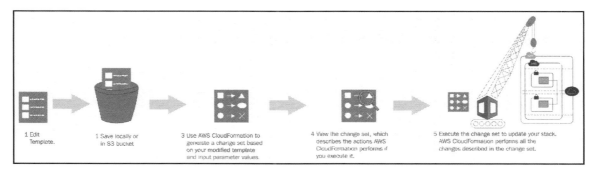

Figure 15.2: Workflow for updating a AWS CloudFormation stack

Reference URL: https://docs.aws.amazon.com/AWSCloudFormation/latest/UserGuide/images/update-stack-diagram.png

AWS CloudFormation stacks can be easily deleted. When the stack is deleted, all the AWS resources created during stack creation is alo deleted. While deleting a stack there may be a situation when partial AWS resources are required to be retained for future use. With the help of the deletion policy such resources can be retained. For example, while deleting a stack, you may want to delete an EC2 instance but retain the EBS volume attached to the instance. You can control such behaviour using deletion policy.

Deletion policy can have following three attributes:

- `Delete`: When you specify this attribute in `DeletionPolicy`, CloudFormation deletes the associated resource on stack deletion
- `Retain`: When you specify this attribute in `DeletionPolicy`, CloudFormation retains the associated resource even after the stack deletion
- `Snapshot`: When you specify this attribute in `DeletionPolicy`, CloudFormation creates a snapshot of the associated resource before deleting the stack.

The following is an example how you can specify deletion policy in a CFT:

```
"NewEBSVolume" : {
"Type" : "AWS::EC2::Volume",
"Properties" : {
"Size" : "200",
"Encrypted" : "false",
"AvailabilityZone" : { "Fn::GetAtt" : [ "Ec2Instance", "AvailabilityZone"
] },
"Tags" : [ {
"Key" : "Name",
"Value" : "DataVolume"
} ]
},
"DeletionPolicy" : "Retain"
}
```

Template structure

The following table helps us understand the basic AWS CFT structure in JSON and YAML format:

JSON structure	YAML structure

{
"AWSTemplateFormatVersion" : "version date",
 	
"Description" : "JSON string",
 	
"Metadata" : {
template metadata
},
 	
"Parameters" : {
set of parameters
},
 	
"Mappings" : {
set of mappings
},
 	
"Conditions" : {
set of conditions
},
 	
"Transform" : {
set of transforms
},
 	
"Resources" : {
set of resources
},
 	
"Outputs" : {
set of outputs
}
}
	--- 	
	AWSTemplateFormatVersion: "version date"
	
	Description:
	String
	
	Metadata:
	template metadata
	
	Parameters:
	set of parameters
	
	Mappings:
	set of mappings
	
	Conditions:
	set of conditions
	
	Transform:
	set of transforms
	
	Resources:
	set of resources
	
	Outputs:
	set of outputs

Basic AWS CloudFormation template structure in JSON and YAML

Reference URL: https://docs.aws.amazon.com/AWSCloudFormation/latest/UserGuide/template-anatomy.html

Having a basic understanding of any one of these two data interchange formats, JSON or YAML is advantageous for writing a quick, efficient, and effective AWS CFT.

A CFT is divided into nine sections. Out of these nine sections, the Resources section is the only required section to successfully execute an AWS CFT. Each Resource section must have at least one resource definition to create with essential properties. For example when creating an EC2 instance, AMI ID and instance type are essential parameters. We will understand the usage of each of these CFTs sections.

AWSTemplateFormatVersion

AWSTemplateFormatVersion section is an optional. It identifies capabilities of the template. The latest and currently supported version is 2010-09-09 and must be defined as a literal string (that is, enclosed in double quotes). In any case, if this section is not specified then by default the latest template format version is assumed. This template version is different from the API or **Web Services Description Language (WSDL)** version.

Example in JSON:

```
"AWSTemplateFormatVersion" : "2010-09-09"
```

Example in YAML:

```
AWSTemplateFormatVersion: "2010-09-09"
```

Description

Description section is optional in a template.. It makes it possible to write meaningful comments from 0 to 1024 bytes long for CFTs. In the future, it helps other developers to understand the purpose of the template. For example, in the future when changes are required to be carried out in the existing infrastructure, it would be very important for architects and developers to understand the purpose of the template. Description section should always be next to the AWSTemplateFormatVersion section.

Example in JSON:

```
"Description" : "Provide meaningful description about the template."
```

Example in YAML:

```
Description: >
 Provide meaningful
 description about
 the template.
```

Metadata

Metadata is an optional section in a template. It can be used to write extra details in the form of JSON or YAML objects. It supports metadata keys, which enables us to retrieve the defined configuration or settings in the Resources section. These keys are defined in a Metadata section. While writing this book, the CFT Metadata section supports the following three metadata keys:

```
AWS::CloudFormation::Init
```

It defines the configuration or settings for the cfn-init helper scripts in the EC2 instance. These helper scripts are executed only once while creating a new EC2 instance to install or configure applications on those EC2 instances. In future, when these EC2 instances are restarted it doesn't execute this scripts:

```
AWS::CloudFormation::Interface
```

It helps to define the grouping and ordering for the input parameters. Input parameters helps to accept values (that is, at template runtime) for resource properties. It helps to make stack creation and modification dynamic:

```
AWS::CloudFormation::Designer
```

A designer metadata key is automatically added to the CFT when it is created using AWS CloudFormation Designer. Usually, it contains information about various AWS resources and how they were laid down on a GUI designer.

Parameters

Parameter section is optional in a template. It can be used to pass values into the template, to be customized while creating a stack. It will allow us to create a stack every time with different values at runtime without changing any code in the CFT. Suppose a template has been written to create a three tier architecture and, based on the infrastructure environment such as test, development, pre-production, or production, the user may want to change the EC2 or RDS instance type. With the help of the parameter section such values can be customized at runtime; stack creation will ask for a parameter to input values for such resource properties. Optionally, it is also possible to provide default values for each parameter. So when the user does not provide any input, it will take that default value. Optionally, also validation can be placed in a parameter to allow the input of only relevant information. No need to write separate CFTs for each environment such as test, development, pre-production, or production.

Basic syntax for parameters:

- Syntax in JSON:

```
"Parameters" : {
  "ParameterLogicalID" : {
    "Type" : "DataType",
    "ParameterProperty" : "value"
  }
}
```

- Syntax in YAML:

```
Parameters:
  ParameterLogicalID:
    Type: DataType
    ParameterProperty: value
```

A maximum of 60 parameters can be defined in an individual CFT. It is essential to declare a unique logical name (that is, `ParameterLogicalID`) for each parameter within the template. Parameter data type can be: String, Number, CommaDelimitedList, or AW-specific type.

AWS-specific parameters

At runtime, when creating a stack from a template, you may require to get values from the AWS environment. For example, an AWS architect or developer has written a CFT for a specific time, as and when required one of the team members needs to run this template to create a stack. While running the template, it requires to identify the AWS region in which it is executed. Based on the AWS region, the template uses a suitable key pair for an EC2 instance. AWS uses a number of pseudo parameters which are populated from the presently available resources in the specific region. For example, the number of AZs may vary from region to region or the list of EC2 key value pairs may vary from region to region and from AWS account to account. For example, when a template that uses such pseudo parameters is executed for creating a stack, it enables an administrator to select desired AZs for creating EC2 instances. The following table helps us understands various pseudo parameters and their usage:

 Most AWS-specific parameters return multiple values in a drop-down list apart from AWS::EC2::Image::Id.

AWS-specific parameters	Description
AWS::EC2::AvailabilityZone::Name	Provides a list of AZs in the current region. Only one value from a drop-down list can be selected. For example: us-west-2a.
AWS::EC2::Image::Id	Provides an Amazon EC2 image ID.. Provides a textbox to enter a valid AMI ID. For example: ami-ff5467egf.
AWS::EC2::Instance::Id	Provides a list of Amazon EC2 instance IDs in the current region. Only one value from a drop-down list can be selected. For example: i-0862FF253e23cfas2.
AWS::EC2::KeyPair::KeyName	Provides a list of key pairs in a region. Only one value from a drop-down list can be selected. For example: test-key.

`AWS::EC2::SecurityGroup::GroupName`	Provides a list of security groups existing in a region. Only one value from a drop-down list can be selected. For example: `launch-wizard-1`.
`AWS::EC2::SecurityGroup::Id`	Provides a list of security groups along with ID existing in a region. Only one value from a drop-down list can be selected. For example: `launch-wizard-1 (sg-28db6c88)`.
`AWS::EC2::Subnet::Id`	Provides a list of subnet IDs along with its CIDR range in a region. Multiple values from a drop-down list can be selected. For example: `subnet-31hj765a (172.31.48.0/20)`.
`AWS::EC2::Volume::Id`	Provides a list of EBS volume IDs along with names that are available in a region. Only one value from a drop-down list can be selected. For example: `vol-010968da1fwd265d8 (TestVol)`.
`AWS::EC2::VPC::Id`	Provides a list of VPCs along with IDs, CIDR range, and names available in a region. Only one value from a drop-down list can be selected. For example `:vpc-6c5fe40a (172.31.0.0/16)(DefaultVPC)`.
`AWS::Route53::HostedZone::Id`	Provides a list of hosted zones along with domain name and ID, in a AWS Route 53 service. Only one value from a drop-down list can be selected. For example: `testdomain.text (A5EF6W8F6S8FF)`.

`List<AWS::EC2::AvailabilityZone::Name>`	Provides a list of AZs in the current region and multiple AZs can be selected from the drop-down menu. For example: `us-east-1a us-east-1c`.
`List<AWS::EC2::Image::Id>`	Provides a list of Amazon EC2 AMI IDs. For this parameter type, the AWS console will not show a drop-down list. It will show a text box.
`List<AWS::EC2::Instance::Id>`	Provides a list of existing EC2 instances in a region along with instance ID and name. Multiple EC2 instances can be selected. For example: `i-0862FF253e23cfas2 (Test1) i-0862FF253e23xfax2 (Test2)`
`List<AWS::EC2::SecurityGroup::GroupName>`	Lists the security groups only with names available in the AWS region. Multiple security groups can be selected from the drop-down menu. For example: `launch-wizard-1 launch-wizard-2`.
`List<AWS::EC2::SecurityGroup::Id>`	Lists the security groups with names and IDs available in the AWS Region. Multiple security groups can be selected from drop-down menu. For example: `launch-wizard-1 (sg-28db6c88) launch-wizard-2 (sg-56hs9g45)`.

`List<AWS::EC2::Subnet::Id>`	Lists all the subnets along with IDs, CIDR range, and names. Multiple subnets can be selected from a drop-down menu. For example: `subnet-5d9d652 (172.31.16.0/20) (DefaultSubnet-1C) subnet-a6sd325s (172.31.32.0/20) (DefaultSubnet-1E)`.
`List<AWS::EC2::Volume::Id>`	Lists all the volumes along with ID and name in the region. Multiple values can be selected from a drop-down menu. For example `vol-369a8sd6689sd4587 (Vol1) vol-98df536rt9as3thc3 (Vol2)`.
`List<AWS::EC2::VPC::Id>`	Lists all the VPCs in the region along with IDs, CIDR range, and names. Multiple VPCs can be selected from a drop-down menu. For example: `vpc-65d3f69s (192.192.192.0/24) (Custom) vpc-69sd32rt (172.31.0.0/16) (DefaultVPC)`.
`List<AWS::Route53::HostedZone::Id>`	Lists all the hosted zones available in the region in AWS Route 53. Multiple hosted zones can be selected from a drop-down menu.

AWS-specified parameters and their usage

All AWS-specified parameters starting with list allows to select multiple values from a drop-down menu, accept `List<AWS::EC2::Image::Id>`.

Optionally, one or more properties can be defined for each parameter. It helps to make the user interface much more natural at the time of creating a stack from the template for example providing a dropdown list for valid values, showing * for each character when sensitive information is entered such as password. The list of various allowed parameter properties are defined as follows:

Properties	Description
AllowedPattern	**Required**: No Specify regular expression for a String type, to validate manually entered string by the user at the time of creating the stack. For example: accepting username or password.
AllowedValues	**Required**: No Restricts the user to entering only valid values that are specified in the list of values in an array. For example: EC2 instance type can be only [t2.micro, m3.large, m4.large].
ConstraintDescription	**Required**: No When user input does not match with the constraint message to be displayed, it can be defined here. For example: username or password can only contain [A-Z, a-z, 0-9]+.
Default	**Required**: No It specifies a value to be used, when the user has not provided any value as input.
Description	**Required**: No It describes the parameters; up to 4,000 characters can be written.
MaxLength	**Required**: No It defines the maximum number of characters to be allowed for String type parameters. It can be defined by specifying the integer value.
MaxValue	**Required**: No It defines the allowed largest value for Number types. It can be defined by specifying the integer value.
MinLength	**Required**: No It defines the minimum number of characters to be entered for String type parameters. It can be defined by specifying the integer value.

MinValue	**Required**: No It defines the allowed smallest value for Number types. It can be defined by specifying the integer value.
NoEcho	**Required**: No By enabling this property sensitive information can be masked by *.
Type	**Required**: Yes It defines the data type for the parameter (data type). It can be defined as String, Number, List<Number>, or CommaDelimitedList.

List of allowed properties in parameter sections

The following example shows how to parameterize the EC2 instance type at the time of creating a stack from a CFT. The drop-down list allows you to choose any one EC2 instance type from t2.micro, m1.small, or m1.large. The default value is t2.micro.

Example in JSON:

```
"Parameters" : {
  "InstanceTypeParameter" : {
    "Type" : "String",
    "Default" : "t2.micro",
    "AllowedValues" : ["t2.micro", "m1.small", "m1.large"],
    "Description" : "Enter t2.micro, m1.small, or m1.large. Default is
t2.micro."
  }
}
```

Ref. URL:
https://docs.aws.amazon.com/AWSCloudFormation/latest/UserGuide/p
arameters-section-structure.html.

Example in YAML:

```
Parameters:
  InstanceTypeParameter:
    Type: String
    Default: t2.micro
    AllowedValues:
      - t2.micro
      - m1.small
      - m1.large
```

```
    Description: Enter t2.micro, m1.small, or m1.large. Default is
t2.micro.
```

Reference URL: https://docs.aws.amazon.com/AWSCloudFormation/ latest/UserGuide/parameters-section-structure.html.

In general, a function is available to be used only in a specific programming language; its implementation is handled specially by the compiler and is called as intrinsic function. AWS CloudFormation provides several built-in functions to help manage the stack such as Fn::Base64, Condition functions, Fn::FindInMap, Fn::GetAtt, Fn::GetAZs, Fn::ImportValue, Fn::Join, Fn::Select, Fn::Split, Fn::Sub and Ref. These functions can be only used in specific parts of a template such as resource properties in the Resources section, Output section, metadata attributes, and update policy attributes.

Intrinsic function	Description
Fn::Base64	This function converts parameterized string to the Base64 representation. Ideally, it helps to pass encoded data to Amazon EC2 instance using UserData property.
Condition Functions	Conditional functions can be helpful while creating a CloudFormation stack based on some conditions. While creating a CloudFormation stack, there may be a need to build few resources based on certain conditions. For example, if the target environment is *Staging*, EC2 instance type should be micro and if the target environment is *Production*, EC2 instance type should be large. Set of conditional intrinsic functions such as Fn::If, Fn::Equals, and Fn::Not can refer to other conditions and values from the Parameters and Mappings sections of a template to conditionally create or update a stack.
Fn::FindInMap	It helps to find appropriate value corresponding to a two-level map declared in a Mappings section. For example, in your CFT, you can write a mapping to use an appropriate AMI in respective region. Depending up on the region, CloudFormation can take an appropriate AMI ID for creating an EC2 instance.

Fn::GetAtt	It is a very common need to refer some attributes of a other resources for creating a new AWS resource. For example, a template needs ELB endpoint to create a CNAME in a Route 53. For such scenario, Fn::GetAtt intrinsic function can be used to get the value of an attribute from another resource created in the same template.
Fn::GetAZs	It is used for fetching a list of AZ in a region where the function is executed.
Fn::ImportValue	It is recommended to create a multi-layered CloudFormation stacks. In a multi-layered CloudFormation stack, it may be required to refer the resources created in another stack. The function Fn::ImportValue returns the value of an output exported by another stack.
Fn::Join	This intrinsic function helps to concatenate a set of values into a single value.
Fn::Select	This intrinsic function simply returns a single object from a list of objects.
Fn::Split	This intrinsic function is opposite to the Fn::Join. This function splits a given string into a list of string values based on a given delimiter.
Fn::Sub	This intrinsic function substitutes a variable in an input string with specified values.
Ref	This intrinsic function returns the value of the specified parameter or resource referenced by this function.

While writing a template, customized value for a parameter can be retrieved using Ref intrinsic function as shown in following code example:

Example in JSON:

```
"Ec2Instance" : {
  "Type" : "AWS::EC2::Instance",
  "Properties" : {
    "InstanceType" : { "Ref" : "InstanceTypeParameter" },
    "ImageId" : "ami-2f726546"
  }
}
```

Reference URL: https://docs.aws.amazon.com/AWSCloudFormation/
latest/UserGuide/parameters-section-structure.html.

Example in YAML:

```
Ec2Instance:
  Type: AWS::EC2::Instance
  Properties:
    InstanceType:
      Ref: InstanceTypeParameter
    ImageId: ami-2f726546
```

Ref. URL: https://docs.aws.amazon.com/AWSCloudFormation/latest/
UserGuide/parameters-section-structure.html.

Another example of parameter properties: Two parameters DBPort and DBPwd are created using parameter properties such as Default, Description, MinValue, MaxValue, NoEcho, Description, MinLength, MaxLength, and AllowedPattern respectively.

Example in JSON:

```
"Parameters" : {
  "DBPort" : {
    "Default" : "3306",
    "Description" : "TCP/IP port for the database",
    "Type" : "Number",
    "MinValue" : "1150",
    "MaxValue" : "65535"
  },
  "DBPwd" : {
    "NoEcho" : "true",
    "Description" : "The database admin account password",
    "Type" : "String",
    "MinLength" : "1",
    "MaxLength" : "41",
    "AllowedPattern" : "[a-zA-Z0-9]*"
  }
}
```

Reference URL: https://docs.aws.amazon.com/AWSCloudFormation/
latest/UserGuide/parameters-section-structure.html.

Example in YAML:

```
Parameters:
  DBPort:
    Default: 3306
    Description: TCP/IP port for the database
    Type: Number
    MinValue: 1150
    MaxValue: 65535
  DBPwd:
    NoEcho: true
    Description: The database admin account password
    Type: String
    MinLength: 1
    MaxLength: 41
    AllowedPattern: "[a-zA-Z0-9]*"
```

Reference URL: https://docs.aws.amazon.com/AWSCloudFormation/
latest/UserGuide/parameters-section-structure.html.

Pseudo parameters are predefined by AWS CloudFormation and do not require to be predefined before use in the template. They are used in the same way as custom defined parameters would have been used, with the help of the Ref function. The list of the presently available pseudo parameters are given in the following table:

Pseudo parameter	Description
AWS::AccountId	Returns 12 digit AWS account ID.
AWS::NotificationARNs	It returns ARNs for each resource in the current stack. To fetch a single ARN from the list, the intrinsic function Fn::Select can be used.
AWS::NoValue	When you specify this parameter as return value in Fn::If intrinsic function, it removes the corresponding resource property.
AWS::Region	It returns the name of the AWS region where the resource is being created.

AWS::StackId	It returns the stack ID as specified with the aws cloudformation `create-stack` command.
AWS::StackName	Returns the stack name as specified with the aws cloudformation `create-stack` command.

List of pseudo parameters

Mappings

The Mappings section is optional in a template. This section matches a key to a corresponding set of named values. For example, the AMI ID for an Amazon Linux is `ami-22ce4934` in Northern Virginia and `ami-9e247efe` in Northern California. With the help of the Mappings section we can have a smart template based on the region where it is running and it will take the right AMI ID to launch an EC2 instance.

 In Mappings sections, values from parameters, pseudo parameters, or intrinsic functions cannot be used.

The Mappings section begins with mappings as a key name. It is required to have keys and values, both must be literal strings. The following syntax in JSON and YAML helps us understand this. Mappings in the top line indicates the beginning of a section as a key and the string. `Mapping01` string indicates the variable or parameter to observe for mapping a value. Usually, the output of a pseudo or AWS-specific parameter is stored in such a variable or parameter. `Key01`, `Key02`, and `Key03` could be different possible values in that variable or parameter.

Syntax in JSON:

```
"Mappings" : {
  "Mapping01" : {
    "Key01" : {
      "Name" : "Value01"
    },
    "Key02" : {
      "Name" : "Value02"
    },
    "Key03" : {
      "Name" : "Value03"
    }
  }
```

```
}
```

Reference URL: https://docs.aws.amazon.com/AWSCloudFormation/latest/UserGuide/mappings-section-structure.html.

Syntax in YAML:

```
Mappings:
  Mapping01:
    Key01:
      Name: Value01
    Key02:
      Name: Value02
    Key03:
      Name: Value03
```

Ref. URL: https://docs.aws.amazon.com/AWSCloudFormation/latest/UserGuide/mappings-section-structure.html.

For example, the output of a pseudo variable AWS::Region is stored in a RegionMap variable. If it returns us-east-1 then it should use the appropriate EC2 AMI available in that region; for example here ami-6411e20d. 32 is used as a key value. This value can be anything meaningful to the project or enterprise. Here we have used 32-bit as a key. It can also be 64-bit to use the suitable AMI. As given in the following example, you can use an intrinsic function like Fn::FindInMap for automatically populating suitable value from Mappings section.

Example in JSON:

```
{
   "AWSTemplateFormatVersion" : "2010-09-09",

   "Mappings" : {
     "RegionMap" : {
       "us-east-1" : { "32" : "ami-6411e20d", "64" : "ami-7a11e213" },
       "us-west-1" : { "32" : "ami-c9c7978c", "64" : "ami-cfc7978a" },
       "eu-west-1" : { "32" : "ami-37c2f643", "64" : "ami-31c2f645" },
       "ap-southeast-1" : { "32" : "ami-66f28c34", "64" : "ami-60f28c32" },
       "ap-northeast-1" : { "32" : "ami-9c03a89d", "64" : "ami-a003a8a1" }
     }
   },
```

```
  "Resources" : {
    "myEC2Instance" : {
      "Type" : "AWS::EC2::Instance",
      "Properties" : {
        "ImageId" : { "Fn::FindInMap" : [ "RegionMap", { "Ref" :
"AWS::Region" }, "32"]},
        "InstanceType" : "m1.small"
      }
    }
  }
}
```

Reference URL: https://docs.aws.amazon.com/AWSCloudFormation/latest/UserGuide/mappings-section-structure.html.

Example in YAML:

```
AWSTemplateFormatVersion: "2010-09-09"
 Mappings:
  RegionMap:
    us-east-1:
      "32": "ami-6411e20d"
      "64": "ami-7a11e213"
    us-west-1:
      "32": "ami-c9c7978c"
      "64": "ami-cfc7978a"
    eu-west-1:
      "32": "ami-37c2f643"
      "64": "ami-31c2f645"
    ap-southeast-1:
      "32": "ami-66f28c34"
      "64": "ami-60f28c32"
    ap-northeast-1:
      "32": "ami-9c03a89d"
      "64": "ami-a003a8a1"
 Resources:
  myEC2Instance:
    Type: "AWS::EC2::Instance"
    Properties:
      ImageId: !FindInMap [RegionMap, !Ref "AWS::Region", 32]
      InstanceType: m1.small
```

Reference URL: `https://docs.aws.amazon.com/AWSCloudFormation/latest/UserGuide/mappings-section-structure.html`.

On the same lines as another example, if it is a test or prod environment in the `us-east-1` `region` then use `ami-8ff710e2` and `ami-f5f41398` respectively. And when the region is `us-west-2`, for the test and prod environments use `ami-eff1028f` and `ami-d0f506b0` respectively.

Conditions

Conditions can be used in a template for reusing the same template again and again based on scenario. The template behaves differently based on the conditions satisfied. For example, in the Parameter section when the environment type is selected as test, then the EC2 instance is created with basic capabilities such as small volume size. Similarly when the environment is selected as production, EC2 instance is created with a higher configuration such as larger EBS volumes and larger instance size.

An example template for CloudFormation condition can be found at following URL: `http://docs.aws.amazon.com/AWSCloudFormation/latest/UserGuide/conditions-section-structure.html`.

Conditions in a template can be modified only when resources are added, modified, or deleted.

In order to create a resource based on a condition, it is essential to specify the statement in at least three different sections in a template that is, Resource or Output section, Parameter section, and Condition section. In the Parameter section, you can define the input value which evaluates whether the input conditions are true or false. In the Condition section, you can specify the condition using an intrinsic functions to determine whether to create an associated resource or not.

Finally in the Resource and Output sections, associate conditions with the resources in the Resources section or output in an Outputs section, which should be created conditionally. Use the condition key and the condition's logical ID to associate it with a resource or output. To conditionally specify a property, use conditional functions such as the `Fn::And`, `Fn::Equals`, `Fn::If`, `Fn::Not`, or `Fn::Or` function. Syntax in JSON and YAML is as follows:

Syntax in JSON:

```
"Conditions" : {
  "Logical ID" : {Intrinsic function}
}
```

Syntax in YAML:

```
Conditions:
  Logical ID:
  Intrinsic function
```

Example of CloudFormation Conditions is as follows:

```
{
  "AWSTemplateFormatVersion" : "2010-09-09",

  "Mappings" : {
  "RegionMap" : {
  "us-east-1" : { "AMI" : "ami-7f418316", "TestAz" : "us-east-1a" },
  "us-west-1" : { "AMI" : "ami-951945d0", "TestAz" : "us-west-1a" },
  "us-west-2" : { "AMI" : "ami-16fd7026", "TestAz" : "us-west-2a" },
  "eu-west-1" : { "AMI" : "ami-24506250", "TestAz" : "eu-west-1a" },
  "sa-east-1" : { "AMI" : "ami-3e3be423", "TestAz" : "sa-east-1a" },
  "ap-southeast-1" : { "AMI" : "ami-74dda626", "TestAz" : "ap-southeast-1a"
},
  "ap-southeast-2" : { "AMI" : "ami-b3990e89", "TestAz" : "ap-southeast-2a"
},
  "ap-northeast-1" : { "AMI" : "ami-dcfa4edd", "TestAz" : "ap-northeast-1a"
}
  }
  },

  "Parameters" : {
  "EnvType" : {
  "Description" : "Environment type.",
  "Default" : "test",
  "Type" : "String",
  "AllowedValues" : ["prod", "test"],
  "ConstraintDescription" : "must specify prod or test."
```

```
    }
  },

  "Conditions" : {
  "CreateProdResources" : {"Fn::Equals" : [{"Ref" : "EnvType"}, "prod"]}
  },

  "Resources" : {
  "EC2Instance" : {
  "Type" : "AWS::EC2::Instance",
  "Properties" : {
  "ImageId" : { "Fn::FindInMap" : [ "RegionMap", { "Ref" : "AWS::Region" },
"AMI" ]}
  }
  },

  "MountPoint" : {
  "Type" : "AWS::EC2::VolumeAttachment",
  "Condition" : "CreateProdResources",
  "Properties" : {
  "InstanceId" : { "Ref" : "EC2Instance" },
  "VolumeId" : { "Ref" : "NewVolume" },
  "Device" : "/dev/sdh"
  }
  },

  "NewVolume" : {
  "Type" : "AWS::EC2::Volume",
  "Condition" : "CreateProdResources",
  "Properties" : {
  "Size" : "100",
  "AvailabilityZone" : { "Fn::GetAtt" : [ "EC2Instance", "AvailabilityZone"
]}
  }
  }
  },

  "Outputs" : {
  "VolumeId" : {
  "Value" : { "Ref" : "NewVolume" },
  "Condition" : "CreateProdResources"
  }
  }
}
```

Reference URL: `https://docs.aws.amazon.com/AWSCloudFormation/`
`latest/UserGuide/conditions-section-structure.html`.

Transform

The Transform section is optional in a template. This section carries statements to condense and simplify template authoring. For example, in hundreds of lines of CFT, a resource declaration of multiple lines can be replaced by a single line. These statements are declarative statements and tells AWS CloudFormation *how to process the template*. It uses simple and declarative language with a powerful macro system. All transform functions are resolved again and again on every change set created for a stack. At the time of writing this book, the following transform declarative statements are supported:

```
AWS::Serverless
```

It is a specific version of an **AWS Serverless Application Model (AWS SAM)**. It helps us deploy an AWS Lambda-based application, also referred to as a serverless application and composed of AWS Lambda functions triggered by events.

```
AWS::Include
```

It helps to include a separate template snippet. For example, to perform a common repetitive task a separate CFT . In an enterprise application it may be required to create a web server for various projects. With the help of this transform it is possible to call the web server template in a main template for that particular project.

Resources

The only section required to run any AWS CFT is the Resources section with at least one resource to create and include in the stacks. One template can have only one Resources section; in that one Resources section, multiple resources separated by a comma can be specified. When the stack is created from a template, all the specified resources will be logically grouped in the same stack. The syntax for the Resources section is as follows:

Syntax in JSON:

```
"Resources" : {
    "Logical ID" : {
        "Type" : "Resource type",
        "Properties" : {
            Set of properties
```

```
        }
      }
    }
```

Syntax in YAML:

```
Resources:
  Logical ID:
    Type: Resource type
    Properties:
      Set of properties
```

In the following table, Resource fields are explained:

Resources fields	Description
Logical ID	Each logical ID must be unique within each template and can contain only alphanumerics (A-Za-Z0-9). It is always suggested to give meaningful and relevant logical names. Logical ID of one resource can be used to perform further tasks on the same resource. For example, a logical ID of an EC2 instance can be used to add an extra EBS volume in the same template.
Type	Resource type specifies the type of AWS Resource that is being created, for example AWS EC2, EBS, VPC, Subnet, and so on. A detailed list of Resource type can be obtained at https://docs.aws.amazon.com/ AWSCloudFormation/latest/UserGuide/aws-template-resource-type-ref.html.
Properties	Resource properties configure the characteristics of the AWS resource that is being created. For various AWS resources some properties are essential to define and the rest can be optional. For example, in the case of creating an EC2 instance, ImageId is one of the parameter that must be specifed.

Resource fields

Outputs

The Outputs section is optional in a template. This section can be used to declare values to be used in another template, return a response (to describe a stack call), or to view the AWS CloudFormation console, for example, to display a public or private DNS name to access an EC2 instance.

In the following syntax we can see that it begins with the key name Outputs. In a single template, a maximum of 60 outputs can be declared.

Syntax in JSON:

```json
"Outputs" : {
  "Logical ID" : {
    "Description" : "Information about the value",
    "Value" : "Value to return",
    "Export" : {
      "Name" : "Value to export"
    }
  }
}
```

Reference URL: https://docs.aws.amazon.com/AWSCloudFormation/latest/UserGuide/outputs-section-structure.html.

Syntax in YAML:

```yaml
Outputs:
  Logical ID:
    Description: Information about the value
    Value: Value to return
    Export:
      Name: Value to export
```

Reference URL: https://docs.aws.amazon.com/AWSCloudFormation/latest/UserGuide/outputs-section-structure.html.

The following table describes each Output field:

Output fields	Description
Logical ID	It is required, must be unique for each output within the template ,and can be only alphanumeric (A-Za-z0-9).
Description (optional)	It is an optional String type and atmost 4 K in length.
Value (required)	It is required and it can have literals, parameter references, pseudo parameters, a mapping value, or intrinsic functions.
Export (optional)	It is optional and can be declared to export a resource to be used in another stack. In other words for a cross-stack reference. A few important points to remember when exporting a resource are: • With an AWS account, Export names must be unique within a region • Cross-stack references can be created for use within one region only. Intrinsic function Fn::ImportValue can only import an exported value in some stacks • Stack can't be deleted when one or more resource is cross-referenced by another stack • It is also not possible to modify or remove an output value referenced by another stack

Description about each of Output fields

The following code example helps us understand the Output section. It is called StackVPC and returns the ID of a VPC, then exports the value for a cross-stack reference with the name VPCID appended to the stack's name.

Example in JSON:

```
"Outputs" : {
  "StackVPC" : {
    "Description" : "The ID of the VPC",
    "Value" : { "Ref" : "MyVPC" },
    "Export" : {
      "Name" : {"Fn::Sub": "${AWS::StackName}-VPCID" }
    }
  }
}
```

Reference URL: `https://docs.aws.amazon.com/AWSCloudFormation/latest/UserGuide/outputs-section-structure.html`.

Example in YAML:

```
Outputs:
  StackVPC:
    Description: The ID of the VPC
    Value: !Ref MyVPC
    Export:
      Name: !Sub "${AWS::StackName}-VPCID"
```

Reference URL:
`https://docs.aws.amazon.com/AWSCloudFormation/latest/UserGuide/outputs-section-structure.html`.

Sample CloudFormation template

The following reference URLs provide various ready to use CFTs to match the general needs of an enterprise. These templates can be used directly or modified as per the actual business need. Once templates are written, partial code can be referred, or copied and pasted into another template to write a template writing quickly.

The following are important reference URLs for sample CFTs:

- CloudFormation sample templates, region-wise refer to `https://docs.aws.amazon.com/AWSCloudFormation/latest/UserGuide/cfn-sample-templates.html`
- AWS CFT solution for various AWS services; refer to `https://docs.aws.amazon.com/AWSCloudFormation/latest/UserGuide/sample-templates-services-us-west-2.html`

CloudFormer

CloudFormer can automatically generate a CFT from existing AWS resources in your AWS account. It stores the CFT in a target S3 bucket specified by you. Unlike writing a template from the scratch, CloudFormer performs a reverse engineering task and makes your life easier by generating a template from existing AWS resources in you acount. This template can be used as is for DR or you can use them for customizing your infrastructure based on your needs. At the time of writing this book, CloudFormer is still in beta version. The more about CloudFormer can be found at the following URL: `https://docs.aws.amazon.com/AWSCloudFormation/latest/UserGuide/cfn-using-cloudformer.html`.

Rolling updates for Auto Scaling groups

AWS CloudFormation provides you with a mechanism to control how an Auto Scaling group updates your resources using the `UpdatePolicy` attribute. If you do not configure your settings correctly, rolling update on an Auto Scaling group may perform unexpectedly. You can address such scenario by using `AutoScalingRollingUpdate` policy, which supports a number of options to configure your template.

Here is an example of update policy for rolling update which can be found in official AWS documentation at following URL: `https://aws.amazon.com/premiumsupport/knowledge-center/auto-scaling-group-rolling-updates/`. You can also refer to a very good article on rolling update with CloudFormation at following URL: `https://cloudonaut.io/rolling-update-with-aws-cloudformation/`.

CloudFormation best practices

CloudFormation best practices are as follows:

- Always give meaningful and relevant names to AWS CloudFormation templates and resources.
- Make sure the resources used by a CloudFormation template does exist in the region where it is being executed to create a stack. For example resources such as an EC2 keypair. It can be also be created dynamically using templates but, if it is hardcoded; make sure it exists in the relevant region.

- Write a template and create a stack for each layer for example a separate stack for web servers, application servers, networks, and so on. It will help us minimize downtime and efficiently manage and maintain infrastructures.

- It is a best practice to use a cross-stack reference. It helps us integrate resources from multiple templates into one template, especially when a separate stack is created for each layer.

- It is a best practice to provide essential IAM privileges to the IAM user executing a CloudFormation template to create a stack. It may involve creating or manipulating various AWS resources. Make sure sufficient permissions are granted.

- At the time of creating a stack, AWS CloudFormation only validates the syntax. It doesn't check for required IAM privileges or soft limits for resources that are being created. Make sure executing a template to create a stack doesn't attempt to cross a soft limit. If so, ask AWS to extend it.

- Reuse the whole or part of the template as and when required with adequate modifications to meet business requirements.

- Use a nested stack to perform common template patterns.

- It is advised not to embed credentials or sensitive information in any template.

- Parameters constrains, AWS-specific parameters, and properties can be used effectively to use the same template dynamically and to avoid invalid user inputs.

- A set of Python helper scripts is maintained and periodically updated by AWS to install software and start services on an Amazon EC2 instance. It is recommended to always use the latest helper scripts.

- Before creating a stack, validate the template syntax (JSON/YAML).

- Stack resource updation, deletion, or modification should be carried out by modifying a template rather than directly performing the action.

16
Elastic Beanstalk

Traditionally, deploying a web application on AWS may have required spending time on selecting appropriate AWS services such as EC2, ELB, Auto Scaling, and so on, and creating and configuring an AWS resource from scratch to host a web application. It could be difficult for developers to build the infrastructure, configure the OS, install the required dependencies, and deploy the web services. AWS Elastic Beanstalk removes the need to manually build an infrastructure for the developer and makes it possible for them to quickly deploy and manage a web application on AWS of any scale. Developers just need to upload the code and the rest of the things such as capacity provisioning, building, and configuring AWS resources such as EC2 instances, ELB, Auto Scaling, and application health monitoring will be taken care of by Elastic Beanstalk. The developer still gets full access to each of the underlying AWS resources powering a web application to fine-tune configuration over applications. In this chapter, we will learn about the following topics:

- Elastic Beanstalk components
- Architectural overview
- Deploying web applications to Elastic Beanstalk environments
- Monitoring the web application environment

At the time of writing this book, Elastic Beanstalk supports web applications developed in Java, PHP, .NET, Node.js, Python, Docker, Ruby, and Go. It also supports web servers such as Apache, nginx, Passenger, and IIS. An easy way to start working with AWS Elastic Beanstalk is through AWS web console. AWS also supports CLI, API, and SDKs to work with AWS Elastic Beanstalk. There are no additional charges for using AWS Elastic Beanstalk, charges only apply for using the underlying resources such as EC2, ELB, and Auto Scaling.

Most of the deployment and infrastructure tasks such as uploading a newer version of a web application, changing the size of the Amazon EC2 instances, can be done directly from the Elastic Beanstalk web console. The following *Figure 16.1* helps to understand the application deployment life-cycle in Elastic Beanstalk:

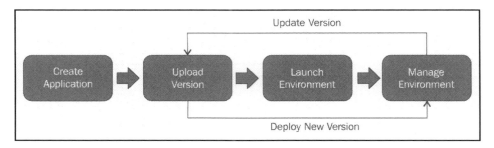

Figure 16.1: Application deployment and lifecycle management on AWS Elastic Beanstalk

Reference URL: http://docs.aws.amazon.com/elasticbeanstalk/latest/dg/images/clearbox-flow-00.png

The preceding figure, at a very high level, describes the way web application is deployed on AWS Elastic Beanstalk. Initially, a web application is developed with a preferred programming platform on a developer's machine. Once it is developed, the source code is converted into a source bundle, for example in Java, source bundle is converted into a `.war` file. This is an initial version of a web application. Once the initial version of the source bundle has been uploaded, Elastic Beanstalk automatically launches and configures the underlying infrastructure for running the source bundle. With time, as the business requirement changes, it is also possible to upload a newer version of a web application.

The main purpose of AWS Elastic Beanstalk is to set developers free from creating and configuring AWS resources (that is, infrastructure) and purely allow them to focus on application development. If they are comfortable to create and configure AWS resources to host a web application, they can use CloudFormation to write templates and create a stack.

Elastic Beanstalk components

The following are various Elastic Beanstalk components that work together to make it possible to deploy and manage custom applications easily in the AWS cloud:

- **Application**: This is a logical collection of Elastic Beanstalk components, including environment, versions, and environment configuration. For easy understanding, it can be imagined as a folder.

- **Application version**: This refers to a specific source code version for a web application. It points to an Amazon S3 object containing deploy code such as a Java .war file. Application version is part of an application. Each application can have multiple versions. Generally, application runs with the latest code version. At times, multiple versions of an application may run simultaneously for catering to users in different geography or for testing purpose.

- **Environment**: There are two types of environments: web server environment to listen and process HTTP(S) requests, and worker environment to process a background task that listens for messages on an Amazon SQS queue. Each environment runs only a single application version at a given time. Creating an environment automatically creates underlying resources to run a specific application version.

- **Environment configuration**: This is a set of parameters and settings, it defines how an environment and its associated resources will behave. Elastic Beanstalk will automatically apply changes from the environment configuration to the existing resources. If required, it may delete existing resources and create new resources to match with the environment configuration change.

- **Configuration template**: This is a starting point for creating unique environment configurations. Environment configuration can be created or modified using the CLI or API.

Architectural concepts

In this topic, let us understand some architectural concepts. As you understood from core concepts that environment is an essential component to deploy a web application. Creating a new environment requires selecting the appropriate environment tier, platform, and environment type. Broadly, environment tiers are divided into two environments:

- **Web server environment**: This hosts a web application and handles HTTP(S) requests. This environment is called a web server tier.

- **Worker environment**: This hosts a web application and handle long-running, or scheduled background processing tasks. This environment is called a worker tier.

 At any given point of time, each environment can support either of the environment tier. The technical reason behind this limitation is that at any given point of time, Elastic Beanstalk can handle only one Auto Scaling group. Each of the environment tiers requires one dedicated Auto Scaling group to host a web application.

A detailed description about these environment tiers are as follows:

Web server environment tier

The following *Figure 16.2* helps to understand the working of the web server environment tier:

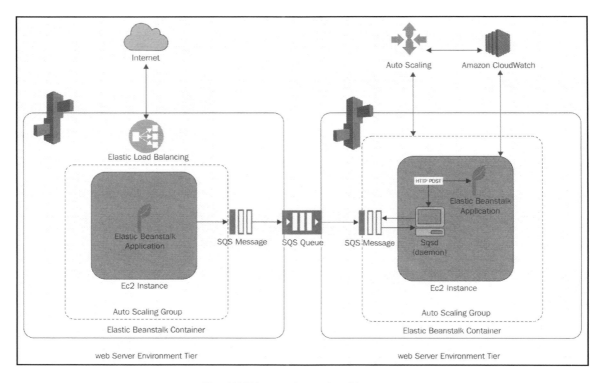

Figure 16.2: Web server environment tier and it's components

Reference URL: https://docs.aws.amazon.com/elasticbeanstalk/latest/dg/images/aeb-architecture2.png

The environment is a key component in an application and it is highlighted as a solid blue line in the preceding figure. It provisions the underlying required AWS resources to deploy and run the web application. The resources in the environment includes such as ELB, Auto Scaling group, and at least one or more EC2 instances.

Every environment has a CNAME and an alias in the Amazon Route 53 pointing to the ELB. The registered domain name (for example, `myapplication.com`) will forward the end user's request to access the web application on the CNAME. The CNAME points to an ELB where ELB is a part of the Auto Scaling group and it sits in front of the Amazon EC2 instances. Based on the actual load on the application, the number of EC2 instances will be scaled in and out.

The container type plays an important role. It decides the software stack to be installed on each EC2 instance and its infrastructure topology. The software stack may include one or more components such as programming language (such as Python, PHP, Java, and so on) web server (such as Apache web server, and so on), web container (such as Tomcat, Passenger, and so on), and Docker containers.

In each environment, each EC2 instance runs one of the container types along with a software **host manager** (**HM**). Later in this chapter, we will see in detail about containers. HM is indicated in the preceding *Figure 16.2* as a circle on the top right-hand side corner in each EC2 instance. The HM is responsible for the following:

- Aggregating events and metrics for retrieval using web console, API, or CLI
- Deploying the application
- Monitoring the application log files for critical errors
- Monitoring the application server
- Generating instance-level events
- Patching instance components
- Rotating applications log files and publishing them to the S3 bucket

By default, Elastic Beanstalk creates a security group and attaches it to the EC2 instances. The security group acts as a firewall and allows anyone to connect on port 80 HTTP. It is possible to customize security groups as per the web application's actual requirement.

Worker environment tiers

The worker environment tier includes an Auto Scaling group, at least one or more EC2 instances, and an IAM role. Optionally, it also creates an Amazon SQS queue, in case of not having one. Each EC2 instance in an Auto Scaling environment gets installed with a daemon and the necessary support files for the programming language of choice. The primary function of the daemon is to pull requests from an Amazon SQS queue and then send data to the running web application in the worker environment tier to process those messages. In case of having multiple instances in a worker environment tier, each instance has its own daemon. They all read from the same Amazon SQS queue. The following *Figure 16.3* helps us to understand the components of the worker environment tier at a very high level:

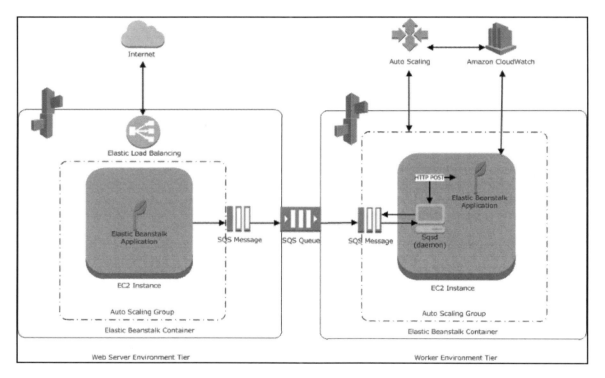

Figure 16.3: Worker environment tier and its components

Reference URL: https://docs.aws.amazon.com/elasticbeanstalk/latest/dg/images/aeb-architecture_worker.png

Elastic Beanstalk supported platforms

The platform defines the instance software configuration. Platforms are broadly divided into two categories:

- **Preconfigured platform**: This is also called an Elastic Beanstalk supported platforms. These platform are available in multiple configurations of various programming languages, Docker containers, and/or web containers. Based on the selected platform, Elastic Beanstalk will install the specific stack of software on one or more Amazon EC2 instances. At present, all Linux platforms are running over Amazon Linux 2017.03 (64-bit). At a very high level, preconfigured supported platforms are as follows:

    - Packer builder
    - Single container Docker
    - Multicontainer Docker
    - Preconfigured Docker
    - Go
    - Java SE
    - Java with Tomcat
    - .NET on Windows Server with IIS
    - Node.js
    - PHP
    - Python
    - Ruby

- **Custom platform**: It allows to create a custom platform based on one of the supported AMIs for OSes such as RHEL, Ubuntu, SUSE, and so on to create a customized platform. This customized platform is created using a Packer tool. It is an open source tool and runs on major OSes. It makes it possible to create a customized platform with a customized language or a framework which is not currently supported in Elastic Beanstalk. The primary function of Packer is to build a machine and container for multiple platforms from a single configuration.

Creating web application source bundle

Whether deploying a new web application, or updating a version for an existing web application in Elastic Beanstalk, it is essential to prepare a source bundle of source code. In general, the characteristics of source bundles for any programming language are as follows:

- It should be a single ZIP or WAR file
- In case of having multiple WAR files, it can be packed in a single ZIP file
- Overall file size should not exceed 512 MB
- It can have subdirectories but not parent directories

 To deploy a worker application in a worker tier, the application source bundle also must include the `cron.yaml` file.

Detailed understanding for preparing a source bundle can be obtained from the following URL: `https://docs.aws.amazon.com/elasticbeanstalk/latest/dg/applications-sourcebundle.html`.

Getting started using Elastic Beanstalk

With the help of the following steps, an easy Elastic Beanstalk web application can be created, viewed, deployed, updated, and terminated.

Step 1 – Signing in to the AWS account

Sign in to the AWS account with the IAM user having sufficient privileges to work with AWS Elastic Beanstalk. In addition to the privileges to manipulate resources at Elastic Beanstalk, the IAM user also requires privileges to create, modify, and delete underlying resources in various AWS services such as EC2, ELB, S3, Auto Scaling, and so on. The requirements of such AWS service privileges totally vary from application to application.

Make sure the appropriate AWS region is selected from the right-hand side top toolbar, as shown in the following *Figure 16.4*:

Figure 16.4: Select the appropriate AWS region to deploy custom web application using Elastic Beanstalk.

From the AWS dashboard, select Elastic Beanstalk from the **Compute** group, as shown in the following *Figure 16.5*:

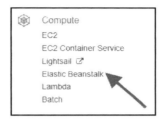

Figure 16.5: Select Elastic Beanstalk from the Compute group

Step 2 – Creating an application

Creating a web application and preparing the source code to deploy a web application varies in each of the supported programming languages such as Java, .NET, Node.js, PHP, Python, and Ruby. In this example, we have used a sample application provided by Amazon Elastic Beanstalk. It is very important to remember that AWS does not charge you for using Elastic Beanstalk service but you need to pay for the resources you use for creating an application such as EC2, RDS, and so on. The steps for creating sample application is as follows:

1. To create and deploy a sample web application on Elastic Beanstalk, follow the preconfigured URL provided by AWS: `https://console.aws.amazon.com/elasticbeanstalk/home#/newApplication?applicationName=getting-started environmentType=LoadBalanced`.

 It will require you to log in to the AWS account with valid credentials and privileges to create and manipulate Elastic Beanstalk and underlying resources.

2. The AWS Elastic Beanstalk ;**Create a web app** dialog box will appear as shown in the following *Figure 16.6*:

Figure 16.6: Create a sample web application by using the preconfigured link provided by Amazon Elastic Beanstalk

Usually, it is first required to create an application as it is a logical container for the Elastic Beanstalk components. Once application is created, create the environment tier to deploy the web application. But in this sample URL, everything will be created in one go only.

3. Choose the appropriate platform and click on **Review and Launch**.

Configure the following parameters to review and launch the preconfigured sample web application.

It is required to select an appropriate platform. In this sample web application, **Tomcat** is required to be selected as shown in the following *Figure 16.7*:

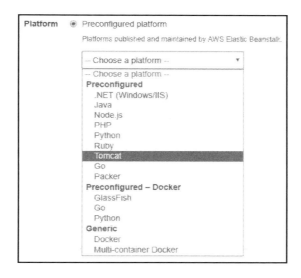

Figure 16.7: Select appropriate platform

If the platform parameter is not configured, an error message will be raised, as shown as follows:

Figure 16.8: Preconfigured platform is required to configure

The preceding sample web application may take a few minutes to complete the underlying resource creation. The default configuration to create AWS resources is as follows:

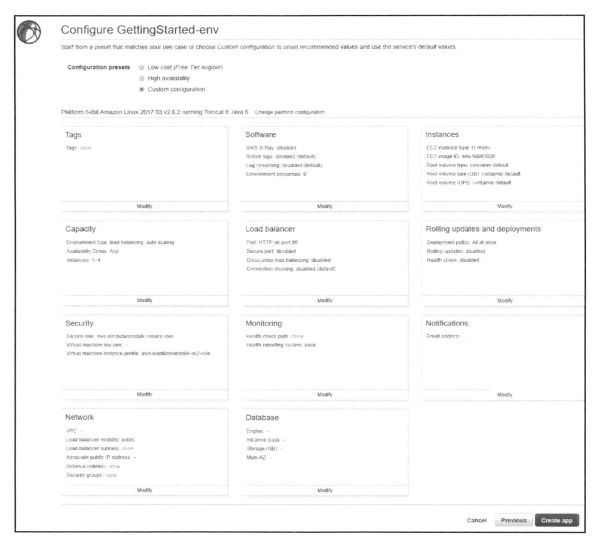

Figure 16.9: Configure and create resources for the web application

From the preceding *Figure 16.9*, major configuration, and creation options along with their parameters are shown as follows:

Configuration	Parameters
Tags	**None** (In current configuration no tags are given. Depending up on the tags used, it appears in the configuration)
Software	**AWS X-Ray**, **Rotate logs**, **Log streaming**, and **Environment properties**
Instances	**EC2 instance type**, **EC2 AMI ID**, **Root volume type**, **Root volume size (GB)**, and **Root volume IOPS**
Capacity	**Environment type**, **Availability Zones**, and **Instances**
Load balancer	**Port**, **Secure port**, **Cross-zone load balancing**, and **Connection draining**
Rolling updates and deployments	**Deployment policy**, **Rolling updates**, and **Health check**
Security	**Service role**, **Virtual machine key pair**, and **Virtual machine instance profile**
Monitoring	**Health check path**, and **Health reporting system**
Notifications	**Email address**
Network	**VPC**, **Load balancer visibility**, **Load balancer subnets**, **Associate public IP address**, **Instance subnets**, and **Security groups**
Database	**Engine**, **Instance class**, **Storage (GB)**, and **Multi-AZ**

AWS resources and configuration along with parameters

By default, Elastic Beanstalk creates an application named **getting-started** and an environment named **Custom-env** with the following AWS resources:

- EC2 instance to run the web application on a configured platform. In this sample web application, it is Tomcat.
- Security Group for an EC2 instance. By default, allows everyone to connect on HTTP port 80.
- A ELB accepts all incoming end users request to access the web application and distributes to the underlying healthy EC2 instances.
- Security group for load balancer allows traffic on HTTP port 80. By default, traffic is not allowed on other ports.
- Auto Scaling group replaces an unhealthy EC2 instance and scale-out and scale-in according to the end users request load to access the web application.
- S3 bucket to store source code, logs, and other artifacts.
- CloudWatch alarms to monitor load on the instances in the environment. It works with Auto Scaling to help in scale-in and scale-out EC2 instances.
- AWS Elastic Beanstalk uses the CloudFormation stack to create underlying resources and change the configuration.
- A domain name that routes the end user's request to the web app, in the form of subdomian.region.elasticbeanstalk.com.
- Elastic Beanstalk creates a new web application version with a name sample application. It refers to the default Elastic Beanstalk sample application file.
- Deploys the sample application code to Custom-env.

 It is possible to change the default configuration by clicking on **Modify**. For example, in case of having a compute-intensive or a memory-intensive web application, it is possible to change EC2 instance type from t1.micro to c4 or x1 instance types respectively.

As shown in the following *Figure 16.10*, Elastic Beanstalk will track the environment creation progress:

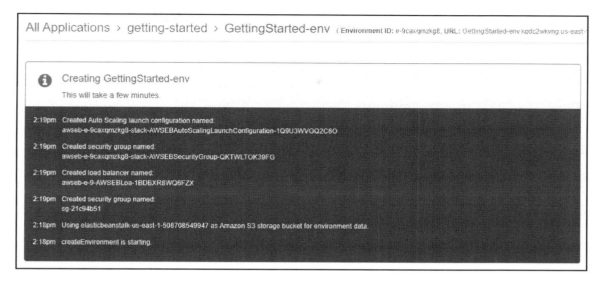

All Applications > getting-started > GettingStarted-env (Environment ID: e-9caxqrnzkg8, URL: GettingStarted-env.kqdc2wkvng.us-east-

Creating GettingStarted-env
This will take a few minutes.

2:19pm	Created Auto Scaling launch configuration named: awseb-e-9caxqrnzkg8-stack-AWSEBAutoScalingLaunchConfiguration-1Q9U3WVGQ2C6O
2:19pm	Created security group named: awseb-e-9caxqrnzkg8-stack-AWSEBSecurityGroup-QKTWLTOK39FG
2:19pm	Created load balancer named: awseb-e-9-AWSEBLoa-1BDBXR8WQ6FZX
2:19pm	Created security group named: sg-21c94b51
2:18pm	Using elasticbeanstalk-us-east-1-508708549947 as Amazon S3 storage bucket for environment data.
2:18pm	createEnvironment is starting.

Figure 16.10: Elastic Beanstalk tracks environment creation progress

Step 3 – Viewing information about the recently created environment

Once the Elastic Beanstalk application is created, it is possible to view information about the underlying resources from the environment dashboard in the Amazon Elastic Beanstalk management console. The environment dashboard shows the application health, application version, and the application's environment version. The Elastic Beanstalk environment indicates **Pending** state until the underlying AWS resources are created and related web application is deploy on the environment.

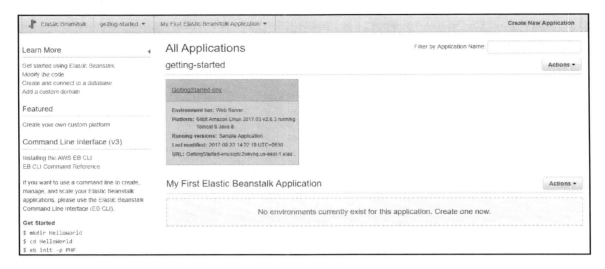

Figure 16.11: Amazon Elastic Beanstalk dashboard

The preceding *Figure 16.11* shows the basic AWS Elastic Beanstalk dashboard. Only one sample `getting-started` application and `GettingStarted-env` exist. By clicking on the `GettingStarted-env`, it is possible to see the **Configuration, Logs, Health, Monitoring, Alarms, Managed Updates, Events**, and **Tags** as shown in the following *Figure 16.12*:

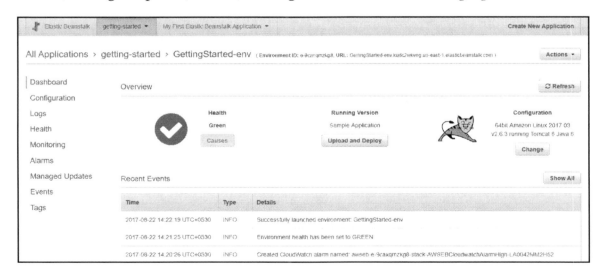

Figure 16.12: Elastic Beanstalk application specific dashboard

Step 4 – Deploying a new application version

Over time, business needs change and a new version of a web application is developed. Elastic Beanstalk allows you to upload the new version of application over an existing application. Elastic Beanstalk creates a new application version upon deploying a newer source bundle for an existing web application. As long as no update operations are in progress, you can deploy new version of your application over an existing application. Let's see the steps to update a newer version for an existing web application:

1. Download the web application's updated source bundle from the URL: `https://docs.aws.amazon.com/elasticbeanstalk/latest/dg/samples/java-tomcat-v3.zip`.

> In the case of a custom-developed web application, it is required to create a source bundle with the updated source code.

2. Go to the Elastic Beanstalk dashboard.
3. Select the application `getting-started` and `GettingStarted-env` environment.
4. Select **Upload and Deploy** from the **Overview** section, as shown in the following *Figure 16.13*:

Figure 16.13: Application Overview

5. We can now upload the new code as shown in the following *Figure 16.14*:

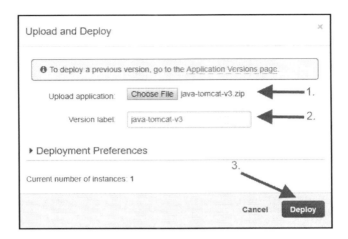

Figure 16.14: Upload and Deploy application

6. Click on **Choose File** to upload our source bundle.
7. By default, the version label will be the filename of the uploaded file. In this example, the filename is `java-tomcat-3`. It can be changed to a meaningful and relevant name.
8. Finally, click on **Deploy** to deploy a new web application.

While Elastic Beanstalk is deploying a new version of a web application, it is possible to see a status of deployment on the web console. Once the deployment is completed, **Running Version** will be changed from sample application to `java-tomcat-v3` under environment's **Overview** as shown in the following *Figure 16.15*:

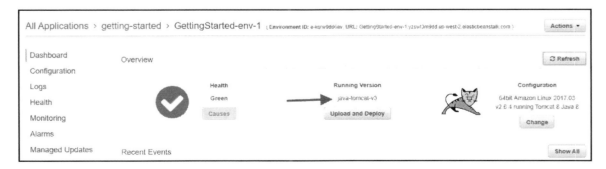

Figure 16.15: Application overview

Step 5 – Changing the configuration

Amazon Elastic Beanstalk allows us to customize the web application environment at runtime for better performance. Some of the configuration changes can be simple and can take place quickly while others may require us to delete and recreate the AWS resources, which can take several minutes. In the event of replacing any underlying resources, it may cause web application downtime. Elastic Beanstalk will warn you about the same before finally reflecting the configuration changes. For example, in the following steps, we are modifying the minimum number of EC2 instances from one to two in the Auto Scaling group. Also, we will verify that the same changes have reflected in the existing environment. The steps for changing configuration are discussed as follows:

1. Go to the Amazon Elastic Beanstalk console.
2. Click on the `getting-started` web application and then `GettingStarted-env`.
3. Go to the **Configuration** tab.
4. Select **Scaling**, by clicking the setting icon on the top right-hand side corner as shown in following *Figure 16.16*:

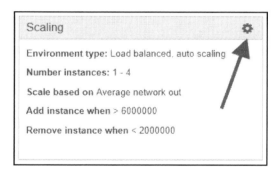

Figure 16.16: Modify Scaling configuration

5. Under the **Auto Scaling** section, modify the **Minimum instance count** from 1 to 2 as shown in the following *Figure 16.17*:

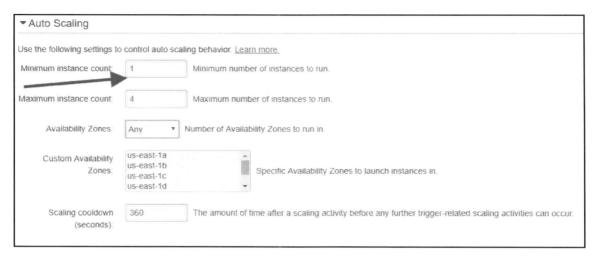

6. At the bottom of the configuration page, click on the **Apply** command button.

 Once the configuration has been changed and applied, it may take several minutes to get reflected in the application stack. The time taken to reflect changes depends on the configuration modification type.

Verifying the changes on the load balancer:

7. In the left-hand side pane select **Events**. After some time, there will be an update regarding recent configuration changes in the Auto Scaling group. The update should be Successfully deployed new configuration to environment.
8. Go to the EC2 console.
9. Select **Load Balancers** under **LOAD BALANCING** on the left-hand side pane.
10. Identify the load balancer, part of the web application deployed at Elastic Beanstalk.

11. In the lower pane, under the **Instances** tab, we can clearly see that two EC2 instances are part of the same ELB as shown in the following *Figure 16.18*:

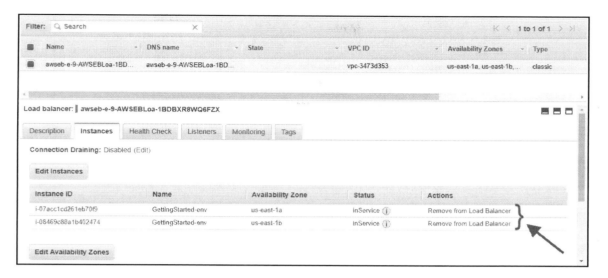

Figure 16.18: Elastic Load Balancer, under EC2 console shows modified minimum number of instances

Step 6 – Cleaning up

It is essential to delete all unwanted versions, environment and application from Amazon Elastic Beanstalk, to prevent incurring unwanted charges to the AWS account.

Version lifecycle

Elastic Beanstalk creates a newer application version upon uploading a newer source code bundle. Creating a newer version and not deleting the old unwanted application version leads to hitting the application version limit. As a result, it does not allow us to create any newer web application version.

The default Elastic Beanstalk limits are as follows:

Resource	Default limit
Applications	75
Application versions	1,000
Environments	200

With the help of the application version lifecycle policy for an application, hitting an application version limit can be avoided. Consistently, it will manage the number of available application versions at any given time. Once the lifecycle policy is enabled, it will keep either the total count of recent versions (that is, the last 200 versions of the application) or the versions which are not older than the specified age in the terms of days (that is, 180 days). Application lifecycle can be configured using the web console, CLI, or API.

Deploying web applications to Elastic Beanstalk environments

Elastic Beanstalk allows you to create a new web application using the web application tier or worker tier, updating an environment with a newer web application version, or redeploying an earlier uploaded web application version:

- Deploying a new web application is very quick. It creates an underlying required AWS resources and deploys a web application.
- While updating a newer version of a web applications perform the in-place updates. This means that the already deployed web application will be updated with a newer source bundle and may result in restarting the web container or the web application server. As a result, the web application may be unavailable for a while.
- When an environment has more than one EC2 instance, in such a situation, a newer version of a web application can be deployed in a rolling manner. It helps to avoid total unavailability of a web application. It will deploy a newer version of a web application in instance batches.
- With the help of immutable updates, it is possible to always deploy a newer version of a web application to new instances rather than updating an existing instance. In this scenario, Elastic Beanstalk will create a new Auto Scaling group, the newly created Auto Scaling group will serve traffic along to the earlier created instances, till the newly created instances pass the health checks.

- In a normal scenario, deployment of a newer version of a web application, Elastic Beanstalk performs an in-place update. As a result, the web application is totally unavailable till the deployment of a newer version completes. Blue/green deployment is a solution to avoid such unavailability. In this development method, a new infrastructure is created and on successful deployment of a newer version on a newer infrastructure, it just changes the CNAMEs of the old environment to the new environment to redirect traffic to the new version instantly.

Details of the various deployment methods can be obtained from the following table:

Deployment policy	Impact of failed deployment	Deploy time	Zero downtime	NO DNS change	Rollback process	Code deployed to
All at once	Leads to web application downtime	Least	X	✓	Re-deploy	Existing instances
Rolling	Deploys new web application version in an instance batch	Moderate	✓	✓	Re-deploy	Existing instances
Rolling with an additional batch	Offers minimal impact in case of failure of the first batch or else it is similar to the rolling deployment	Moderate to higher	✓	✓	Re-deploy	New and existing instances
Immutable	Minimal	High	✓	✓	Re-deploy	New instances
Blue/green	Minimal	High	<p>✓	X	Swap URL	New instances

 Actual deployment time for rolling and rolling with an additional batch depends on the batch size.

Monitoring the web application environment

Once a web application is successfully deployed, it is very important to monitor the performance. It helps to find if any infrastructure bottlenecks create a performance issue or underutilized resources to save monthly billing. Elastic Beanstalk web console gives a high-level overview in terms of figures and graphs as shown in the following *Figure 16.19*:

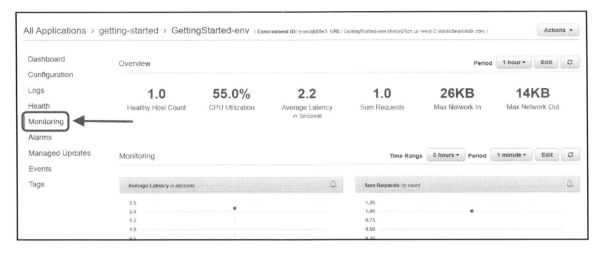

Figure 16.19: Monitoring Dashboard

- Elastic Beanstalk also offers various other methods to monitor a deployed web application, such as basic health reporting, enhanced health reporting and monitoring, managing alarms, the Elastic Beanstalk environment's event stream, listing and connecting to server instances, and viewing logs from the Elastic Beanstalk environments EC2 instances. Detailed understanding of various monitoring methods can be obtained from the following URL: https://docs. aws.amazon.com/elasticbeanstalk/latest/dg/environments-health.html.

Elastic Beanstalk best practices

Web application deployment on Elastic Beanstalk ultimately uses AWS services such as EC2, ELB, ASG, SQS, S3, and many others. Points such as scalability, security, persistent storage, fault tolerance, content delivery, software updates and patching, and connectivity should be kept in mind when designing applications to deploy on AWS Elastic Beanstalk:

- Web applications should be as stateless as possible, fault tolerant, and loosely coupled to efficiently scale out and scale in as the end users request increases and reductions respectively.
- On AWS, security is a shared responsibility. AWS is responsible for providing as and when required physical resources to make the cloud a safe place to deploy our application and we as cloud users are responsible for the security of the data coming in and out of the Elastic Beanstalk environment and the security of the application.
- Configure the SSL certificate to encrypt sensitive information transmission over a public network such as the internet.
- Elastic Beanstalk deploys an application on an Amazon EC2 instance that does not have persistent storage. Applications should be designed to store data in a persistent data source such as Amazon S3, EBS, Amazon DynamoDB, and Amazon RDS.
- It is highly recommended to design an application capable of auto recovering from failure. Deploy an application and database across multi-AZs. For a mission-critical application and database for the enterprise, also design the DR site.
- End users may be accessing web applications from across the globe and various networks. They may experience poor performance due to higher latency; Amazon CloudFront can be used to avoid such poor user experience.
- Periodically, Elastic Beanstalk updates its underlined platform configuration with the latest software and patches. AWS recommends to upgrade your application environments to latest software and patches. These environment updates can be applied on all server at once or you can apply it in smaller batches such that your entire application environment does not go down.

17
Overview of AWS Lambda

In AWS, compute resources such as AWS EC2 is used to host small to large enterprise applications. Infrastructure configuration complexity in enterprise applications may vary from application to application in different organisations. Handling day-to-day operational activities on such compute resources may be time consuming and requires additional resources for managing the tasks. Even if an organisation automates such tasks, any periodical manual intervention in the activity may also create hindrance for management and maintenance of such resources. To address such organizational issue, Amazon provides a hosted compute service called Amazon Lambda. The sole purpose of Lambda service is to abstract server management and simplify building on-demand applications. Lambda provides an abstract layer for hosting application function and manages underlined servers in the background. A piece of code can be uploaded in an AWS Lambda. It is called Lambda function. Lambda function gets executed against an event on AWS resource. Such events can be *a new object uploaded into an S3 bucket* or *new data added in a DynamoDB table* and many such similar events. AWS Lambda supports a wide range of events for a variety of AWS services.

Let us understand AWS Lambda with with more details. This chapter talks about following topics:

- Introduction to AWS Lambda
- What is Lambda function?
- Lambda function invocation type
- Writing a Lambda function

Introduction to AWS Lambda

AWS Lambda is a serverless and event-driven compute service. It allows you to upload a piece of source code to execute against a valid event. The uploaded piece of code is called a Lambda function. At the time of writing this chapter, AWS Lambda supports Java, Node.js, C#, and Python programming languages. In case of EC2 instances, you are charged for each running seconds. It is important to note here that till mid 2017 AWS used to charge on hourly basis for EC2 instances. In the case of AWS Lambda, charges apply for code running time in increments of 100 milliseconds. Charges are not applicable for uploading code. AWS does not charge you for just creating and keeping a Lambda function. You are charged for the duration it takes a Lambda function to run.

You can create Lambda functions that runs on events such as any new object placed in an S3 bucket, a new record inserted into a DynamoDB table or you can directly invoke a Lambda function using an API call. It can also execute a code at a scheduled time just like a cron job on a Linux server. Lambda functions run on a highly available compute resources, having balanced CPU, memory, network, and other resources. Lambda automatically scales from a few requests per day to thousands per second based on the actual load to the Lambda services in real time. AWS Lambda sets IT professionals free from creating an EC2 instance, server maintenance, patching, code monitoring, Auto Scaling, and so on. It eliminates the need of managing servers for operations team in an organization.

 Lambda does not provide a complete control over a base OS like EC2 instances provide. It is not possible to log in to a Lambda instance to customise the OS level parameters. On the other hand, AWS Lambda supports securely running native Linux executables by calling out from a supported runtime.

What is a Lambda function?

AWS Lambda functions includes source code along with all dependencies. Each Lambda function has its own configuration informations, such as runtime, environment variables, handler, IAM role, tag(s), memory, timeout, VPC, and many other details that are defined at the time of creating.

The amount of memory that can be allocated to a Lambda function ranges between 128 and 1536 MB. The minimum memory that can be allotted to a Lambda function is 128 MB. Based on the requirement, you can allot more memory in increments of 64 MB. Depending up on the allocated memory, AWS automatically allots proportional CPU power and other resources for executing the specific Lambda function. In the background, AWS uses general purpose M3 instance type for Lambda service, which is opaque to the end users.

Lambda function can be configured to execute in between 1 to 300 seconds. Lambda function execution time is called timeout. If the Lambda function is running after the defined timeout, it is automatically terminated. The default configured timeout for a Lambda function is 3 seconds

Source code can be written using code authoring tools and editors. When creating a Lambda function using a web console, it automatically prepares a deployment package before uploading the source code. The steps to create a deployment package varies from one supported programming languages to another. At the time of creating a Lambda function, you can configure the amount of memory for executing the function. AWS automatically allocates proportional CPU power and other resources for executing the specific Lambda function. For example, a Lambda function with 256 MB memory may be allocated twice as much CPU as a Lambda function with 128 MB allocated memory.

Lambda is widely used by many organisations for deploying small to large scale applications. These applications range from small event driven applications to large big data architecture for implementing stateless infrastructure.

While creating a Lambda function along with memory, here are few more parameters that need to be defined:

- **Maximum execution time (timeout)**: The maximum it can be 5 minutes. It helps to prevent the Lambda function from running indefinitely. When timeout has been reached, the Lambda function execution terminates.
- **IAM role (execution role)**: Lambda can assume an IAM role at the time of execution. Based on the privileges granted to the IAM role, the Lambda function can inherit the privileges for executing the function.
- **Handler name**: It refers to the method name to be used by AWS Lambda to start the execution. AWS Lambda passes an event information that triggers the invocation as a parameter to the handler method.

For testing purposes, Lambda functions can be invoked on-demand from the AWS Lambda console or by using the CLI.

To troubleshoot AWS Lambda function, AWS Lambda automatically monitors functions through CloudWatch metrics. This provides several metrics such as **Invocation count**, **Invocation duration**, **Invocation errors**, **Throttled invocations**, **Iterator age**, and **DLQ errors**. To manually validate the behavior of a code, it is possible to insert logging statements in a code. Automatically, Lambda will push all logs from the code to CloudWatch Log groups.

Lambda function invocation types

AWS Lambda supports two invocation methods: synchronous and asynchronous. The invocation type can be only specified at the time of manually executing a Lambda function. This Lambda function execution is called on-demand invocation. Examples are calling a Lambda function from a custom application or manually executing it using a CLI/GUI.

On-demand invocation is done by the *invoke operation*. It allows you to specify the invocation type, synchronous or asynchronous. When a Lambda function is triggered using an AWS service as an event source, the invocation type is predetermined for each of the AWS services and it cannot be changed. For example, Amazon S3 always invokes a Lambda function asynchronously and Amazon Cognito always invokes a Lambda function synchronously.

A synchronous method blocks a thread's execution until the client receives a response from the Lambda function. An asynchronous method returns control immediately, giving control back to the calling thread without waiting for a response from a Lambda function.

Writing a Lambda function

At present, while writing this book, AWS Lambda supports Node.js, Java, Python, and C#. Irrespective of the programming language used to write the AWS Lambda function there is a common pattern to write a code for a Lambda function. It includes the following core concepts:

- Handler
- The context object

- Logging
- Exceptions

A handler needs to be specified at the time of defining a Lambda function. It points to a function in a source code. On an occurrence of a configured event to execute, the Lambda function starts executing the code by calling the handler function defined in the code. At the same time, AWS Lambda passes event data to the handler function as a first parameter. It is recommended to write a handler function which is capable of processing the incoming parameters. Based on the supplied parameters, the function may invoke any other subsequent function or method.

The context object, logging, and exceptions are explained in subsequent pages.

 It is possible to write direct Lambda function logic in a handler function. It is a best practice to write separate functions to incorporate a core logic from a handler.

Lambda function handler (Node.js)

The general syntax of handler function is as follows:

```
exports.myHandler = function(event, context,) {
...
}
```

The `callback` parameter is optional, based on whether it is required to return information to the caller:

```
exports.myHandler = function(event, context, callback) {
...

// Use callback() and return information to the caller.
}
```

Here is a list of components that are part of the syntax:

- `event`: This parameter is used by AWS Lambda to pass event data to the handler function.
- `context`: This parameter is used by AWS Lambda to provide runtime information from an executing Lambda function to the handler function, such as the remaining execution time before AWS Lambda terminates.

- callback: Optionally, callback is used to return information from the executing Lambda function to the caller. Otherwise, by default it returns null value.

 Node.js v0.10.42 supports context methods (done, succeed, and fail) to gracefully complete Lambda function execution. Node.js v6.10 and v4.3 supports callback.

- myHandler: This is a function name and acts as an entry point to invoking the Lambda function.

Lambda function handler (Java)

The general syntax of handler function is as follows:

```
outputType handler-name(inputType input, Context context) {
    ...
}
```

Here is a list of components that are part of the syntax:

- inputType: This can be an event data or custom input that is provided as a string or any custom data object. To successfully invoke this handler, the Lambda function must be invoked with the input data that can be serialized into the defined data type of the input parameter.
- outputType: When the Lambda function is invoked synchronously using the RequestResponse invocation type, it is possible to return the output of the Lambda function using the valid and supported data type.

If you invoke the Lambda function asynchronously with the help of Event invocation type, the outputType should be void. For example, event source Kinesis, Amazon S3, and Amazon SNS invoke a Lambda function in an asynchronous using the Event.

inputType and outputType can be one of the following:

- **Predefined AWS event types**: They are defined in the aws-lambda-java-events library.
- **Plain Old Java Object (POJO) class**: It allows to create own POJO class. Lambda function automatically serializes, deserializes input, and output on the POJO type or JSON.

- **Primitive Java types**: It supports primitive Java types such as `String` or `int`.

If handler function is overloaded (that is, multiple methods with the same name), based on the following rules, handler method selection will take place:

- Method with the largest number of parameters
- When two or more methods in a Lambda function have the same number of arguments, the method that has `Context` as the last parameter gets selected

 If the overloaded handler methods do not have a `Context` parameter, the behavior is unpredictable.

Lambda function handler (Python)

The following syntax can be used to write a handler function in Python:

```
def handler_name(event, context):
...
return some_value
```

Here is a list of components that are part of the syntax:

- `event`: AWS Lambda passes event data to the handler by this parameter. It is usually of the Python `dict` type.
- `context`: AWS Lambda passes runtime information of the executing Lambda function. It is of the `LambdaContext` type.

Optionally, the handler can return values based on the invocation type to invoke the Lambda function.

- In a synchronous execution using the `RequestResponse` invocation type, Lambda function returns the result of a Python function call
- In an asynchronous execution using `Event` invocation type, the return value is discarded

Lambda function handler (C#)

You can write a Lambda Function handler in C# as a static method in a class or as an instance. You can access a Lambda context object with the definition of `ILambdaContext` type as given in the following syntax:

```
returnType handler-name(inputType input, ILambdaContext context) {
    ...
}
```

Here is a list of components that are part of the syntax:

- `inputType` - This can be event data or a custom input, provided by an event source or string respectively
- `outputType` - When a Lambda function is invoked synchronously using `RequestResponse`, it is possible to return the output of Lambda function using any of the valid and supported data type

When invoking the Lambda function asynchronously with the help of `Event` invocation type, `outputType` should be void. For example, event sources such as Kinesis, Amazon S3, and Amazon SNS invokes Lambda function asynchronously using `Event`.

Since now we understand what is a handler function, let us have a brief understanding of other core concepts in AWS Lambda, which includes the context object, logging, and exceptions.

- **The context object and how it interacts with Lambda at runtime**: As a second parameter, AWS Lambda passes a `context` object to the handler function. It can help the source code to interact with AWS Lambda runtime. It can help to find remaining execution time before AWS Lambda terminates. In addition, asynchronous programming languages such as Node.js use callbacks. It supports additional methods on this `context` object method to tell AWS Lambda to terminate the function and optionally return values to the caller.
- **Logging**: AWS Lambda functions can have logging statement depending on the programming language used to write a source code. These logs are written to the CloudWatch Logs.
- **Exception**: AWS Lambda functions needs to return the invocation state in terms of success or failure. Exceptions may be raised at the Lambda function initialization or function invocation. If there is an exception at function invocation, each supported programming language has different ways to return the success or the fail of Lambda function execution. With synchronous execution, AWS Lambda forwards the result back to the client.

Deploying a Lambda function

A Lambda function can be created using the inline editor provided in the Lambda function dashboard or you can create a function in your location machine and deploy it on Lambda. When you create a Lambda function in your local machine, you need to create a package that can be uploaded to Lambda for deployment. AWS Lambda function configuration requires a source code in a .zip or .jar file consisting of a source code along with dependencies. Creating a deployment package varies for each supported programming language. For example, in Node JS, you simply zip up the content of the directory along with all the dependencies in a zip file and upload it to Lambda for deployment.

As shown in following *Figure 17.1*, you just need to zip up all the files in MyFunctionFolder that includes index.js and node_modules folder. Remember, you should not zip up the MyFunctionFolder itself. The zip should contain only the index.js and all the dependencies but not it's parent folder:

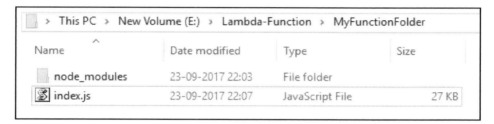

Figure 17.1: Deployment package

It is essential to create a deployment package to create a Lambda function. A deployment package can be created in two ways:

- It is possible to prepare a deployment package manually
- Write code directly in a Lambda console and the console will create a deployment package for you

Once the source code is converted into a deployment package, it can either be directly uploaded to Lambda from the local machine or first to an Amazon S3 bucket. The S3 bucket should be in the same region where the Lambda function is being created. Specify the same S3 link URL while creating a Lambda function.

AWS Lambda function versioning and aliases

Lambda function versioning makes it possible to publish one or more versions of a function code. It makes it possible to use a different function version in a different environment, such as development, testing, pre-production, or production. Each lambda function has a unique and immutable ARN.

It is possible to create an alias for each Lambda function version. Each alias is a pointer to specific the Lambda function version. Just like Lambda functions, an alias is a resource and has a unique ARN for a function version to which it points. Alias are mutable. They can be modified to point to a different Lambda function version.

 An alias can only point to the function version. It cannot point to another alias.

Aliases primarily help to abstract the process of promoting the Lambda function version from one environment to another. To simplify this, for example, the Amazon S3 bucket is an event source; when some new objects are created in a bucket, the Lambda function gets invoked. For triggering an event on S3 bucket, you need to configure the Lambda function ARN in the bucket notification configuration. The configured Lambda function is invoked on a new object event on the bucket. Normally, every time a new version of a Lambda function is created, a function with new ARN is generated. New ARN for the function forces you to modify the bucket configuration where the event is configured. To avoid such repeated S3 bucket configuration modification, it is recommended to use Lambda function alias. Lambda function alias can point to an ARN of any Lambda function. ARN of Lambda function alias remains intact as you don't need to change it. You can configure this alias ARN in S3 bucket for triggering the event. Every time you create a new version of a Lambda function, you just need to update your alias pointing to the ARN of newly created Lambda function. As a new version of a Lambda function is promoted from one environment to another, we just need to change the alias pointing to the latest stable Lambda function version and don't need to update the notification configuration in Amazon S3 bucket.

If you need to roll back a modification from newer Lambda function version to an older one, it can be done easily by changing where an alias is pointing. This avoids the need to update the event source mappings in the S3 bucket.

Environment variables

Reusable and efficient code often requires passing dynamic values at runtime. Such runtime values may be environment type, file paths, path to store logs, table name, and so on. With the help of environment variables, Lambda functions allow us to pass dynamic values at runtime. As a result, the code becomes reusable without making any changes to the code. Environment variables are key-value pairs and these key-values pair are encrypted/decrypted using the AWS KMS. Key-value pairs can be defined at the time of creating a Lambda function. Externally configured environment variables are also accessible within the Lambda function using standard APIs supported by the different programming languages. For example, Node.js functions can access environment variables using `process.env`. The `process.env` refers to an object in Node.js. In Node.js, process is the global object and `env` is the sub-object of process which provides all environment variables.

The rules for naming environment variables are as follows:

- Lambda functions can have any number of environment variables, but the total size should not exceed 4 KB
- First character must be a [a-zA-Z]
- Consecutive valid characters are [a-zA-Z0-9_]

Specific environment variables such as `MemorySize` and `Timeout` are saved as a snapshot for each Lambda function version. These settings are immutable.

Tagging Lambda functions

Tagging is useful when you have many resources of the same type, which in the case of AWS Lambda, is a function. By using tags, customers with hundreds of Lambda functions can easily access and analyze a specific set by filtering on those that contain the same tag. Tags are key-value pairs. They are associated with a Lambda function to organize them as well as to find other details such as frequency of invocation and the cost of each function invocation. Primarily, tags help to group, filter, and allocate cost.

Lambda function over VPC

Deploying AWS resources inside an Amazon VPC makes sure that they cannot be accessed over the public internet. By default, Lambda function code is invoked within a VPC. To enable Lambda function to access other AWS resources deployed in a private VPC, it is essential to provide details such as VPC, subnets, and security groups at the time of configuring it. VPC details are used by the Lambda function to create ENIs to connect securely with other private VPCs.

 AWS Lambda does not support connecting to resources within dedicated tenancy VPCs.

When a Lambda function requires internet access, rather than deploying in a public subnet, deploy it in a VPC in a private subnet with a NAT gateway or NAT instance in a public subnet.

Building applications with AWS Lambda

In a serverless architecture, the main components are the event source and the Lambda function. The event source could be custom applications or AWS services. Each of the AWS services event source uses a specific format for event data. At present, AWS Lambda supports the following AWS services as event sources:

- Amazon S3
- Amazon DynamoDB
- Amazon Kinesis Streams
- Amazon SNS
- Amazon Simple Email Service
- Amazon Cognito
- AWS CloudFormation
- Amazon CloudWatch Logs
- Amazon CloudWatch Events
- AWS CodeCommit

- Scheduled Events (powered by Amazon CloudWatch Events)
- AWS Config
- Amazon Alexa
- Amazon Lex
- Amazon API Gateway
- Other event sources: invoking a Lambda function on demand
- Sample events published by event sources

These supported AWS services are broadly divided into two categories:

- Stream-based services
- Regular AWS services

 Out of all the supported AWS services, Amazon Kinesis Streams and Amazon DynamoDB streams are the only stream-based AWS services. The rest of the services are regular AWS services.

Apart from the preceding mentioned supported AWS services, a custom user application can also create an event to trigger the Lambda functions invocation.

Event source mapping for AWS services

Regular AWS services publish events to invoke a Lambda function. It is also called a push model. A push mode has following behavioural characteristics:

- Regular AWS service resources maintain event source mappings with event source. AWS provides APIs to manage event source mappings. For example, S3 bucket notification configuration API enables us to configure an event source mapping on a bucket. This configuration mapping identifies the bucket event which is published to a Lambda function that is configured on the bucket.
- As the event source invokes the Lambda function, it is essential to grant the necessary privileges to the resource, using a resource-based policy. This resource-based policy is referred to as a *Lambda function policy.*

The following *Figure 17.2* explains how Amazon S3 pushes an event to invoke a Lambda function:

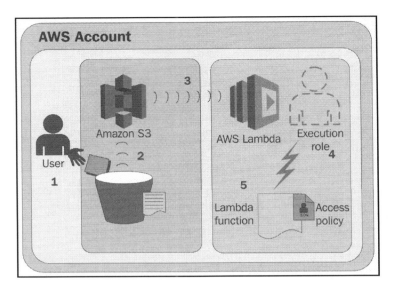

Figure 17.2: How Lambda Function is invoked

Reference URL: https://docs.aws.amazon.com/lambda/latest/dg/images/push-s3-example-10.png

In the preceding figure, S3 pushes an event for each new object created in a bucket to execute a Lambda function:

1. As you can see in the preceding figure, a privileged user creates a new object in an S3 bucket.
2. As soon as the object is created in the bucket, S3 detects the object creation event.
3. The Lambda function which is configured on the bucket is invoked according as per the event source mapping defined in the bucket notification configuration.
4. In the subsequent step, an attempt is made by the event source for invoking the configured Lambda function. Immediately after the invocation call, the Lambda function refers to the attached policy to ensure that the Amazon S3 has the necessary permissions.
5. After successful verification of the attached permission policy on Lambda function, finally the Lambda function is executed.

Event source mapping for AWS stream-based service

The following *Figure 17.3* explains the way a custom application writes a record to a Kinesis stream and the way Lambda polls the stream:

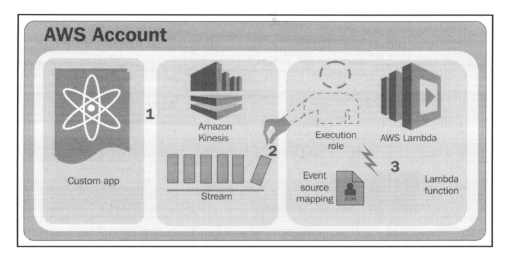

Figure 17.3: Event source mapping for AWS stream-based service

Reference URL: https://docs.aws.amazon.com/lambda/latest/dg/images/kinesis-pull-10.png

The steps for the preceding figure are as follows:

1. Initially, the custom application writes records to an Amazon Kinesis stream.
2. At the same time, AWS Lambda continuously keeps polling the stream. As soon as, it detects a new record on the stream, it invokes the AWS Lambda function. Based on the event configuration, it decides which Lambda function is to execute against which event source.
3. It also verifies that the attached IAM permission policy to the Lambda function allows it to poll the stream. If it is not true, then the AWS Lambda function is not invoked.

Event source mapping for custom applications

A custom deployed application in an AWS account can also directly invoke the Lambda function. The following *Figure 17.4* explains this. Create a Lambda function in one of the IAM user accounts and the same credentials will be used to invoke the Lambda function. You do not require additional permissions to invoke the function:

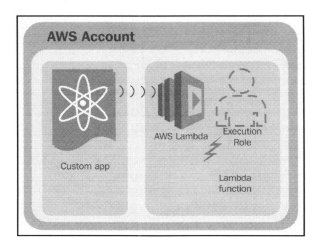

Figure 17.4: Custom application publishes events and invokes a Lambda function

Reference URL: https://docs.aws.amazon.com/lambda/latest/dg/images/push-user-app-example-10.png

It is also possible to deploy a custom application in AWS account A, and invoke the Lambda function from AWS account B. AWS account B (that is, where the Lambda function is) must have cross-account permissions in the policy associated with the Lambda function. The following *Figure 17.4* explains this:

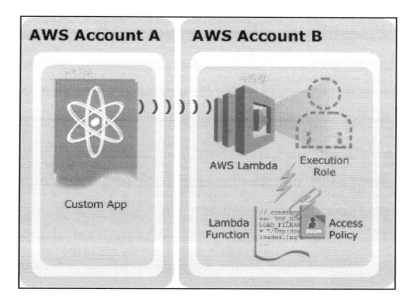

Figure 17.5: Lambda function execution in cross account

Reference URL: http://docs.aws.amazon.com/lambda/latest/dg/images/push-user-cross-account-app-example-10.png

AWS Lambda best practices

The AWS Lambda best practices are as follows:

- It is best practice to write a AWS Lambda function in a stateless style. It should not have any affinity with the underlying compute infrastructure.
- Persistent state should be stored in another cloud service, such as Amazon S3 or DynamoDB.
- It is a recommended to separate core logic from the Lambda handler as the handler is generally used as an entry point to the function.
- When a Lambda function is deployed over a VPC, it is a best practice to avoid DNS resolution for a public hostname, as it may take several seconds to resolve and it adds several billable seconds.
- It is recommended to specify at least one subnet in each AZ with the Lambda function configuration.

- It is recommended to make sure sufficient subnet IPs are free to allow Lambda functions to scale. If there aren't any free subnet IPs, Lambda functions will not scale and Lambda function failure will increase.
- Rather than re-initializating variables or objects on every invocation, use static initialization or constructor, global, or static variables and singletons. It helps to improve the performance of the Lambda function.
- Where possible, keep alive and reuse connections such as database or HTTP that were established in an earlier invocation.
- To cope with frequent changes in the operational parameters, pass them using environment variables to avoid frequent changes in a Lambda function.
- It is a best practice to pack all the dependencies in a deployment of a Lambda function. Where possible, control the dependencies in the Lambda function to minimize the overall size and execution time.
- If you are using a Java programming language, put dependencies in a separate /lib directory rather than putting all functions, source code in a single jar with a large number of .class files.
- It is highly recommended to use a simple framework and minimize the complexity of the dependencies to quickly load the container startup.
- It is a best practice to use Lambda metrics and CloudWatch alarms to monitor Lambda functions health rather than creating and maintaining custom metrics from Lambda function code.

18
Mock Tests

Mock test 1

Question 1: Monthly billing for Lambda is based on what?

- A: Number of uploaded functions in the AWS account per region
- B: Number of uploaded functions in the AWS account per region plus the execution time in minutes
- C: Execution request and the time is rounded to the nearest 100 ms
- D: Execution request and time is rounded to the nearest 1 second

Ans. C

Question 2: Which is a compulsory section in the CloudFormation template?

- A: Outputs and Resources
- B: Resources
- C: Parameters and Outputs
- D: None of the above

Ans. B

Question 3: If an EC2 instance with instance store volume is stopped or terminated, any data on the instance store volume is lost:

- A: True
- B: False

Ans. A

Question 4: Which of the following statements is true about AWS regions and AZs?

- A: Every region is independent, consists of at least two or more AZs and AZs within regions are interconnected through low-latency dedicated network
- B: Each region is independent and has only one AZ
- C: You can create as many AZs as required from AWS console
- D: Regions and AZs are only required when hosting legacy applications on the cloud

Ans. A

Question 5: Is it possible to stop an RDS instance?

- A: Yes, it is possible to stop for maximum 7 days when it is in single AZ
- B: Yes, it is possible to stop for any time duration when it is in single AZ
- C: Yes, it is possible to stop for maximum 7 days when it is in multi-AZ
- D: Yes, it is possible to stop for any time duration when it is in multi-AZ

Ans. A

Question 6: Which of the following statements are true? (Select 2)

- A: A group can contain many users, and a user can belong to multiple groups
- B: Groups can't be nested; they can contain only users, not other groups
- C: Both, users and groups can be nested
- D: Groups can be nested but users cannot be nested

Ans: A and B

Question 7: What is the maximum size of an item in DynamoDB table?

- A: 400 Bytes
- B: 400 KB
- C: 400 MB
- D: 400 GB

Ans: B

Question 8: Which of the following statements is true?

- A: NACL applies at the EC2 level and security groups apply at the network level
- B: Security groups apply at the EC2 level and NACL at the network level
- C: It can be implemented interchangeably depending on the project's requirements
- D: None of the above

Ans. B

Question: 9: Which of the following AWS service supports infrastructure as a code?

- A: CloudFront
- B: CloudFormation
- C: CodeCommit
- D: None of the above

Ans. B

Question 10: When RDS instance is configured in multi-AZ, what happens when primary instance fails?

- A: Automatically, standby replica database becomes primary database
- B: You need to manually failover control from primary database to secondary database in different AZ
- C: Automatically CNAME pointing to the primary DB instance changes to standby DB instance
- D: All of the above

Ans. C

Question 11: An organization Example Inc, runs their website on Amazon S3 named `https://www.example.com`. They have kept their corporate images in a seperate S3 bucket which is accessed on endpoint: `https://s3-us-east1.amazonaws.com/examplecorpimages`. While testing the website, the Example Inc found that the images are blocked by the browser. In this scenario, what should the company do to resolve the issue such that the images are not blocked by the browser?

- A: Make the bucket `examplecorpimages` as public where the images are stored
- B: Enable versioning on the bucket `examplecorpimages`

- C: Create CORS configuration on `examplecorpimages` bucket for allowing cross-origin requests
- D: You can't do anything as S3 does not allow to host images in different bucket

Ans: C

Question 12: Which encryption method is supported by AWS EC2 and S3 by default?

- A: 256-bit Advanced Encryption Standard (AES-256)
- B: RSA
- C: 128-bit AES
- D: DES

Ans. A

Question 13: What is the purpose of `cfn-init` helper script in CloudFormation?

- A: Install and configure application and packages on EC2
- B: Sends a signal to CloudFormation when EC2 instance is successfully created
- C: Detects changes in resource metadata and runs user specified action when change is detected
- D: All of the above

Ans. A

Question 14: A Load balancer can span across:

- A: Multiple AZs
- B: Multiple regions
- C: Multiple AZs and optionally multiple regions
- D: Depends on the region

Ans. A

Question 15: AWS IAM is:

- A: Region-independent and free to use
- B: Region-dependent and free to use
- C: Region-dependent and the charges vary from region-to-region
- D: None of the above

Ans. A

Question 16: Which of the follwing CloudFormation template section matches a key to a corresponding value?

- A: Transform
- B: Mappings
- C: Metadata
- D: Conditions

Ans: B

Question 17: Which of the following statement is true?

- A: VPC can span across multiple regions
- B: VPC can span across multiple-AZs
- C: VPC can span across multiple-AZs and multiple regions
- D: VPC spans across AZs and optionally across regions

Ans. B

Question 18: What happens when the password policy is changed or newly implemented?

- A: It is implemented immediately, but is effected the next time an IAM user attempts to change the password
- B: It forces all the AWS IAM users to change the password immediately whose password do not comply with the new password policy
- C: Optionally it can be configured to apply only to a few IAM users
- D: None of the above

Ans. A

Question 19: Billing alerts are triggered by which AWS service?

- A: AWS Billing dashboard
- B: CloudWatch
- C: SES/SNS/SQS
- D: All of the above

Ans. B

Question 20: What is true about Elasticity?

- A: Elasticity refers to the provisioning of news resources to match increase in demand
- B: Elasticity refers to automatically provisioning and deprovisioning of resources to match the workload demand
- C: Elasticity refers to the deprovisioning of resources due to decrease in demand
- D: None of the above

Ans: B

Question 21: How do you move/transfer an EC2 instance from one region to another?

- A: It is not possible to move an EC2 instance from one region to another
- B: It can be done only by a root user
- C: Shut down the EC2, take AMI, and copy it in another region to launch the new EC2
  instance from the AMI
- D: Raise a support request to AWS
- E: None of the above

Ans. C

Question 22: Which of the following services are recommended for transferring petabytes of
data between on-premises data center and AWS?

- A: Snowball or Snowmobile
- B: S3 Transfer Accelerator
- C: S3 multipart upload
- D: S3 Import/Export
- E: Direct Connect

Ans. A

Question 23: RRS stands for what?

- A: Reduced Redundancy Storage
- B: Reduced Risk Storage
- C: Reduce Resource Storage
- D: None of the above

Ans. A

Question 24: What can be used to provide internet connectivity to the resources residing in a private subnet?

- A: NAT instance or NAT gateway
- B: Internet gateway
- C: Virtual private gateway
- D: Elastic Load Balancer

Ans. B

Question 25: Which of the following statement is true for CloudWatch metrics?

- A: It can be manually deleted when the CloudWatch alarm is no longer used
- B: It cannot be manually deleted
- C: It doesn't create any metrics for any custom CloudWatch alarm
- D: All of the above

Ans. B

Question 26: What subnet is usually recommended for hosting a database instance in RDS?

- A: Public subnet
- B: Private subnet
- C: A and B
- D: None of the above

Ans. B

Question 27: What is true about IAM policies?

- A: IAM policies cannot be modified
- B: When IAM policies are changed, it immediately reflects in privileges of all users an groups
- C: IAM policies can be changed only by AWS root account
- D: You need to raise a support request to AWS for changing IAM policies

Ans. B

Question 28: Which of the following AWS services is suitable for data archival?

- A: S3
- B: EMR
- C: Glacier
- D. All of the above

Ans. C

Question 29: What is true about deploying SSL on ELB?

- A: It is not possible
- B: It is not the best practice to deploy SSL on ELB as it may increase the load on the EC2 instance
- C: It is suggested to deploy the SSL certificate on ELB to reduce load on the EC2 instance
- D: Use of SSL is not required with ELB, as it automatically looks after encryption and decryption

Ans. C

Question 30: What is true about IP addressing in AWS?

- A: You can access an EC2 instance over the internet using a private IP address
- B: Public IP address of an EC2 instance does not change when you stop an instance and restart it
- C: Private IPs can be accessed only within the VPC
- D: None of the above

Ans. C

Question 31: Which of the following feature is supported by DynamoDB?

- A: ELB
- B: Auto Scaling
- C: A and B
- D: None of the above

Ans. B

Question 32: One EBS volume can be attached to?

- A: Only one EC2 instance.
- B: Multiple EC2 instances.
- C: Depends on the type of the EBS volume.
- D: EBS cannot be attached to the EC2. It can only be attached to the RDS.

Ans. A

Question 33: Data stored in a S3 can be accessed from?

- A: Within AWS
- B: Within the same region
- C: Within the same AZ
- D: From anywhere across the internet

Ans. D

Question 34: Which statement is true?

- A: Every region has at least two AZs and each AZ is isolated but inter-connected with low-latency dedicated connectivity
- B: Every region may have one or more AZs and each AZs is isolated but inter-connected with low-latency dedicated connectivity
- C: Every region has at least two AZs and each AZ is isolated but inter-connected through the internet
- D: Every region consists of only one AZ which automatically provides highly available infrastructure

Ans. A

Question 35: Which of the following AWS service offers a NoSQL service?

- A: RDS
- B: Simple database
- C: EC2
- D: EMR
- E: DynamoDB

Ans. E

Question 36: What can be done to reduce cost of a mission critical production application hosted on EC2 instances?

- A: Spot instances can be used
- B: Reserved instance can be used
- C: On-demand instance can be used
- D: None of the above

Ans. B

Question 37: What is the largest individual object size supported by S3?

- A: 5 GB
- B: 50 GB
- C: 5 TB
- D: Any size

Ans. C

Question 38: Which AWS service helps to perform log analysis and resource monitoring?

- A: EC2
- B: Lambda
- C: CloudWatch
- D: Any of above

Ans. C

Question 39: What is true about indexes in DynamoDB?

- A: GSIcan have a different partition key and sort key compared to it's base table
- B: LSI can have a different partition key and sort key compared to it's base table
- C: GSI should have the same partition key as it's base table
- D: All of the above

Ans. A

Question 40: What happens when CloudFormation stack creation fails?

- A: It rolls back the stack and deletes any resources that have been created
- B: Skips that resource creation and continues
- C: Depends on the region in which stack is being created
- D: None of the above

Ans. A

Question 41: What is session affinity in an ELB?

- A: Ensures that the ELB stops sending requests to instances that are deregistered or unhealthy, while existing connections are open
- B: It enables to carry source connection request information to the destination
- C: It enables ELB to bind user's session to a specific EC2 instances
- D: It distributes incoming user's request evenly across registered AZs with ELB

Ans. C

Question 42: By default, which of the following metrics are not supported by CloudWatch?

- A: DiskRead/Write operations
- B: NetworkIn/Out
- C: CPU usage
- D: Memory free/used

Ans. D

Question 43: Which of the following statement is true for Lambda?

- A: Security groups and subnets can be assigned with Lambda functions
- B: Only subnets can be specified
- C: Only security group can be specified
- D: Neither security groups nor subnets can be specified

Ans. A

Question 44: By default, a newly created object in S3 is what?

- A: Private and only accessible by an owner
- B: Private and only accessible by IAM users
- C: Public, anyone can access it
- D: All of the above

Ans. A

Question 45: Which of the following AWS services helps to use AWS storage as a local storage to the applications installed in the data centers?

- A: AWS storage gateway
- B: Direct Connect
- C: AWS Snowball
- D: None of the above

Ans. A

Question 46: Which of the following AWS service provides a relational database as a service?

- A: RDS
- B: DynamoDB
- C: RedShift
- D: EMR

Ans. A

Question 47: Which of the following queues in SQS can target messages that can't be processed (consumed) successfully?

- A: Fresh queue
- B: Broken queue
- C: Dead-letter queue
- D: All of the above

Ans. C

Question 48: What consistency model is used for scan operation in DynamoDB?

- A: Strongly consistent
- B: Eventually consistent
- C: Read after write consistency
- D: Above all

Ans. B

Question 49: Which of the following AWS services can be used for various notification types?

- A: SES
- B: SNS
- C: SQS
- D: All of the above

Ans. B

Question 50: Which of the following platforms does not have in-built support on AWS Elastic Beanstalk?

- A: Java with Tomcat
- B: IIS
- C: Java SE
- D: Go
- E: C/C++
- F: Nginix

Ans. E

Mock test 2

Question 1: What is the maximum execution time for Lambda function to run that can be assigned?

- A: 1 minute
- B: 3 minute
- C: 5 minute
- D: Depends on the complexity of the function

Ans. C

Question 2: Which of the following AWS services is used along with S3 to enable S3 Transfer Acceleration?

- A: EMR
- B: SES
- C: SQS
- D: CloudFront

Ans. D

Question 3: Which of the following features is supported by DynamoDB?

- A: Supports relational databases
- B: Supports nested JSON
- C: Supports A and B
- D: None of the above

Ans. B

Question 4: How many IPs are reserved in a VPC CIDR range?

- A: 10
- B: 5
- C: 2
- D: 1

Ans. B

Question 5: Which of the following programming languages is not currently supported by Lambda?

- A: Node.js
- B: Java
- C: Python
- D: Scala

Ans. D

Question 6: Which is the efficient way to server high-volume read-only application traffic in RDS?

- A: Create one or more read replicas to server read-only application traffic
- B: Deploy the Database in multi-AZ
- C: Create memory enhanced RDS Instance type
- D: None of the above

Ans. A

Question 7: What is the primary purpose of using AWS SQS?

- A: Decoupling application components
- B: Building server less architecture
- C: Building micro service architecture
- D: Building monolithic applications

Ans. A

Question 8: AWS EC2 instance store volume provides:

- A: Permanent block storage
- B: Temporary block storage
- C: A and B
- D: None of the above

Ans. B

Question 9: Which statements is true about DynamoDB?

- A: DynamoDB uses a pessimistic locking model
- B: DynamoDB uses conditional writes for consistency
- C: DynamoDB restricts item access during reads
- D: DynamoDB restricts item access during writes

Ans. B

Question 10: Which of the following AWS storage services supports object storage?

- A: EBS
- B: EFS
- C: S3
- D: All of the above

Ans. C

Question 11: Which of the following helper scripts cannot be used while bootstrapping an instance during stack creating in a CFT?

- A: `cfn-get-metadata`
- B: `cfn-put-metadata`
- C: `cfn-init`
- D: `cfn-hup`

Ans. B

Question 12: Which of the following terms attracts CEOs and CTOs to select cloud computing rather over on-premises infrastructure?

- A: They adapt cloud computing as everybody is adapting
- B: Cloud converts CapEx to OpEx and better ROI
- C: Cloud computing does not require hardware and software
- D: Cloud is more secured over on-premises environment

Ans. B

Question: 13: Which of the following statements about SWF is true?

- A: SWF tasks are assigned once and never duplicated
- B: SWF requires an S3 bucket for workflow storage
- C: SWF triggers SNS notifications on task assignment
- D: SWF requires at least 1 EC2 instance per domain

Ans. A

Question 14: Which is the default consistency model in DynamoDB?

- A: Strongly consistent
- B: Eventually consistent
- C: Occasional consistency
- D: All of the above

Ans. B

Question 15: Which of the following engine is not supported by RDS?

- A: Cassandra
- B: MySQL
- C: Oracle
- D: MS SQL

Ans. A

Question 16: The default interval for CloudWatch metrics is what?

- A: 10 minutes
- B: 1 minute
- C: 5 minutes
- D: 2 minutes

Ans. C

Question 17: Which of the following notification mechanisms is not supported by SNS?

- A: Pager
- B: Email
- C: SMS
- D: All of the above

Ans. A

Question 18: Which of the following is an example of a good DynamoDB hash key?

- A: User ID, where the application has many users.
- B: Status code, where there are only a few possible status codes.
- C: Item creation date, rounded to the nearest time period
- D: Employee Name, where there are many employees with similar name

Ans. A

Question 19: By default, what privileges does a newly created AWS IAM user get?

- A: Inherits all root privileges
- B: Inherits administrator privileges
- C: Depends up on the AWS region where the user is created
- D: Does not have any privileges

Ans. D

Question 20: What is the purpose of the `cfn-init` helper script in CloudFormation?

- A: Download and install the packages and files described in the template
- B: Retrieve metadata attached to the template
- C: Initialize bootstrapping command
- D: Signal that stack is ready

Ans. A

Question 21: How many number of objects can be stored in each bucket?

- A: 500 objects/bucket
- B: 50,000 objects/bucket
- C: Virtually unlimited
- D: None of the above

Ans. C

Question 22: What is true about EC2 instances?

- A: An EC2 instance can be part of only one target group
- B: An EC2 instance can be Part of multiple target groups
- C: An EC2 instance cannot be a part of any target group
- D: All of the above

Ans. B

Question 23: How do you obtain AWS security compliance documents?

- A: You can ask to initiate a third-party inspection at AWS data center
- B: Schedule a visit to the AWS data center and ask for the document
- C: Obtain the compliances documents from the AWS compliance reporting service
- D: Every compliance agency across the globe are automatically sent AWS compliance report

Ans: C

Question 24: Packt publication stores periodic log data from it's high traffic book subscription portal to S3. Which object naming convention would give optimal performance on S3 for storing the log data?

- A: instanceID-log-HH-DD-MM-YYYY
- B: instanceID-log-YYYY-MM-DD-HH
- C: HH-DD-MM-YYYY-log_instanceID
- D: YYYY-MM-DD-HH-log_instanceID

Ans: C

Question 25: Which of the following AWS services provides a schemaless database?

- A: RDS
- B: Simple database
- C: DynamoDB
- D: All of the above

Ans. C

Question 26: What can be done to avoid a single point of failure in AWS?

- A: Create a multi-AZ architecture with ELB
- B: Create a multi-region architecture with ELB
- C: Create a multi-AZ with multi-region architecture with ELB and Auto Scaling
- D: AWS automatically takes care of single point of failure

Ans. A

Question: 27: What can be the maximum size of an SQS message?

- A: 1 MB
- B: 512 KB
- C: 128 KB
- D: 256 KB

Ans. D

Question 28: Each datpoint in a cloudwatch requires to have a valid time stamp. This time stamp can be :

- A: Two weeks in the past and up to two hours into the future
- B: Two hours in the past and up to two weeks into the future
- C: Two hours in the past and up to two hours into the future
- D: Two weeks in the past and up to two weeks into the future

Ans. A

Question 29: Which of the following statement is true for an internet facing web application?

- A: Web server should be hosted in a private subnet and associated database should be hosted in a public subnet
- B: Web server should be hosted in a public subnet and associated database should be hosted in a private subnet
- C: Web server and database server, both should be hosted in a public subnet
- D: Web server and database server, both should be hosted in a private subnet

Ans. B

Question 30: What is the secured way to access an RDS database from an application deployed on EC2?

- A: Embed access key and secret in the application source code
- B: Use IAM role with the EC2 instance
- C: Directly specify Database User ID and Password in application configuration file

- D: Store credential file on an encrypted object in S3 and access it from application for user id and password

Ans. B

Question 31: Swathy Mohan, working for Packt Publication, is repeatedly trying to launch an EC2 instance in organization's AWS account, however, the instance gets terminated as soon as it is launched. What could be the possible reason behind the issue?

- A: The snapshot used for launching the instance is corrupt
- B: The AMI used for launching the instance is corrupt
- C: AWS account has reached the maximum EC2 instance limit
- D: The user does not have permission to launch an EC2 instance

Ans. C

Question 32: Abhishek is unable to SSH an EC2 instance which is launched in Packt Publication's AWS account. What could be the possible solution to resolve the accessibility issue?

- A: Modify EC2 instance's security group to allow incoming TCP traffic on port 443
- B: Modify EC2 instance's security group to allow incoming ICMP packets from your IP
- C: Modify EC2 instance's security group to allow incoming TCP traffic on port 22
- D: Apply the most recently released Operating System security patches on the EC2 instance

Ans. C

Question 33: Which AWS service triggers scale-in and scale-out in Auto Scaling?

- A: SES
- B: SNS
- C: SQS
- D: CloudWatch
- E: All of the above

Ans. D

Question 34: How do you change the EC2 instance type?

- A: Directly change it using EC2 console, API, or CLI
- B: Stop the EC2 instance and change the instance type using EC2 console, API, or CLI
- C: AWS does not allow to change EC2 instance type once it is created
- D: EC2 instance type can be changed only for specific instance type family

Ans. B

Question 35: Which AWS service can be used to store archival data in a cost effective way?

- A: AWS RRS
- B: AWS S3
- C: AWS RDS
- D: AWS Glacier

Ans: D

Question 36: Packt publication needs to process a big chunk of data stored in S3 using a data analytics process. This process needs to run periodically on an EC2 insatnce and does not need to have the EC2 instance running after the data is processed and stored back in S3. Which of the following instance type would be cost affective for running these processes?

- A: On-demand EC2 instance
- B: Reserved EC2 instance with full upfront payment
- C: Reserved EC2 instance with no upfront payment
- D: Spot EC2 instance

Ans: D

Question 37: Which of the following AWS managed services makes it easy to coordinate work across distributed application components?

- A: EMR
- B: SWF
- C: RedShift
- D: SNS

Ans: B

Question 38: Which of the following AWS services supports a volume that can be mounted on multiple EC2 instances at a time?

- A: EFS
- B: EBS
- C: Glacier
- D: S3

Ans. A

Question 39: Which of the following AWS service is not supported as AWS Lambda event source?

- A: Amazon alexa
- B: AWS config
- C: Amazon lex
- D: EMR

Ans. D

Question 40: What is true about Amazon SQS queues?

- A: Standard Queue guarantees A-least-once delivery and FIFO queue guarantees exactly-once delivery
- B: Standard Queue guarantees exactly-once delivery and FIFO queue guarantees A-least-once delivery
- C: Standard Queue and FIFO queues do not provide message delivery guarantee
- D: None of the above

Ans. B

Index

URL 313
outputs, template
  references 490

P

Paravirtual (PV) 168
percentile 221
petabytes (PB) 298
pilot light 55
Platform as a Service (PaaS) 24
platforms, Elastic Beanstalk
  custom platform 501
  preconfigured platform 501
policy simulator
  URL 96
policy
  about 91
  Active Directory Federation Service (ADFS) 96
  ADFS, integrating with AWS console 97
  elements 94
  IAM policy simulator 96
  inline policies 92
  managed policies 92
  resource-based policies 92
  resource-based policy, example 95
  URL 94
  web identity federation 98
PostgreSQL
  about 301, 313
  URL 313
primary key
  about 339
  partition key 339
  sort key 339
Protected Health Information (PHI) 390
provisioned IOPS SSD (io1) 186

Q

queries
  URL 370
queues
  attributes 391
  CloudWatch metrics, for SQS 411
  creating 392
  deleting 404

logging 411
message, deleting 400
message, sending 397
message, viewing 400
monitoring 411
purging 402
SQS API actions, logging 413
subscribing, to topic 405
types 390
user permission, adding 407
working 388

R

Reduced Redundancy Storage (RRS) 262
Regions 22
Relational Database Management System
  (RDBMS)
  about 305, 331
  NoSQL 333
  SQL 332
  SQL, versus NoSQL 336
Relational Database Service (RDS) 8
  about 301
  best practices 330
  components 302
  engine types 304
  instance type, modifying 324
  instances, monitoring 321
Requester Pay model
  about 252
  enabling, on bucket 253
RFC 4632
  URL 111
root account credentials 64
root device 167
root user
  URL 39
  versus non-root user 39
route table 141

S

S3 console
  URL 260
S3 storage classes
  about 262